ON THE CROFT

In Search of the Cleara

DAVID CRAIG

BIRLINN

This edition published in 2010 by
Birlinn Limited
West Newington House
10 Newington Road
Edinburgh
EH9 1QS

www.birlinn.co.uk

First published in 1990 by Jonathan Cape, London
First published by Birlinn Ltd in 2006

ISBN: 978 184158 801 8

British Library Cataloguing-in-Publication Data
A catalogue record for this book is available
from the British Library
Facsimile origination by Brinnoven, Livingston

Printed and bound by Grafica Veneta
www.graficaventa.com

For John Manson
poet and crofter

We're sailing west, we're sailing west
To prairie lands sunkissed and blest –
The crofter's trail to happiness.

Emigrant jingle,
Canadian Pacific Railroad Archives

CONTENTS

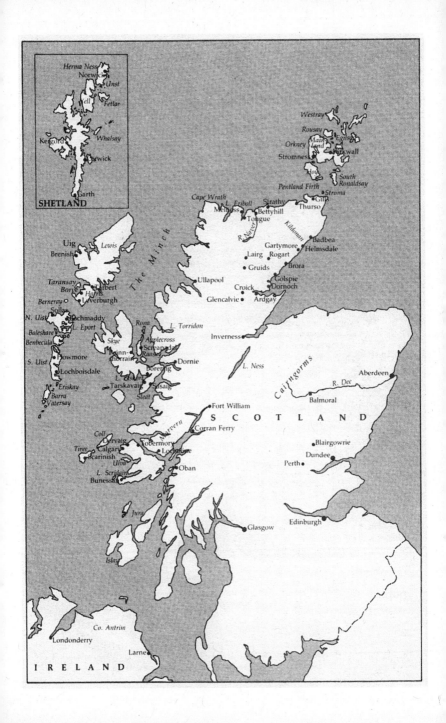

SHETLAND

Herma Ness
Norwick
Unst
ell *Fetlar*
Whalsay
Kergord
rwick
Garth

Westray
Rousay
Egilsa
Orkney Mainland
Stromness Kirkwall
Hoy South
Ronaldsay
Pentland Firth
Stroma
Gills
Cape Wrath L. Eriboll Strathy Thurso
Melness Bettyhill
Tongue
R. Naver
Kildonan
Badbea
Gartymore Helmsdale
Lairg Rogart
Uig *Lewis* Gruids Brora
Brenish The Minch Ullapool Colspie
Croick Dornoch
Taransay *Harris* Glencalvie Ardgay
Borb *Harris*
Berneray Leverburgh
Sollas
N. Uist Lochmaddy
L. Eport *Ronn* L. Torridon
Baleshare *Skye* Applecross Inverness
Benbecula Scrapadal
Howmore *Raasay* L. Ness Cairngorms
roman Boreraig Aberdeen
Lochboisdale Dornie R. Dec
Eriskay L. Balmoral
Barra Tarskavaig *Susa*
Vatersay *Sleat* Fort William

S C O T L A N D

Corran Ferry

Coll Blairgowrie
Dervaig Dundee
Tiree Calgary Tobermory Perth
carinish Lochbuie
Ulva Oban
L. Scridain
Bunessan

Jura

Glasgow Edinburgh

Islay

Co. Antrim
Londonderry
Larne

I R E L A N D

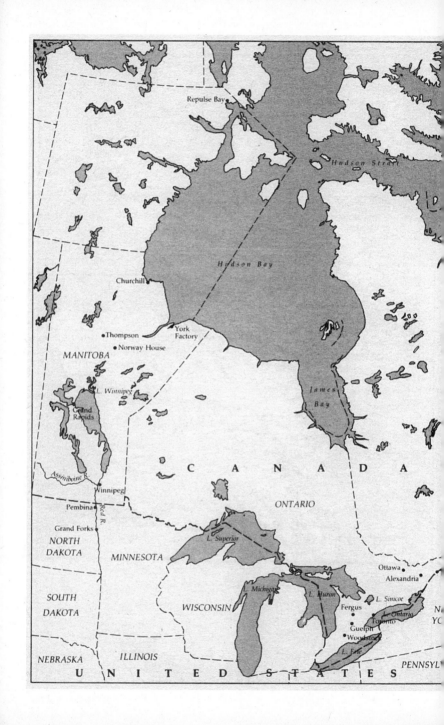

Repulse Bay

Hudson Strait

Hudson Bay

Churchill

York
Factory

•Thompson
•Norway House

MANITOBA

*James
Bay*

L. Winnipeg

Grand
Rapids

Assiniboine R.

CANADA

Winnipeg

ONTARIO

Pembina

Red R.

Grand Forks•

NORTH
DAKOTA

MINNESOTA

L. Superior

SOUTH
DAKOTA

WISCONSIN

L. Michigan

L. Huron

Ottawa
Alexandria

L. Simcoe

Fergus
L. Ontario

Toronto

Guelph
•Woodstock

NEBRASKA

ILLINOIS

L. Erie

PENNSYL

U N I T E D   S T A T E S

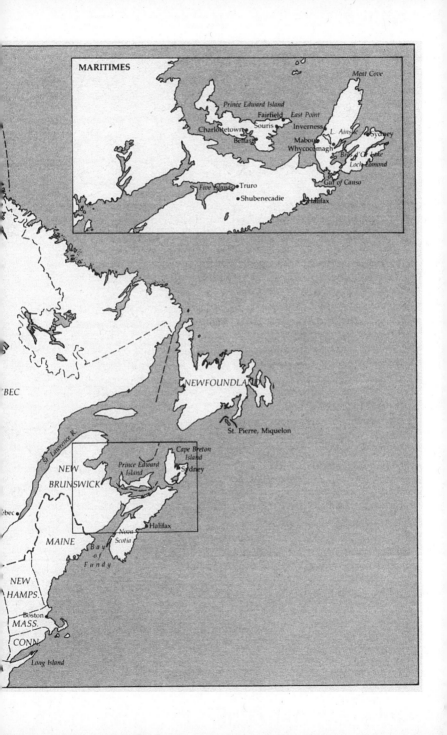

MARITIMES

Meat Cove

Prince Edward Island
Fairfield   East Point
Charlottetowne   Souris   Inverness
Bellast   L. Ainslie   Sydney
Mabou   Bras d'Or Lake
Whycocomagh   Loch Lomond
Five Islands   Truro   Gut of Canso
Shubenecadie   Halifax

BEC

NEWFOUNDLAND

St. Pierre, Miquelon

Cape Breton
Island
NEW   Prince Edward   Sydney
BRUNSWICK   Island

QUEBEC

MAINE   Nova   Halifax
Scotia
Bay
of
Fundy

NEW
HAMPS.
Boston
MASS.
CONN.
Long Island

FOREWORD TO
THE 2010 EDITION

When the North Assynt crofters bought 21,000 acres of their land from a bankrupt Swedish company in 1993 and set up a form of communal ownership, I was unaware whether to see it as a single splendid coup against the old regime, of symbolic value rather than practical and wide-ranging significance. It was good to stay in a B&B in Stoer owned by one of the committee and to hear news of the hydroelectric scheme they were setting up. Would the new Trust last? And would it thrive?

It is still there, doing well, and similar buy-outs and new community set-ups have come into being in Skye, Knoydart, Lewis, North Harris, South Uist, Eigg and elsewhere. So crofters are getting full title to their land at last (if they want it) and harvesting the full fruits earned from their own resources – wind and water (for sustainable energy), the landscape (for the visitors), as well as the age-old ones – the fields, the pasture and the sea.

A Runrig song that has always resonated strongly for me is 'Recovery', sung by Rory Macdonald on the album of that name:

Still the morning comes in on the land
See the new sun red and rising
See the corn turn ripe in the fields
See the growth in the glen
And MacPherson's in Kilmuir tonight
What a night for a people rising
Oh God not before time
There's justice in our lives

And I can't believe
That it's taken all this time

I can't believe
My life and my destiny
After the clans, after the clearings
Here I am recovering.

(© 1981 C&R Macdonald/Storr Music)

Twenty-nine years later this no longer sounds like well-meaning rhetoric.

A further heartening development has been the setting up of cultural centres where Highland archives and exhibitions can be housed, for example at Lochmaddy on North Uist, Kildonan on South Uist, Castlebay on Barra and Gairloch in Wester Ross. As the people's memoirs on which this book depends inevitably shrink and disperse, at least they can be supplemented by the pictorial and other records which are being lovingly collected in those places.

David Craig
January 2010

INTRODUCTION TO
THE 2006 EDITION

As I worked on the new edition of this book in the early summer of 2005, the papers and television were constantly reporting the Zimbabwe government's clearance of people from their homes in Harare, Bulawayo, and other towns, and their dumping in transit camps: more than 50,000 families, more than 300,000 people. From time to time President Mugabe's spokesmen used the phrase 'slum clearance'. The Highland Clearances happened piecemeal, over seventy years, and were less thorough – they came before the invention of the petrol engine and the centralised police force, the bulldozer and the truck, among other things. Although the culture and politics of the two countries were unalike in many ways, the patterns of personal experience had a good deal in common: the helpless outrage, the nightmarish hardships, as those in power solved their problems by more or less draconic means.

Still closer to the Scottish events described in this book were earlier cases in Rhodesia/Zimbabwe. In the 1940s the colonial government was clearing African farmers off their land to make way for British settlers. In 1997 Ephraim Nyakujare, aged 83, recalled his eviction from the Nyanagudzi river valley, where he grew maize, soya beans, sorghum, and rice on 'good red soil'. His detailed memories are exactly the same as hundreds I have gathered in the Highlands and Islands and Canada, and reproduce in the following pages: 'We carried things on our heads and packed belongings in a cart. We had six cattle then. The Rhodesians destroyed our huts as we left. Anyone who resisted was arrested and their belongings destroyed. We tried to come back to see our ancestors' graves, but they wouldn't let us.' They were 'settled on a smaller plot, with many rocks, poor soil and less rainfall.'[1]

With that – apart from the rain – compare the clearance situation on South Uist and Eriskay, or Assynt and Coigach, or the north coast of Sutherland: the gruelling ordeals are the same, the razing of houses, the trashing of household goods, the relocation to bleak terrain. And the emotional wrenching is the same. Although the evicted people had often been living in cramped houses on tiny smallholdings, harried by shortages and sometimes famine, home was home and the clinging onto it was desperate. A boatman from Rona, north of Raasay, remembered seeing people 'going to the churchyard in their grief at being separated from their homes, and taking handfuls of the soil and grass that covered the graves of their kindred, as mementoes.' This was typical. The son of a man from Howbeg in South Uist took earth from the floor of his father's house to be put in his coffin when he was buried in France. A man from Rum who left with fifty-four others at the final clearance in 1852 came back from Canada around 1860, hoping for 'the site of his two soles of a bothy and the breadth of his two shoulders of a grave in the land of his heredity and the land of his fathers'. Denied these, he went back to Canada with a handful of earth from St Michael's burial ground in South Uist, which a 102-year-old woman cleared from Ormacleit had asked him to bring back so that he could place it on her heart on the day of her death.[2]

This kind of deep-seated ritual was ingrained in Highland life, in longstanding habitation of a place. Early in the 20th century, a Lewisman, William MacKenzie of Shulishader in Point, emigrated to Thunder Bay in Ontario after his wife's death. Before leaving, 'he visited his wife's grave in Aignish where he pulled a tooth from his head and buried it in her grave, so that something of him would remain in Lewis with her.'[3] Such efforts at belonging are as international as human nature itself. In the autumn of 1956 a Hungarian called Gergely Pongratz who had been fighting the Soviet invasion was fleeing into Austria with his family. Near the border 'his mother stopped to salvage a fistful of Hungarian earth, which she wrapped in a handkerchief. The soil was eventually buried with her when she died in the United States.[4]

Such stories, or memoirs, are to my mind the prime stuff of history because they bring home to us what it was like to experience a cruel or trying point in a social process, what it felt or smelt like, what you had to do to stay alive, how you swallowed (or nurtured) your worries or your anguish. Such memoir is still there, in spite of one historian's suggestion that 'The events [of the Highland Clearances] have now receded into the distant past', and the crass assertion of another that Highlanders 'largely lacked ... the ability of fluent self-expression', so that we cannot find out their 'motivations'.[5] In Skye and Tiree and Yell, in Ardnamurchan and Sutherland and Harris and Mull, I have again and again been brought close to the evictions, and the later fight-backs against them, as I have listened to crofters and teachers and retired people as they recalled their forebears' experiences, often in words passed down through anything from one to six generations.

The cumulative testimony of the crofters and their people is far-reaching and often highly expressive. In the first place as witnesses at two government commissions (Napier in 1883, the Deer Forest Commission in 1892), people poured out facts and hearsay concerning their recent past, its trials by land hunger, hardship, emigration, and eviction. Sometimes they recite the names of destroyed townships like a litany. Or they specify cases of land loss, or unreasonable harassment and denial of rights. Or they recall the leaving of homesteads, including the behaviour and even the remarks of the laird's agents. In a supreme example of fluent self-expression – recorded by Alexander Carmichael the Victorian exciseman, the most fruitful of all Highland researchers – Catherine MacPhee of Iochdar, in the north-west corner of South Uist, spoke this lament for the terrible disruptions of the middle 19th century:

Many a thing have I seen in my own day and generation, many a thing, O Mary Mother of the black sorrow! I have seen the townships swept, and the big holdings made of them, the people being driven out of the island to the streets of Glasgow and the wilds of Canada, such of them as did not die of hunger and plague and smallpox while going across the sea. I have seen the women putting their children in the carts which were sent from Benbecula and the Iochdar to Lochboisdale when their husbands lay bound in the pen, and were weeping, without power to give them a helping hand, though the women themselves were crying aloud, and the little children wailing like to break their hearts. I have seen the big strong men, the champions of the country, the stalwarts of the world, being bound on Boisdale quay and cast into the ship as would be done to horses and cattle. The God of Life, and He only, knows all the loathsome work of men on that day.[5]

Every detail here is distinct, nothing is misleading. This has to be said, partly because it is always hard to be sure what happened unless, or even if, you were there yourself, partly because it has been customary to discredit crofter witnesses. Lord Napier started it when he spent a page of his Report disparaging 'tales that pass from mouth to mouth' of the 'poorest and least educated class' as 'loose and legendary'. This prejudice bedevilled his Commission from the start. At Balmacara in Wester Ross, on 2 August 1883, the Lochalsh teacher read out a statement by the crofters of three townships. They testified that the evicting factor had said 'Go you must, even though you should go to the bottom of the sea.' The crofters said they were being 'driven out of the country like noxious vermin' and 'crowded into barren promontories or boggy hollows which were useless [even] for sheep'. These the Commissioners thought were 'expressions of rather unnecessary bitterness'. They wondered if this was what the people had actually said and whether the translation might be at fault. It took four long questions-and-answers before the words were allowed to stand, with the substitution of 'wild animals' for 'vermin'.[7]

This sort of discomfiture at heartfelt speech seems to spring from the habits of managerial and academic persons. They incline to the official and the dispassionate because they are used to the orderly and comfortable and they benefit from it in their own lives. When a stonemason (Donald MacLeod of Strath Naver) who himself lost his home and saw his wife maddened by eviction describes hardship graphically, the historian calls him 'melodramatic and sensational' – then admits that his account is 'considerably corroborated' by the contemporary reports.[8] This same academic expert, a decent and thorough scholar, has also written to me that he requires 'a degree of parallel contemporaneous corroboration' before he accepts the sort of memoir I have brought to light and relied on in this book and in *The Glens of Silence*, which David Paterson and I made two years ago. Well, when a crofter on North Uist tells me what his grandmother told him about the burning of their loom at the eviction with the tweed still in it, or a retired teacher on Mull tells me what her father told her about seeing the day's milk poured onto the fire to force them out of their house in Sleat, or a lobster fisherman on Loch Eishort tells me how his great-grandmother's neighbour was lured from her house by estate heavies to fetch them fresh water and came back to find her roof burning, 'contemporaneous corroboration' will probably be hard to find. No government officials were present in Sollas in 1849, or Boreraig in 1853, or on Yell in 1870. Journalists were just beginning to get into those parts – most notably Donald Ross, who covered clearances in Skye, Knoydart, and Strath Carron for the *Northern Ensign* – and press photography had not yet been invented. What we have are such snatches and glimpses of eye-witness memoir as have survived the tattering of history.

The stories I have gleaned, from people and from printed records, amount to probabilities or possibilities. They are not facts, they are social likelihoods. We can give them credence, and respond to their poignancy, according to their ring or weight as utterance and also according to our knowledge of how the powerful have treated the powerless in other parts of the world, in the Kandyan region of Sri Lanka, at Pari-haka in New Zealand's North Island, in Gran Canaria, in St Kitts and Hispaniola in the Caribbean, in Rhodesia and Florida and Arizona and the Andes: almost everywhere.

Notes

1. *The Observer*, 14 December 1997.
2. *Minutes of Evidence Taken Before the Royal Commission (Highlands and Islands, 1892* (1895), Question 361; *Evidence Taken by her Majesty's Commission of Inquiry into the Condition of the Crofters and Cottars in the Highlands and Islands of Scotland* (1884), Appendix A, pp. 460–1; Camille Dressler, MS History of Eigg, p. 260.
3. *West Highland Free Press*, 11 September 1998.
4. *The Guardian*, 5 June 2005.
5. Eric Richards, *The Highland Clearances* (2005), p. 3; J.M. Bumsted, *The People's Clearance* (Edinburgh, 1982), p. xiv.
6. Alexander Carmichael, *Carmina Gadelica* (1900), II, p. 256. Recently spoken to music as 'Fichead Bliadhna' on Runrig's album *The Highland Connection* (Edinburgh, 1979), side 1, track 4.
7. Napier *Commission of Enquiry* . . . Report, pp. 2–3; *Evidence*, Questions 30, 56–65.
8. Eric Richards, *A History of the Highland Clearances* (1982), p. 415.

PREFACE

Most of the material in this book was given me by crofters and descendants of crofters. I have kept to their words as exactly as I could. Nothing has been added to their stories and statements; they have only been edited to trim away um's and ah's and minor repetitions or digressions. Working with the tapes and notes that represent hundreds of conversations, I was often chagrined to find that, ideally, I should have gone back to the source to check a detail. It would certainly have been delightful to revisit Churchill in Manitoba, or Loch Lomond on Cape Breton Island, or Mid Yell in Shetland, or ... Short of becoming permanently nomadic it can't be done, so I hope my hosts and informants around Scotland and Canada will forgive me if I have called a great-great-grandmother a great-grandmother, or mistaken a year, or even swopped the occasional gender. Second and last disclaimer: what follows is not exhaustive in its coverage either of cleared places or of the migrants' destinations. Many Scotsfolk made for areas such as British Columbia, South Carolina, and New South Wales which I have been unable to visit so far. Perhaps this book will lead their descendants to get in touch with me, which would be most welcome.

Printed sources are listed in the Notes under the relevant chapter and page.

Most of the people who helped me are named in the course of the narrative. I owe a further and special debt to the following: Margat MacGregor of Gartymore, Echan Calder of Port Gower, and John Manson of Rhemusaig, for help with leads and information regarding Sutherland; Margaret and Norman Johnston of Lochmaddy, for

North Uist; Dr Alasdair Maclean, for South Uist; Niall and Chrissie MacPherson, for Barra; Sorley and Renee MacLean and Rebecca Mackay, for Raasay; Alastair MacKinnon of Sasaig, for Sleat, Skye; Ann Manson of Kirkwall, for Orkney; Jim Johnson of Bettyhill and John Graham of Lerwick, for Shetland; Dan Gillis of Philadelphia, and Harry Baglole of Charlottetown, for Prince Edward Island; John Shaw of Glendale, for Cape Breton Island; Hugh MacMillan and Ed Cowan of Guelph, Ontario, for western Ontario, Glengarry County, and Manitoba; Kay Gillespie of Winnipeg, for the Red River area, Manitoba; John Ingerbertson and his son Mark for Churchill, Hudson Bay. Sandy Fenton, fellow-runner during our green days in Edinburgh and Research Director of the Royal Museum of Scotland, helped me to find sieves, tongs, and other tools. Morland Craig helped me with maps and information as did Ann Craig. Peter Craig and Anne Spillard read parts of the manuscript with a fastidious eye and Anne helped me by her companionship on many journeys. The Public Libraries of Guelph, Winnipeg, and Kirkwall were particularly helpful, as were the National Archive, Ottawa, the Lancaster University Library, the Shetland Museum, Lerwick, Brian Smith of the Shetland Archive, Lerwick, the Highland Folk Museum, Kingussie, the Strathnaver Museum, Bettyhill, the Scottish Agricultural Museum stores, South Queensferry, and the Comunn Eachdraidh, Paible, North Uist.

I am grateful to the following organisations for grants towards travel and subsistence: the Nuffield Foundation, the Iona Foundation (Philadelphia), Northern Arts (Newcastle), Lancaster University, and the British Council.

Special thanks are owed to my publisher, David Godwin, who suggested this book; Karl Miller of the *London Review of Books*, who published the germ of it in his correspondence and review columns; and John Prebble, whose work among the grass roots of Scotland's history is now cherished by people there from every walk of life. As we parted after a marathon conversation over malt whisky in a Pimlico hotel, he said to me, 'I envy you' – for having found good reasons to travel all over the Highlands and speak to people who know about what happened there. His five chief books about Scotland are an abiding landmark for everyone who believes that cruxes in our history can still be realised with the distinctness of personal experiences.

CHAPTER ONE

WATCHING THE PEOPLE'S MOUTH

This book describes my travels in eastern Canada and the Scottish Highland and Islands in search of people whose forebears emigrated at the time of the Clearances, sometimes within Scotland and sometimes overseas. After fifty years of walking among the shells of houses, abandoned oases of green grass amongst moorland, stripes of the old narrow plots or lazybeds on the sides of glens and islands, I began to think there was still one thing to be done in order to know that prolonged agon of the Gaelic people, which was to hear it from them in their own words – not Gaelic ones, which as a Lowland Scot I do not understand, but in their other language, English. A huge proportion of the people we now call 'the crofters' were banished from their homelands for the sake of economic progress, yet to this day (in the view of their best historian, James Hunter) 'the people upon whom estate managements imposed their policies have been almost completely neglected'. He remarks that we can recover the events but 'not the emotions' of the people's history from the documents, and that is some deficiency. George Ewart Evans, chief oral historian of the English countryfolk, advises us to listen to their word-of-mouth testimony if we want to hear not only the facts but 'what they *think* of the facts', and that is some advantage. For several years, therefore, I have been talking to people in Sutherland, Shetland and Orkney, Perthshire, the Outer and Inner Hebrides, in Cape Breton Island and Prince Edward Island, Ontario, Manitoba, to find out what they still remember about the experiences of their forebears during the great exodus. It is a diaspora which has many recent counterparts (that of the Jews from Germany and Poland, the

3

Okies from the American Middle West, and on and on all over the world) but the Scottish one means most to me because it happened in places that I love.

How much of the story survives, four to six generations after the diaspora? (How much do most of us know about the detailed behaviour of our great-grandparents?) Some inklings of what is left came to me in the winter of 1982 on North Uist. I was writing a historical novel about a real carpenter from Lochaber, called Angus Cameron. In 1797 he found himself at the head of a rising in Strath Tay against a conscription act passed in July that year. He was arrested, hustled off to Edinburgh by a detachment of dragoons, interrogated; then, amazingly, given bail – which he at once jumped. He was outlawed in January 1798 and disappears from history, apart from a glimpse in 1823 when he appealed, successfully, to have his citizenship restored. I felt very near him in the Scottish Record Office reading the yellowing rolls of evidence taken down by a clerk as Cameron spoke with his masterly ironical reticence (rather like Brecht before the UnAmerican Activities Committee). Where had he gone to ground during that quarter century of being a non-person? Refugee militants from Scotland sometimes lay low in Holland or Lower Saxony, but there would be no tracing him there. Cameron was a native Gaelic-speaker – might he not have hidden in the Outer Isles, which were famously unpoliced? Could I invent a life for him under another name somewhere over there? Perhaps I could connect him with another great defiance of heartless law, the battle against eviction by the people of Sollas on the north shore of North Uist in 1849, when the women fought with stones and tangle-stems against policemen's truncheons until they were left lying at the high-tide mark with bleeding scalps.

My partner Anne and I followed by car the route Cameron would have been likely to take in the guise of a cattle drover, by the Moor of Rannoch and Glencoe, Fort William, Glen Garry and Glen Shiel. An intense frost had iced over Grimsay harbour in Benbecula, we were told later, and in the high moors of north-west Perthshire skulls of bluish ice bulged out of the heather where the moss-boils had frozen solid. At dusk, as we zig-zagged north to spend the night with friends in Wester Ross, we saw the surface of Upper Loch Diabaig as one complete black pane which flexed to the smiting of the wind. The face of the Highlands had turned alien – yet was this Arctic look not more real than the summer-holiday scene of caravans and anglers'

Volvos? Now the few vehicles and people belonged here and the land itself bulked up hugely, dour and unspectacular, tweed-coloured in saturated browns and blaes and duns, the dull cinnamon of withered fescue grass, the dark claret of birch forests bristling in the gloaming. The night before we sailed from Uig in Skye, from the end window of Renee and Sorley MacLean's house at Peinnchorran, we watched clouds like aged hair trail over the high draped snowfields of Sgurr nan Gillean. The Cuillins had withdrawn into their ice-world, everything had withdrawn, lobster boats to harbour, otters into their dens, holidaymakers to the Lowlands or England. The time of the next lambing, peat-cutting, or housebuilding was a long way off.

In the cafeteria of the *Columba*, on the four-hour crossing to Lochmaddy, there were no visitors, only regulars. A black-coated minister in his thirties, with a long orange scarf thrown over one shoulder in a desperate effort to be young, conversed awkwardly with a chubby crofter's wife. 'Let us hope the gale warning will prove a false alarm, Mrs MacKenzie!' Her man, who had a beard like a charred hedgehog, snapped his dark eyes as though to ban all such pleasantries. Presently, the iodine-blackened skerries of Lochmaddy slid into place around us. The town looked as raw and scattered as some anchorage in the Canadian outback. Would there be anywhere for us to lodge among these kit bungalows and cement-grey council houses and metal-roofed sheds? As I asked about this in the post office, a black-haired woman who was buying stamps along the counter spoke up: 'You can have a room with us if you like – the house is along that way,' pointing out of the window at a straggle of houses along an inlet. 'Look for the Old Court House.' This was the first move that led me step by step until I seemed to be seeing, hearing, and smelling the Clearances as they happened. Our landlady was Margaret Johnston. Soon her husband Norman (Tormod MacIain, as he signed himself in his fine collection of scholarly books) was telling us that this massively compact late eighteenth century house had been the prison where the four Sollas men arrested for defying eviction in August 1849 had been kept in handcuffs on their way to trial in Inverness:

You'll be driving up to the north end tomorrow, no doubt. Well, where the road bends round the bay at Malaclete, just past Sollas, near what we call the dentist's house, go down into the heather between the road and the shore, and you will see a big stone –

we call it Big Alasdair's Stone, because he was the strongest man in Sollas, Alasdair Matheson, and the estate men were afraid of him, so when they came to burn the village they made sure he was away. They were giving out meal at Lochmaddy – or was it over the hill at Paible? Anyway there was great hunger at that time, so Big Alasdair was away getting the hand-out for his family when they were all evicted. He was so strong, you see, that he was the only one could lift that stone, though all the men would have a try. We had it marked recently, with some red paint, because we think these things should be remembered.

Norman is a quarry worker and has been a county councillor, a social worker before that, and before that a policeman in Edinburgh. He teaches piping to a group of teenagers in Lochmaddy. His jet-black hair and blue eyes show you the features of a people quite distinct from the east or south of Scotland, descended from the Iberians, perhaps, who colonised Ireland and came into Scotland across the stepping-stones of the Hebrides. As he talked, the events of five generations ago started to sharpen into visibility like a photographic print in its bath of transparent developer:

My family had come in here from Skye – the estate brought them over because they were weavers and they established a mill for the tweeds in Malaclete – it was beside the burn near where it runs into the bay there. I think that may be why they were not cleared out with the rest of them in 1849. And the four who were put in prison, they were lodged inside these walls, of course, and a man I spoke to in Sollas was telling me that his father always hated the sight of this place, because he remembered the noise, the thud-thud-thud of the hammers the prisoners used, to soften the fibres of the oakum.

As Norman spoke, we could see through the window the rows of Brussels sprouts in his kitchen garden and surrounding it the thick, seven-foot walls of what would have been the prison yard. The clearance was coming nearer and nearer, and seemed only just beyond the hills next day as we travelled north and west to Sollas, the small isles of Pabbay and Berneray hospitably green on the sea nearby (but only Berneray has houses now) and Harris lifting its mountains in the middle distance. Sollas still exists but it is not right. A row of houses, well apart from each other, was built seventy years ago when the land taken from the crofters to make into large farms was restored to crofting after the Great War. Many of them lack screens or curtains in the windows or whitewash on the walls – few washing-lines, no fresh paint or grass mown close around the doorsteps. The shop, a Co-operative Foodstore, is a windowless hangar made of breezeblock and corrugated asbestos. The school, where some excellent history lessons are taught, is like a cross between a small telephone exchange and a blockhouse. Some organised life has come back to the razed community but not enough amenity and not enough future.

Here and down the slope towards the coastal meadows the people's homes had clustered among the communal fields of the runrig system – the subsistence economy which was eaten and swept away between 1770 and 1850. In the aftermath of the Forty-five the Highland chiefs evolved into landlords, bent on maximising the income from their estates. Big sheep from the Lowlands, often managed by Lowland or English farmers and their shepherds, invaded a way of life in which families with small lands grew their own food and fattened black cattle for the market. The big sheep, *caoraich mhòr*, must winter on the best grass – the glen bottoms, lochside meadows, and coastal machair where the villages had been. For a time the crofters took part, as wage labourers, in the kelp boom, when seaweed was cut and burnt to make industrial chemicals. The population rose enormously and lived on the newly allotted smallholdings or crofts. When kelp was replaced by raw materials from Spain after the end of the French Wars, the Highland industry collapsed. And the crofters paid too little rent (£20 or less for 95% of northwest Highland tenants) to satisfy their masters. From the early 1800s onwards, peaking after 1815 and again after the Potato Famine in 1846, the estate managers drove the families out by the thousand, serving eviction orders, using fire and force if need be, and they joined the influx to the industrial cities, the efflux to the New World and the Antipodes.

Clearance is what happens to smallholders, in Cuba and Ceylon last century, in Stalin's Soviet Union, in Brazil today. Like any major historical process, it has a benign face and a vicious one. To the survivors on the ground it feels like a bereavement and a banishment – 'banish' is the crushing old word they still use – because they have to make their homes today among the wreckage of houses and fields, harbours and fish-traps, where the deed was done. Their grandparents saw the flames crackle through the thatch while the fires on the hearths hissed and died.

I glimpsed this in two letters that reached me from Skye and Sutherland and finally convinced me that the experiences of clearance were still vivid enough to be caught and fixed. In August 1987, Alastair MacKinnon, postman at Sasaig in Skye, wrote to say that his grandmother, Kirsty Robertson, had been among the people cleared from Suishnish in 1853. She had lived at No. 11:

> The eviction was carried out forcibly throughout the township of Suishnish with the usual cruelty by the land officers of Lord MacDonald's estate. The milk basins being poured outside and the cottages wrecked so that the people could not return . . . However, my ancestors did not leave the township by the route taken by most of the people, which was towards Torrin and Broadford. They went towards Boreraig and Heaste along Loch Eishort side and finally to the Sleat road just beyond Drumfearn. Here they spent the night (in the open) and milked their cows. My grandmother, Kirsty MacPherson by then, used to relate this experience to my mother saying her eyes shed more tears that evening than she received milk from the cows.

With these details the clearance became almost palpable – the wet smack of milk on grass, the lank udders of exhausted animals. Could the same be done for the first wave of clearance, a generation before?

In September, Bridget MacKenzie wrote from Lednabirichen, west of Dornoch, to say that the great-great-grandmother of her second cousin, a retired shepherd who lives north of Lairg, had seen the clearance of Lettaidh in Strath Fleet from her home at Inchcape, high on the slope opposite:

> She remembered being woken by her mother and taken to the window, and she looked out into the darkness and saw a red glow in the hills opposite. She asked what it was, and her mother said in a grim voice, 'They are putting fire to Lettaidh. The people have been put out.' The child was frightened, naturally enough, since they had relatives in Lettaidh themselves, but she was reassured when told it would not happen to her house, since all the men

were still there. All the men from Lettaidh had been recruited, by the Sutherland estate factors, to go to fight in the Napoleonic wars, and then the factors seized the chance to evict the women and children without fear of resistance.

I had been far from sure that a veritable memory of the burning would come to light (1814 is called *Bliadhna an Losgaidh*, the Year of the Burnings). But of course it did, and there was more to come. The memory of so genealogical and tradition-minded a people could not have lost the image of so momentous a turn in their history.

CHAPTER TWO

'THE THING THAT WOULD MAKE DROSS OF MEADOWS'
Applecross, Wester Ross

The exodus from the Highlands and Islands is not entirely a far-off thing. It was still happening when I was young. In the middle of summer 1956, a friend and I were plodding up the brae which lifts the coastal path to a height of 550 feet just north of Applecross in Wester Ross. The MacBrayne's launch had brought us from Kyle of Lochalsh through the heaving black waters of the Inner Sound and set us down in the scant shelter of Loch Toscaig. As we walked north by an untarred road, seaweeds broke the surface to our left, then slumped into heaps of rubbery orange foliage as the sea ebbed still further. To our right, small broken crags defended the unknown land behind a scatter of shut-looking croft houses. Between Camastearach and Camusteel we passed the simplest of churches, a narrow stone house with a little belfry and a bell-rope rapping on the seaward gable. Our rucksacks, 45 lb. loads of socks and jerseys and sleeping bags and tinned food, bruised deep into our shoulders and the black metal tentacles round the base of mine (Commando type, ex-W.D.) clutched my kidneys. There was also the liver – 1½ lb. of it carved from the innards of an ox. We had bought it in Mallaig, with a very post-War, post-rationing wish to store up supplies against whatever shortages lay ahead. Now it had taken on the aura of the old mariner's albatross, but flayed – too much of it, too pink, too wet.

We were making for Torridon and its terrific mountains, fifteen miles to the north. Scrutinising the Ordnance Survey map in Aberdeen before setting off over the passes of the Lairig Ghru and the

Corrieyairack, we had argued the options: why not save eight out of fifteen miles round Applecross by cutting north-east from the bay, straight through the hinterland? We might even climb the unknown mountain of Cròic-bheinn with its scarp that beetled darkly attractive on the map. But all that rising ground was invisible now in a fume of white rain, and the start of the path was hard to find. The policies of Applecross House, waist-deep in soaking green hay and screened by taller limes and beeches than any I had seen this far north-west, barred the way with that unmistakable façade of the expensively owned.

Later I found that it all belonged to a Wills, a maker of cigarettes, and was available to princesses for short holidays with their lovers.

So we crossed the delta of the Applecross, where the Torridonian sandstone is milled by the rushing water into shingle round and red as nectarines, and set our minds and legs on automatic for the trek up the rather blank coast. It follows the meridian for nine miles with only one break or haven of any kind, at Sand, a sheltered inlet pointing south-west.

Fifteen years later Sand became the site of a naval installation. A tarred road now cuts straight down to a pair of steel gates and some squat concrete buildings. These are not marked on the O.S. map.

In a way it had been cowardly to choose this well-drained 4 foot 6 inch track instead of the louring unknown to the east. But if we had struck inland we would not have seen the long berg of Raasay, parallel with us on the sea between the mainland and Skye, shaping and firming as the water-vapour ceased to blow past in droplets and condensed in layers that lifted, parted, peeled – a beancurd landscape, oriental in its intricate dovetailing of blue lands and white mists. And then again, if we had not followed the coast we would not have met the refugees.

We were each of us in a cocoon of sweat and ache and drizzle as we homed on the Youth Hostel at Lonbain – a little red triangle on the map that offered cosy security. Then, as the gloaming thickened, we were passing through something like the relics of a war, familiar from so many newsreels and photos eleven years before: stone shells of cottages, which in the poor light looked like shattered outcrops. Over the next two miles I counted over a hundred. I saw nothing like it again until Anne and I travelled through the Mani, far down the

11

middle finger of the Peloponnese, where each Maniot town as you approach, with its roofed and unroofed carcases of houses, collapsing lean-tos and truncated towers, looks as though armies have fought through it – in fact, the people have abandoned their thousands of cunningly masoned terraces and fields to thorn and thistle and gone away for good to Athens or Australia.

From childhood I had taken it for granted that the last few farms up any glen, or above a certain contour, were deserted – unlike the more-or-less thriving state of the hill farms I later grew accustomed to in the Yorkshire dales and Cumbria. But dereliction on this scale, on what seemed a workable shelf of coastal land, was new to me, and we looked at each other with a shivering of doubt.

The hostel turned out to be an old square school and schoolhouse half a mile beyond the village. It was unlit, cold and equipped with greasy Primus stoves most of which refused to fire. However would we stew, or possibly scorch, the albatross out of its raw and bleeding state? A notice – apparently aimed at people heading *south* – told us helpfully that the well was two hundred yards back the way we had come. And we must have water; we were beyond washing but we did have to brew tea and hydrate our powdered milk. As we clambered about in the dark looking for a stone trough among so many useless stones, a bright thought occurred: why not look for some real milk in the village? There had been a few black stirks and a brown cow chewing away among the rocks. (But there had been neither hens foraging nor washing getting still wetter on a line.) We picked our way down to a row of cottages facing out to sea. Orange light glimmered in one glazed window. We peered in dubiously. In front of a hearth where bits of driftwood flamed, a small very old hunched man in a blue jersey and a sailor's cap was lurching up and down in a ricketty dance.

Quite haunted now, we passed on down the 'street'. A two-storey house looked intact. On the threshold, sticking out beyond the edge of one leaf of the door, the toes of two boots were just visible. As our boots clumped on the grass-grown track we must have been audible. *His* boots never moved. He was a middle-aged man with short, greying hair and a face shaved shiny red, in an old grey pullover and dirty tweed trousers. He was contemplating the dark-blue reef of Raasay. When we stopped opposite him, and our eyes met, he said nothing. Was it possible to buy some milk from him, we wondered? 'No,' he said. Or anywhere else nearby? 'No,' he pronounced again. When we said goodbye and turned back, chastened and thirsty, towards the well and the hostel, he said nothing at all.

Were these the last two people to live in what had been a populous township? It seems likely. Next morning, two miles north, we arrived at Cuaig, a cluster of crofts on level ground that had been well grazed and cultivated – the kind of green oasis among heathery browns and purples which marks a crofting site even two centuries after the people left or were evicted. At Cuaig there were hens, calves, children – a civilisation still active. When we asked at a house for water, the family insisted on giving us an old ginger ale bottle of fresh milk and half a Burnett's plain white loaf from Inverness, wrapped in its greaseproof paper. And utterly refused payment. As we talked it turned out that these were not their homes. They were, in effect, refugees – people from the slightly larger Fearnmore, on the headland two miles north, who had despaired of winning the conditions for a reasonable livelihood in their native Applecross and were now trekking southward with their stock to the nearest roadhead and harbour.

At that time Scotland lost about 44,000 people every year by emigration. When the North Sea oilwells opened, this figure was halved.

We said goodbye to these folk, who had nothing and had given us something, and walked on north by east to Rubha na Fearn. We could have taken two-thirds off the distance left by cutting east across the peninsula but Tony knew a crofter in Fearnbeg, Mrs MacBeth, who had given him lodging the year before and he wanted to take her some tea and chocolate biscuits to say thankyou. When we arrived at her house, she had just been hefting a half-hundredweight sack of Indian corn for her hens up the hundred foot of steep path from the shore where the merchant launch from Shieldaig had left it for her. She was in her fifties at least, in black widow's skirt and jumper and cotton apron, and her tanned cheeks and forehead had a sunset flush. At once she made us a *strùpag*, the Highland snack for the wayfarer – tea and soda-flavoured flat scones with strawberry jam. Her house had the perfectly plain interior which is almost unknown now that Highland homes are richly stocked with furniture and ornaments from the catalogues. The walls were varnished tongue-and-groove boarding and the sole ikons (no doubt she was Presbyterian) were two very small colour photos of the Queen and the Duke of

Edinburgh, about a yard and a half apart, he in naval uniform, blue-and-gold with a white peaked cap, she in a red jacket and a hat with a black cockade – that same photo which we students would not stand to worship when it was screened along with the national anthem at the end of the evening's showing at the cinema. Presently the photos became the subject of our conversation. Mrs MacBeth dropped her voice and looked troubled. 'Do you think', she asked us (as bringers of knowledge from the Lowlands), 'that he is *kind* to her? I think he has a hard face.'

'I'm sure she has an extremely comfortable life,' I said, intransigently republican, conceding nothing to the human side of things. But it did half-strike me at the time, and has been with me very much ever since, that it was wholly poignant for Mrs MacBeth, on her own and hunched with work in that extreme environment, to be so warmly and innocently concerned about the wellbeing of her chieftain.

The feudality of it came home to me richly twenty years later, three miles across Loch Torridon in Diabaig, when the royal yacht, long and immaculately white, anchored in the sea-roads during its summer progress through the islands. In the harbour below our camp, an old seine-net boat was the base for a team of scallop fishers, who were stripping the undersea reefs of those most succulent and expensive shellfish. The deck was one-third covered with bulging sacks of them. Presently a pinnace from the *Britannia* tied up at the quay and a royal underling negotiated briskly, then took a whole sackful back to his employers. Some hours later – in keeping with the ancient, not to say barbaric style of the occasion – the pinnace called again with payment in kind: a case of malt whisky for the fishermen.

Mrs MacBeth may well be dead now, her house empty for good or awaiting conversion to a holiday home for relatives or Lowland incomers. Her township could have been saved. For several years in the Sixties, looking across from Diabaig, we saw puffs of dust like shellbursts springing from that coast where Tony and I had walked the switchback path. Four men with a second-hand bulldozer were slowly cleaving and blasting a road from Shieldaig west to Ardheslaig, Kenmore, Arinacrinachd, Fearnbeg. The townships showed as toy white oblongs across the water. Very few were lit at night. The home-made road was slow to build because no government funds were forthcoming and because each landlord in turn resisted the work which might yet save the townships before they all went the way of Fearnmore, Cuaig, and Lonbain. These landlords were not exactly clearing or evicting people. They were not behaving like the Duchess of Leeds, who owned Applecross in mid-Victorian times. In August 1859 her ground officers evicted a tailor, his ill wife, and their baby by manhandling them outside and padlocking the door of their house against them. But these present-day landlords were not helping the crofters to stay. The only people they had much use for were gamekeepers and servants – employees to drive the Land Rovers to the end of the track and cart back the dead deer – since 'sporting' income is so much higher than crofting rentals.

At last, the home-made road reached Kenmore, and then the houses looked bright white from across the water. They were being freshly Snowcemmed and a new family with young children had moved in, just months after two households had flitted south for good. Now the butcher's and greengrocer's vans could get there, the trucks bringing in new beds and cookers, an ambulance in time of need. The path we had toiled along, plunging and climbing between the green-bristled and bronze-boled stands of Loch Maree pines, had been obliterated or bypassed. A few miles short of Mrs MacBeth's we had paused to chat with the County Council path-mender, a quizzical man with a yellowish complexion and a mouthful of eroded brown teeth. His tools were a shovel and a pick and he travelled on a Royal Enfield pushbike with rod brakes and a khaki mackintosh folded over the handlebars, tied with a leather strap. 'It is hard work right enough,' he agreed. 'But if you do it well, you will be getting a smooth ride home on it yourself.'

Finally, his work was made redundant. The Inner Sound became a torpedo range and proving-ground for Polaris-carrying submarines. In 1976 I swam off Red Point, five miles north, and swivelled in the water to look through the wave-crests to the tabular blue headlands off Trotternish in Skye. A tar-coloured steel whale with a blunt, featureless conning-tower slid from left to right across my vision. We saw it again in 1982 as we drove down the new road which the government had commissioned for the sake of armament when it would do no such thing for people.

A seal would lift its head
and a basking-shark its sail,

15

but today in the sea-sound
a submarine lifts its turret
and its black sleek back
threatening the thing that would make
dross of wood, of meadows and of rocks,
that would leave Screapadal without beauty
just as it was left without people.

So now a road swishes straight past above Lonbain, where one
man danced crazily beside his hearth and another could hardly
bear to meet a stranger – past the naval depot which is a non-place
on the map. Ach, the ill-kept secrets of the state, how they typify
our age! As we drove up to Kyle in the middle of that freezing
winter, we failed to get lodging in the ice-bound inn at Cluanie,
then dropped down to sea level at Dornie on Loch Duich as night
fell. In the hotel bar, as we waited for a meal, five men were well
away already, their table crowded with drams and half-drunk pints.
They called for champagne with their meal and the landlady went
to fetch it from a shed in the back garden. At the bar I stood next
to a bulky six-footer with large, glazed black eyes. When my CND
badge came into focus, he swung back to the bar, swung round to
me again, and said abruptly, 'You don't own your own house, do
you? No – you don't!' When I assured him that I *was* a householder,
and that in spite of this stake in the British way of life I thought that
nuclear weapons were more dangerous than what they defended us
against, he changed tack, but not a lot, and said in a menacing voice,
'Some people want us to lie down on our backs with our legs in the
air and let the Russians walk all over us.' Then he carried the tray of
whiskies back to his mates. In the morning they were subdued and
blotchy and one of them was scared because he couldn't remember
where he had left the official Land-Rover the night before. Who
were they? Engineers installing hi-tech equipment for the Navy perhaps, or sappers setting up yet another military base, drinking and
concreting their way round the world from Belize to Diego Garcia
to Stornoway. As I have travelled round the Highlands and Islands
in the past few years, and in the Canadian Maritimes and northern
Manitoba, I have been forced to realise how, all over our world, it
is often this defence industry, this preparedness for war, that has
kept the remoter places inhabited and capable of yielding a modern
wage.

CHAPTER THREE

POURING AWAY THE MILK
Sleat, Skye

In the autumn of 1987 I went straight to Sleat, at the southern-most end of Skye, drawn by the force of Alastair MacKinnon's news about his forebears:

> About the same time [as the eviction of his maternal grand-mother's people from Suishnish] my other grandfather Alexander MacKinnon, whose name I bear, was being evicted with his family from Morsaig which is opposite Boreraig in Strath. With several more families, they had been removed from Boreraig only ten years previously. My grandfather, quite a number of years afterwards, got this half croft of 4 Sasaig but his two brothers were forced to emigrate with their wives but they died on the voyage to North America. Their wives landed in North America, both widowed and each with babes in arms born on the voyage.

Alastair recapitulated these atrocities with a kind of imperturbable calm. We were sitting in his caravan perched among the birch and alder above the road from Isleornsay to Armadale while his wife covered the table with tea and fruitcake and chocolate biscuits. (In the holiday season they let their house to visitors.) Under his calm the hurt abides: 'I read half way through Alexander MacKenzie's book about the Clearances, but I had to stop – it was too painful.'

The MacKinnons and the Robertsons had been a few among the thousands banished from their homesteads during the years after the 1846 potato famine, when the Highlands became a scene of crowded destitution not unlike East Africa today. The evictions did not end with that nightmare time. They whimpered on into the doldrum years before the Land War. Then the crofters fought back. In 1886 with the help of the five M.P.'s they had elected, the Act was passed which gave them security of tenure and a review (usually a reduction) of rents – but still not enough living-space. On Skye alone, between 1840 and 1883, 1,740 notices to quit were served at the bidding of the estates. The sordid or vicious chivvying behind that statistic, on all sorts of pretexts, came out in Alastair's final story:

A great-grandfather Archie Campbell was evicted from No. 6 Teangue, the adjoining township to this one. He was fifty years old and was able to emigrate to New Zealand with his family all except my grandmother, Catherine, who eventually married Alexander MacKinnon at 4 Sasaig. The emigration took place in 1871 and the eviction, probably the previous year, was due to Archie Campbell having fallen foul of the estate land officers. One of them shot his dog at his heel as he was about to open a gate while taking a short cut through Knock Farm on his way home. When they were evicted, they were charged a removal fee – the ground officer took this money . . .

Knock and Ostaig were the two large sheep farms at the north and south ends of the district. (Sabhal Mòr Ostaig, the big barn of Ostaig, now houses a Gaelic-language college of business studies.) It was for the sake of their swollen rents that the estate was clearing out the tenants of single crofts. To reach beyond his own family Alastair now sent me out along that network which is actually the matrix of this book: the people with unbreakable ties of kin and shared experience who still live in the beach-heads of shallow soil to which their forebears were consigned.

Sleat is 'the Garden of Skye'. I had first sampled its fruits twenty-nine autumns before on an unhurried journey from Uig down to the Mallaig ferry at Armadale, cooking a lunch or a high tea of scrambled eggs over a little petrol stove on the foreshore and following that with many handfuls of glistening black brambles, both tart and sweet, picked from canes curving over stone dykes upholstered with herb-Robert and saxifrage. That luxuriant seaboard, tilted away from the severest Atlantic winds, feels unHighland because it is not stark, it has both shade and shelter. The very air feels enriched by the bunched leaves, whether they grow on the invasive trees of the old jungle, the birch and the alder, or on the monumental planted beeches, sycamores, and exotic conifers surrounding Armadale Castle. Here the MacDonald chiefs steadily ruined themselves in the most stylish manner possible. Even the stables have a battlemented tower at their centre and the 'castle', completed in 1815, was dreamed up as a hulking *schloss* in full Gothic fig. (A single staircase window cost Lord MacDonald £500.) It burned down in 1855. The remnants of the front wall now lour between the treetrunks like the backdrop of an expensive, rather old-fashioned production of *Rigoletto*. As for the stables, they have become a 'Taste of Scotland' restaurant, perfectly refurbished in mahogany and naked stone, where women in skirts and bodices with a discreet proportion of tartan serve you smoked salmon and malt whisky. This is the Clan Donald Centre, known locally as The Clan, created with the help of money from an American corporation so rich it was able to fund the building of a state freeway when the state's own funds ran out. The Clan has created fourteen jobs, with more to come. In the words of the wisest thinker about the Scottish countryside, Fraser Darling, 'the working capital of the Highlands is its scenery', so it is pointless to repine if a land which once housed a self-sufficient culture must now live by displaying itself as a piece of 'heritage'. Equally we should remember that what Darling calls 'one of Europe's best bits of wilderness' is fringed by a *civilisation* – settlements dug out of what they call 'black moor' by the work of women and men who were then forced to evacuate these cramped bridgeheads.

Such a settlement was Dalavil, on the west coast of Sleat, and such was Caradal, opposite Dalavil across the mouth of Allt a' Ghlinne. This is a 'wilderness area', according to one writer in the *West Highland Free Press*. The 'Walks and Talks' brochure available at the Clan refers to 'the lost wood of Dalavil'. Some years ago a learned geographer wrote that Gleann Meadhanach, which runs due west across Sleat to Dalavil, was 'an interesting example of underpopulation' – i.e. it's empty – since 'there is evidence of ancient cultivation'. If he had watched the people's mouth, he would have discovered that Dalavil and Caradal were cultivated in next-to-living memory and were cleared at the time of the Education Acts of 1870–2. Donald MacDonald of Mavis Bank, a near neighbour of Alastair's, told me:

It was for the children to get their schooling. It was cheaper to clear the crofters than to build a school there. It was quite isolated – there was no road to it, just a path over the hill. They missed their old crofts just the same. It was a very good place for fishing, plenty of mackerel, and ling, and again there was shellfish too, and there was a lot of [sea]weed for their crops, for their potatoes and whatever they were turning.

To visit Dalavil, I left the road from Ostaig across the hills and followed the brown pools of Abhainn a' Ghlinne Mheadhanaich through heather infested with bracken. Nearby the whiteness of a sheep showed and for once it didn't startle away. It was a lamb lying helpless on its side, hidden from the shepherd's eyes by the smothering bracken. The ground next its feet was thrashed and stirred into a sticky brown quag. I took it by its horns and boosted it gently a short way onto wholesome grass. It couldn't stand without help and I had to leave it there, its eyes fixed, its breath coming in slow heaves. Dalavil in the west looked a long way off through the dim air of late September. Presently the glen expanded into wide level fields with the remains of a house looking seaward across them, its walls still six feet high and its chimney-stack erect, the plume of a rowan growing out of the flue. Now the thread of a sheep-trod I'd been following entered a wood which grew densely down to a loch used by whooper swans. It felt aboriginal, choked with growth – scrubby saplings thinning upward towards the light, mature trees blown down but still nourishing foliage through the few roots left in the earth, still older trees rotting where they'd fallen. Masonry loomed – a single house strangled by honeysuckle and scrub hazel. It became difficult to keep a westward line and the growth festooned thickly enough to conjure up the 'green hell' of Amazonia and that monstrous photo of an anaconda rearing, a deer's antlered head crammed in its jaws . . . Soon, the translucency of light over the sea began to sparkle between the branches and Dalavil opened out around me with that singular welcoming and softening of the atmosphere which never leaves a settlement.

A stretch of the river-bank was revetted with packed shingle-stones. A drystone dyke with a turf-and-heather top divided the moor from the old fields and to my right the last roofed house stood up, apparently used as a bothy by crofters dosing their sheep or herding them back for the autumn lamb sales. A brown enamel teapot stood in the remains of a fireplace and a dangerous ladder led upstairs. Through boggy grass beside the river, purple flares of heather conducted my feet, signalling drier, firmer ground – the line of an old path. The heart of the croftland was a broad, shallow swell of still pure grassland, surrounded by a tweed of russet and green – the warp and weft of the old lazybeds where potatoes or oats were grown. Now heather grew along their tops and rushes in the runnels between them. Caradal on the far side looked as though it must always have been a narrow and hard place to live in, squeezing up the burn of Bealach na Ceàrdaich. Down here it was all habitable. A fisherman's hut had been built up with boulders against the side of a little knoll, a dyke stretched out into the shallows of the bay to keep in the grazing animals. On a rock rib a dozen cormorants and great black-backed gulls stood silhouetted in a row, like the knobs on the krang of a beached whale, and a heron flapped off just above the wavelets, an unusual white bar on each wing. The crowds of fat birds confirmed Donald MacDonald's report of good fishing, as did the bulky shells they had left in the heather after gulping the meat. The mussels were fist-sized and I measured a whelk 2¾ inches long and nearly 2 inches in diameter.

Beside the croftland there were three heaps of small stones, evidence of laborious field-making, and I remembered Bill Brooker, geographer and climber, telling me how in the back glens of the Tilt, south of the Cairngorms, people moved from elsewhere – perhaps in the clearance of Upper Deeside to make room for Queen Victoria – would break in ground from the moor, levering out boulders, hacking ditches, chopping up the rooty soil, making a croft from wilderness. Oats and potatoes would be growing and the laird's factor would come along and say, 'Weel, weel, that's a fine wee place ye have here now! How much rent is it ye're peyin? Five bob! Michty me, it's worth mair than that! We'll be needing £3 from you the next time . . . ' Of course they couldn't find that much, and out they had to go. And their work had been monumental.

Here in Dalavil the people (MacKinnons, MacGillivrays, Robertsons for the most part) had prayed and sung psalms to the sound of running water. Children as they grew older looked up at the terraced black drop of Doire na h-Achlais where wild water sheds its veils and jets of spume and wondered, 'When will it stop? Why does it come in jerks instead of smoothly?' And thought this over and over again as their senses curled out to understand the world. The mothers and fathers loved and hated each other, the conditions allowed of no daily escape, to the pub or down the motorway – although the men (and the single women) could escape for seasons at a time if need or fancy drove them over as guest-workers to the mainland, where they lifted potatoes in the big fields of Ayrshire and Angus or brought in hefty harvests with their own sickles that they had carried with them over the kyle and over the mountains.

You could say that here humanity tried to establish itself and failed, over a period small in the eye of time but long in the minds of the tyauving families. The final families at Dalavil did not fail, they were terminated (with extreme prejudice, to use a C.I.A. term). And the lack of a school was only an excuse. The estate and the incoming farmers wanted the best land, the broad well-grassed glen bottoms, for the wintering of their sheep and they wanted the hill land – the crofters' traditional common grazings – for summer pasture and later for sport. 'We had a little glen here above Sasaig,' Alastair told me. 'It was just part of the common grazing. Well, my grandfather's people were told by the estate to fence it, and they couldn't afford it, so it was taken into Knock farm.' To them that have . . . When the Victorian gentry were seized by the urge to kill everything that moved, they bagged thousands in a day, not only grouse, partridges, and pheasants but curlew and woodcock, pigeons and snipe, rabbits and hares and deer and seals. The sportsmen came ravaging over the croftlands, serviced by a corps of estate workers organised by gamekeepers. 'The keeper was worse than the landlord,' says Donald MacDonald. 'They would shoot a dog, or a cat – if they saw a cat, and it was mousing or something, they would shoot it. Protecting the birds.' When I asked in amazement, 'What birds?' – because the hills of Sleat are quietly empty now – he recalled the abundance of game at one time:

> Och, I remember, between here and the road, you would start up a covey, and another one before you reached it. Grouse, and partridges, and blackcock – a beautiful bird – that tail! And when the shooters came down, it was bang-bang-bang! And if we had the horses near in, tethered, they would be rearing up, and running round and round – we would have to go out to them and shift them into a safer place.

The crofters were being curbed on all sides, left with minimal room and minimal resources. All through the summer of 1883 they retailed the ordeals of the previous sixty years to the Parliamentary Commissioners under Lord Napier who sailed from Argyll round to Easter Ross and interrogated hundreds of crofters. 'To those who told the tale, and to their fellows who heard it, the effect was one of profound psychological liberation, at both personal and communal levels, while to the world at large the social and political conditions it exposed, and the manner of their exposure, were of no less shattering importance. Facts which had for generations lacked a means of expression were now, for the first time, articulated in public . . . ' The evidence from Sleat, given to the Commissioners at Isleornsay, where we were lodging, is desperate in its pleas for rights: the right to cut heather for thatch (but this would jeopardise the grouse); the right to collect seaweed from the shore for fertiliser without paying the estate factor. They badly needed a pier to give the fishermen safe harbour and some chance of competing with the east-coast boats which came through the Pentland Firth or the Caledonian Canal and scoured the herrings of all sizes and ages out of Loch Hourn. The fish were salted down in barrels and exported to Russia to feed its needy peasantry. And the 'peasants' of Skye? From the sheltered and soft lands of eastern Sleat they were squeezed out into the narrowest coastal lands. It was an intricate game of Monopoly, practised by the estate managers who planted a house here, removed two there, but never quite managed to buy a hotel on Park Lane with the proceeds. Donald Robertson, a 65-year-old fisherman from Sasaig, told Napier how he had been brought up in Kilmore, where the slope is easiest and there is a very old settlement with a church in the midst of a hummocky graveyard. Fourteen years before there had been 'two lots cleared there. Two widows were cleared off there, and a widower . . . without any reason whatsoever [i.e. no rent arrears], but just to make room for another man who was a ground officer.' These men were small tenants themselves as well as being on the estate payroll. A few months later in the Uists I learned that the nickname for a ground officer was *abhag*, 'terrier': 'The weak ones were the worst devils,' I was told. 'If they were of lower status in the estate, they were more dangerous – they wanted to make a name for themselves.' In Sasaig Donald Robertson was allotted a half croft but no house: 'I was put into a small bothy that had been built for a stable and a byre, and I sometimes could take the snow off the bed with my hand while in bed. I dared not open my mouth about that.' And there he lived for eight years.

Donald MacDonald told me how his folk had been cleared from Ferindonald just north of Kilmore:

> They had come from Glencoe a few years after the massacre. My ancestor was Paul, and he landed at Armadale there down behind the pier, what they call Rubhà Phòil. He was the leader and so they called them MacPhail, the sons of Paul, but they were MacDonalds – that was the idea of them coming to Sleat, because it was the MacDonald's [i.e. it belonged to that chief]. The eldest son had to go off to the landlord's regiment, to some of MacDonald's regiments or else the family would be evicted. Och, they were fighting these battles in the Napoleonic Wars and the Spanish Peninsular Wars – my grandfather was wounded in it, he had only one arm, it was a hook he had. But he was a very good joiner – he built a boat of his own in a cave by the seashore.

This family was cleared to No. 20, Tarskavaig, a township above a bay on the west side which is so beautifully the calendar image of a crofting village that it has been a magnet for photographers from Robert M. Adam, working in black-and-white before the War, to the colour postcards of recent years. In these photos it looks as though a broad bright quilt in sap-green and bluish green, olive and ochre and brassy yellow, has been spread over rugged ground, filling the hollows, shrugging round outcrops, stretching smoothly down the slopes. White houses with twin gables like eyebrows on their front roofs look out over their trim rectangles of potato rigs, hayfields dotted with drying stooks, late-ripening oats, and ley fields freckled with flowers. Beyond, across the sound where Loch Slapin and Loch Eishort funnel out towards the ocean, the toothed and striated massifs of the Black Cuillin and Blaven, Garbh Bheinn and Marsco, rise in a tremendous barrier of Hebridean blue. The colour and texture of the township have simplified to an even green. Only a few potatoes are grown and the place is becoming a haven for retired people, mostly original families along with several of the incomers dubbed 'goat people' or 'white settlers' who have come to escape the poisons of mainland Britain.

Alastair had sent me to his second cousin, another descendant of Paul of Glencoe, called Archie Gilleasbaig MacDonald, a retired headmaster who had just built himself a fine house on the family croft. His hands still showed the wear and tear of the heavy work. He was a man of bristling strength, mental as well as physical, and adept at phrasing mordant observations on how his people were mistreated. His feeling was that the chiefs had betrayed their people:

> The MacDonalds were outbred for generations to the English aristocracy. So they were no longer part and parcel of the people amongst whom they lived. It would be the same if I bred my Highland cows to shorthorns. After four generations it would be shorthorns I'd get.

The value he set on the native and rooted qualities of this part of the world came out as he spoke about Highland cattle in the literal sense:

> It was cattle they had here, before the sheep – sheep were the worst thing that ever hit the Highlands, though I keep them myself. The Highland cattle were small, before the breeders turned them into horns and hair, and they matured slowly. Black, brindled, a few reds, the occasional yellow. All of them had a needle stripe down their back, a lighter streak like you see on a horse. We milked them out there on the hill. They were quiet. You could keep the bulls among the cows in the byre and let them out into the field in the morning. Those bulls were the only ones the Department of Agriculture would allow without a ring in their nose.

For all this practical affection Archie Gilleasbaig doesn't romanticise the old crofting culture. He emphasised the hardship of it:

> They were poor – very poor. There's a green morass up in the hill there, the name of it is 'the Flowing of the Blood'. They drove the cattle into the bog and cut a vein in their throats and drew it off and mixed it with oatmeal, like a black pudding, and then the animals could get away. Och, they were very poor, and they had these hunting dogs foisted on them by the keepers. Every house had to feed them for a fortnight, whether you wanted to or not. There was a neighbour of ours who could hardly feed her children but she had to feed the dogs. They *kept* them poor, it was their idea. Down at Arisaig, when they were getting cockles from the sand to eat, the landlord sent his men to plough up the

beach so that the birds would eat them, to discourage the people from getting them.

Such poverty was endemic in the marginal land of the islands but it was felt to be acute only in famine years and Tarskavaig veterans testified in 1883 that the place was 'in a pretty comfortable condition' before the Clearances. Archie lent me his daughter's thesis on the township and this laid bare a history which could be matched all round the coasts. Tarskavaig was planned in 1811 and laid out in rectangular lots ruled onto the map regardless of contours. The original five little farms had grown to eleven by the time of the lotting. Presently, there were 31 crofts, 30 less than three acres and only four worth rent of more than £1. The population trebled while Sleat's as a whole rose by a half. By 1883, out of nine crofts recently subdivided only three involved natural increase, to make room for a son: that is, the rest were being sliced up by the estate to make room for incomers evicted from elsewhere. What the estate had needed from its Tarskavaig property was kelp rent. The crofters cut seaweed to make the industrially valuable chemical and paid their rent in tons cut at a price fixed by the managers: 'as more kelp was gathered, the rent would increase proportionately.' Even if the people worked harder, they could never increase their income. The ingrained bitterness of a people forced for generations to labour like Sisyphus with stones that could never reach a resting-point came out when Archie Gilleasbaig showed me out through his grassy front garden and gave the ground a hard thump with his boot. 'That's what they gave us to live off,' he said. 'Rock six inches down.'

Although Archie is still in his prime, he has a direct line to the middle nineteenth century. Sitting amongst later twentieth century comfort, picture windows and modern fabrics, he can recount at only one remove the exact hardships of his cleared forebears:

My MacKinnon relatives were evicted from Morsaig [ten miles up the coast] in the early 1850s. The place was burnt while all the men were away at the fishing. When they came here they had to spend all night on the green because the other people hadn't been shifted out to make room for them. Well – unless you get it from some old folk there is no knowing the wanderings of these displaced people. My grandmother told me about it. I knew her so well. She would have been about 102 when she died in 1932, when I was ten. She knew absolutely no English. She was a servant girl up at Ord House and her wage was £6 a year and tea – the MacDonalds there had been planters so there was plenty of tea. They fed the servants on braxy mutton, where the sheep had had that illness. They used to say it was fit to eat if you took up the carcase by the legs and swung it round your head and it stayed in one piece!

The exact spot where they lived in Morsaig was marked by a big ash tree growing at the end wall of the house. They cut it down a few years ago and my father was furious. They were piling them into this village, people were living in little huts by the shore. And then they built themselves houses – you could tell them, they all faced north and east and the back wall was the rock. And then my grandmother's brothers, Charles MacKinnon and I think it was John MacKinnon, they wouldn't lift their bonnets to Lord MacDonald, because their grandmother had been cleared. So they were kicked out.

The wanderings of the displaced people: I badly wanted to follow their actual routes, as nearly as you can today. The line that most drew me led from Suishnish and Boreraig eastward along the north shore of Loch Eishort to Drumfearn. Alastair MacKinnon's people had been unusual in retreating that way. Most went north to Broadford through Strath Suardal and were seen there by a young Lowlander, Archibald Geikie, later renowned as a geologist:

A strange wailing sound reached my ears at intervals on the breeze from the west . . . I could see a long and motley procession winding along the road that led north from Suishnish . . . the minister [of Kilbride] with his wife and daughters had come out to meet the people and bid them all farewell . . . There were old men and women, too feeble to walk, who were placed in carts; the younger members of the community on foot were carrying their bundles of clothes and household effects, while the children, with looks of alarm, walked alongside. When they set forth once more, a cry of grief went up to heaven, the long plaintive wail, like a funeral coronach, was resumed . . . the sound seemed to re-echo through the whole wide valley of Strath in one prolonged note of desolation.

That lacerating passage and the contemporary newspaper and pamphlet account have been quoted more than once. We know how Flora Matheson, aged 96, had her house barred and padlocked against her and was helped by her grandchildren to crawl to a byre, where they lived for months. Here her son joined her when he came home from harvest work on the mainland. When he fell ill in the cold and damp and died, he lay with his head at the door, his black hair waving in the wind, till he was coffined. We know how at Suishnish three men, a MacInnes and two Macraes, fought with the ground officers – were taken in irons to Portree – walked voluntarily to Inverness to be tried for deforcement – were acquitted, then evicted five days after Christmas. Their mother was dragged out into the snow on a blanket. As her grandson aged seven said that night, '*O nam bitheadh m'athair an seo an-diugh, cò aig an robh a chridhe seo a dhèanamh oirnn!*' ('If my father was here today, who would dare to do this to us!'). But none of these accounts mentions the milk: the sadistic wasting of it at the eviction, the daunting failure of it that night when the cleared folk lay down exhausted among their animals at Drumfearn.

It turns out that what the estate men did with the milk was even more obliterating than Alastair's memoir had already told me. In the spring of 1989, on Mull, I visited Mary Morrison at Penmore Mill near Dervaig, expecting to hear memoirs of clearance in that area. Within minutes she was describing the clearance of Boreraig, as she had been told it *by her father*. He was a Macrae, born in the 1840s, a boy in 1853:

One thing that he always used to mention, he remembered the bailiffs putting out the fire with the basins of milk – you know that they set the milk for cream to make butter, and they put out the fires with the basins of milk, and I suppose a small boy would remember that, because in those days milk was very precious at that time ... And he had a story of a very old lady who was ill and had to be lifted out from her house on a litter. He mentioned her by name, she was a Matheson, in fact he was related to her.

The fire will have been in the centre of the house, on a stone hearth set in an earth floor, the smoke going up and out of a chimney-hole in the roof. The custom was that there was always at least one fire burning in the village. In spring, when the soot-caked thatch was taken off the roofs and littered over the fields to fertilise them, this was done in turn so that by the time the last house came to shed its thatch the first was already roofed again and its fire re-kindled. The keeping in of the fire was so close to the heart of their way of life that people said a prayer as they smoored it – built turfs over it at night so that the embers would still be hot in the morning:

> I smoor the fire
> As the Son of Mary would smoor it.
> Blessed be the house and the fire,
> Blessed be all the people.
> Who is on the floor? Peter and Paul.
> Who must keep the watch tonight?
> Gentle Mary and her Son.
> The mouth of God said, the angel of God tells.
> An angel in the door of every house
> To shield and protect us all
> Till white day comes in the morning.

It is no wonder that the words 'hearth' and 'heart' are so like each other and no wonder that the evictors chose to strike there, as they did in Knoydart opposite Sleat, on Barra, in Lewis at Dallmore ('Had you seen it, you could scarcely bear the sight') and Great Bernera and Shawbost (while the woman was away getting her baby vaccinated), in Harris and Strath Naver (water poured down the chimney-hole which 'created a volume of smoke, mingled with ashes, that filled the whole place, and made breathing most difficult') . . .

Such was the work of the estate men who were dubbed, in Sutherland, the 'fire brigade', led by Donald Bannerman whose nickname was 'Sgrios' – destroy. For all the fires of a township to be quenched – forever – was fundamental. It must have been experienced as a breach in something eternal, a snuffing-out of the life-possibility itself, and to do it with the clean and precious milk, from the wooden cogs scoured with fresh water and stones rubbed to a high finish, linked the obliterations of food and fuel, warmth and nourishment, in a single unholy rite. Imagine it: the slopping of the milk as it was carried indoors – the hiss-and-dunt of the explosion as the liquid hit the flaming peats – the obscene stench like flesh scorched – the fizzing and curdling of the last few bubbles around the embers.

I set out for Suishnish and Boreraig from the road-end at Camus Malag, the home of Mary Morrison's mother, where her father went to fish lobsters and presumably to court his bride – Mary called it 'a tiny cove, a beautiful little place'. A track climbed and twisted southward, built when the Board of Agriculture briefly re-crofted Suishnish after the Great War. Attuned to the history of the place, my eyes were seeing traces of the old life everywhere. Up in the hollows of the moor on my left, the map shows only an ancient remnant, a dun or Iron Age fort at Kearstach. When I quested up there, drawn by a faint corduroy of lazybeds in the heather, I found an entire village strung out along a rib where the land lifted clear of the bog. Each house was visible as an oblong of big grey stones, the corners rounded, a green lawn still girdling the homestead. 'It was a bleak country,' says the modern historian. But the cleared lands were usually the antithesis of 'bleak'. Suishnish presently opened out on both sides of the track in an ample spread of good grassland, a gently inclined plateau between moor and cliff, seventy or eighty acres of field still scarcely smirched by weeds. On the inland side, which was clearly the old core of the place, a pattern of paths knitting houses to each other and low stone dykes topped with turf made sense of the terrain as features articulate a human face. The houses – mere hollow cairns now – were well back from the cliff edge where the sea-winds would make a withering updraught. The one modern house, still roofed in crinkly tin painted raw red, was on the seaward side of the track. It looked to be a shepherd's bothy: black iron bedstead with mildewed mattress, splayed ricketty chairs, torn tongues of wallpaper lolling off the walls, a few brown glass bottles, a copy of the National Farmers' Union weekly for August 1985 yellowing on the window-sill. As I approached, a figure in a khaki anorak, head bowed and hooded, walked slowly into a lean-to fifty yards off the track. As I drew level, I saw him moving about in the half-dark inside and waved my hand. No response. A minute later I looked back. The lean-to might as well have been deserted.

One hundred and thirty-one years before, Alastair's grandmother and her people had abandoned No. 11 up amongst the fields and trekked off eastward. Perhaps they hoped for shelter among the Macraes and MacInneses of Boreraig. The *abhagan*, the terriers, might be leaving it alone – who could tell? Better risk that than accept a passage on an emigrant ship like last year's Suishnish contingent. They had sailed from Campbeltown on the *Hercules* and suffered terribly from smallpox. The passage between hill and sea-cliff narrows. The steep ground to the left rears into Carn Dearg and Creag an Daraich, the red rocky hill and the cliff of oaks, armoured in very old hard sandstone. Here is the drop, 350 feet to the sea, a place they rarely passed if they could help it, marked by a boulder jutting into midair, its face streaked with tears of rain. The updraught has carved a funnel-mouth out of sandy clay. The brown-legged girls and boys go first, gripping the stones with peat-stained toes, posting themselves with their sticks to bar the way against the cattle which drive their hooves through the turf and stand at bay rolling their eyes, flinching at a gust from the sea immediately below. They half plunge down the stony chute, backbones sloping and straightening. The dogs snap at their houghs, are jerked back by snarls from the men. The young women follow the cattle, creels lurching on their backs, pale or flushed faces of babies peering over the rims. The older women bow under the weight of the tools, foot-ploughs and flachter-spades for the peats tied in bundles with heather-ropes, spinning wheels, black pots and slowrie-chains for hanging them above the fire, the wooden cogs for the milk. Nobody looks back to the padlocked houses.

From below, the slowly twisting-untwisting ravel of figures, shawled or blue-bonnetted, bare-headed or wearing the white mutches of married women, the hindmost silhouetted in the vee of the wind-funnel, the leaders blending into the scree of the descent, look like a file of charred angels falling in slow motion out of the heavens – like Israelites with no milky or honeyed Canaan on their horizon.

Down at sea level, a few yards of turf with shingle bulging through make a footway between the southernmost scarps of Beinn Bhuidhe and the salt waters of Loch Eishort. The scarps are blackish, degenerate stuff, a coagulation neither earth nor rock, 'heights decaying never to be decayed', crawling with ivy in their nether reaches. They piss soil and shit stones down spouting cascades of a horrible beauty, curving out of the ground at eighty or a hundred feet in twists of snow-white water, demon-haired. A mile and a half to go before the old dun of Boreraig raises up its green mound topped with weathered stones. The cattle put down their heads to browse. The boys clatter at their rumps. The men swear. A few babies cry for the breast as their stomachs cramp but most keep still, feeling their mothers' backbones shift and give as their feet feel for balance.

The level arable triangle of Boreraig reaches back into the steeps of Beinn a' Mheadhain, smiling like an oasis. The sandstone outcrops are so blocky that from a distance they seem to double the number of houses, which have tall gable-ends, doors that make you stoop less than in most villages, with good thick lintels and sometimes two windows between door and house-end. Ashes and sycamores, dwarfed by sea-wind, bunch their thick foliage along the middle burn. The turf round their roots is trodden dusty-hard as a threshing floor by cattle craving shade on the hotter days. The leaves are seared by five months' salty winds but they still layer densely, mixing their greens and browns in a rustling camouflage. The oats are pale yellow, the shaws of the potatoes rusted – ready to reap and lift. No blue smoke makes the air fragrant above the roofs. The doors are all chained up or barred and nailed. The people are huddled against the gable-ends or sheltering their babies in the entries of the roasting-kilns, their eyes shocked and emptied. A MacInnes woman is rocking and crooning while her man slowly beats his forehead against a cornerstone of his house. From the little they can make themselves say it seems that Factor MacDonald has been and – there was a bit of a fight – the MacRae brothers have been dragged away in handcuffs. The rest lack even the milk and oatcake to offer the Suishnish folk a *strùpag*.

Nothing for it but to trail on past Neill Kelly's place beside the roaring white waterfall which bounds the clachan on the east. It is two wet hummocky miles to Loch an Eilean Heast, three more to the head of Loch Eishort. Beyond the few poor houses at Heast, a thread of a path, rarely used, melts into the bog. Ahead, in the gloaming, someone thinks they see a grassy way twisting through the heather – they make a beeline for it through bushes deep as a child – it is only a narrow morass which winds down to the burn of Allt Lòn Bhuidhe. This is a bad dream now, endless. If the floodtide has filled into the mouth of the Abhainn Ceann, they will never win across to the grassy haugh land north of Drumfearn. There is nothing for the cattle hereabouts, only the tough brown deer's-hair sedge pricking through the heather. And if they feed them the few sheaves of corn the men tore out of the fields, then there will be no seed to plant, and that will be the end . . . The black, ripping current makes the cattle stall. The boys force the beasts into the shallowest part where it ruffles over stones. They stagger but they keep moving and the people follow. Now they feel, rather than see, the softer ground beside the track south to Kilmore. Slowly, with hardly a word to each other, they lie down among the tussocks, beyond hunger, desperate for a nourishing drink, putting fingers into the babies' mouth for something to suck.

The banishment must have been unassuageable for many of the evicted. Mary Morrison's father expressed it in what he sang:

My father had an emotional feeling for that part of the island all his life, and I think it came back more when he was a much older man. He lived till he was 93 [about eighty-six years after the eviction] and he used to sing old songs that they sang away back, and he used occasionally to repeat verses – verses that he had heard as a child. So there was an attachment. I can remember one that he sang I think because he liked the places, and I picked it up because I liked the sound of it, and it was [she recited in Gaelic, then translated]

> Kilmarie under the wing of the ocean,
> Cold Camasunary of the bens,
> Romisdal of the grey [unripened] corn,
> I would like very much to be there.

The exodus from Suishnish/Boreraig was completed for me by Peggy MacKinnon of No. 13 Heast. The township straggles down a narrow glen at the dead-end of a road south from Broadford. It has the look of a place where people lived perforce rather than by choice. Peggy, a retired teacher living in a neat, substantial house well furnished with books and pictures, recalled that the main drainage ditch which had made Heast arable was planned by the landlord to provide work for needy crofters and was known as the Starvation Ditch. She is the great-granddaughter of Neill Kelly who had had the croft in Boreraig next to the waterfall. He was away at sea when the evictors came. His wife had little twin sons, and when she asked the men where the boys were to sleep that night if the door was barred up, one of them answered, 'Throw them into the loch!' This is what I call Fascist humour, the jeer that accompanies a brutal act. Is it because the bully is genuinely tickled? or because he is covering real unease with a hardboiled mask? It shows through in the records we have of evictors at work. Patrick Sellar, burning a house in Strath Naver in 1814, jeers at the householder, 'There's a bonfire for you!' The Duke of Sutherland's manager James Loch advises a tenant in Strath Fleet to clear off 'to America, Glasgow or to the devil if he choosed'. Here is the idiom natural to a class who are so powerful and so contemptuous of those who are in their power that the normal restraints on greed and cruelty count for nothing. You can still meet people who believe that the Highland laird enjoyed *droits de seigneur* and would hang his hat outside the door of a house where he was bedding a new bride. I suppose we will never know. More telling in its ordinariness is the evidence of a woman from Fraserburgh in Aberdeenshire who as a girl used to follow the herring round to Skye and gut fish for a wage on the shore at Loch Eishort, where she lived in a turf hut. She was angered by the meekness of the evicted people, which she blamed on their cultural subjection: 'If they had teached them in their own tongue they would be more self reliant and have a greater pride in their heritage . . . if somebody attempted to burn my house, I would have lifted their skull with the sharpest stone I could lay hands on, and organised the others to do the same.' What she noticed about the factor when he came to collect rent for their bothy was that he was above the law:

One day I noticed the factor and his groom lift a barrel of herring onto their gig. I asked what they were doing. They said, 'Just taking a barrel of herring.' I told them to put it down; if I stole vegetables from his garden he would have had me up before the court. He said, 'Didn't I know he was the factor?' I told him I did not care though he was Prince Albert: if he did not put it down I would go up to Broadford and get the police.

Peggy MacKinnon's people had carried away with them from Boreraig burdens even heavier than I had imagined. They included house stones to help in the building of new places at Drumfearn, Morsaig, and wherever else they found themselves. Some people went back to the clachan once the bully-boys had gone, sheltered as best they could, and lifted the potatoes they had had to leave in the ground. What I got from talking to her went beyond information. We were talking about the difficulties of making a livelihood in the place. I thought of the spruce salmon farm I'd passed down at Loch an Eilein, the crates of fat gleaming fish, the quite young men I'd asked the way across the moor, and out of some wish to make the best of things I said that at least there was some new employment going on. She gave me a look from her salt-blue eyes, set in an almost ivory complexion, and said with a severe lean of her head, 'Oh aye. But *whose* is the sea? *Whose* is the ground?' Until then I had seen myself as the questioner, setting the agenda, receiving the information determined by my line of questioning. Peggy MacKinnon's alert intellect and rooted implicit conviction that whatever good can be got from the country should be the commonweal of those who live there – these altered my set by reminding me that I was in the Highlands not to amass data but to talk to people and to learn from their ideas as well as from their memories.

CHAPTER FOUR

HANDFULS OF EARTH
Raasay

Skye the following spring was rinsed by primrose light. Sap was almost visible in the hazel and birch buds but there was no leafage yet, even in luxuriant Sleat, to hide the clean structure of trunks and branch or the craggy edges of rivers. Summer would blur them with its drenching rains, its draped foliage, the distraction of caravans and tentage and queues for the ferry (a million bed-nights are sold annually on the island). Now, in early April, a pristine wellbeing could begin to rise and spread, melding with the warmth of revisiting friends and acquaintances – the irony being that these good feelings were occurring on a quest for memoirs of epic hardship, displacement, and endurance which, if they happened today, would leave most of us crushed. This double feeling was chronic; it came with the territory. Reaching Skye late in the evening, we went in hurriedly to eat at the hotel in Sconser on the south shore of Loch Sligachan. It is an old shooting 'lodge', that is to say a monumental *schloss* in a style of leaden baronial pastiche, enlarged to house shooting parties in the Victorian heyday of deer-stalking. Its grounds and the 9-hole golf course nearby occupy the croftlands of two townships, Tormichaig and Mol, which were brutally cleared to extend Lord MacDonald's deer forest. It felt bizarre – it felt like bad faith – to sit eating farmed oysters from Loch Harport and drinking *Macon Villages* in a high-ceilinged dining room which looked out over that evacuated green bareness. I was only a little relieved by the thought that 'anybody' can now come in to buy a meal in a place where once only the landowner's guests could enjoy the fat of the land.

This duality dogged me as we nestled again into the delicious civilisation of Renee and Sorley's sitting-room – walled with vivid, innocent paintings and with poetry of all vintages, its end window looking straight across and up the loch to Sgurr nan Gillean's fretted profile (the 'fire dragon with its four rugged headlong pinnacles', as he calls it in 'The Woods of Raasay'), the main window looking out across the Clarach to the dark length of Raasay – and discussed at our leisure the butchery at Culloden (would better tactics have saved the Highland army?) and the expulsion of Sorley's crofter forebears. Even this worriting is a kind of luxury – the twentieth-century Western person anxiously checking up on whether his conscience is in good working order.

Sorley's people were from Skye and Raasay. His vision of the Highland agon, in the poems called 'Hallaig' and 'Screapadal' (both Raasay townships) and in the long, unfinished sequence *The Cuillin*, had inspired me to watch the people's mouth and listen to how the men and women of Gaeldom remember that agon themselves.

It turned out that every near branch of his forebears had suffered clearance:

I was aware of the Clearances when I was a boy because my MacLean great-grandfather was evicted from Screapadal and went to Fearns, then evicted from Fearns to Balachuirn, and his son was *damn near evicted from Balachuirn too*. Because there was a rumour – you see, the hill ground that Balachuirn had [i.e. common grazing] was drastically cut down, and there was a rumour that Rainy [George Rainy, owner of Raasay 1846–63] was going to take the crofts from them too. And actually in one year my MacLean great-grandfather's people – he was married to a Mary Matheson from Braes – in one year he planted potatoes on his brother-in-law's croft in Braes because he expected to be cleared from Balachuirn.

As Sorley told his chronicle, he was closing his eyes and allowing an oddly impersonal and prolonged voice to issue from his mouth – surely the way in which the Hebrew bards delivered the genealogies common in the Old Testament. At acute moments the pitch would rise and his eyes would open in a dark challenge:

I'm not sure if it was at Screapadal or at Hallaig or at Fearns

— as far as I can make out they were grand-aunts of my father, and their house was knocked down. They lived for a while under boards propped up against the wall. The roof was taken off. It would be in the 1840s or early 1850s. I heard that from my father's sister Peggy — she was born in 1869 . . .

My Nicolson grandfather, after whom I'm called — he was a Somhairle son of Iain son of Somhairle — *his* grandfather was a piper in the Peninsula. He was wounded in the hands, he caught frostbite in the retreat to Corunna, and was invalided out on a pension.

A piper with frostbitten fingers would seem to be a deserving case; he was evicted from Scorebreck. The Matheson father of Sorley's grandfather's wife Mary was a miller who had been cleared from between Auchtertyre and Strome in Wester Ross and settled at Stenscholl in Staffin, near the north end of Skye, and was evicted from there to Scorr across the bay from Portree, 'a dumping ground for people cleared from better places'. His maternal grandmother, a MacLeod, was cleared from Tormichaig:

They poured the milk onto the fire there. The fire would have been at the centre of the house. We were told about it on Raasay. That particular tradition about the removal *is still known* — as an *offence*. The families are *still alive* — the families who were cleared, and the family of the landlord, *and* of those who put out the fires.

Here he closed his eyes again and was silent for some time, in a clear signal that the names of the evictors were not to be asked for, that this wound in the culture of the people was not to be further opened (much as people may well feel a century hence that it would be gratuitous to ferret out the names of the volunteers for the firing-squads at Auschwitz, who took the work for five cigarettes and 200 cc. of vodka). His final summary was comprehensive: 'The MacLeans, the Mathesons, the Nicolsons, and the MacLeods *were all cleared against their will.*'

Sorley had been brought up, the son of a tailor, in Oskaig on the west side of Raasay and we now crossed the sound to stay there with his cousin Rebecca Mackay whose husband was a Forestry Commission ranger, Calum Don. Their humour and wit made conversation with them a delight. At breakfast one day the talk turned to swearing in Gaelic and English. Rebecca, passionately patriotic, insisted that Gaelic didn't have such 'bad words' as English.

'No sexual words at all?'

'Well, a few – but not such bad ones.'

'Not "cow", as a term of abuse?'

'Yes, like that.'

' "Bitch"?'

'Yes, they say that – "a bitch of a boat", or "bitch of a house". But it's more like saying "Oh sh-h-hugar!" ' '

Calum (pawkily): 'And there's nothing sexual about sugar. Especially white sugar . . .'

And Rebecca happily scored off crass incomers in her anecdote about a young blood from the royal yacht *Britannia* who came past as she was working in the garden and called out, 'Do you speak English?'

'Well,' said Rebecca, 'I speak French, German, Norwegian, Gaelic – and English. What do you want to know?'

At first, for me, Raasay *was* Hallaig. I had first seen Sorley's sublime symbolist poem in a magazine called *Calgacus* edited from Dornie on Loch Duich by Ray Burnett, illustrated with a desolate black-and-white photo of empty pasture fringed with woods. The fourteen Gaelic quatrains, ending in full rhymes and vowel-rhymes, are translated by Sorley himself into a resonantly 'foreign' English and I had begun to know them by heart when I shared a reading with him at the Lancaster Literature Festival in 1979. The poem crystallised in him many years after 'The Woods of Raasay' (early 1940s) and differs from the earlier poem in speaking distinctly about the clearing of the island:

> The window is nailed and boarded
> Through which I saw the West . . .

This is the opening and the note of it sounds down the poem: 'every single generation gone . . . the heartbreak of the tale . . . the grass-grown ruined homes'. The symbolist logic of 'Hallaig' consists of imagery which can stand either for the people who were there once or for the trees that remain:

> The men lying on the green

> at the end of every house that was,
> the girls a wood of birches,
> straight their backs, bent their heads.
>
> Between the Leac and Fearns
> the road is under mild moss
> and the girls in silent bands
> go to Clachan as in the beginning,
>
> and return from Clachan,
> from Suishnish and the land of the living;
> each one young and light-stepping
> without the heartbreak of the tale.

The one-line epigraph, by MacLean himself, says: 'Time, the deer, is in the wood of Hallaig.' The poet exerts his will to abolish the deer – to stop Time, or History, which has undone the people by wiping out their community:

> . . . when the sun goes down behind Dun Cana
> a vehement bullet will come from the gun of Love;
>
> and will strike the deer that goes dizzily,
> sniffing at the grass-grown ruined homes;
> his eye will freeze in the wood,
> his blood will not be traced while I live.

This image was most extraordinarily confirmed the very moment I entered Hallaig after walking the five miles down the east coast from Screapadal.

At first you walk, or sleep-walk, through a dense Commission forest. It lasts a mile. Silence under the conifers. Paralysed subculture of moss and rusted needles shaken down by a generation of winters. Your eyes look for life in the shadow-layers, baffled by the eclipse. The absence of birds is visible as holes in the air. Even the stones freeze in the green morgue. Barked branches lie dismembered, skinned bones, abattoir remnants. From these sere galleries, these sunless corridors of a mouldering mansion, the family has gone (to a war? to Eldorado? fleeing a plague?) and draped this forest hastily over the rooms, pretending (expecting) they would (never) return.

One cottage skulks in the gloam, an oblong with rounded corners, a home from the old time, spent as the carcase of a stricken horse too sick to accompany the forced retreat after the final battle. Oh the inertia of each moist brown limb! Oh the depth of the dereliction drowning the stunted walls! The words of the people, the praying, the crying, the wailed notes of the psalms have foundered into the humus, gone to America in the handfuls of earth in the holds of the hulks, leaving the essence of their anguish lodged in each generation of heads. Voices from Strath Fleet, North Uist, Strath Naver: 'They are putting fire to the clachan ... The thatch was dry, the sparks were coming through ... O *teine* – oh, fire ... Whose house is burning now? *Save the people!*'

The visitor hurries finally through, looking neither left nor right. There is nothing to see or hear. The forest transpires silently, its texture deafening the eardrums to the sough of the wind above. Light is ahead, a blazing sapphire slot in the dusk of noon. The way is barred by a fence of galvanised wire split by a stile. A sunlit alp expands, stretching green from the eastern shore to the western skyline, sloping as purely as the profile of a snowdrift, planing across the dolomite tower behind it. In the dazzle rabbits nibble and bounce and sheep mow closely, plucking the last few blades from the bedding of the moss. It is gentle underfoot. The drench of winter has not waterlogged it. Parallel ditches comb its slopes and, curving upward to meet the knobbed spine of the island, the broad base and narrow tussocky crest of the ring-dyke bound the soft domain of the runrig, definite as a Roman road, strong as a pyramid.

The goodness of Screapadal, still so palpable, had been expressed in the evidence of a 35-year-old crofter, John MacLeod from Braes on the west side, to the Deer Forest Commission. Testifying in Gaelic through an interpreter on April 18th, 1893, he called Screapadal 'fine green grassy land', one of the two 'best townships that have been cleared to my knowledge'. He was being practical, not wishful. When he was asked how many families Screapadal would support, he reckoned that 'it would suit four well'. In the 1841 Census there had been seventeen (and I counted 36 ruins, about half of which will have been houses). The beauty of Screapadal belongs to civilisation, not to nature: that is, to nature refined. The admiration for the 'fine green land' is given lyric form by Sorley MacLean in 'Screapadal':

Screapadal in the morning
facing Applecross and the sun,
Screapadal that is so beautiful,
quite as beautiful as Hallaig . . .

Rainy left Screapadal without people,
with no houses or cattle, only sheep,
but he left Screapadal beautiful;
in his time he could do nothing else.

There is nothing 'literary' about this emphasis on beauty. Rebecca's mother, who had been brought up on the little island of Eilean Tighe off Raasay's northern tip, had missed the outlook over the sea when her family moved to Kyle Rona on the mainland: 'We were looking across to Rona and all the other little islands,' she recalled fondly. Roderick MacLeod, a crofter born on Rona who now lives in Eyre at the south end, spoke warmly of the vista over the Inner Sound to Applecross: 'Kalnakill and Lonbain were only five miles away. We could hear the cows mooing, and the grouse and the cocks crowing, and the dogs barking.'

As I walked on southward, Applecross and its abandoned crofts were a hazy cinnamon foreground for the Arctic massifs in Shieldaig and Torridon – Baosbheinn and Beinn Alligin and Liathach white as salt under the dimmed blue of an old Italian painting. On the Sound's bright face a Ministry of Defence vessel stood still, working away quietly for the British Underwater Test Evaluation Centre, Europe's leading facility for the sea trials of the latest torpedoes, Stingray, Tigerfish, and Spearfish, and of the 'stealth' hulls designed to make nuclear-powered submarines less detectable. The hydrophones on the seabed are blamed for scaring away the lobsters, but then, there is so much more money in weaponry than in seafood (£1,000 million spent by the U.S. in 1988 on undersea research).

Surrounded by the snowbound mountains of Skye and the mainland and a sea prepared for war, Raasay that morning looked like an enchanted zone. I walked all over the Screapadal crofts, reluctant to leave, feeling the last vibrations of hospitality and husbandry in the clustering ruins, then struck off south. The cliff that Sorley calls Creag Mheircil (on the map it is Creag na Bruaich) rears up three hundred feet, a gate-tower at the boundary of township and woodland, ochre and clay-grey rock with deep horizontal corrugations. I itched to climb it but when I ventured twenty feet up one slim buttress, a huge biscuit broke off as I tested it. I forced a way up the gully behind it, teetered over a slowly-disintegrating bridge of rocks and turfs to its perfectly level top for a last look back at Screapadal's goodly fields and the deathly forest lurking behind them. Then I picked my way down into the steeply-angled woods through which a sort of path strays south towards Hallaig, Leac, and Fearns. Primroses like pats of butter, like a speckling of yellow sunlight, dappled the steep little banks beneath the rowans and the birches. These were of all ages, straight young boles whose eider-pink and silver skin was still as fine as satin, terminally aged trees undermined by landslides, black toes still dug into the crumbling ground. A few more of the sheep for which Screapadal and thirteen other townships were cleared came down out of the warren of dells and ravines below the cliff and gathered into a flock which I involuntarily shepherded for a quarter of a mile until they felt hungry again and dispersed to graze among fox-gloved pastures under the slabby barrier of Druim an Aonaich.

Sheep and deer: Donald Macrae of Balachuirn testified to the Deer Forest Commission that 'the best townships have been cleared, and now form a huge sporting preserve. Deer, rabbits, pheasants, and black game do incalculable damage to us.' Calum Don's father had told me that this was 'more or less the sanctuary of the deer, they make their home there, at the rock where it's dense with natural wood'. It seemed more like a garden, everything little and pretty, the yellow breasts of the blue-tits, the petals of primroses and celandines, the sharp high whistles of birds unseen amongst the wine-red tracery of the birch twigs. Then, as I reached the entrance into the north end of Hallaig where a low dyke bars the way between foreshore and inland cliff, a deer lay dead at the side of the path. I had never before seen such a thing. It was a full-grown hind. Its legs were lodged in a swathe of bramble and withered ferns. Its head lay among celandines in the grass. Its eyes were eaten out but otherwise it was unmarked by any 'vehement bullet'.

In another quarter of an hour I was amongst the gently-descending lawns of Hallaig. The lay-out was intricate, looping round and dropping below an outcrop like the whinsill at Hadrian's Wall, spreading back deeply into the hill, stepping down seaward in natural terraces. It was marred only by what I found to be the stigma of a cleared township: a big square field, its walls, built of stones from the wrecked homes, falling down already. Gathered above the sea was 'the congregation of the girls/ keeping up the endless walk' – the well spaced out birchwood among whose branches the cobalt waters shone like lozenges of stained glass. The trenched lines of the old drainage and the wrinkles of the fail-dykes (turf dykes) were engraved, as at Suishnish, on the face of what was now pasture. A blue-and-turquoise figure was moving up there, heading north. I hailed her – it was Anne coming to meet me by the 'road of mild moss' from Fearns.

To walk towards the sun on Raasay is to reverse the direction taken by most of the cleared families. As the population swelled in the later eighteenth century, townships pressed up into the limit of the easily habitable part – Kyle Rona on the last bony joint of the north end, Umachan on its east coast, Dryharbour and Doire na Guaile on Rona, Torran and Arnish at the isthmus where the island is less than half a mile across and narrows off into an extremity which should never have been colonised. As John Cummings, Rebecca's uncle, put it, 'It was all animals to the south, people to the north' – a drastic model for the entire Clearance process. As Alexander Gillies, a crofter from Kyle Rona, told the Deer Forest Commission, 'I know that there is land on the other side of Raasay, of the breadth of the sole of my shoes, which would be better than half an acre of land I have now. It is not soil but rocks we are occupying.'

I made my own way northward via Manish Beg, which on the O.S. map is a scatter of the hollow squares that stand for roofless buildings. On the skyline ahead a stag performed a peculiar skittish prancing with its forelegs, like a triumphal gesture on behalf of the wild game who had ousted the people. In the village I found at least seventeen houses with the old rounded corners and the division into 'but' and 'ben' rooms (living and best rooms) still distinct in the shells of stonework. The crofts nearby were broad hollows between ribs of rock and to the north, down by Manish Point, a wide plain of arable showed, grooved by parallel ditches. From here, as from the other thirteen townships south of the isthmus, the families were driven out by all possible means:

You were not allowed to marry without the consent of the laird. And this man Donald MacLeod, he was a young man and he was wanting to get married, and he wouldn't be allowed by the proprietor, and he wouldn't get a place to build a house or anything else. So in spite of all he got married and he built himself a wee house, and they had a baby a while after that, so then they cleared that end as far as Arnish, and if the people wouldn't clear out of the houses they were just setting fire to them, and this couple went to Australia ... They weren't all for going, because some of them – they were telling us that, especially the young women, they were just tugging the hair out of themselves, weeping, when they went aboard. There was a woman Catherine MacSweyn, her great-grandchildren are here yet – actually it was her mother, I believe, that saw this event from the hills, when they were embarking there.

In the age before the clearance, when emigration was less involuntary, a Mrs MacKinnon had told Boswell, during his tour of the Hebrides with Dr Johnson, that in the previous year (1772), 'when the ship sailed from Portree for America, the people on shore were almost distracted when they saw their relations go off; they lay down on the ground and tumbled, and tore the grass with their teeth.' Very rapidly, it seems, people inured themselves to this, that is, they repressed their anguish: 'This year there was not a tear shed. The people on shore seemed to think that they will soon follow. This is a mortal sign.'

Beyond Arnish the highway up and down the grain of Raasay becomes a linear memorial to billions of steps taken in all weathers. In the steeper and wetter places it is paved and palisaded with stones. It breasts stiff braes, stepping-stones its way through bogs, squeezes between crags and over passes, creeps under cliffs of Lewisian gneiss like flayed carcases jutting out of the moor, skirts the black straight lips of old peat cuttings. Hardly enough continuous grass grows anywhere to make a golf green but not a furlong passes without evidence of settlement – a stone dyke in a ravine between crags to stop herds straying, the bottom three courses of a stone cell to shelter travellers, brown heather stripes of lazybeds fitted into a cramped plot. From the east side of Beinn na h-Iolaire (eagle mountain) the small, short-lived village of Umachan showed as a grey scar on a green patch at the far end of a narrow glen, like an image through the wrong end of a telescope.

By this amazing route the children of Eilean Tighe, Kyle Rona, Eilean Fladday, and Umachan traversed the wilderness twice every day to school at Torran, four miles there and four miles back: a penance imposed on the people of the north end by the clearances. Rebecca's mother recalled that 'you got a sandwich in the morning and that had to do you all day. We were allowed to be an hour late if it was bad weather. But if it rained after you had left home you had to sit all day in wet clothes.' They made the best of it. Sometimes they played in the pools beside the path. They eked out their food with hazelnuts picked in the groves above Torran – no mean snack, since hazelnuts are worth 110 calories an ounce and were once a staple Highland food, sold by the sackful in the markets of Easter Ross. The worst thing seemed to have been waiting at the end of the day, 'shouting for the boat, when you were starving'. The people of Eilean Fladday, a roomy island just offshore to the west, for many years petitioned for a bridge to save the schoolchildren waiting until the ebb to cross the channel dryshod. They never got it. I crossed over at low tide and walked about on the fine close grass, wishing life back into the three good houses which still stand, deserted since the 1960s, clusters of daffodils lighting the turf with their sunny yellows and three decorative spruce trees taking the bleakness out of the air.

At the very north end, at Eilean Tighe, I was lucky again with the tide and crossed the slipping and popping bunches of bladderwrack to reach this island off an island off an island off an island. John Cummings revelled in the memory of the food to be got here: 'When the cuddies appeared in Loch an Sguirr we just got into the sea and herded them into the narrows between Eilean Tighe and Kyle Rona – we were shovelling them ashore with our hands!' As his memories brimmed, and high days shone out, he made the island sound like a northern Land of Cockayne:

We ate cormorant, if the dog brought one in. Lovely broth with a cormorant in it – it was not fishy at all, more like a chicken or a grouse. And a wild duck now and again. Father used to row out to a wee island and take seagulls' eggs – they were lovely. If they divided a cow, or a big fish, the flesh was put into four heaps. And we used to kill otters and sell the skin – stretch it on a door and dry it, and fold it up and send it away. Of course we had to depend on the boat from Portree for our supplies – we had to buy our meal. But we could have visitors properly when the tide was out, especially at night, with lanterns.

The harbour where they landed is a double line of black boulders with the boatway still clear and shingle-floored between them. Over a little rise a broad saddle of grassland between outcrops keeps the unmistakable resilience underfoot of ground that has been worked and two ruins look over the fields, their backs to the shelter of the crags. From here the people gravitated south again. Mrs Mackay, who now lives at Inverarish a mile from the ferry, moved to Kyle Rona from Eilean Tighe when a grandfather died. She lived first in a house whose lintels and gable-end still stand, built of a fine-grained, beef-red stone that had been ferried over from Applecross, and then in the one house which still has a roof. I went into it to lunch off a packet of Ribena and some chocolate. When it turned out to have been Mrs Mackay's home, I felt I should have asked permission. It has whitened walls, a blue door and window-frames, and a roof red with rust. The living-room is thickly cluttered with bottles of Warburton's 'world-renowned remedy for liver fluke', and rusty hammers and screwdrivers, and empty McEwan's cans, and trestles and tins of tar and paint and old clogged brushes and tartan short-bread tins and mugs and cups from the plainest and most timeless to Seventies supermarket jobs. The white-painted tongue-and-groove walls are a Visitors' Book that goes back to at least 1951: no witty or dirty graffiti, just names or initials, date, and place of origin, Dingwall, Achnasheen, Aberdeen, every one of them Scottish. Over the fireplace was one poignant remnant of home-making, nailed in place: a stem with two leaves carved in cigar-box wood, rising to a machine-made rosette of plywood, and nailed in the middle of it, nicely positioned, the tin top from a 'John Walker of Kilmarnock' whisky bottle.

The reoccupation of Raasay's south end was undertaken by the men of Rona who came back from the Great War in a state of fearless anger at their people's mistreatment by landlords and neglect by government over the previous eighty years. The story was told me by Roderick MacLeod down at Eyre – Ruairidh Mòr, Big Rory, still strong in his early eighties with thickly-tufted black eyebrows and a kiss-curl of white hair which he patted into place on his forehead when I asked if I could take his photograph. His brother had been one of the land raiders in 1921 when the raids were once again spreading like muirburn in Lewis, North Uist, Benbecula, South Uist, Vatersay, to name only the places where I got word of them myself. It was the culmination of the Land War started in the 1870s, the Crofters' War. For Ruairidh Mòr's people the struggle had been constant since the last quarter of the eighteenth century. His mother's people were Mackays from Sutherland:

> This Mackay, he was out on the hill one day, looking for the cattle, and he had young family, I think one of them was in the cradle. And when they came back after seeing the cattle on the hill, and when they came in sight of the house, the house was ablaze. They ran as fast as they could and the wife met him outside the house and he asked her, 'How did the house went on fire?'
>
> 'You weren't long away when three men came and set fire to the house.'
>
> 'Which way they went?'
>
> He went after them and battered them half dead, the three of them, and the factor was one of them! But when the landlord heard of it: 'Clear out!' They had no place to go but he made his way to Skye and they were in Skye for years.

His father's people were builders, who came from Caithness to work on the famously expensive extensions to Raasay House – what Sorley MacLean in 'Screapadal' calls:

> such debt
> as the social climbing put
> with its burden on James MacGille-Chaluim
> and brought exile on his son
> with the largeness and the beauty
> that they added to the Big House.

The son was the MacLeod of Raasay who struggled against indebtedness, evicted half-heartedly, then sold up and emigrated to Australia. James, the father, was typical of his generation of chieftains, splashing out on a grandiose scale in the years of recovery after Culloden, when a punitive detachment had visited Raasay and burned all its villages and all its boats. Ruairidh's grandfather and great-grandfather were cleared from Screapadal to Rona, another brother to Kyle Rona, and a third to Arnish. His Mackay forebears were cleared from Eyre, his father's mother from Leac. As he retails all this, he punctuates it with a 'heh-heh-heh' like the last notes of a grouse's call, not so much mirth as a way of adding a salt of irony to the sheer piteousness of the old tale. He was born on Rona and came back to the good level homeland at Eyre on the heels of the land raid:

My elder brother and some of them, they came down here in a boat and planted the potatoes here and the crops, and they built themselves huts on the place here. They were going home mostly every weekend to Rona and there would be a stand-by left here, watching the crops before the sheep and the deer would come in. They brought the cattle down from Rona in open boats, two at a time. Well, the police came on a Sabbath night. They got them in bed. And the men from Braes [on Skye south of Portree] came to the pier here, to batter the police. Oh, they stood by them to the hilt, the Skye men! But a fight would have done them no good – I don't believe it would.

Seven men were brought to trial at Inverness and Ruairidh's father William got off through a technical blunder:

They read out his name in the court – 'William MacLeod, son of Donald MacLeod deceased,' and my father got up and says, 'My Lord, my father is not deceased.' 'Discharge that man out of the Bar!' And his cousin was the same, name taken down wrongly, and these two got clear from jail.

After nearly two centuries of mismanagement Raasay has seen off its last landlord (an eccentric and ill-natured doctor from Surrey) and settled down into better stewardship under the Department of Agriculture. When the writer Derek Cooper was there some years ago, people told him that they wanted 'no more changes' in the island's way of life. This is always impossible, a beleaguered ethos of turning in on yourself to at least keep what you have, but it is understandable after a history in which change after change was for the worse. It is an island intensely conscious of itself as a homeland. A boatman from Rona, Ronald MacLennan, recalled in 1893 that during a clearance 'I have seen them going to the churchyard in their grief at being separated from their homes, and taking handfuls of the soil and grass that covered the graves of their kindred, as mementoes'. As mementoes and as binding rites. A handful of earth in the *Gàidhealtachd* was a *fàd seilbh*, the 'turf of

49

ownership', a pledge given by one party to the other when land changed hands. That last digging with their fingers into their homeland was a passionate reflex which had in it generations of accustomed life. Let us hope that the handfuls survived to be planted again on the other side of the water.

CHAPTER FIVE

THE LOOM AND THE TWEED
North Uist

The hours on the 35 miles of rolling and pitching waters between Skye and North Uist allow you ample time to be seasick or to write a poem – in January 1982 I had done both simultaneously. Despite the gulf between the two islands it is typical of the *Gaidhealtachd* that the Skye and Uist people know each other as near neighbours would elsewhere. The MacLeans of Peinnchorran know all about the MacDonalds of Cnoc na Luib, near Clachan on North Uist. During a summer hurricane on North Uist twenty years before, the MacDonald boys, then students, had given us, a family of strangers arriving out of the night, a whole house to live in with a full load of peats for the cooking range and an outlook over the sinuous channels of Claddach Cumhang where snail-sized buckies ('winkles' in English) clung in clusters under the fronds of the seaweed and supplied a full meal in an hour's gathering. Now Sorley was able to tell me that the 'boys' had become headmasters in the island schools.

He also knew the intimate detail of North Uist's recent past. In 1982 I had several times come across one story which displayed the island at the climax of clearance in a single melodrama. The property – and the Hebrides *were* now property – had passed out of the hands of the spendthrift chieftain, MacDonald of Sleat, and was managed by a trust. The factor was James MacDonald of Balranald, who rented a large farm on the west side and was bent on clearing all the crofters from the north-coast townships. His daughter Jessie was the belle of the island and had fallen in love with a young farmer neighbour, Donald MacDonald of Balelone, third son of a debt-ridden house in Skye. The villain now appears – Patrick Cooper, law agent for the trust, an advocate from Aberdeen twice Jessie's age. Black beard bristling, he asks old MacDonald for Jessie's hand in marriage. Young MacDonald had briefly acted as factor. Now he was sacked – Jessie's father resumes the factorship – Donald and Jessie promptly elope in a small boat and set off across the Sound of Harris, making for Rodel where she has family. The villainous Cooper bribes some local men with promises of land to form a posse and give chase. Jessie's wicked uncle locks her up in his rambling mansion and young James has to send for some heavies from his father's house and force her release at gun-point. The clouds part, the sun breaks through, the young lovers get away to Skye and emigrate to Australia (where hundreds of evicted crofters also ended up three years later). When I mentioned this story to Sorley, he knew it well, of course, and he was able to cap it: 'Oh yes, Jessie and her young man passed through Portree, and my grandmother saw them at the harbour, and she said Jessie was wearing a little blue hat.'

So it was no myth, or even a legend – it was the nineteenth-century history of North Uist crystallised as a perfect true scenario. I also went to the Uists in July 1988 with my imagination alerted by two classic myths. They were told to me by Alasdair MacLean, Sorley's brother, who had been a doctor on South Uist for twenty years. As a part-time historian and genealogist he had found his way into some inner passages of the island memory. He had heard that before the day of a clearance waterspouts would come up out of the sea to the east and drop a shoal of fishes onto the moor. Donald MacIntyre, a crofter at Loch Eynort, remembered his father, a shepherd at Liathadhal, talking about it as having happened around 1845. And a man called Big Neil MacIsaac who lived on the far side of Beinn Mhòr, South Uist's highest mountain, saw a file of the 'great sheep', the hated Cheviots, passing through the embers of the fire under his cooking-pot. Not long after, sheep came to the island in large numbers – though they were not Cheviots, as Alastair pointed out, but black-faced crosses.

What a myth does is to signal the deep-seated importance of its theme for the community. If it was trivial or irrelevant, it would not be able to gain currency in an image or a tale. From that point on I was on the look-out for clearance myths, as well as memoirs and facts, although I found no more full-fledged ones until I went to Sutherland in the autumn. The kinds of material I was searching for ran from fact through to memory (perceived facts) to what I call 'memoir' (memories handed on) to legend (a story which unwittingly garbles the historical original under the influence of some strongly-held belief) to myth (something that could never actually happen but surfaces in the consciousness and speech of a people because it symbolises their deeper fears or longings). By 'memory' I mean a first-hand recollection, which implies immediacy but does not guarantee accuracy, and by 'memoir' I mean someone else's recollection retailed at second or third or even more indirect hand, 'edited' no doubt but apparently not distorted in essentials. By 'legend' I mean, for example, the following story about defying eviction which was told me by a crofter called Donald MacQueen of Balgarva, Iochdar, in the north-west of South Uist. He was over seventy and his maternal grandmother, Marion Ferguson, had lived through the final devastating clearances in the middle nineteenth century. Had she talked about them? Not very much. Did he remember anything in particular that she said?

I remember about this soldier, he was wounded in – I think it was the Crimea, that war, I don't remember right ... He had the bone of the eyebrow cut off and that was kept in a silk handkerchief to go into the coffin along with him when he would be buried. And he had an honour, by saving the fort: he could produce his sword at any time – an honour from royalty, the king I suppose. At the time of the Clearances he was going to be evicted along with the rest. Well, he was waiting for the trap with the lawyers coming and so on, to clear them out, and he had this overcoat on and he was fully armed with the sword, and he just showed them the sword: 'Come off that road! Come off that track! Or I will make widows of the wives of every one of you!' Well, they bypassed him, and he was taken to court, to Lochmaddy, because he was, you know, against them. And the Sheriff asked him, 'Did you produce a sword to these people while they tried to enter your house?' And he says, 'I did, and I have got full permission to produce it in any public place. And as a matter of fact it's here, and your head will be the first one, if I am cleared out.' So he was never evicted. He was never put out.

Another version of this story that I heard at Creagorry, Benbecula, from Mr MacKenzie, a retired minister, was the same in essentials but added the fine details that the Crimean hero, who was always called Iain Saighdear, Iain the Soldier, had strutted to and fro brandishing his sabre along the outer thickness of the walls of his black house – that favourite place for householders to sit and take their ease – and that he had said, 'I have never put this sword back in its scabbard but it was running with blood.'

Considered as a story, it is a grand legend of triumphant defiance. Considered as history it is riddled with doubtful points. If the war in which Iain Saighdeir had done heroic things was the Crimean War, it would have been a queen, not a king, who awarded the honour, and it cannot have happened during the clearance, which preceded the Crimean War by five years. It also seems unlikely that Iain Saighdear would have been allowed into court with a sabre dangling from his belt. And Donald MacQueen told me the story as an event that happened in Sollas. The house was actually ten miles from there down the west side, near Paible. What the mistakes leave intact is the core of the legend: on this island, around the middle nineteenth century, for once an eviction was resisted, by means of a warrior's prowess.

To try and verify such a story is probably a fool's errand, although I did make the attempt. Iain the Soldier's daughter, I was told, was still alive in her hundredth year and lived in the old people's home near Carinish. I found her sitting in the day room, leaning forward in her chair and looking at the floor, deeply abstracted. Her face was a mask of yellow skin stretched tightly downward, making her nose a beak. She had small dark blue eyes and dark hair drawn firmly past her ears. Her hands were freckled kipper-brown and she was wearing a printed cotton blouse and a skirt of blue tweed. Her neighbour, a butcher's widow from Grenetote near Sollas, confirmed that this was Iain the Soldier's daughter, still known as Jessie an t-Saighdeir after her father, who had won three medals in the Crimea and had one of them stolen in Glasgow.

Jessie now said something in Gaelic, in a high penetrating voice. She was asking if I was the doctor, because she wanted news of her mother, who was drowned. Her neighbour explained the code: her 'mother' was her daughter, who had looked after Jessie for thirty years. She had gone away on holiday, leaving Jessie bereft. 'My mother is drowned,' she repeated over and over in English, in a surging falsetto. 'The boat will not come ashore, because it was a very bad storm. Do not be telling me she will be coming, because the storm was very bad. My husband said it was, and what will I do without my mother?'

A woman in the corner, behind a Zimmer frame, said in a deep hoarse voice, 'She has not drowned, she has gone to the New Forest.'

But Jessie still lamented, then paused and said, looking at the floor, 'You are all looking at me as if I was a crow.' Presently the supervisor told me that Jessie was often clearheaded, in which case she might either tell me the story of her father or else simply say 'No!' At present her daughter's absence had upset her but perhaps next time ... When I came back to the island the following year, I was told that she had died.

Her story lives on; an informant's being very old need not mean that her or his story too is frail and about to die out. People constantly said to me, 'I'm afraid most of the old people have gone' or 'There was old John, he knew a lot of things but he died last year,' the implication being that 'old age' and 'history' are one – only old people know the history – so when they die out the history dies with them. The same could have been said at any time during the past six generations. Fortunately, and naturally, each generation tells its story to the next one. Not everyone pays attention. Time and again people said to me, 'If only I had listened to my father, or my grandmother! But when you're young you've no interest in that kind of thing.' Then, too, members of a family are less or more receptive. Hugh MacLean, a crofter at Barrapol on Tiree, knew perfectly well that of his two sons one, a radio-station maintenance man, had taken in much less of his father's historical knowledge than the other, who drove earth-movers and ditching tractors. Certainly, overall, there is a grievous and irreversible loss of memoir. A vital event, embroiling (say) 300 people over a month in 1851, has often been reduced by now to a single story of a hundred words. At least the reduction has a distilling side to it and the result may well be a potent quintessence.

What I was chiefly looking for on my visits to the Uists was memoir of *Blàr Sholais*, the Battle of Sollas, and of the devastating clearance of South Uist soon after the Potato Famine. At Sollas, in the late summer of 1849, for once an outright stand was made against eviction. Over several days, the women of the townships near the shore fought estate men and constables with piles of stones and the hard stems of sea-tangle. The stones ran out, and tangle stems, as I found out when I tried thrashing them on boulders the shape of policemen's helmets, give a stunning enough blow but break at the same time. The people were forced out and tried at first to settle six miles to the south-east, at Langass on the north shore of Loch Eport, but 'That was too good for them,' as one man said to me, and they were moved on to a wet moorland site on the far side of the loch. After a starving season there they finally accepted banishment and sailed for Australia on a ship ridden with smallpox. On the three month voyage from Campbeltown in Argyll to Adelaide in New South Wales there were at least 38 deaths and repeated suicide attempts. One islander wrote in a letter home: 'Oh, Sandy, throwing out my two into the deep sea, it will never go out of my heart. The youngest died with the measles crossing the line, and the other six days later with a bowel complaint.' So many were evicted (117 families) that it seemed too much to hope that any memories had survived in the little broken chain of houses overlooking the long trough of good arable land and the blond crests of the dunes. But in 1898 a knighted gentleman called Campbell-Orde redivided the farmland into half-crofts and this, with the Board of Agriculture's purchases and recroftings for the benefit of Great War veterans, had the effect of restoring Sollas to at least a few of the families who had lived there before the battle.

Murdo McCuish of Middlequarter, beside the road down to the sea, had been told about the evictions by his grandmother, who was eleven at the time and died in 1929:

I remember her telling me that they were making a tweed and hoped to have it finished. They knew that they were to be evicted, they had been warned that they would have to leave, but it came as a surprise when a posse of police came to their house. And they got as much of the furniture out as they could, but they knew they wouldn't have much time to get the loom out, so they were just going to leave the loom in and cut the tweed out of the loom. But the next thing they knew, they had fired the thatch, and it was so dry the sparks were coming in through the thatch, and they had to evacuate the house. The loom and the tweed were burnt in the house. They hadn't even time to cut it clear. They had expected at least to be allowed to salvage that much. They got what furniture they had, which wasn't very much, they got that out, and the bed-clothes. As a boy hearing her talk about it, that's always stuck in my memory, how they'd burnt the loom, with the tweed in it.

Murdo is a short, self-contained man with a full head of black hair, although he is seventy, and the words came from him with unfaltering certainty. He was not given to fiery comments but he was tersely caustic at the expense of factor and minister:

> She was angry about it – she would never trust the factor again, the estate factor, because they firmly believed that the factor had more to do with it than Lord MacDonald himself. And the minister at that time came round and advised people to leave – that would be Finlay Macrae. That didn't go down well either, that he would come round advising people that it was God's will they should leave.

How many of us know who our parish clergyman was one hundred and forty years ago? The Rev. Finlay Macrae is remembered for his treachery, and this is ubiquitous. All over the Highlands, people (including some incumbent ministers) made the same criticism of those complaisant ministers of the Church of Scotland. Macrae, like many of his kind, was a substantial tenant farmer. He would not only dine with the laird but rent properties from him and these were not crofts and therefore not liable to be claimed back by the estate for conversion into large farms. Macrae had three farms, at Baleloch and Griminish to the west and on Vallay, the shapely island of well-drained sandy ground which lies across the mouth of the little bay. It has the benign protective aspect of St Martins or Tresco in the Scilly Isles. Its undulating pastures and range of dunes fringed with marram look aglow even when the day is overcast. Once I swam over to it through the river of the ebbing tide and delighted in running barefoot over its springy machair. Murdo recalled going over to its outer shore and finding lobsters under the tidal boulders when his mother needed something for the pot. From this vantage point the Rev. Finlay Macrae was well-placed to dispense his opiate advice: 'It's rather surprising that the *men* weren't organised to resist. But I think the minister had much to do with that. People at that time looked up to the minister.'

Sorley MacLean writes in *The Cuillin* about:

> chiefs and tacksmen plundering,
> with the permission of divines shearing,
> clearing tenants and planting brutes . . .

Such bitterness is still near the surface in Sollas. At the Post Office Mrs Macaulay told me that a letter had come to the school from a boy in New South Wales, asking for a pen-friend. When it turned out that he was the great-great-great-grandson of Finlay Macrae, people said, 'Do nothing about it – Macrae was a bad man' until one of the mothers insisted that the young Australian had nothing to do with his scorned forebear. The bad blood is slow to clear. According to Mrs Macaulay, the old saying about Vallay was, 'You could live on the smell from the Big House but you get nothing from them.' The clearance itself has become *the* byword for heartless government. Mrs Morrison of Struan – the semi-circular group of new council houses which have at last brought back a look of physical togetherness to the gutted township – said to me, 'Forever there's a sense of wrong. You've heard of local primary schools being closed of late years in Uist. And they always say, "It's just like the evictions, this closing of schools over the children's heads," so it's still very sore in their memories.'

Mrs Morrison, teaching in the school, had found out much of what she knew preparing history lessons for the children. She had taken them to see the ruins, including the house of Alasdair Mòr, the strong man who was lured away on the day of the battle. Her husband, who spoke to me in the evening dressed in the American-looking peaked cap and bright blue denims which have replaced the old flat cap, dark tweed jacket and trousers, has taken on himself the role of *seanchaidh*, the annalist of the community, and the details he preserves are wonderfully distinct. Thus history tells us (i.e. it was in the *Inverness Courier* in August 1849) that the women of a family called Monk were put out of their house by force and one of them threw herself on the ground and barked and yelped like a dog for some minutes, while another pleaded to have a roof left over the loom – their sole immediate source of income. Here the frame freezes. Archie Morrison was able to tell me that the Monks were able to save their tweed by cutting it from the loom. (A descendant of this family, now living in Kintail, actually called at the Morrisons' while I was there.) He also knew that six or seven of the men who helped to destroy the houses came from Houghgarry on the west side – which is at a discreet distance and is also next to Balranald, the factor's headquarters. It was he who called them the *abhagan*, the fox terriers. The good house along at Dunskellor, near the sad little graveyard on its knoll among the bents, had been meant for Jessie of the little blue hat and the villainous Cooper who planned the clearance (and later wrote a book defending it). When Jessie escaped the fate worse than death, the house went to one of the incoming farmers.

Archie's most telling story was another legend of defiance, if he will pardon my calling it a legend. Before he told it he took off his cap and settled himself with a deliberateness and a seeming unawareness of the hearer which I came to recognise as the way of the *seanchaidh*:

There was a blind man, they called him MacCuish the Catechist [an uncle of Murdo's grandmother], and this man was blind since fifteen years of age, and he went to listen to a man that came to preach the gospel here, and he was converted. So he was a great man as far as religion was concerned. Anyway, when Captain MacDonald [of Balranald] came to put this man out of his house he had one of his henchmen with him, Donald MacDonald, and when they came in he said, 'Oh I know Captain MacDonald, and he is going to put me out of the house. But this is the house and this is the croft that God gave me and he will not put me out of the house, or the croft, until He takes me away.' And oh, he was taken aback, the Captain, then, and he says, 'Oh Donald MacDonald, you must put him out.' But Blind MacCuish says, 'I know him, and his croft will not have any of his relations on the croft in a few years' time, and neither will any of your relations be on Balranald in a few years' time, and the man that sent you here will be as blind as I am today, and he won't have any relations on his croft.' And so it came about that that happened, and Balranald today is divided into crofts, and that man Donald MacDonald, there is another man on his croft, none of his relations, and that man that sent him there, he was as blind as a stone before he left this world, and there's no relations of him on the croft.

As I heard curses like this throughout the Highlands and Islands, I came to see that they were the commonest form of the black poetry of the Clearances. Almost without exception I was told about curses that had worked – no doubt it would be too dispiriting to recall the failures. In any case these curses are 'the heart of a heartless situation, the sigh of the oppressed' since they enact a symbolic revenge on those who because of their legal power over property are beyond the reach of more practical retaliation or resistance. In 1849–52 Sollas was defeated. The single most poignant thing Archie told me as we walked over the cleared ground between the present road and the shore was the name of the little burn which cuts its way down a green sprinkled with wild irises and the low, stony humps of the ruined houses. Here the women who did the fighting came to wash their lacerated scalps which the constables had split open with their truncheons. Since that day it has been called Abhainn na Fala, River of Blood.*

The curse on the MacDonalds of Balranald was not made good without some further human intervention. The last of them was held in low esteem and still is. In Murdo McCuish's words, 'I don't know how the devil he was a captain, because he went round [during the Great War] taking horses off the old people – that was his job, commandeering them. And one of them said to him, "Why are you not in the Army?" "Because of my bad eyesight," he says, "they wouldn't take me." "Well," the man says, "you recognised me half a mile down the machair." ' The men who had been doing the fighting came back a few years later hungry with the Highland desire to reclaim their own lands. In North Uist, as on Raasay, they wanted back the crofts cleared in their grandparents' time. The story of it was told me by the last surviving raider, Angus Alick MacAulay, who lived (he is dead now) at Paiblesgarry a mile south of Balranald. He was a tall man of 92 who sat upright in a chair facing the kitchen range, wearing a tweed jacket, a handknitted grey zip-up cardigan, and glasses that hugely magnified his sore red eyelids. As soon as I asked him how the raid started, he began to talk fluently – history made audible in a quavering, phlegmy voice. He warned me that he was getting confused but his wit and grasp of detail were nearly intact:

I left the Army when the war was over, and some of us approached the Land Office in Edinburgh to know whether they had a job

---

* On Sunday April 9th, 1989 in Tbilisi, Georgia, Soviet troops attacked a crowd of demonstrators and left 18 dead, most of them killed by CS gas and beating with truncheons and entrenching tools, 14 of them women ranging in age from 16 to 70.

or anything at that time, and was there land to be divided, so that we might apply for it. So eventually we all got back to the island, you know, one at a time, maybe three or four at a time. So we had a meeting over at one of the old townships. They'd passed the word around that the meeting was to be at Alasdair MacDonald's house, and when Alasdair asked them who told them the meeting was to be there, they said to him it was Donald Matheson. And Alasdair says to Donald Matheson later, 'Well,' he says, 'MacAulay' – that's me – 'and MacDonald' – another that went to prison – 'they're Bolsheviks!'

We wrote to the Office in Edinburgh, but no response, so there was an election on at the time and the Member that was elected, Dr Murray we used to call him, he was a real fellow, that would talk to anybody, and we approached him one day. 'Ah well,' he says, 'I'm very sorry, boys . . . ' I told him that the only response we got from Edinburgh was a printed postcard. 'I believe that,' he says. 'I don't know how to involve you, but if I was on one of the places there I wouldn't write to the Office at all. The only way you can get land is by raiding it – by *raiding* it.' So that was all right.

We raided the place about a fortnight after that, about fourteen of us. Some of the other fellows – their dad had a croft, so they had an excuse for not taking part. We started seaweeding. One of Captain MacDonald's workers was at the seaweed then, it was very plentiful at the time. So we paraded ourselves through the sand dunes down there. And they all came and as soon as we saw them we decided what to do. We were going to tip over their carts with the seaweed. So that's exactly what we did, and I still remember, and it's quite a long time ago, the old man that I came to, I told him that I'd come to tip his cart, that we weren't allowed to be growing crops by Captain MacDonald – to own the land – when we had *fought* for it –

He sobbed at this point, shaken by 70-year-old traumas.

So we went and tipped his cart, and the man said, 'Good for you, boys. I thoroughly sympathise with you.' And Captain MacDonald came on his horse and we just chased him back home. One of the boys had a big tangle, and he held it [Angus Alick mimes a vigorous brandishing movement] and it was as hard as a brick and Captain MacDonald was coming near, and he gave the horse a flick on the leg – the horse went up into the sky and Captain MacDonald came walloping down.

Well – the people working on the machair next day were told not to go near the land, and if we did interfere any more with the land we would be charged with breach of interdict. But we did, because we didn't know what it meant anyway! So we carried on, and eventually we were called to Lochmaddy to the – where the sheriff was. And they advised us we should join the Territorials, because it would help our cause if we showed we wanted to stand up for the British. But they sent us home, because there wasn't room in Lochmaddy [Courthouse], it's only a small place, at that time anyway, and I hope it *will* be!

Sixty days we were given, without the option of a fine. We had joined the Camerons, you know, the Territorials, because they didn't care who you were as long as you passed the medical. So we went to prison, and we were told to take our kilts off immediately – it was a disgrace to wear them in prison! There was a man from Knockline – one, two, three from Balemore – four from Balemore – five from Knockintorran – and one from Paiblesgarry. And when we got back they gave us a great welcome here. There was bonfires in every place.

Mr MacAulay's daughter Morag Murray had left the hayfield, where she was turning swathes with a tractor, to let me into the house. During our conversation she sat on a stool beside the kitchen range exactly opposite her father, absorbed in his words, prompting or explaining occasionally. Their two profiles, against a window full of clear sunlight, were identical – aquiline nose, chin gathered up under the lower lip, mouth broad and downturned; his right and her left profiles presented to me as mirror images. She has recently helped to work up her father's and other material on the Balranald land raid into a Gaelic play which has won awards in the island drama competition and the Mod in Glasgow. In it she herself (in an otherwise male company) plays the role of her father. This seems exactly right: she was, in a perfectly visible and material way, his reincarnation. Their double image stays with me as the type of the Gaelic culture which maintains the plait or weave of the generations against all efforts to cut and burn it out of the loom.

I now had to move south, following the drift of the Sollas

refugees, and live for a little while at Loch Eport where they had found a brief refuge. I went by the Committee Road in a slant across low hills from Claddach Vallay to Claddach Kyles, built by the crofters during the Hungry Forties in exchange for meal from the Central Fund for Relief of the Destitute, paid off in road-work at a penny-halfpenny a day for a man and a penny for his wife. Like its many counterparts in Ireland it is a monument to labour that should have been ploughed back into the crofts. As I drove over it, past glistening black parallels of peat cuttings, twelve red deer, six stags and six hinds, trotted briskly across the crumbling tarmac and a short-eared owl quartered the moor nearby with wafts of its lissom wings, its round feather mask turning this way and that, scanning for prey. The road reaches the west coast on a course parallel with a dozen tracks up into the hills – exactly parallel because this stretch of hinterland displays classically the relentless, spreadeagled pattern of crofting townships as they were lotted early in the nineteenth century. It is a bald coast in any case, with no shelter from rising ground, let alone woodland. The houses are placed every mile or so, on rectangular crofts bounded by wire fences with square wooden posts that stalk off drearily into the moor.

Once, the people lived in clusters of houses surrounded by fields on the run-rig system. The pieces of ground for corn and root crops were reallocated among the families every so often by agreement (or disagreement). This was democratic and fairly unproductive – there was too little incentive for a family to improve their ground if it would no longer be theirs next season or the season after. When the crofting system was imposed, the villages or clach-ans dispersed, and the land laid out on a geometrical pattern, it was not done for the commonweal but to organise the people as wage-earners whose work at cutting and burning seaweed for kelp made a profit for the laird-turned-capitalist. The outcome is the cheerless arrangement of the townships today, strung out along the roads, not grouped near each other or near the shop, pub, church, or mill. It is a painful contrast with the close-knit villages of the Yorkshire dales, say, or with the French villages whose main streets alternate house doors with massive barn doors made of broad bleached timbers (and a Peugeot inside, no doubt, instead of a hay-wain). The Hebridean people remain strongly neighbourly but it is in the teeth of the arrangement that has set them apart.

Pre-Clearance clachans huddled together: 'tenants lived companionably together in loosely clustered settlements' and their siting was 'entirely a matter of immediate conditions of slope, shelter, and aspect'. A plan drawn up for North Uist by the estate in 1799 provided for the lotting of farms into crofts as the population grew but 'the rectangular croft boundaries were superimposed on the plan' when it was carried out. 'On the ground today one may still discern the meandering lines of old turf-dykes, corresponding to the old boundaries mapped by Reid in 1799, but the modern boundaries correspond to the regularised lines drawn over Reid's plan.' Another geographer points out that the agents of such changes were the land surveyors: 'The earliest members of this professional group, around 1730, were schoolmasters (often mathematicians).' It happened all over. Up in Bettyhill, Sutherland, where the people burnt out of Strath Naver were dumped from 1814 onwards, rectangular plots supposed to accommodate them were ruled onto the map against the lie of the land, which is extremely steep and broken. In Iochdar, South Uist, four farms were lotted as six crofting townships and 'the clusters disappeared'. Even in Canada the merciless grid ruled. Along the Red River where Winnipeg is now, 'Surveyors began to lay out square lots on the Ontario township system [derived from Scotland] across the long and narrow Métis [French-Indian] river-lots. The Métis, who held no legal title to the lands they occupied, were understandably alarmed.' Significantly, lots with a river frontage of only three chains had to be provided for the 'Sutherlanders of Kildonan' [cleared in 1813–19] so that 'the settlers' houses would be closer together'. There was a felt human need to be near, not strung out on whining wires like telephone poles. This was still being voiced by crofters generations after the alienation: by Donald MacKinnon of Halistra in Skye, who told the Napier Commissioners that people 'lament it to the present day', by Donald Morrison of Geocrab in east Harris, who told them 'I have seen a woman weeping at being separated from her neighbours by the division of the crofts,' by John MacAulay of Illeray, Baleshare, North Uist, who told me, 'When the crofts were made the women didn't like it, because if anything went wrong they had only to go around the corner, but after the breaking-up of the congested place they had to walk two miles.'

Balranald, headquarters of the local tyrants from the lovely Jessie's father down to the captain toppled from his horse by the land-raiders, is a square slated house, large in an island of cottages, squat as a fort and palisaded like one behind its high walls of shingle and mortar. It is still rented in the summer by fishin' and shootin' gentry but it has that shunned and blighted look of a house where an unforgettable crime has been committed – like Buck Ruxton's house in Lancaster, which stood empty for half a century after he butchered his wife and the maid and was never lived in again, or the arch-evictor Patrick Sellar's house at Syre in Strath Naver, which today is unkempt and full of junk. MacDonald and Cooper, Jessie's overweening suitor, consigned the Sollas people to 'black moor' on the shore of Loch Eport. Neil MacVicar, a man from Claddach Vallay whom I searched out in retirement at Garry-du, Grimsay, amongst the labyrinth of islets and inlets between Uist and Benbecula, said dourly:

Oh aye, we heard about the clearances. They jumped on an old woman and broke her ribs. It was *boorishness*, what they did. It is difficult to understand the cruelty that's in man's heart. And it goes right down through the animal kingdom. They went to Loch Eport, and first they were on the left side [Langass] but they had to move and the estate got them to sign a paper that they agreed to go to the other side – most of them couldn't read, they just signed a cross. There was nothing there, they made the houses out of turfs. They had no light, so if they had to go into the next house they carried a peat on a wire.

Mrs Macaulay at Sollas Post Office had heard that an old man went south 'carrying a bag of crumbs'. John MacDonald, a teacher who crofts at Sidinish on Loch Eport, had heard that the ground inside the huts was so soft that when the children played at long-jumping indoors the winner was not the one who jumped furthest but the one whose feet sank in deepest. Earth floors were standard but when a house had been built in its own good time the neighbours were invited to a ceilidh so that the trampling of many feet would pack and harden the earth. The result can be seen in the replica black house in the Highland Folk Museum at Kingussie on Speyside – a floor which is smooth, tough, and slightly resilient – and I have seen the same in well-kept wattle-and-daub huts in the Dry Zone of Sri Lanka. The demoralised people at Loch Eport in the winter of 1850 may well have lacked the will to found good homes.

They had come there by a sort of forced march. Mrs Morag

MacLean of Sidinish, whose grandmother's uncle was the Boyd imprisoned after the battle ('a terribly strong man – I'm sure he must have made a fight of it'), had heard that the people had to ford the upper reaches of the loch by 'a sort of deer-crossing, which is dry some of the time'. This is still the deer's way: one night at Langass I saw two stags embarking on the water to get over to good grazing on the headland of Ruidinish, their elegant legs and antlers sharp black against the gold shine of the water like Inuit pictures scratched on walrus ivory. This maze of waters is fed by the sea through a mouth eighty yards wide, five miles to the east. For three days, at the house of Mrs Flora MacLean, I was mesmerised by the wide views from my window of the flow and the ebb. It looked like the passage of time made visible. In the last half-hour of gloaming the seaward movement of the water resembled steel-blue panes of ice sliding over the surface of a gelatinous mass. As the backwaters emptied between the low stone piers of the many bridges or causeways, the current rippled like the mane of a running horse and the ultimate interpenetration of sea and land showed in the rare sight of natural peat banks blotched with clumps of orange seaweed. The sea-loch must have been the one advantage of the place. It is rich in fish, which the families bartered for barley-meal from the more arable west-side townships. My family and I had once caught enough fish to feed us all for two days in a single evening's work with hand-lines. The usable land, however, is the merest rim and had supported only three families before the Sollas folk arrived. Then it was forced to make room for 34. Seven people of Sollas origin live there today.

To try and survey this weird waterland, I made for Clachan Burrival beyond the end of the road, below a little square-headed mountain proverbial as the remotest place in eastern Uist: 'Chluinnte fuaim do chaolain/ Am Biùrabhal 's 'a Bhallaigh' – (The noise from your guts could be heard / From Burrival to Vallay). From its summit, only 461 feet above sea-level, the landmarks of the Hebrides wheeled all around in a fragmented blue continent. Turning clockwise I could see: Lord MacDonald's Forest on Skye. The Black Cuillin, serrations just smoothed by cloud. Distant mainland summits, perhaps in Knoydart. Rum and Eigg, hull-down to the south. A spur of South Uist beyond the shoulder of Eaval, North Uist's highest peak. Benbecula's moorland, a low dark shoal, and to its west Balivanich and its airport showing the one urban profile hereabouts. The lowlands of Baleshare, where kelping was first practised in the Islands. The dark finger of the lighthouse on Heisgeir whose keeper had carved 'Eternity oh eternity' on a stone now lodged in the church wall at Paible. A verge of sea beyond Sollas in the north with Pabbay and Berneray sunlit. To their right Beinn Bhreac, where I had climbed down to a deserted golden eagle's eyrie on a cliff blossoming with honeysuckle, bell heather, and wild roses. The little rockery of the Shiants in the middle of the Minch. On the mainland just an edge of the gradual moors south of Gairloch. Skye again and the strange tablets of reef off Minginish ... Each separate land, dislimned by distance, signalled 'Come, here is a place to live ... ' On the sea, lapped in the same ideal atmosphere, reflected cumulus clouds shimmered like white whales about to surface. At my feet, derelict stoneworks on the shore at Clachan Burrival showed what pains had been taken to make the place yield a livelihood. The sides of an inlet built up with hefty boulders to make a dock. A curved sea-wall to shelter the boats. A path neatly revetted with stones. Big stepping-stones across a tidal channel where the mussels bristled so thickly, mussels on top of mussels, that the rock was invisible. A most original fish-trap, a natural basin on a reef filled only at high tide, its outer rim supplemented by a low wall to keep back the fish as they tried to swim seaward again on the ebb. An old man here had kept a cat; when it came back with a mackerel, 'it was giving the news out' that abundance had come again.

The last house at the road end at Druim Sidinish is the home of Peggy Morrison. Her people had been MacCuishes from Sollas and when I said to her 'One of the four imprisoned at Inverness was Roderick MacCuish,' she tapped her breastbone and said 'My grandfather'. Her father had died aged 90 in 1944 and must therefore have been born in the fourth year of the settlement here to parents who decided against Australia. According to Peggy, 'My father told me that his father "could not bear to see the burning of the houses",' and as she said this her chin trembled and her eyes shone with tears. She herself is 88, eyes bleached-blue behind heavy lenses, spine bent double with arthritis, but not in pain: 'I'm sometimes unsteady, but I get there.' She has a rich conceptual vocabulary and used it to make forthright points: 'If I had had the wisdom and experience that I have now, I would have listened more to what my father said about these things.' As it was the Sollas exodus remained with her as a few stark facts. She had heard that a loom and a tweed had been burnt but not, till I told her, whose loom it was, which itself is evidence of the chaos on that day and the fracturing of the community afterwards:

> When they were putting them into the boats in Lochmaddy, they were taking the women by their long hair and swinging them in. It was like Africa. When they came here they were making clod shacks. They had nothing at all. There was only heather . . .

And surrounded by heather and loch she still lives, in a stone house built on a knoll of rock covered with thin soil and grazed by sheep. Her son comes three times a year or so, 'to cut the peats at Easter and bring them home in July', and coloured photos of many grandchildren decorated her living-room walls. Her image of life is sturdily positive:

> My father told me, when they went to get the tangle they had two carts, and they went when the star was on the sky, and they took bannocks of barley meal, and all the food they had was to dip the bannocks in the sea, to soften them, and they were sweet and very good.

Now she was spring-cleaning in expectation of family arriving for a summer holiday. She looked set to be self-sufficient to the end of her days. My image of her is also of a person cast out to the back of beyond who deserved to be living in a *neighbourhood*.

CHAPTER SIX

'BANISHED FROM EVERYWHERE'
South Uist

During the next two years I made two stravaigs through South Uist, searching for memoirs of the deportations of 1851 and getting used to the island's split terrain. To the west of the north–south road: level machair, based on shell-sand, open and unrelieved, the houses moored like little square-ended boats on a pale-green marina of pasture and old arable. To the east: steep-gullied moors and mountains that approach 700 metres, with a deserted coastal world beyond them which the islanders call 'the back of the hill'. The long view down the plain, two miles wide and twenty miles long, makes everything look miniature and far-off – the pencils of the phone-poles, the dinky cattle browsing, the stubs of 'big houses' which presided over farms made at the sacrifice of the old nucleated clachans, North Frobost, Milton, Kildonan, Ormaclett, Stoneybridge, Bornish. 'It was all to the landlord's benefit, because before the lotting into crofts you could only sting them [charge rent] for the father's land. After, you could sting each son as a lot-holder.' This took place in 1818 and created a labour force of kelp-cutters. After 1830 the kelp income died out as foreign minerals were imported by permission of a government with no care for the Highlands and Islands. The crofters were expelled from the machair lands; farms were made, to be run by shepherds from the mainland, Stewarts from Perthshire, Grieves and Elliotts from the Borders. 'By 1886, nine-tenths of the population of South Uist were occupying two-fifths of the land – the remaining and best agricultural land was in farms.'

After the Great War these farms were divided again, in response to vigorous land raids, often led by a piper. The 'big houses' now have almost the air of pre-Civil War mansions in the Southern states of America, marooned among obsolete plantations. One that I visited was early-Georgian in its proportions. A staircase curved up from its hallway in a handsome wide spiral. The 80-year-old sister and brother who were ending their days here lived in a tin-sided extension at the back. They sat in a room kept stifling hot by a Raeburn, the bare walls relieved here and there by colour photos of the Pope, apparently giving an audience to a deferential crofter in his best suit, 'In Memoriam' photos of dead relatives, and an ornate Roman Catholic calendar. The man said nothing; his sister gave me long stares from her large now milky-blue eyes, and her most telling remark was that she had spent forty years down in London, in Lewisham, and still missed it, especially the shops.

The Clearance history of South Uist centred for me in the terrible expulsions after the Potato Famine, when it was owned along with Barra by Colonel Gordon of Cluny in Aberdeenshire, Scotland's richest commoner. I made little sense of the ins and outs of the matter until I spent two sessions with Donald and Jill MacLean of Howmore, a motley village that includes a thatched house and an old wooden bus studded with seashells, nesting among the lochans and little old fields near the north end. She has taught geography; he is a lobster fisherman with a hoary crinkly beard who fishes out of Loch Skiport at the north-east corner and is boatman for the lighthouse at Creag Dhùghaill, the easternmost point. Between them they have become learned in island history and between anecdotes they covered the sitting-room floor with sheaves of documents and photostats.

Howmore itself, they told me, had not been cleared. By an unusual arrangement the minister early in the nineteenth century, who was a well-connected farmer with a monopoly of kelp production, had imported six Presbyterian families from the north as sub-tenants of his farms: 'He wanted labourers to work for him – to exploit, if that is the word, and I think it is. They would have to work for him without actually being on his payroll': that is, they would have to give him forty days' work on his farm while paying rent for their own. The church and burial ground for the north end are at Howmore and Donald knew that people cleared from the back of the hill down to rocky Eriskay, off the south end, preferred to bring back their dead in coffins to Howmore, a two-day trek. The carpenter-cum-coffinmaker was an indispensable craftsman and a house that became vacant in the pre-Clearance clachans would be offered by the villagers to a carpenter. James Wilson, a retired docker and crofter I spoke to in the old folks' home at Daliburgh, recalled that his great-grandfather Hector MacIsaac, a carpenter up at Iochdar, only escaped eviction because of his trade – he used to saw coffin planks out of square timbers, a specially hard job when the wood was wet.

Looking across South Uist today, you would think that the machair was the prime land and the deserted east side impossibly hilly. Donald opined that it had once been the more habitable:

> It's very recently that the machair has stabilised into grassland from blown sand. In Iochdar there, it was suggested they did not plant potatoes in case it destabilised it in a certain part. The glens round at the back of the hill were good for cattle, the Minch was fish-rich. When I was hauling my creels yesterday, I saw lazybeds in places where if you were planting potatoes and it didn't fall into its hole it would roll down into the sea. The holes in the rocks where they pounded the shellfish, the limpets, to break them up [for ground-bait], they were really deep, they must have had a lot of use. And you can see where the rabbits have dug out shingle stones, way above the shore. Now, those stones must have been carried up and spread out for the fish, to lay the fish when they were drying them. Corodale Bay, Hillisdale, Usinish – they were evicted from there *because* it was prime sheep country.

– that is, it was made over to the 'great sheep' which Big Neil MacIsaac saw passing through the embers of his fire.

All the eastern side was cleared. The overseer to the Census enumerators in 1841 notes: 'This area [from Loch Eynort to Loch Skiport] has lost 168 people'. James Wilson believed that from Loch Eynort north to the Point of Usinish 'five hundred people were banished, they were banished from everywhere'. They had either to break in barren land in the Lochboisdale area, where the modern services, hotel, supermarket and school, now cluster, or accept small lots on the almost uninhabited island of Eriskay, or leave the country for good. 'If you had been here in 1840 [in Daliburgh] you wouldn't see a house between here and the pier. It was only Dalabrog common grazing at that time, and Kilpheder grazing – only heather.' James himself 'might easily have been a Canadian, born in Canada' but his grandfather James broke a leg when the whole family were on the eve of embarking for Cape Breton Island and he stayed behind and learned the trade of shoemaker. A few years later Gordon of Cluny's deportings were in full force and 'they were catching them and securing them with ropes. There was no pier or wharf at Loch Boisdale, so they were taking them out to the ships in small boats.'

The thought of peaceable folk being manhandled and tied up still stops one dead. It was the most brutal and enslaving of all the clearances and was protested against in print, in the *Quebec Times* in 1851, in *Gloomy Memories in the Highlands of Scotland* (Toronto edition 1857) by the Strath Naver stonemason Donald MacLeod, himself three times evicted, and thirty years later in *The History of the Highland Clearances* by the campaigning journalist Alexander MacKenzie. It was more like the shipping-off of the Polish and other Jews in cattle trucks than anything in recent British history. People who had provisionally agreed to emigrate, then changed their minds, were seized by constables and ground officers, handcuffed, dragged screaming to the shore, dropped into boats like bales, hunted with dogs through the hills and islets – much of this under the supervision of a Barra minister called Henry Beatson, an associate of Gordon's manager William Birnie. A ship's captain from Arran, John Crawford, had to repel the bully-boys with a marlin spike when they demanded to search his boat. Young men dug burrows into earth banks near the shore, with breathing holes at the inner end, to escape capture. Surely all this would have left a strong trace in the word-of-mouth tradition?

Those details are all from print except the final one, a story from Donald MacQueen of Iochdar, and it is unclear whether it applies to flight from a pressgang or from the ground officers. Donald MacLean had a profound point to make about this which I have used many times to console myself when a trail has gone cold: 'These things are talked about in a community. It takes a while to build a community. If you're moved from the back of the hill – and then to Eriskay – and then to Canada – you haven't ever got a community and you haven't got a tradition.' Nevertheless two stories did surface which typify the harrowing of the island. They were told me by John MacInnes of Daliburgh, an old friend of Dr Alastair MacLean's, and they drew on family memoir – his grandfather had been at Lochboisdale in that summer of 1851 and was 'asked to tie a man who wouldn't emigrate. And the answer my grandfather gave, he always told me

– "No," he says, "but we'll tie anybody who *does* tie him!" It was like gathering sheep, the way they were sending them across.' His first story, like Christian Watt's on Loch Eishort, testifies to the seigneurial rapacity of the landlords in their usual practices, never mind the Clearances:

My own great-grandmother in Kilpheder, she was married to James MacInnes, my great-grandfather, and James [he pronounced it like the Irish Seamus] died when he was a very young man and his children were very young. And the first thing that a proprietor used to do then was to take any good stock that a person had, and preferably his best horse – what was known in Gaelic as 'side of the door' – the best horse was kept there. So in any case she sensed they were going to take some stock off her and she decided to go to the factor, to complain to him. He was in Nunton [the small mansion on Benbecula from which the MacDonalds of Clanranald organised the Young Pretender's escape with Flora MacDonald] and Nunton was about 26 or 27 miles away. Well, however she got there, the factor was not at home, and his wife was in bed, and she went up to her room. I don't know what she said to her at that time. Anyway, when the factor came in his wife said, 'No wonder,' she said, 'if I am ill, the way you're treating these poor people.' So he gave the woman a letter to ask the ground officer here not to disturb her. But the letter was no use, because they'd already set her house on fire before she arrived. That was the way it was.

This commandeering or thieving of the crofters' animals, calmly and as of right, is to be found on all sides in the Napier evidence.

Another woman took in her children while she was away and they *also* got *her* out of her house. So she was sent out of Lochboisdale to a place called Lasgair, pretty near the school that's just now been closed by the Education Authority. And she got a little croft there, and they built a house down at the side of the sea, and the sea there was the opening into a narrow bay which led to the river which comes up from Loch a' Bharp, which is a salmon and seatrout loch. So they got a net, and she used to have a little string coming in at the end of the house. If anything big came in the string vibrated and she got a salmon.

Well, she was on a good ticket until she gave half a salmon to a lady on the west side of Loch Boisdale. There was a colony of cottars and squatters in Lochboisdale and they were all at death's door with hunger and that, and this water watcher came in and smelt the salmon, and he got it and saw it – the woman had to admit who gave it to her, and they set fire to her and sent her over to South Lochboisdale. They got there, you see – 26 acres of rock and stones, and it was all black heather at that time. And that's the sort of thing that was happening, you see, day in day out. And that was the way it was.

John MacInnes was an almost managerial figure: retired from local government, dressed in a neat dark suit, speaking to me in a well-decorated, old-fashioned sitting-room full of oak and mahogany furniture, in a detached house whose garden with its high privet hedges would have looked at home in the Edwardian suburb of a mainland city but is rare in the wind-scathed Hebrides. Most other conversations I had in the north, we would be sitting in the front room of a kit bungalow, built from ready-made plywood sections, surrounded with breeze-block, then harled and Snowcemmed, with a picture window, a patterned nylon carpet, a coal fire framed in beige tiles, brass fire-irons at the ready with three-masted sailing ships for handles, and every available niche ornamented with amazing, gleaming Things. Such as – I'm making this one up but I know it's waiting for me somewhere – a black Scotty-dog in glazed pot, sitting on its hunkers and smiling a Mickey Mouse smile, red tongue lolling roguishly, a tartan bow-tie round its neck, and dangling from its extended forepaw a wee calendar with tear-off leaves. Or an aluminium stag with an ashtray lodged helpfully in its antlers. Or a small pot 'Frae Bonnie Dunoon' in the guise of a tree-stump girdled by a pot ribbon holding a bunch of pot white heather. The whole scene is the antithesis of thirty years ago, when plainness was, not universal but certainly common. The walls were tongue-and-groove board, varnished brown or painted cream. There were few ornaments – a Scottish countryside calendar, a framed photo of a daughter or son in graduation gown or of a son in the uniform of the Navy or of a Highland regiment. The hearth was a blackleaded (or sometimes an enamelled) range, fed more often with peats than with coals. In the last few years I have been inside such a house just once – the home of an unmarried man in his seventies who is reputed never to have left the island of Tiree.

Now that more cash is circulating (from Development Board grants, from work at fish farms, seafood factories, airstrips, oil-rig docks, and of course from tourists like myself), the more tangible face of Highland life has been absorbed into the southern-mainland style and your landlady feeds you gammon or salmon steaks from her freezer instead of mince from the butcher's van. She is also unlikely to serve you a cup of creamy milk from her own cow to sup along with the porridge, such as I enjoyed on Skye thirty years ago. The room you sit in – apart from that great, broad, purely natural vista of brown mountains or of breakers arcing in against a long white beach – could as well be in Dundee or Nottingham. There are still differences. The pictures almost always include some good framed colour photos of Highland scenery and there are liable to be one or two excellent books – Thomson and Grimble's *The Future of the Highlands*, for example, or *John Prebble's Scotland*, or a well-used wildlife encyclopaedia – since this is a people who still live next to or *in* their place of work and continue to have a deep and educated absorption in their own culture.

It was in such respects that John MacInnes, a retired 'white-collar worker', seemed to be at one with the 'manual workers' I mostly met. He spoke in the same idiom and accent and had the same frame of reference. The spirit of all that he said inclined to the underdog. In his awareness of social wrongs and his detailed knowledge of how gruelling life had been for most people here I felt I was meeting face to face that ethos of the Gaidhealtachd which is egalitarian to the core and impels them again and again to vote against the ruling-class, usually for the Liberal, sometimes for Labour.

John's own stories turned on resistance as well as on dispossession:

Two of my grandfather's brothers were there at Loch Eynort at the time of the clearance, Alexander MacRae and his brother James, and whatever sort of land they had of their own it must have been rather restricted. There's an island called Calvay which belonged to a farmer, which was part of the South Uist estate – well, they made a patch of potatoes there, and they were hauled up before the court, and they were imprisoned in Edinburgh, for thirty days or six days or something of that sort. And the story of their imprisonment went round. Some minister of the Church of Scotland went and took an interest and began to collect some funds. There was some method at that time, you could get decent feeding in the prison if you could pay for it. And when he got a fair sum, wherever he got it, he came to tell them. And Alexander MacRae was looking to the future, you see. 'Now,' he says to the minister, 'would you mind if we just carried on the way we are doing, we can probably manage,' he says, 'but it would be handy to have that money when we came back and got settled again.' So the minister says 'Okay', he says, and he came away. And when they got back they got land in Craigastrome in Benbecula, of 250 acres, a joint tenancy.

Two hundred and fifty acres seems impossibly big – although that part of the island is one-third water, and perhaps the acreage included a good deal of hill grazing. The beauty of the story for me is in the mild, almost humorous courtesy with which Alexander, in prison hundreds of miles from home, strikes the best possible bargain to recoup his set-back.

The fiercer face of resistance to the proprietors came out in a fine curse which John told me:

They had a house in that area at a place called Ceann a' Gharaidh, which is up against the south end of the Uist hills where they taper down to the Sound of Eriskay, and a prophecy had been made to the laird that had been so bad to his people: 'One day the people of Uist will be walking on the stones of your house.' And this house *was* taken down for some reason in 1907, when the crofters went to the place and just started to help themselves to the stones. And then in 1936 a road was built to the Ludag jetty – what the crofters didn't take the road took.

Of course it is a loss to the culture of the Highlands that so many of the larger houses have gone – and not mostly sacked by the people: in the aftermath of Culloden Butcher Cumberland's army burned houses, destroyed libraries, paintings, archives, orchards, in a planned *blitzkrieg* against the Gaelic civilisation from which it has barely recovered. Supported by the newspapers who were calling the people of the Highlands vermin, monsters, beasts, mountain savages, 'enemies to all civil society', he proposed to Scotland's principal law lord, Duncan Forbes, a policy which is a trailer for the Clearances: whole clans should be transported to the American colonies 'because it is feared, and I believe with great reason, that while they remain in this island their rebellious and thievish nature is not to be kept under without an army always within reach of them'. Highland society was not allowed to evolve continuously and a mark of this is its lack of large houses, as in Midlothian, say, or the Vale of York, which have the look of being in harmony with the country around them. There are 'castles' enough in the Highlands, fantasies in stone, put up in the short heyday of the sporting estate when tobacco millionaires, owners of chain shops and shipping magnates wanted to imagine, at least from July to September, that they were warrior chieftains with battlements, trophies, and daggers in their stockings. The *Highlander* magazine, published from Chicago, still advertises kilts, hose, banners, claymores (full size $119). Now those baronial follies have been kicked to pieces by Commandoes during the War, unroofed to avoid rates, or refurbished as 'Clan centres': that is, tourist attractions for Americans seeking their roots. What is rare in the Highlands is a big house which has survived for a good many generations as an accepted sinew of the social fabric. In view of what the proprietors did to their tenants, this is not at all surprising.

CHAPTER SEVEN

'THE ISLE OF CONTENTMENT'
Prince Edward Island

Prince Edward Island and Cape Breton Island in the Canadian Maritimes made a kind of beach-head for migrant Highlanders. They were bound to because 'New Scotland', Nova Scotia, was after Newfoundland the first feasible landfall on the far side of the Atlantic after the six-week voyage. The original migrant from Europe was the land itself, when Pangaea started to split 200 million years ago and Laurasia slowly separated into North America and Eurasia with the gulf of the Atlantic deepening between them. Today the kinship between Scotland and Canada is cultural, personal – embodied in the many thousands of families who now have members on both sides of the water. The ground of this relationship is the rock of the two lands, the pre-Cambrian granites which form the old continental masses of both northern Europe and the Hudson Bay area and are markedly different from the young folded mountains of the Alps and the Rockies. This prehistory may seem remote but it fairly came home to me as I spoke to a very old farmer on Cape Breton and he said, laughing, that his North Uist forebears had felt at home when they landed there because 'both the places were full of rocks.'

My chief goal in the Maritimes was Cape Breton, in particular an area I knew simply as 'Loch Lomond' because Murdo MacCuish in Sollas had told me about his great-grandfather's brother, An Saor Mòr, the Big Carpenter, who had led his people to Cape Breton in 1828 because 'they are going to clear us off the land anyway, so we had better be prepared'. Our first stay, which turned into a kind of enchanted interlude, was on Prince Edward Island, by courtesy of a remarkable man, Dan Gillis, a college teacher of Classics in Philadelphia, who runs a centre for Highland studies called the Iona Foundation on P.E.I. each summer. His forebears came from Morar, which I had explored in the autumn of 1976. It was one of the most gruelling walks I ever undertook. We made our way through the mountains north of Loch Eilt in Arisaig, west of Fort William, and slept – or failed to sleep – on the floor of a derelict boathouse on Loch Beoraid, near a cave where the Young Pretender had also doubtless failed to sleep. For a nightcap, instead of his brandy, we used Teacher's whisky. We reached Loch Morar at a macabre sporting settlement where the wooden vents of a larder for hanging gutted deer gaped in the mossy shadows and a Bren-gun carrier rusted in the shallows of the loch. We then struggled for six pathless miles along the huge cleft where the 2,000-foot mountains continue their plunge straight into the deepest fresh water in Europe: the underwater contours go down to 1,000 feet.

The birch and heather jungle on either side of us climbed into the trailing fringes of cloud slashed by white lightning-forks of waterfalls in spate. At the head of the loch, on the far side, the loneliest house I had ever seen was dwarfed by the weeping brows of Sgurr Breac, the speckled peak. On our side the dung-sweetened turf of an old settlement called Oban, the bay, was an oasis by the shore with the usual ruined grey walls making a monument to the people of long ago. It seemed an endlessly discouraging place to live in. Twelve years later, talking to Dan Gillis at Iona House, I found that this outpost at the head of Loch Morar had been the home of his forebears. They seem to have been forced out as much by the discomforts of being Catholic after the 'Forty-five as by hardship and remoteness. His great-great-grandfather had been known as Donald Oban and he had emigrated to Antigonish County, Nova Scotia, in 1801.

On August 7th, 1803, 800 people arrived in Prince Edward Island, most of them on a two-masted square-rigger called the *Polly*. Most were from Skye with some from Raasay, North Uist, Mull, and the mainland. One of them, a bard called Calum Bàn MacMhannain, made a song called 'Emigration of the Islanders' which catches the experience of people setting out for North America with the immediacy of soundtrack on film. His people left Flodigarry at the northernmost point of Skye to escape the extortions of a 'miserable vulture' of an estate factor: that is, they were not exactly cleared

– the fraught distinction between eviction and free emigration will concern us later. The song mixes the sheer impetus of setting sail with the first pang of yearning for the abandoned homestead:

MacFadyn from Digg
Shouted to me,
'She will veer down towards Trodday!
The most capable man
Had better take the helm
Till she gets beyond Soain . . .
Leac na Buinne there,
Rubha 'n Aiseig beside it,
Mol a' Mhaide with its hard-set boulder –
Take the greatest care
To keep well above them
And clear of Rubha Hunish with its dangerous current.'

A north wind got up
When we were above Fladda Chuain.
Then she hummed along,
Sailing rapidly
As she tacked around
To take the open sea she knew so well.
I glanced behind me
Towards Rubh' a' Chàirn Lèith
And saw nothing but mist.
Then MacPhail said
Looking upwards,
'That must be the top of the Storr.'

Oh Mary, how often
I spent time in its shade
In Rigg – it was perfect for the cattle.
When March came,
The herd was in Carn
And the grass grew with the flowers.
Fresh new rushes
Stood deep in the burn
Under the fragrant pretty banks . . .

At that time the voyage took twelve weeks on the worst crossings. We flew, of course, six hours from Stanstead to Montreal, then chose the marathon by rail, a 500-mile trundle through the forests of north Maine and New Brunswick in order slowly to get used to the terrain and to feel its sheer extent. After a time the journey came to seem gradual as the Continental Drift itself. A friend from Halifax, Alison MacLeod, whose forebears came from Skye, had warned us that Canadian railroads were 'leisurely'. At times during the seventeen hours, immersed in the night-time forest with no visible movement of trees past windows, it was as though the sleeping-car was standing there like an exhausted ox, shuddering and groaning a little but not actually making headway. In the chasm ahead between tattered stands of black spruce and silver fir, aspen and birch, a nearly-full moon, orange as cheddar, rolls slowly across the sky, lighting up dream images: meres full of rotting spars, like a Paul Nash painting of the Somme, huge white cement-tanker wagons, never with the VIA logo of the new amalgamated railroad but always with titles redolent of the great trucking continent – Nationwide Boxcar Pool, or Ashley Drew & Northern Railroad Co., Serving Southern Forests. The free magazine on our recliner seats, dynamically titled *Directions*, assures us that 'VIA has no intention of favouring one region over another'. Funnily enough, however – and this made us feel at home – the Montreal–Toronto Corridor (for which read London–Birmingham Intercity) has the exclusive enjoyment of all the boasted improvements, a First-class lounge, cellular phones, a complimentary light meal ... The best thing the magazine did for me was to introduce me to Nicholas Morant, retired photographer to the C.P.R. He had worked along the railroads for nearly half a century, standing his tripod in seething salmon rivers or waiting half a day in winter fog for the sun to shine through and light a remote signal box or a curve of lakeside track. One of his images seemed to typify my own subject: 'Immigrant Farmer, Manitoba 1931': a man with a seamed face and stubbly chin, eyes looking far off under the rim of a crumpled felt hat, work-thickened fingers resting on a scythe blade set in a home-made haft. If he had been born in 1880, his father could have been cleared from the Hebrides in the Hungry Forties and learned the North Uist emigrant song about Manitoba, 'Land that's cold, no coal or peat there'. Later, corresponding with Mr Morant, I learned that this farmer was probably from Central European stock but he sent me a photo taken near Digby on the Bay of Fundy which shows beautifully the likeness between the maritime croftlands of the two Scotias, Canadian and Hebridean.

Fifty-two hours after leaving home we were delivered from the last of many upholstered wombs and cast out by the ferry bus at Port Borden on Prince Edward Island. Were we still in the real world? and if so did anybody care? If there really was a man of flesh behind the 'Dan Gillis' signature on the letter from 'Iona Foundation, St Columba, P.E.I.', no such being existed here where we needed him (desperately!) at an Irving filling station on this sleepy, sunny island. I ring his number in St Columba, wherever that is. No reply (but somewhere in the Maritimes that phone is ringing). From the directory I work out that it's in the South Lake telephone area. Where's that? The shop woman has never heard of it. Neither South Lake nor St Columba is on the large-scale tin map nailed to the wall. I search the South Lake columns again, avid for an address. Gillis! Daniel! He's at Fairfield – the eastern extremity of the island. There is no hotel here, or lodgings, or service bus, or taxi. We have got off at the wrong place.

As we sit on our luggage in a resentful stupor, trying not to blame each other, feeling the green miles all around us humming with homelessness, a man with a wall eye, greasy black hair hanging in shreds, and three days' stubble comes over from his car and says, 'What's the pro'lem? Wanna getto Charlottetown? I'll drive ya – gimme ten minutes while they fix on my tailpipe.' Soon we're chugging off in his huge clapped-out Oldsmobile. Exhaling a reek of neat bourbon, he talks continuously about how people have helped him in his time, confides that he wants to sell up and buy a lot downtown but only if his aunt will move. 'She's in a wheelchair, but *I* don't look after *her* – *she* looks after *me* though she *is* in a wheelchair!' We get to Charlottetown some time after the ferry bus, on which of course Dan will have been expecting us to arrive. The station is emptying, the ticket office and snack bar are closing. No Classics professor of Highland origin materialises to greet us.

More phone calls. Silence in distant Fairfield. He must be late and still on the road – or on the road back, having given us up – or in the ditch, having swerved to avoid a skunk and broken his neck . . . A grey-haired woman, an ex-islander home for a holiday (it's Down Home Week), is concerned about us but can't suggest anything. Then the other bystander comes over and says that he and his wife have a Tourist Home; he'll drive us there for the night and after breakfast in the morning – er – well, in the morning we can decide what to do, maybe phone some more. Worn out, we agree.

Our host is actually called Gallant, which turns out to be a common name on the island. His house is a new bungalow in an expansive grassy suburb east of Charlottetown which looks so temporary I expect it to have disappeared again by morning. The verandah and the steps up to the Gallants' are covered with bluish-green astroturf and on the stoop a shrine displays a blue-robed Mary backed by a triptych of mirrors. Mrs Gallant is wearily waking up on a settee among holy pictures and statuettes. She's a nurse, about to go on night duty. Mr Gallant was a foreman builder but seven years ago 'It all broke up on me and I fell twenty feet onto the concrete deck in this position' – he mimes a sitting position. 'I got five injured vertebrae, a nerve blockage at the neck, a nerve block further down. Five years I been fighting for fair compensation and now they say I'll get it if the hospital says to *them* what they said to me. I'm an alcoholic and I haven't had a drink for fourteen years. I do this work, down at the VIA station every day, telling people about our Tourist Home – they don' like you to do that – I can put a sign on my car roof but not go right up to people. So I jus' keep goin', jump in the car, get on the bus station, jump in the car 'n' *drive* all day – why, at night I jus' flop straight out, too tired to even think about booze . . . '

At night we hear him vomiting in the bathroom. In the morning, when it's already 70° and humid, he's walking about in his stocking soles and singlet, blowing out exhausted sighs and clutching his belly as though to hold himself together. 'I'm wore out – I was still finishin' that grass at midnight – it's too much for me.' He and his wife have always wanted to see Scotland. 'This year I thought we'd make it. But my wife's got a bad heart. She c'n *work* but she's nervous about flyin' . . .' The Gallants were only two of many lodging-keepers for whom we bled, helplessly. What this episode really triggered in me was an unnerving fantasy of what it would be like to fetch up oneself in such a backwater of adversity and realise that this was it, your lot, The End (like a friend of ours, exiled first from South Africa, then from England, whose nightmare is to end his days alone in a certain old people's hostel on the road from Amherst to Northampton, Massachusetts). But by now we had got through to Dan at Iona House and two hours later he turned up, a middle-aged man with a trim white beard, and drove us the eighty miles to the eastern end of the island in his softly-wallowing Pontiac-Nissan Bonneville. When we arrived, we stepped gently through the looking-glass.

To the west, lapped in sunlit air like a fine syrup, a few scattered frame houses were becalmed amongst meadows vivid with magenta and butter-coloured flowers. Cable was strung against the yellowish glare on poles weathered so deeply that the nodes where branches had once sprung stuck out like horns. Invisible in the meadows that dipped off to a bristle-topped forest, unidentifiable birds chirrupped. There was a sense of infinite seeds swelling in their pods, warmed seas lipping the low red sandstone bluffs, clams closing and opening, lobsters manoeuvring along the channel of the St Lawrence a few hundred yards to the north. The fieldscape was Scotland and not Scotland, akin to Angus or the softer parts of Perthshire in the interleaving of fir plantations and crops of oats, alien in the style of the isolated houses sided in white board. They looked closed and out of time, as though in any one of them you might find Antony Perkins crooning to his mother's corpse in the boiler room. Iona House was a benign version of such a place, three storeys high, with wings, a verandah, steep-pitched roofs and generous eaves, flaking slowly among grasslands deep in vetch, white dog-rose, dwarf rhododendron, ox-eye daisies withering in the prolonged drought, and grasses with seed-heads solid as wheat.

The house was 108 years old and it had been here since 1985. It used to be the priest's manse across the road at St Columba's. 'It weighed,' Dan told us, '300 tons – the heaviest building they've ever moved on P.E.I. It took them three days just to jack it up onto a pair of low-loaders. It was too big for them at the church. They needed the land to make room for the corpses of the future.' The church hall that went with it, a simple building like a large shingled barn with four windows on each side, had been thrown in for $1 and Dan had had it moored fifty yards to the south-west. He named it Margaret Campbell Hall after his mother, a Scots-Catholic girl from the island who had met and married his father down in Massachusetts, and he uses it for fiddlers' ceilidhs and the like. He was still not satisfied, though. He wanted to add more buildings to his colony. It became a standing joke, driving with Dan down side roads among the fields and forests to look at more deserted manses, all ripe for uprooting. He even went to the length of finding out what it would take to move one from fifteen miles away but seemed to balk a little when he found that about a hundred and twenty cables across the roads would have to be taken down temporarily to let the house pass. Trying to accustom my mind to the notion that a house could move about, like a boat or a marquee, I realised that, coming from the granite of Aberdeen and the limestone of Cumbria, having always lived in houses made out of the same rock that lay under them, I think of them as more rooted even than trees, their stone integral with the strata. In Canada, it seemed, even the houses were migrants.

Over the next week, speaking to dozens of islanders, I came to realise that the people proudest of their immigrant lineage were those whose families had arrived on the *Polly* in 1803. This contingent was led by Lord Selkirk, the entrepreneurial nobleman from the south-west of Scotland who did his best to think out and provide for the social needs of people transplanted from one outlying island to another. He learned Gaelic, which must have helped in his very delicate persuadings of people to choose lots. It meant that he did not have to go through an intermediary, as did, say, the MacDonald who inherited South Uist when he was a teenager at Eton and ruined himself on the proceeds at the gaming tables in Brighton. Selkirk tried to overcome the worst alienation by laying out the new settlements as villages occupied by related-family groups. He was a speculator in real estate, who later bought up most of northern Canada, but humanly he was at the opposite pole to an absentee landlord like Gordon of Cluny who sent the people of South Uist to sicken in droves in the quarantine sheds and cholera islands of Quebec and Montreal.

In 1803 P.E.I. was far from being virgin land. In 1767 it had been raffled off in 20,000-acre lots to rich speculators in London. A few Scotsfolk had settled in 1770 and had lifted the first recorded potatoes on the island in 1771. By then it had been for two thousand years a summer fishing station for the Micmac (correctly Megumaage) people, who called it Abahquit or Abegweit, 'parallel-with-the-shore'. To the French it had been Ile St-Jean. Cartier had admired it from his ship in 1534 – 'the fairest land it's possible to see!' – and it had been settled in 1719, then grabbed by the British in 1758. They deported most of the Acadian French, except for a few who fled into the forest and then to the deserted northern coast. Two generations later their descendants sailed the island's schooner fleet and one of them told Selkirk, according to his diary for late August 1803: 'We be all farmer – all fisher – dat be de veri ting dat make us all began.'

These tidal flowings and clashings of peoples ran as a theme through our stay in the Maritimes. To have occupied one place for more than a few generations began to seem a rarity. Battles, flights, undertakings and breaches of them, long-drawn-out flittings by boat and on foot, a violent jostling for meadows, herds, harbours, mines – here was the exact mixture of what it has cost the human tribes to stay alive.

Calum Bàn from Skye came to see the island as a paradise:

> This is the isle of contentment
> Where we are now.
> Our seed is fruitful here:
> Oats grow,
> Wheat in full bloom,
> Turnip, cabbage, and peas.
> Sugar from trees
> May be got free –
> We have it in large chunks.
> There is fresh red rum
> In every home and shop,
> Abundant as the stream . . .

No agrarian region can be at its ease any longer. Next year, in Ontario, I read constantly in the *Toronto Globe and Mail* about the urgent worry on P.E.I. that the federal government would close the big naval-air base at Summerstown in the west of the island and that the thousands of jobs lost would torpedo the economy. In our eastern haven we didn't even know it existed. At times of worship each day, a miniature tape revolved on the deck of the P.A. system in St Columba's little white-sided church across the road, sprinkling the notes of a hymn like seeds of sunlight broadcast among clover and vetch in the fermenting meadows. Only a few were ever there to hear the lorn lyric appeal from this ark stranded in shallows of half-ripe oats and potato flowers. Often only a single worshipper came to Mass, a visitor in clean white slacks and a flowered blouse, drawn by the bell and the bones of her parents, MacEacherns or Doucettes or MacInneses, lying together among a hundred and sixty years of burials, farmers, servicemen from World War Two, the crew of a Finnish barque. On Sundays the farmers and the North Lake fisherfolk were almost outnumbered by holidaymakers. Getting a priest, I was told, was hard – 'Why, Father Dollinger comes from Kentucky!' He seemed most fulfilled when he was cutting the grass around Dan's house with his motor mower. The islanders leave for Boston and New Bedford, for Detroit and Philadelphia. Beyond the reach of the bell, at the end of the island, an iron buoy hoots in the salty blur. The St Lawrence and the Northumberland Strait mingle their waters, the sea's blue rapids plait like the generations, baffle each other in a cross-grained seethe of overfalls, and the saint's white house rocks lightly, a migrant ship awaiting permission to moor and ballasted by the dead.

Each morning, preparing for a talk or history workshop or poetry reading that night with the help of Dan's fine small library, I sat on the verandah in the honeyed air, bothered only by the black flies which suddenly bite and leave a thick blood-streak as a leech does after being picked off. (Lord Selkirk had had the same trouble on August 8th, 1803: 'The muskettoes made a vehement attack on us, & were much worse than the little black flies which we met at Cape Breton tho' these were more sharp in their bites.') I was using passages of Sorley MacLean's to tune me in to the voices of the past:

> Screapadal in the morning
> facing Applecross and the sun,
> Screapadal that is so beautiful,
> quite as beautiful as Hallaig . . .
>
> The sound is blue in the sun
> and the skies naked
> and the white bands of Creag Mheircil
> glittering to the south
> above the wood of birch and hazel . . .
>
> filling the steep slopes,
> their laughter a mist in my ears
>
> and their beauty a film on my heart
> before the dimness comes on the kyles . . .

The burden of Sorley's laments epitomised all I had been hearing in the Hebrides. The refugees from those harshest clearances came not to P.E.I. but to the huge vacant lands of the eastern

87

prairies by way of the St Lawrence and it could be imagined that the tranquillity of this island stems partly from its less traumatic heritage. The people we met were proud to have been part of the migration rather than troubled that it had ever been necessary, as we found when we drove to Belfast, on the broad southern peninsula between Montague and Charlottetown, by way of Rock Barra and Gowan Brae, past Glen Martin and Priest Pond and Harmony and Sturgeon, past Petro-Canada Quik-Mart Avec Service (& Avec ICE) and Rachel's Motel & Cottages and the British Royalty Collection, past Edna MacSwain's letter-box and the letter-boxes of A. Macrae and Mrs Beaton and Mrs Buchanan and Duncan MacMaster, past the Mud Puddle Pottery And Crafts and Jack's Deep-sea Fishing and the Cherry Grove Tourist Home and Knox's Clover Farm, past Caledonia and Culloden and Strathcona and Kilmuir, past Creamer Realty and the Magic Fingers Craft Shop and Lorin Panting Car Wash and the Gladstone Tent & Trailer Park, past the New Harmony Demo. Woodlot and Black Pond Table & Seed Potatoes and the Mrs Rubble Collection, past Family Hairdressing Regular & Stylecuts and the Centre Accueil des Visiteurs, past the Fore & Aft Schooner Art Gallery and the Royal Canadian Legion Eldon Branch No. 7, past Wood Islands Pioneer Cemetery – but no, we stopped there and went along a raw-red dirt lane between spruce and aspen to see the century-and-a-half-old graves of Munns and Curries and MacMillans, many of them from Colonsay, with eloquent pious epitaphs, for example John MacQueen's (died November 5th, 1879 aged 73):

> Take comfort Christians when your friends
> In Jesus fall asleep
> Their better being never ends
> Why then dejected weep

or Euphemia MacMillan's nearby:

> Weep not for her you love
> O weep not o'er her tomb
> Her flesh soon to corruption gone
> Immortally shall bloom

and on and on again past the Harvey Moore Wildlife Management

Centre and the G&G Chipwagon and The Old General Store and Islay Mist Hsk. [i.e. housekeeping, i.e. self-catering], past Baltic and Red Point and Cape Bear, past Koleszar Pottery and the Blue Fin Motel and Unit 4 School Bus Maintenance Depot and Ideal Muffler (Lifetime Warranty) and Jay C's Icecream & Take-out and so at long last past Lord Selkirk Cove and the Belfast Tire Department to St John's Presbyterian Church, where we went to a service. When had I last been? In 1942, around the time when my brother and I discarded the notion of God. Not much had changed. The minister wore a light dove-grey summer suit, instead of the black robes which used to strike me with their morbid ugliness, and during Intimations he made jokes about the local ball team, at which the congregation laughed merrily. But 'Praise, my soul, the King of Heaven' was still a favourite and I found I remembered the first three of the five verses.

Our purpose in going to St John's – Dan's idea – had been to meet members of the Historical Society which I would be speaking to, and learning from, a day or two later. The sub-culture was so close-knit that the Church and the Historical Society were almost one. St John's had been built in 1824 mainly by people from the *Polly*, which had made its landfall near here. At the Annual Pot-luck Dinner after the service I met a man whose blacksmith great-great-great-grandfather had hand-forged the nails that fixed the shingle to the walls – the same shingles are still there, freshly whitened. The locum preacher for next month, a chicken farmer, was directly descended from *Polly* settlers from Skye. In a day or two I met some of this congregation again at Iona House when a surprising number of people, Catholics as well as Presbyterians, appeared out of the dusk to attend a workshop on the Clearances. I had no great hopes of hearing eviction memoirs but a woman of South Uist antecedents, Helen MacIsaac, who lived a few miles away at the harbour town of Souris, had brought a 140-year-old letter which we spread out gingerly on the table. It was brown and brittle as a winter leaf, flaking where the single sheet of paper had been folded to make an 'envelope'. It had been sent to Archibald MacIsaac, the first cousin of Helen's paternal grandfather, who had emigrated to Cape Breton in 1832 with his brother Angus and moved across to P.E.I. two or three years later. He was a tailor and Helen still has his scissors, which are made of brownish metal, with one sharp and one broad point, forged by J. Askham in Sheffield. The writer of the letter was Archibald's cousin John MacIsaac, a crofter at the clachan of Ardnamonie. I wondered which had been his house among the grass-grown rickles of stones near the road when I went to see Donald MacQueen, just north of Loch Bee with its fleets of snow-white swans. There was no telling, but as I read the neat, sloping script the man's voice came audibly through the courteous phrasing.

The letter is dated June 30 1841 and subscribed 'South Uist, Dunvegan, North Britain': that is, it had to be sent via Dunvegan on Skye, and had been stamped there on July 21st. There being no Canada then – the federation was set up at Charlottetown in 1867 – the address was simply 'Prince Edward Island, North America'. The phrasing is often heartfelt and shows how the Canadian connection had become a lifeline for the suffering community on Uist. Archibald's letter the month before had been only thirty days on sea and was 'the most satisfactory letter that came to this place from that quarter for the last thirty years':

> You will be sorry to hear that the people in your native country are becoming poorer and poorer every year since you left. Colonel Gordon, who is now sole proprietor of all South Uist, Benbecula and Barra seems to be a very hard and selfish man and the opinion generally entertained of him is that the sooner people are quit of him, the better for them. Considerable numbers are going to America from Benbecula and some from Iochdar this same season and many more are likely to go next season.

John himself would have gone in 1841 but his father was very old and required 'all the kindness and kind attention I can pay him'. In the nine years since Archibald sailed for America, 'fifty two persons full grown' had died in Iochdar, John's in-laws of 'fever' and 'inflammation of the brain', an aunt of 'consumption'. The impression is of a person stoical but quietly desperate to get away. At the heart of the letter is a candid plea:

> I request of you most earnestly to write me again soon after you receive this letter and let me know how far my uncles Neil and Donald MacAulay will assist me for the first twelve months after my arrival there. If these good men cannot or will not help me to support myself, my sisters and my wife I cannot venture to go there at all –
>
> All the means which I possess will do no more than clear me

out of this Country and pay our passage money but we are all
healthy and trust we would not be a burden upon our Relatives
there longer than the first year and therefore I shall be preparing
to emigrate.

As further evidence of the family's self-sufficiency he tells Archibald
that his (Archibald's) nephew Angus

is now twenty years old a stout fellow and a good shoemaker
to trade. Mary the second eldest daughter is a smart promising
girl and a good weaveress though only 13 years of age – Donald
desires me to ask you would those two of his children do well in
your Island by their handicraft . . .

Everyone is leaving or wants to leave. Archibald's stepmother and
her son have been 'overjoyed by the encouragement your letter gives
them in regard to America – they will be preparing to go next year'.
The writer himself can't wait. The final sentence, the most resonant
in the letter, hints just one qualification: ' . . . [words flaked off]
you will all continue attentive to the priceless Holy Religion and
ever bear in mind if America is a very good place, the Kingdom of
Heaven is infinitely better.' Is this the customary warning not to be
besotted with the things of this world? Or is it tinged with envy of the
good life over there, alloyed with discomfort at being dependent on
those who had already made the crossing? Such mixtures of feelings
flickered between the lines of many letters from would-be emigrants
which I found later.

During these workshops at Iona House, and at Belfast and
Charlottetown, a rich brew of conversation heated up as everyone fed
in what they knew about their forebears. 'I'm a South Uist MacInnes,
from Garrynamonie' would be a typical introduction, or 'We're from
Carnan Iochdar' – said by someone whose people had lived in Nova
Scotia or Pennsylvania for at least a century. A very old man with
a husky ruined voice, a member of the Charlottetown Caledonian
Club, told me that a Hebridean forebear of his mother's had been
'born on the Atlantic'. A middle-aged woman, 'a MacDonald from
South Uist', knew that hers had been a tacksman [tenant farmer]
who was able to buy lots 37 and 38 of the original 20,000-acre
properties, a huge spread even at the giveaway prices of the time;
when Selkirk supervised the division in 1803, a 200-acre lot was

standard. Mr McGowan 'from Kilmuir in Skye' said humorously but decidedly, 'I'm not one of the *Irish* McGowans!' and told me that his parents, seventy years ago, still spoke Gaelic but *only when they wanted to baffle the children*. This farcical guttering-out of a whole language was something I heard wherever I went in eastern Canada.

The racial melting-pot – in Canada it is quite officially dubbed 'the mosaic' – mixed many nationalities. A swarthy, well-groomed man with the formidable alertness of a barrister introduced himself and his wife as the Mischks, from Princeton, Kentucky, and explained that they were Moravians, descended from the Protestant sect whose passage out to America had been organised by a Saxon count who had given them asylum from Roman Catholic persecution. A forebear had run what was now 'the oldest tobacco shop in North America' (in fact a rebuilt tourist attraction in a museum 'village') and had been allowed to trade in this wicked substance because he was disabled. The Mischks cared for 'roots', like all the people here, and had been to Winston-Salem in North Carolina to find the graves of their pioneer forebears, which were all meticulously listed from Year One of the new life, men buried separately from women. When they cleared away the leaf-mould, the names and dates showed up as sharply as though they had been chiselled yesterday.

The most poignant glimpse of migrant experience was the sort of sidestep into an unexpected area that became familiar as the trail led from place to place. On a hot afternoon we had gone to the fishermen's co-operative at Basin Head for the annual Fish Feed. Barbecued fish, ten kinds in all, redfish and smelt and sole and trout and rock-eel and clams, were heaped together on our platters and we ate at wooden tables in a new-mown field, above a creek with bronze beaches where blue herons, larger and more luminously coloured than their British relatives, flew up-river as the sun went down and roosted in the crowns of the spruces. When we got back, a woman in her seventies had arrived in a Dodge Estate to continue her researches for a book about her family antecedents. She was master of the lowdown on a manic laird of Boisdale who waxed rabidly Presbyterian and gave 'his people' the option of converting from Catholicism – their religion from St Columba's time – or getting out. As we discussed the difficulty of getting memoirs of the most traumatic episodes of migration, for example of famine times, she told me how she herself had been an orphan, brought up by a great-aunt who was also an orphan. Her people had come from Ballylongford in Ireland – left in hungry despair and settled on Alderney – had to leave again when the island was being fortified against Napoleon and settled at Tredegar in South Wales. It was known in Dorothy's family that her Irish great-great-grandmother, crazed by starvation, sat in the corner and when her daughter doled out food to the children but not to her, she held herself with her arms crossed over her breast and rocked and cried for food like a child. The unbearable image recalled a story I had heard from a Jewish refugee from Westphalia. Her mother had been taken away to a concentration camp in Belgium in 1940. For years after the War, living with her daughter in England, she used to hide little packets of food in the wardrobe and recovered herself only in her late eighties when she 'sat down at the piano and played Beethoven once again'.

Dorothy Morris had 'been back': that is, she had gone to South Uist, and had been so moved that she had been writing poems about it ever since. She told me an anecdote which illustrates the defensiveness which has become ingrained in crofters by generations of insecurity. The eight owners of the island recently decided to sell up and were offering to sell their crofts to their tenants. A couple on Loch Eynort, he working on a fish farm, she doing Bed and Breakfast, were discussing what they should do. 'It's come at last!' said Dorothy. But Chrissie said, 'What! Buy in and be like *them*?' And Archie agreed with her: 'We'd be fools to. We can benefit by the schemes [Development Board grants] – build our houses, make up the road. If we were owners, we'd get none of that *and* pay taxes. So let the owners pay.' It was understandable; it also seemed a sad come-down from the militancy of the crofters on Skye, Tiree, and elsewhere in the 1880s who argued that the land was their own and always had been: 'The earth belonged to the people and not to the Duke of Argyll or any landlord . . . The earth is mine . . . The earth He hath given unto the children of men . . . If the landlords consulted Moses or Joshua, they would find there substantial evidence as to who are the rightful owners of the soil.'

Dorothy Morris lived at Poplar Point on the south coast. Our visit there gave us our last strong flavour of Prince Edward Island before we flew across to Cape Breton. The river-mouth just downstream from her house was strung across with the white floats of mussel-ropes but a hundred yards upstream it became the Canada of our imaginings, the forest pressing right down to the shore in a bristling texture of conifers, every generation of them from 6-inch saplings to 80-foot spires, the long grey bones of their dead cast up by floods to bleach on the shingle. Dorothy enjoyed discussing historical issues at length – why, say, the people of the Maritimes were Loyalists in the American War of Independence – but she was as likely to recall things that brought home to us how near the people here still are to the forest Canada of Arctic frosts, wild animals close around, and guns on the nails in the parlour wall.

The downstream end of her house had been 'Dan MacDonald's smithy – I like to think of all those horses getting shod in the sitting-room'. It had been moved bodily across the road, then built onto. Their only problem had been to defend it against skunks. 'We stacked up seaweed against the walls there for insulation against the frost but the skunks ate right through it three winters ago, first time in twenty years. Anyways, I'm running out of elderly bachelors to haul seaweed.' What she did was fix welded mesh all round the base of the house, twelve inches down and then twelve inches along, 'because the skunks dig down and down and then when their noses stop hitting wire, they start digging forwards'. Squirrels were less trouble but they stole the hens' food so one day she went out with the rifle to knock them out of the trees. When she came back in, her husband said, 'I heard *four* shots. You *miss* 'em?' 'No, I di'n't,' she said triumphantly, 'I got the four!' And she told us about black foxes fighting on the moonlit ice when the river froze over, and about looking up from the table straight into the eyes of a fox, level with hers as it crouched on the snowdrift outside. Her conversation was beautifully Canadian and it was already of the past, as the Maritimes lose their people and turn into Have-Not States, as the farmhouses at the east end of P.E.I. begin to empty. In another generation many will be holiday homes, lived in for a few summer weeks. The car number-plates, making the best of things, proclaim in blue letters 'Nova Scotia: Canada's Atlantic Playground' – a counterpart of the name given to the Hebrides in the Highland ferry company's brochures – 'Scotland's Pleasure Isles'.

CHAPTER EIGHT

'BOATS AGAINST THE CURRENT'
Cape Breton Island

The Big Carpenter of Sollas had singled himself out as the person whose trail we would try to pick up on Cape Breton. Would it be a farmhouse? a gravestone? a descendant? How likely was it that any trace at all was left among these scabs of old mine-workings, these shaggy forests that clothed the hilly terrain like buffalo-robes? My one clue was in a remark of Murdo MacCuish's in Sollas: 'They took the sheep over with them, some of them. And strangely enough they didn't lose anybody going over there, or the first year. He was a carpenter and they made a boat and sailed it round Loch Lomond looking for suitable places to go ashore and make their houses there, and that is what they did.' I still had no idea why the McCuishes and MacDonalds had lit upon that particular beach-head in the maze of waterways and little forested glens.

We hired a small Dodge and bought a motor map at Sydney airport. The fretted blue blot of Loch Lomond was thirty miles off to the south-west, past a mountain with the perfectly Gaelic name of Sgurra Bhreac, a perfectly American range called The Big Barren, and a perfectly French river called the Gaspereaux. Across an eastern arm of the Bras d'Or, Cape Breton's inland sea, lay a memento of South Uist, the Boisdale Hills. The skylines fledged with conifers, the meadows enclosed by forests bathed in resinous warmth, were a world away from the stark terrain of the Hebrides. At Big Pond, opposite Indian Islands, the map directed us to turn off down a dirt road made of rolled red marl. The forest closed in behind us and for an hour there was nothing but the pink dust-cloud behind us and on either side massed hemlock and spruce. The sun-dappled ground below them was rich in wild raspberry and goldenrod, the antithesis of the brown, dead floors of the planted forests back in Scotland. Apart from the road the land looked as intact and inscrutable as it must have done to those first settlers – a place before history, where trees and fish evolved obliviously. On that warmed green fabric ruffling away in all directions, anything or nothing might one day be imprinted; for now it was still itself. Yet we knew it had been colonised.

Where the pink channel of the road divided we forked left for Enon. Why not right? Perhaps because there was a stretch of water ahead called Lake Uist. Pale-blue arms of lake, or loch, shone between islands and headlands furred with forest. A large white wooden church appeared at the roadside with a black-lettered notice proclaiming 'Presbyterian Calvin Church 1910', but no village or single houses even from which worshippers might come, nothing but a single timber barn staggering sideways among scrub spruce, like Noah's ark long, long after the Flood. According to the map we had reached Enon Lake. Loch Lomond was three miles ahead. A quarter of an hour later, oppressed by a sense that we might have lost the trail for good, I walked down one of several short gravel tracks that led to the waterside and a comfortable woman with no teeth came out onto the verandah of a chalet decked with flags and strings of pennants. Had she heard of a McCuish graveyard? or the Big Carpenter of Uist? She waved her arms in various directions and said, 'Just past the monument – that's where it is – it's all graveyards on the shore road by East Bridge. Back there, just past that mill they're trying to start, if you turn right you'll find a small place in the woods with the graves of four McCuishes.' And there it was, between pillars of shingle-stones labelled in metal letters 'Pioneer Cemetery', a little slope of ankle-deep grass among clusters of birch and aspen from which crows were abusing a broad-winged raptor, eagle or buzzard, as it sailed above. The most poignant epitaph read:

Philip Ch Morrison
Died Dec 29th 1882
Aged 14 Years
6 Months & 19 Days
Short Spring
Endless Autumn

A nearby headstone for a pilot officer killed in Holland in 1943 bore a line of Gaelic: 'Earb às an Tighearna le d'uile chridhe' (Trust in the Lord with all your heart). But none of the stones were anything like early enough for the first settlers.

Baffled, we backtracked to the 'mill', a gaunt deserted gravelworks, and I quested on foot down a track to another holiday cabin. It was clearly hopeless. It also felt fairly silly to be roaming a Canadian forest asking after a man who might or might not have been here 160 years ago. I opened the mosquito-screen door, went in, and said to a massive paunchy man who was sitting in a singlet, enduring the heat, 'I'm trying to find out about the Big Carpenter . . . ' With just a trace of a Dublin accent he answered at once, 'Go back past the church and turn up on your right to a white house. Johnny Allan MacDonald – he knows all about that. He's 98 or 99. But don't get out of the car till they tell you – there's a German Shepherd dog.' We drove back, turned off, and stopped the car between a brown shingled barn and a white house of the oldest vintage. A woman in curlers came to the screen door and when I said, 'I'm looking for Johnny Allan MacDonald,' she answered, 'Well, you've found him,' and ushered me in.

At an oil-clothed table, near a massive stove with chromium feet and handles, a very tall man in a tartan shirt and braces, with huge hands and one eye creased shut, was sitting watching a chat show on television. I said, 'I've been trying to hear something about the Big Carpenter.' He towered to his feet, took my hand in a crushing grip, and said, 'My great-grandfather.' Then in a ringing voice, 'The lords, in those days they had the whole country in their hands' – here his voice rose and his fists turned on each other – 'and if they wanted you off a place to give to someone they liked better, well, they could do what they willed.' Then he sat down and told me about his great-grandfather, Angus the Saor Mòr from Sollas:

> It was in 1828, and the Big Carpenter called a meeting of all his friends and relations, that it was just as well they'd prepare to be leaving, they'd be driving them out anyway. And in about a year he'd try and have his favourite vessel for to take them over across to Canada. So he told them whatever they could get along without, to sell it now, whatever they'd get for it, because the time of leaving wasn't the time to sell things at all, and they could get along with very little, you know, for a year. When the

time was come he had a vessel called the *Commerce* engaged for to take them across, and it took them six weeks and six days to come to Sydney.

It was all right for them here – most of them could have 100, 200 acres and over in Scotland they couldn't have a damn thing. The land was granted, and granting 100 acres at that time wasn't very much, I think it was $10. So they settled about four miles from here. The Big Carpenter and his daughter – she was married to another MacDonald and it was here they lived, in this place here. Of course it was only a log cabin they had in the beginning. They were just travelling in the wilderness and what puzzles me is, where did they get the *axe*? They would have brought some tools but there was no forest over there – there was at one time, because they ran into stumps down at ten or fifteen feet. But they managed to make boats here – over in Middle Cape they were building boats.

The time that they came in September, it was too late for planting and they stayed in Middle Cape for the winter. And then half of them went to West Bay, the men, and the other half stayed between here and the Bras d'Or lake, and then they were to meet on a certain day at Irish Cove. And when they met, Dugald Buchanan MacNab, land surveyor, he met them there, he was following up all the streams for sites of mills and he told them about this place here, a chain of freshwater lakes, littered thickly with trout. And indeed he told the truth. My mother would say, Well now, John, it would be nice to have a couple of trout for breakfast. I'd go down there and throw a hook out anywheres, and I never took but three, never did. Worm on the hook, or a piece of trout, made no difference what you did you'd get trout.

The people that came here, so long as they got some trees chopped down and burnt, they planted potatoes there. It was quite a time before they could have a herd of cattle. It was oxen they had for hauling stumps and ploughing, any work there was, and pulling logs to one side so they could carve them up to burn them.

Johnny Allan's accent was making me feel at home. Its Hebridean undersound was unmistakable, as marked as the North-American nasal, and single words were pure Highland, for example 'peat' and 'eight' which he sounded with a guttural before the final 't'. 'Right' came out almost Irish with a breathed 'h' after the 't'. When I asked him about Gaelic, he said, 'I have the Gaelic as well as anybody, and just as good as they'll have over there.' This was not a mere boast; he had been to North Uist twelve years before and had 'visited every corner of it'. He went on, 'I was as big as I am today before I knew what "yes" or "no" meant. Because I'd be left in with my grandmother and she didn't have any English.' She, the Big Carpenter's daughter, had been sixteen when the family came over and had died in 1905 when Johnny Allan was fifteen; his knowledge of the first settling had been heard directly from her:

> The Big Carpenter had two brothers and one of them was learning to be a wheelwright so he stayed back for a year because he had a year to go. And they went to Upper Leeches Creek, because they didn't know where the others had landed, because they didn't have much transportation at that time. And they found at last where they were.

As time went by I found nothing more telling, as evidence of the sheer obstructive density of the virgin forest, than these stories of how difficult it had been for scattered members of families to unite again: a story from Glendale for example, about an immigrant who had given up hope of finding his brother and planted his potatoes for the first season, then got news of him, lifted the potatoes, and took them over to plant on the place next to his brother's.

Johnny Allan's final comments were about the land they had settled on:

> In Prince Edward Island they weren't up agen rocks anyway — no. When you're walking outside there you're like walking on a carpet. But here — we had an occasion to go over to West Bay a few years ago and this was on my mind to kind of look things over. The party that went there, they didn't like it. Well, I never seen a pile of stones over in West Bay like there is *here* – all kinds of stone here, *rows* of stone, and that must have been what persuaded them to keep away from West Bay, because all the houses in Uist is stone – and there wasn't enough of it in West Bay!

And he laughed out loud, with pleasure at this solution to a long-standing problem and with wry amusement at the thought of people choosing to live among these rocks which had cost him and his father so much effort to drag out with horses and chains, to crack out by building fires round them, as they struggled to make hayfields big enough to reap with a mower instead of a scythe.

Before we left, Johnny Allan and his daughter-in-law directed us to the real McCuish graveyard by a road between the lakes that he called 'the MacVicar road' – the practice of naming tracks after the first to settle along them – and we went to find it in the dusk. It was the usual peaceful acre, the grass scythed soft and deep, not close-cut by machine. It was named 'McCuish Cemetery' in black Gothic lettering on a white board. The Big Carpenter's grave (if this was it, for Angus MacDonald was a common name hereabouts) was marked by a slightly leaning pillar of the white marble usual up to the mid nineteenth century, with a tapering top. Behind, in a perspective of darkening firs, reaches of silvered water narrowed off into bay after bay dimmed by a foggy atmosphere. Lines came to mind from T.S. Eliot's 'Marina' that might have been secreted by this place:

> What seas what shores what grey rocks and what islands
> What water lapping the bow
> And scent of pine and the woodthrush singing through the fog . . .
> Whispers and small laughter between leaves and hurrying feet
> Under sleep where all the waters meet . . .
>
> What seas what shores what granite islands towards my timbers
> And woodthrush calling through the fog
> My daughter.

We heard no woodthrush at Loch Lomond, but five days later in the Highland Park on the west coast we found a cassette which mixed the thrush's succulent singing with the cries of loons and the churring of peeper frogs. Eliot's poem had originated just five hundred miles to the south-west, in New England, and it was the urban magnets of that seaboard which had pulled the people out of the Maritimes. Johnny Allan, I later learned, had aimed to follow four sisters to the States, or go to the logging beyond the Rockies, but had stayed on Cape Breton to help his parents. The men went south and west to the railroads and fish docks, the girls into domestic service in, for example, Eliot's Aunt Helen's 'small house near a fashionable square', where they 'sprouted despondently at area gates'. What we had been seeing among the East Bay hills was the remnant of a settlement which throve for little more than a century before the forest clearings, broken out with such effort and hope, were absorbed back into the huge vegetable matrix and the forever migrant people into the cities of the plain.

I had not expected, although I should have, that the Scottish crofters would move on, most of them, so soon, having used Cape Breton as a stepping stone to the American Middle West, the Canadian prairies, British Columbia. I had fallen into thinking that after their wrenching severance from Scotland the Canadian landfall must be their final goal. But there is no such thing – unless we believe that we have come to rest in our present cities.

Once, Cape Breton had seethed with migrants: in 1802, 299, the first to come direct from Scotland; in 1817, 382 from Barra; from 1821–30, 6,513 Scotsfolk through the port of Sydney alone, among them presumably the Big Carpenter and the other passengers on the *Commerce*; from 1821–38, at least 20,000 to the whole island. The year before the North Uist people arrived, the poorly-funded government services had begun to fall apart. In the autumn of 1827 170 people arrived on the *Stephen Wright* from Tobermory in Mull, 40 of them seriously ill with smallpox. Those who could walk 'threatened more than once to force a landing; which may have received some encouragement from the impudent conduct of a wrong-headed Priest who ordered a Boat alongside the vessel in direct contradiction and in the very face of the Magistrate who was calling and commanding her return ... The Master of the vessel, who is an obstinate and brutish fellow, declares he will do nothing towards the relief or recovery of his unhappy living Cargoe and in pursuance of that determination perversely refuses to let air into the hold of the vessel where it must necessarily be pestilential.' Next year a ship from Greenock, the *Two Sisters*, arrived in the same hellish state. By the end of the year more than 2,000 people had 'come into this district, from the Western parts of Scotland, many of whom, on their landing, were quite destitute of food ... great numbers of these unhappy people are without friends, or resource of any kind to relieve their necessities, and are begging from door to door, for a morsel of food.' By the end of the Hungry Forties, the government minister who was supposed to make speeches about these matters, Labouchère, told the House of Commons that in one year's migration to Canada and New Brunswick, 'Out of 106,000 emigrants from Ireland and Scotland 6,100 perished on the voyage, 4,100 on their arrival, 5,200 in the hospitals, and 1,900 in the towns to which they repaired.'

Latterly, most of the migrants had been cleared, whereas the Big Carpenter and his people in some sense chose to leave. Of course these overlap: both the evicted and the voluntary share feelings and conditions – the purgatorial voyage, yearning for the homeland, a sense (whether bitter or resigned) that the homeland had failed to afford either livelihood or freedom, the belief that both were to be had in the New World. As one crofter wrote home from Manitoba in 1883, 'We have got plenty of land, very good water, any amount of timber; also we are not under bondage to any man, as we have been in Benbecula. I have also to tell you that I sowed twelve bushels of potatoes, four bushels of barley, half a bushel of white beans, carrots, onions, and turnips, and to look after them coming up is a glory you would not believe, and we are thinking ourselves happy that we left Benbecula in time.' Nevertheless, the discovery of stories about people who had undergone the more acute experience of clearance was still my higher priority, so Anne and I now began to work out a theory of why clearance material was more elusive than that of more voluntary emigration.

Perhaps memories of eviction and its aftermath were repressed. It was dire, not only the torching of the roof and the loom, the quenching of the fire, the physical fight or chase (if any), the violation of your home and your neighbour's but also the flitting with a minimum of provision. Unlike those who chose or 'chose' to go, you had not saved up for the day of your removal nor had you the gratification of at least deciding quite rationally and leisurely that it was time to make for new pastures. If you were cleared, especially in the mass expulsions of the middle century, you might well have to beg in rags through the streets of Tobermory, Glasgow, or Quebec, you might have to spend weeks as an inmate of the quarantine sheds and hospices, as needy and futureless as someone in Germany in 1945 or Hong Kong today. There must have been a severe onus on them to repress all that suffering, need, and humiliation and I have seen the shadow of it, like a reef darkening just below the water, on more than one face. John MacDonald at The Clan in Armadale on Skye knew that his maternal forebears had been cleared but 'My mother would not talk about it' – as he said this he looked down with a clouded face which must have mirrored his mother's expression, and her mother's before her.

On Barra such feelings are well-known. People told me how relatives had consciously suppressed their traumas. A merchant captain's widow at Garrygall, near Castlebay, was emphatic: 'No!' she said vehemently, her blue eyes firing, 'they won't speak up about it – it's like the prisoners of war – there was a P.O.W. in our family and if anybody started up the subject he left the room. It was the same with the people who went away. They used to say, if we're doing all right we'll send you a letter, but if not . . . We had an aunt who went out there [to Canada on the *Marloch* in 1923] and she never wrote, and we used to say to our mother, "Why do we never hear from Auntie?" But she would only say, "Oh, she is not happy." '

I heard the same from Chrissie MacPherson from Buaile nam Bodach in Northbay whose parents had originally been evicted from Pabbay south of Barra. Her parents had been in a contingent persuaded by the priest to go to Saskatchewan. The cold and the distance from the sea had driven them home again after three or four years and 'Mother forbade us to ask our father about it, when we came home from school and started asking.'

The objective face of the same process would be the likelihood that evicted people arriving without money or flocks would find it hard to acquire title to land and would pass on into the vastness of North America without leaving any prints that lasted. They would make their way as soon as they could to where the unskilled work was – digging the Erie canal, driving the railroads west, logging for industrial timber, not carving out their own farms. Generations later they might still know that they had 'come from Sutherland', or from Uist or wherever, but they would be less likely to have detailed stories, for how could these be audible today unless they had been repeated for generations with some satisfaction and interest in the telling? From this point on we suspected that the hardest thing to find in Canada would be memoirs of veritable eviction.

We were now on the way to Glendale, a dot on the map where a knowledgeable man called John Shaw was supposed to live. For some reason I pictured him as a bearded farmer who told stories and played the fiddle. When we found him, via the road map and enquiries at a dusty, neglected filling station, he turned out to be a youngish, brilliantly alert folk scholar from Ohio with a salutary scorn for people who drove about picking up instant folklore. He lives with his family on a small shabby farm on a suntanned slope backed by the forested Craignish Hills. Poultry were pecking in the yard and cut hay bleached in the field but they had run down their stock and the main effort was now going into collecting and translating stories from Gaelic speakers and making subtle analyses of how fiddle music had mutated as it travelled from the Highlands to Cape Breton. So John too was an immigrant, a recent one, and so was his wife Jilly. As I made notes of what he was telling me, I could hear Anne talking to her – casually at first, then with growing interest as they realised they had both lived in London – in the same part of London – and lo and behold! they had gone to the same school. As we talked flies whined outside and lettuce in the well-tended kitchen garden wilted in the golden glare. Many fields below, the atmosphere in the sheltered glen bottom gurled in windless heat. The road was modernised and good and as unused as the East German autobahns. 'Cape Breton is the basket case of the Canadian economy,' John remarked, explaining the tranquil desertion of it all. It is also, according to the Tourist Association material, 'A Masterpiece of Nature', and this figures: the more beautiful, the less work, the more people go back to a place for nostalgic holidays.

Acquaintances of the Shaws were drifting in now, a fiddle player to drink canned beer and make music with John in the living room, a man called Bill Lamey to tell me about his forebears. These were MacVarishes and Stewarts from the seaward end of Loch Shiel in Argyll, where the ten miles of lochwater pour to the sea in a short black river rife with salmon. The township was called Mingarrypark and a grand-uncle had been called Donald Bhreac, after Beinn Bhreac, the speckled mountain, which runs down into the broad moss of Kentra at that point. The family's experience had been in every way a settler epic:

They left there about 1834. And it had not been easy for them in that part. My grandmother told the story, how they had one or two cows, and no meat to butcher, so she used to bleed the cattle to make the pudding, the *marag* [blackpudding]. And there was two children buried there in infancy. But they were very sad leaving, when the boat started pulling away from Fort William – very broken up about it. And my great-grandmother was pregnant with my grandmother coming across. They landed here in the fall of 1834, a place called Craignish down here. They didn't know where they were, just told to get off, that's all.

My grandmother would be the seventh child and she was born shortly after they arrived. But her mother told the story about them coming across in the boat, and in the bowels of the boat, you know, there was squalor, and filth and sickness, and dying and fighting – all crammed up in the boat. And they ran out of water, and they had very little food. They had some potatoes they dare not use [needed for planting], and a bag of oatmeal. So when their water ran out, he [Alexander MacVarish] happened to have a bottle of whisky in his chest, or two. He mixed the whisky with the oatmeal, to moisten it up. And he said that was the happiest time on the way to Cape Breton!

They were dumped right on the ocean – they had no shelter. Just told to get off, that's all. With their trunk and bedding. They had to go into the woods, to cut down a lean-to. And they stayed there for the winter. And my grandmother was born in that shack. And when he went into the woods with the axe on his shoulder he said to my great-grandmother, 'Don't let the children go out into the water and get drowned. But, she said, she was so sick from the voyage, and being pregnant, there was nothing she could have done about it if they had. And she said, 'About dusk when he arrived back out of the woods he was the happiest man I ever saw, to come back.' That spring they came across the mountain, which is probably ten or fifteen miles as the crow flies, and settled up here at a place called Maple Brook.

Bill lives ten miles from Glendale, at Glenora near Lamey Brook – named after the family into which his mother married. Like nearly everyone I spoke to he was modestly disparaging about what he had to tell and he thought of it genealogically: 'This is just the story of my own family. But I'm sure they all had the same experiences.' The details of his family tree showed me how precarious and how tenacious these grapevines are down which the past reaches us. He never knew his grandmother, let alone his great-grandmother, and the entire story had survived only because his own mother listened to the two elder women:

My grandmother died February 11th, 1911, when *her* mother was aged one hundred years. And in those days they made the coffins themselves but they needed to get the shroud. So there was a merchant ten to twelve miles from there, and my uncle went there and the merchant said, 'Well sir, there are the two colours, black and tan,' and he didn't know which to choose, so he brought them both home, and when he got back *she* had died an hour after my grandmother, so they didn't need to return the shroud.

The MacVarishes, Stewarts, Camerons, and MacLeans (from Perthshire) who made up Bill Lamey's Highland forebears had run a kind of gauntlet to reach land at all. His great-grandfather Alexander and a brother of his called Angus had quarrelled so seriously on board that Angus went off to settle in Antigonish, Nova Scotia, and changed his name to MacDonald (of whom the MacVarishes were a sept). People were bound to fight. The 'bunks' were liable to be planks six feet long, three feet wide, and little more than two feet apart; ships that had carried up to 500 slaves were refitted to carry more than 700 emigrants. One ship might harbour three or four hundred rats and the water supply was often foul as well as scanty – the death-rate from cholera, typhus, and smallpox could reach one in six passengers. In an Ontario paper for 1847 I found a note on a captain who kicked away from the freshwater butt a man who was dying of scurvy and kept order among the passengers with a rope's-end. 'During storms a mother would many times take her petticoats and tie the arms and legs of the family into their bunks but she would leave one arm of hers free to hold the baby.' Such glimpses are as rare as memoir of the hunger during the Potato Famine. The most harrowing conditions are repressed so intensely that they barely reach the present day by word of mouth. The words of one sea captain from Skye, concerning the 1850s and copied down in 1911, evoke the exact moment when the repression sets in, in this case at the onset of ship fever: 'The fear of death, when it takes possession of a crowd on board ship, is beyond the power of words to describe. Silence is the prevailing note. The boldest holds his breath . . . ' When the promised land was in sight the families might well be set their final ordeal. Ships bound for the Gut of Canso – the old name for the strait between Cape Breton and Nova Scotia – foundered so often on the island of St Paul's ten miles out from Cape North that it was 'strewn with human bones and other memorials' of the frequent wrecks.

Heedless captains were more concerned to offload the human cargo and take in payload for the return trip than to deliver families to the port named in the contract with the agent in Fort William or Greenock. People were dumped, like Bill Lamey's forebears, in coves and inlets, failed to become known to the officials, and therefore had no chance of qualifying for assistance in the way of tools and a little cash. The economic state of first-generation immigrants tended to be disastrous – they could not get over the exhaustion of the voyage. A businesslike Nova Scotian wrote an assessment in 1849: 'emigrants from the Highlands of Scotland are less skilful and persevering in their industry than their own descendants.' He was not inclined to be charitable and favoured keeping out people with no savings, who had been able to afford only their passage (it could cost £4 or a Highland family's whole income for a year), because they often lacked 'sobriety, industry, and a resolute spirit of enterprise'. In any case, those who had already managed to settle were against letting in any more of 'the poor and labouring classes of Irish'. Such are the dynamics of survival. An almost racist aversion from the next wave of settlers brews up among the first-comers. As I found next year in Ontario, immigrants from the north of Scotland now used 'Highlander' as a dirty word and applied it with distaste and alarm to the refugees from the post-Famine Hebrides.

Bill Lamey's Stewart forebears had come from the south-west end of Moidart, the ancient Catholic country where the Young Pretender saw fit to start his campaign in 1745. According to Bill his people were loyal to the old dynasty and were never at ease after Culloden. This had been among the motives for the exodus of Dan Gillis's forebears from Morar and so it had been for the great-grandparents of the priest I visited two days later on the advice of both Bill Lamey and John Shaw. He lived in the hollow of Glendale, in an ample white-sided presbytery built in 1885 which was like a prosperous elder brother of Iona House on P.E.I. – instead of seeming becalmed on a shoal out of the mainstream, it simmered with the activity of a parish which, for all its spellbound summer look, must have secreted a good many believers among its glades. Helpers and relatives came and went with that camaraderie of a priest's house. When Father John Angus Rankine himself appeared, in a study brimming with books (on the floor), fiddles of all sizes (on the walls, in corners, balanced on piles of LPs), cassettes in elastic-banded piles, a towering music system and large glossy photos of the Father conducting prize-winning choirs, he turned out to be quick with contained vitality, white hair combed back in waves, brown eyes aglow beneath eyebrows bristling black like new paint-brushes, and a fund of thoughts on the condition of Gaeldom since the débâcles, the famines, the exodus of the years from 1750 to the early twentieth century. He also told me a story that made my back shiver. Here was the marrow of migrant experience:

> My great-great-grandfather rowed from Prince Edward Island to Cape Breton Island. Rowed across the strait there from P.E.I. to Mabou coal-mines. And they slept under the boat, turned the dory over and slept under it. And when they woke in the morning, there was a little rivulet on the beach, and they started a fire, just underneath the high tall trees, so she looked up at them and she said, 'Finlay, we're free. This is our country.' Went to the river and somehow or other – it was teeming with fish – caught some fish. They had fried fish for breakfast and whatever else they had in the boat. They were free.

By this time we were already well out in mid-conversation and I realised that, as often, this gem might easily have been bypassed in the windings of spontaneous talk. As he spoke, I was thinking, This is known to me already – a dream? *déja vu?* Of course not – it was the archetypal vision at the close of *The Great Gatsby*:

> ... the inessential houses began to melt away until gradually I became aware of the old island here that flowered once for Dutch sailors' eyes – a fresh, green breast of the new world ... for a transitory enchanted moment man must have held his breath in the presence of this continent, compelled into an aesthetic contemplation he neither understood nor desired, face to face for the last time in history with something commensurate to his capacity for wonder ... It eluded us then, but that's no matter – tomorrow we will run faster, stretch out our arms further ... And one fine morning –
> So we beat on, boats against the current, borne back ceaselessly into the past.

Fitzgerald wrote with the disenchantment of our century. For the Beatons landing on Cape Breton in the early 1800s the future was still positive. From those ringing sentences of Finlay's wife, uttered in that pristine place, it sounds as though she very well 'understood and desired' the 'aesthetic contemplation' of that first landfall on Cape Breton. The thrill of conviction is palpable in her words. The pain for me, undercutting their sublimity, was in having to see that this vision of freedom and belonging was what people could no longer have in the Scotland of the rackrents, the kelping wage-slavery, the exacted services, the shaky tenures of fractional crofts.

Presumably Father John's Beaton forebears had been among the number from P.E.I., known to historians, who were 'dissatisfied with the land system there' and settled in Cape Breton on the coast from Judique north to Margaree. His word for what drove them out of Scotland was 'oppression'. A branch came from Achnacarry, which is where Loch Arkaig's waters run out into the south end of Loch Lochy, an area which is noticeably spruce, well-fenced – and devoid of any real village. Cameron of Lochiel has his big house there and is well connected in the banking world. Father John's people were 'squeezed out because the landlord raised the money [the rent] and they could not produce it from their farm'. He laughed as he recalled that when a minister called Archie Beaton visited Cape Breton in 1979 they found they were third cousins and the Scotsman said to him, 'Och, you're one of the lost sheep!' His relationships seemed to link him with every crux in the Highland diaspora. It was a Rankin forebear who had wakened the MacDonald chief at the start of the massacre in Glencoe on February 13th, 1692 – presumably the Duncan Rankin who was first to be killed, shot in the river. A Beaton forebear had married a MacBain who was sister to 'the only Highlander that Butcher Cumberland ever praised'. As the conversation unfolded, every kind of migrant passed along the horizon. The men who left Cape Breton by schooner from Port Hawkesbury for work in Pennsylvania. The girls who left from Plaster Cove and went south to service in Massachusetts: 'At one time Boston was half Cape Bretoners. In order for the family to survive they had to go. The soil wasn't rich enough to support a large family farm. Generally the bachelor and the old maid would stay at home to look after the parents.' A contingent of MacDonalds (who must have been from South Uist, because they called their settlement Bornish): 'The boat just dropped them off on the New Brunswick coast. Luckily for them they were picked up by some Frenchmen from Arichat [on Isle Madame in south Cape Breton].

But they had a very tough winter, living with people who couldn't understand them.'

In spite of all that daunting flux, the motif of Father John's memoirs was 'freedom'. The story that seemed central to his vision concerned a visit to Cape Breton by Bishop Grant of Argyll and the Isles:

We had a ceilidh for him, some of the Scottish priests, down at Samuel Gillis's, God rest his soul, he's dead too. Five or six fiddlers and singers there were, so we had a kind of supper for him. And I can still see Grant sitting there, next the piano, and once in a while the handkerchief would come out and he'd rub his eyes, you know, and he said, 'Well,' he said, 'you haven't lost the Scottish music, but there's one difference – our music at home is slow, and grave, and sad. Because we didn't go over here. We were not free.' And I thought of my great-great-grandmother: 'We're free.' In other words, we're not pestered by the landlord or the sheriff, or anybody else – this is ours – let's start new now.

So the immigrants were free – to go under or make their fortunes. The anecdotes I heard on Cape Breton ranged from the lowliest failure to success – usually defined vaguely as a matter of becoming 'great men in their field – doctors and lawyers and professors'. Jimmy Mackay in lower Glendale – 'a Mackay from Tongue in Sutherland' – was proud of his grandfather blacksmith, for example, who had never been to school yet read Burns and Scott in bed at night. He was also a connoisseur of the downbeat lives of people who had failed. The man who went to Ohio but came back in the end and found a couple living in his house – they let the man have one end of it and when Jimmy called on him he had to enter head-first through a window because the man refused to treat the door as his. The relative who came back to Glendale with one suitcase after going to make his fortune in the States and when the neighbours got to peek inside while the man was out, 'all there was in it was a collar, a necktie thin as a rat's tail, and a newspaper'. As a transatlantic legend it seemed the perfect antithesis to the Ben motif in *Death of a Salesman*, the man who walks into the jungle at the age of seventeen and comes out with diamonds.

I was speaking to Jimmy Mackay in a house among aspens, screened and curtained against the sun. His grandfather had built it and its board walls were still ox-blood red, as were the big barn and small house, now a shed, a few yards off among parched blond grasses. The smithy had been there and the strong crimson, typical of west Cape Breton, had been made with red ochre from the store mixed with fish-oil. This had been a farm but crops and stock were scarcely to be seen in Glendale. Jimmy's house was an antique shop. Alastair MacLeod the novelist's house up at Dunvegan is a holiday home for his family when they all drive up from Windsor, Ontario, at the start of the summer. Dan Angus Beaton still farms, in the dreamy valley of Blackstone near Lake Ainslie, but he spent many years as an engineer in Detroit. The ex-mayor of Inverness, 'a MacLean from Duart in Mull', was looking after his son's caravan park, MacLean's Camp, where we turned off the road looking for accommodation. Such were the people who told us about their Highland connections during the next few sunlit days as we traced the grapevine of John Shaw's contacts and Alastair's relatives and acquaintances, or just followed our own noses along the simmering roads.

The ex-mayor of Inverness was in his white string vest, reading the paper under a hawthorn tree, and when he asked us to stay for a mug of tea and a doughnut, we sat beside him on a home-carpentered settee upholstered with a moss-peat bag filled with hay. He gave me a cyclostyled history of the Clan MacLean and recalled that when his son visited Castle Duart and was entertained by Sir Charles MacLean, 'he was offered a jigger of whisky. So he knocked it back and took the bottle to help himself to another dram. And the laird said, "Hold on! That's enough, or it winna go roon!" ' This sounds like the laird impersonating the canny Scot to amuse his guests, since I'm sure he doesn't speak Scots normally ... Mr MacLean had no caravans available, and much as he'd have liked to offer us a room in his own house it wasn't really suitable because 'they were taking the scullery apart'. We drove on northward and got a room in the motel at Inverness where long breaths of sea-wind keened in the mosquito screen, ruffled the table-mats in the dining-room, and made the fishing net slung from the ceiling waft and belly and shake its green glass floats. The froth of the breakers on the beach was warm as fresh milk to swim through and even at night, when we drove through leagues of forest with Alastair and Anita MacLeod to a country dance at Glencoe Mills, the air was so close that sweat coursed down our backs and chests as we kept time with the demonic fiddle music. The music, like the heat, was Scots and it wasn't Scots, and although we knew the steps of the reel well enough (or Anne did: I only ever stumble around in clumsy confusion on a dance floor), the solo turns were quite unScottish, they were more like dancing I had seen in Donegal. An acknowledged maestro, woman or man, would take the floor, everyone else drew back, and in the dusty space a metronomic frenzy was let loose, legs shooting forward from the knee, sideways from the knee, feet flying like shuttles, torsoes and heads bobbing but never turning, arms at the sides, only the legs and the feet flip-flip-flipping with the tireless precision of a loom. Outside, young guys lounged in the headlights of big American cars with bleached paintwork and drank Labatt's or Coor's from cans. Inside there was no liquor and the whole community, aged eight or eighty, thudded and whirled together as though some ideal village from past times had been conjured up in the middle of this forest where Mull River ran out of the Craignish Hills.

Alastair had taken a workshop with my writing students at Lancaster and I had read his *Lost Salt Gift of Blood*, in which a country way of life transforms into story with the certainty and physical presence of George Eliot's Warwickshire or Hardy's Dorset. I had never imagined that I'd travel his own back roads under his guidance or go visiting in his company. When I found him in Dunvegan, he was up in the steep field behind his house, gleaning hay with his sons. A neighbour had mowed it for him before they arrived but in the mochie heat it had begun to stale. The place was on a lot that had been quartered among four brothers. Down by the roadside a truncated pyramid of shingle stones commemorated

PIONEER
DONALD MACLEOD
HIS WIFE
JANET MACPHERSON
APPLIED FOR
AND GRANTED 1808–11
A SECTION OF
THIS THE GOOD EARTH
TRADITION AND
CULTURE ENRICHED
THE LAND OF
THEIR ADOPTION

B'I A' GHAIDHLIG AN CAINNT
[Their language was Gaelic]

Not far away was the bare hut where Alastair goes to write his stories. One day he heard a noise at the door and turned to see a deer stepping in. The window with a plank shelf below it where he stands to think and smoke and write looks due north across the sea from which the Arctic winds come, herding the pack-ice, which he describes so bodily that it becomes animal, and shearing close the dwarf cypress and blueberry – which now was thick with fruit. A hollow in the ground nearby was what was left of the cellarage of a house owned by people who bought an acre from Alastair's father and ran in rum from Jamaica by night on their ketch. The clearest relic of this older Cape Breton was the bypassed main coast road – a mere yellow-dust track where dense maple and hazel brushed the wings of the car. From here the lighthouse at East Point, P.E.I., a few miles from Iona House, was visible at night over the sound which the Beatons had crossed to land at Finlay's Point. At Broad Cove churchyard Alastair's forebears were buried among people identified as 'Native of Morar' or commemorated in Gaelic. According to Alastair, a woman 'Born Bay of Fundy' was one of a complete congregation who felt isolated among blasphemers and had walked right across Nova Scotia to settle among fellow Catholics. The houses invisible in the woods are now being bought by Americans but Alastair remembers them in the days when the farm families had driven the first high ten miles to church in a sleigh and the last, low-lying part in a buggy.

The MacLellans at Dunvegan whom Father John had suggested I visit turned out, of course, to be old friends of Alastair's, and his father's, and his grandfather's . . . What he was doing now was gently folding me into the round of visits he makes each summer when news of deaths and migrations is exchanged, the grapevine watered with mild comment – nearly everyone who had died was judged to have been 'a good person' or 'very nice'. The MacLellans were ending their days in an immaculate white farmhouse with a gaggle of red-ochre barns floating beside it among the pale-gold shimmer of hayfields that had not been mown for years. Archie Dan, aged eighty-nine, and his sisters Annie, Jessie, and Flora were all unmarried. We conversed in a living room hung with religious pictures – Jesus seven feet tall with long auburn hair and blue contact lenses, turning his melting forgiveness on the assorted sinners at his feet. Archie was over six feet tall and broad, with a check shirt, a leather belt, and slippers on his bare hairless feet. His eyes had the very old look, the irises paling from their outer edges, as were Flora's, who was deputed to speak to me. She sat in a rocking-chair, her steel-wool hair neatly crimped, her eyes opening and closing in slow motion, and told me that their forebears had come from Swordland in Morar. On the maternal side there had been Gillises from Kinlochmorar – that little house dwarfed by the weeping mountainside that I had seen on our long walk years before. So they were related to Dan Gillis – of whom they'd never heard.

Every five minutes or so Archie Dan asks me where I come from (to which I answer 'Aberdeen', although I left there thirty years ago). 'He's getting forgetful,' puts in Flora quietly. Glasses of cooled ginger ale with little glass rods in them to stir the ice are brought through by Annie, the most active of the four. I thankfully swallow several inches of it and it turns out to be two-thirds Bourbon. In more cautious Scotland a drink at such times is nearly always offered in genteel code – 'Will you take a refreshment?' Abruptly Archie Dan strikes a clear vein and tells me, 'I was wounded in France – 19th April, 1917.'

'What happened exactly?'

'I will not be remembering.' I think he means, I'm no longer clear about this, but no; he means, I refuse to go into grisly detail.

'When did it happen?' I ask.

'Vimy Ridge. 19th April, 1917,' and he pulls up his trouser leg to show a deep bite out of his lower shin, a yellow pit lined with shiny brown scar tissue.

This was a history I was not at all expecting. A year later Alastair wrote to me to say that Archie Dan had died and recalled how that afternoon he had kept mistaking Alastair for his father or grandfather, 'none of it seeming to matter very much to him as we still had enough material to carry on our kind of conversation which was probably the same kind of conversations he had with my father and grandfather. I have thought of that since – that only in such a community could one be sort of interchangeable with men who, if they were living, would now be 91 and 124 respectively.' Now came the disconcerting bit: 'He was one of those men who "missed" the First World War and regretted it. He was eight years old, I believe, when it ended. However, it was very real to him. Once, years ago, he and my father were coming home in a horse drawn buggy and he pulled up his trouser leg to "show" my father where the imaginary bayonet had entered his calf.' So what did cause that hideous gouge? Of course it could have been done by the tine of a hayrake or a steer's horn – an uncle of Alastair's had been unable to go down the Mabou mine to work because a cow he was feeding had raised its horn and put out his eye. But my notes for that day, Saturday August 13th, 1988, record distinctly: 'Later Alastair says he [Archie Dan] has another bad one in his rib cage, from a bayonet wound.' Maybe Alastair was surrounding this with sceptical inverted commas which I failed to hear? A chronicler or genealogist could ascertain the birth date of A.D. MacLellan but since I am writing not a chronicle but a book about how people perceive their history, the thing may be left at that. The war-wound was real for Archie Dan, which may or may not mean that the only really real thing was his wish to have gone and fought, and certainly it can have made no difference to the course of history whether or not he was among the Canadian troops who captured that little hill in Flanders (on the 9th April, not the 19th).

As history and people's perception of it threatened to dislimn in the haze of these old farmlands, I was given a well-focussed memoir by Dan Angus Beaton, whose working farm lay in the grassy vale of Blackstone between the Mabou Highlands and the glittering shallows of Lake Ainslie. As early as 1811, Protestant Highlanders had colonised the eastern side of the lake (from Mull, Tiree, Coll, Muck) and Catholics the western (from Moidart, Arisaig, South Uist). Dan Angus himself, at 85, was tanned, upright, incisive, and his hearing aid worked perfectly. He was a woodsman who almost chanted his praise of the great trees of the west, the redwoods and sequoias, and uttered angry laments for the broad-leaved trees of the Maritimes, beeches and yellow birches 'with stumps four feet across', felled by his grandfather. Both were extinct now because of acid rain. Day after day we had been dismayed by the look of the black spruce and jack pine. Instead of the pristine green canopy we had expected, we drove past hundreds of miles of tattered tops, ten feet of lichenous spar ending in a pathetic tuft of needles. 'There's only no-good stuff like alder left here now,' Dan Angus confirmed. 'And look at the spruce – dying from the crown – spruce-bud worm – the gasoline pollution weakens 'em and the bug gets 'em.' Later, at Hidden Falls in Nova Scotia, we spoke to a woman of seventy whose maples were dying, wiping out her income from the syrup for the first time in her life.

Dan Angus's lounge was all well-carpentered wood, including a singular piece he had made himself: a wooden lobster trap turned upside down, planed and varnished and fitted with a heavy glass top to make a coffee table. The glory of the room, its altar-piece, portrait gallery and archive, was the collage across the entire end wall above the fireplace. Every family photo he had been able to find back to 1880 had been laid out in a tree, complete in all its principal branches, with a postcard in the middle showing the Mother of Sorrows Church at Ashtabula Harbour, Ohio, where he and his wife had been wed in 1934. Great groups of children and grandchildren assembled for their fortieth anniversary flanked the tree. He reckoned that it had cost him $3,000 all told.

Dan Angus was proud to have been in work 'right through the Slump' but in 1941 they had come back to the house of his birth and farmed there ever since. His forebears were from Achluachrach, which is in Glen Spean, and his vision of them was concentrated in one dramatic episode, hinging on a nice double meaning:

Big Finlay, Fionnlagh Mòr, was the youngest in the family and he remained [when his brother Donald emigrated in 1772]. And he was married over there, and he was one of the crofters. And the lord would come to collect the rent, and if you didn't have the rent it would be just too bad. It was pretty hard to have it – it was almost impossible to have the rent they were charging. They'd dowse your fire, and it's very hard to start a fire with this-here peat. But Finlay had it all planned to come over here, because the lord gave him a pretty hard time. However, Finlay sold pretty near everything he had on the farm, and when he came for his rent, 'Well,' he told him, 'I'm just not ready to give you the rent today, I haven't got it all for you. But you come over on such-and-such a day and I'll have it all for you and you'll get what's coming to you.'

And the lord said, 'You *better* have it ready. Or else.'

So the boat was ready – however far Finlay had to go it wasn't far. And the lord came and there was a bowl on the table. Finlay was in alone, waiting for him. And he [the lord] had a beautiful horse, of course – saddled, tied outside. And the lord said, 'Mr Beaton?'

And Finlay said, 'You'll get everything that's coming to you today. The rent is in the bowl and I don't know if I have it all for you but you'll get what's coming to you.' So the lord went down – there was like a pantry, off the kitchen where they were living. There was water in some pails that was there, and he dowsed the fire. That was the sympathy! Well, Finlay never said a word. But he said, 'You count what's in the bowl.' And he counted it, and it was all there, every last penny of it. And the lord said, 'The rent is all here.'

'Yes,' said Finlay, and he moved towards the door. It was wooden blocks that they had for chairs. And he said, 'There's a lot more that's coming to you.'

It was then that the lord understood. 'Oh,' he says, 'but my rent is all here and I've got to go.'

But Finlay says, 'When I'm all through with giving you some of what is coming to you I don't know if you'll ever go.' And he grabbed hold of him – and you can imagine a big raw-boned Highlandman of about 250 or 260 pounds, six foot seven inches, to grab at you! There wasn't much of that fellow left. He just left him flat as a pancake on the middle of the floor. Flattened him four or five times, just made tar-paper out of him in the middle of the floor.

He walked out, threw the saddle off the horse, took the bridle off it, took a whip and let him go to the mountains. Then he left for the boat. Finlay knew he'd just have about twenty minutes before the boat sailed. Got on the boat and the boat sailed for America. Nobody had any knowledge what port he was sailing for, and he might have sailed under any name, you understand – how was he going to trace him? He might have stopped at Montreal, Quebec, anywhere. But he stopped at Prince Edward Island, because he had a brother Donald there twenty years before that.

As we know, they did not stay there, because this was the Finlay whose wife hailed the freedom of the new world in the story told me by Father John Angus, and he was the great-great-grandfather of Dan Angus. The brother Donald, who was much older, had 'fought in the field with the English – what was that called? Culloden. And after the thing was over they caught Donald later at home, and they hung him upside down by his feet in the barn to kill him, but you may be sure someone in the family let him loose, and he escaped to America.'

So the exodus from Lochaber, as Dan Angus has received it and passed it on, takes epic form. Like the Big Carpenter who led his people out of Sollas, Finlay Mòr is tall, cunning, and far-sighted. He resolves the conflict with the chieftain-landlord into single combat – a final act of physical revenge for tyranny. No word of his family, or of his neighbours or the factor or the ground officers. They have all been edited out, leaving the protagonists by themselves on a sparsely furnished stage to fight the class war to a finish which, for the crofter, is both a retreat and a victory.

The hitherto unmentioned presence in the Maritimes is the Indian people. More absence than presence. As we drove west from Iona House on P.E.I., Dan Gillis would point to a series of small, unkempt wooden houses and say, 'A Micmac settlement.' The land nearby would be more or less unfarmed, the car or pick-up only just roadworthy. 'Micmac', or 'Megumaage', means 'land of the true men' – the first name ever given to the Maritimes. I only learned this when we went in for lunch at Whycocomagh on the Trans-Canada Highway in mid Cape Breton. Nearby, a perfunctory tepee – a few poles half-clad in tattered birch bark – signalled the Micmac Basket Shop, where you could buy small varnished tomahawks and canoes six inches long. The restaurant was superb. Subtle prints of dream animals, bird and deer totems, adorned the walls; they were by a sophisticated native-American artist who lived in Toronto. The food, served by a Megumaage woman 'born and bred right here in Whycocomagh', was so richly and purely of this place that it was like being absorbed into the lakeside forests simply to have it in your mouth: Malagawatch eel, whose flesh was succulent and fishy, stewed with fiddlehead fern and eaten with lookineegun bread, which was murlie with a crust like cake; roasted game-hen basted in blueberry and stuffed with wild rice. The place was obviously the pride of a resurgent effort to attain high modern standards. Father John, who was their priest, had said that the ninety families on the reservation were 'doing better now' – those who were in work (builders, teachers, clerks) – although those on government hand-out were 'not in good shape'.

When the waitress saw me studying a wall map which showed the homelands of all the native-American tribes, she gave me a closely-printed leaflet of Megumaage history. From between its lines you could hear a long-drawn-out lament echoing over the bays and forests. 'The Micmac spoke an Algonkian dialect. They were involved with the French and later the English in efforts to stop pilfering by the Beothuk from Newfoundland. The final result was the extermination of the Beothuk.' The new alliances in turn foundered in blood. 'Small groups of Micmac probably settled near Whycocomagh around 1720 when Abbé Gaulin set up a mission at Mirliguèche. Some Indians from mainland Nova Scotia were provided with a haven from the English during the Indian war of 1723.' This sounds like the background to a story told me by Father John which could have come from a pious children's storybook of the later nineteenth century. 'Some Scottish settlers on the shores of the Bras d'Or were fishing. They sensed Indians nearby. Soon they came stepping out of the woods with tomahawks and surrounded them. When the settlers knelt to say their last prayers, the Micmac recognised the sign of the cross, and made friends with them.' A pacific interlude. The peoples could not co-exist for long. *Silent enim leges inter arma*: firepower rules. According to a history of early Nova Scotia which I read at the house of a veteran Gaelic-speaker called Katey Gillis at Mabou, an English party who landed 'were greeted with a hail of musketry from one hundred neutral Indians and French', which is a use of 'neutral' worthy of Joseph Heller. The usual naked struggle for resources was under way and the free lands and peoples of America had to pay for the congestion and tyranny in Europe. 'Invading Loyalists', according to the waitress's pamphlet, 'reduced the supply of game, killing almost 9,000 head of moose and caribou in the winter of 1789.'

This white people's way with game came back to me when we were being told about the Indian way at our most northerly point on Cape Breton, just short of Cape St Lawrence. For miles the dirt road looked about to plunge terminally into virgin forest, then it would recover itself, head slap over a sharp rise, and zig towards the sea-cliffs till finally it gave up at a grassy valley-mouth facing the north-east. A Robinson Crusoe garden of lettuce, shalotts, and dill grew in a little plot amongst knee-high wild flowers and grasses, fenced round by poles with the bark still on. In a home-made wooden house we were served copious crab salads by a tanned woman from Germany who painted bleak blue-and-ochre landscapes and a hippy with stoned black eyes who specialised in paintings of burnt-out wrecks in glittering yellow lagoons. We were at Meat Cove – so named, he told us, because the Indians used to drive the deer through the trees to the cliff edge. They toppled headlong down the layered brown granite and were butchered on the reefs below, just above high tide. This seemed ecologically sound, the small population and absence of guns keeping inroads into wildlife to a minimum.

Now that both native-Americans and white have shrunk back to the parts of the island more accessible from the mainland, the 'game' can resume its own life-cycle. Early one morning as we drove into the Highlands Park past a towering raw-red crag called the Grande Falaise, a white-tailed deer trotted daintily across the road and jumped four feet vertically over dwarf pine, hooves flinging, blonde rump flaunting. Apart from the road the only human trace for fifteen miles was an alluvial fan at the mouth of the MacKenzie River whose close homogeneous green had once been cultivated by Highland settlers. We saw it in perspective down two miles of wooded ravine – like the northern settlements on Raasay, another little beach-head of crofting seen through the wrong end of history's telescope. Our species had been and gone. Naturalness had come into its own again. Between the forest and the sea, these last few days in Canada, a zone of peace, suffused with the oldest legends and names of the country, wrapped itself round us.

En route for Halifax, Montreal, and home, on the Minas Channel of the Bay of Fundy, we stayed in a plank hut, burning logs in an iron stove and rowing on a river like a window of blue glass. Not far away, the Beaver – a sort of Loki or mischief-maker in Micmac myth – had wrecked the garden of the great man-god Glooscap. Glooscap chased him and threw five huge boulders after him. Now they are called Five Islands, and they even look legendary: humps of warm sandstone topped with basalt, each one furry with forest like a coonskin cap, a whole family's headgear left floating on the estuary. It had been a special wish of Anne's to come here for the sake of the tidal bore, the highest and quickest in the world. Up the Shubenacadie River, which flows into the Minas from the south, we got a last elemental gust from the heart of Canada.

A veteran Dutch fisherman with three fingers missing from one hand took us out into midstream in a Zodiac inflatable. As the motor idled, he pointed out the massive treetop nest of a bald eagle. Round the bend downstream a brown tide came charging, not the maximum (the moon was far from full) but rearing in waves three feet high and spinning deep black whirlpools as it met the current. The Dutchman gunned the motor and forced us bucking over the breakers – cut it and let us whirl slowly – then turned upstream and added our speed to the tide's eight knots until the reedbeds and the aspens were fleeing past. Shoals and beaches disappeared as the water rose – we were surrounded by placid farmland and copses, and the sea was in another world.

As we hauled onto a shelf of rippled sand, we asked our captain how on earth the river accommodated the bore when it was frozen over. The ice split here and there, he said, and when the water spewed through the cracks it threw up smelts and salmon onto the ice. Then the bald eagles who wintered here, as many as eighty, circled down from the trees and glutted themselves on the fish as they froze. We had seen the bird just once before, for two seconds. Near Seattle a friend had asked us where we'd like to go one afternoon. I liked the sound of Granite Falls (on a bus route map) and when we went there we saw a bald eagle cruise across the slot made by the river through the cedars and turn its milk-white head, scanning for prey. An hour later, a porcupine rattled off into the undergrowth. Our American friend had never seen either before. As we glided back to base now on the Shubenecadie, we saw broad wings spreading and tilting against blue sky fifty feet above the maples – two young bald eagles learning to ride the thermals – as much a symbol of North America as condors are of the South, joint incarnation of the time when the forests and the rivers and all that lived in them seemed inexhaustible.

CHAPTER NINE

'LOCAL BULLIES AND BAD LANDLORDS'
Sutherland

After Canada the Highlands felt different – older – almost like a pupa case from which the New World had emerged. This soon changed, as I talked to people that autumn in Perthshire and Sutherland who were perfectly at home in and committed to their way of life; but the emptiness is there – Strath Brora is empty, and Kildonan and Ousdale and Strath Halladale and Aberscross, and Strath Naver above all. Until the Countess of Sutherland's gangs came with their writs and torches in 1814 and 1819, there were clachans all along Strath Naver: 64 townships housed 338 families. In 1724, Daniel Defoe had been impressed by the abundant corn that grew there, which was exported to Orkney and Shetland. It is one of the old sites of civilisation in Britain – its population peak was probably reached in the Bronze Age – it could have a civilisation again. Instead, for 150 years, it has had Masters of Fox Hounds from the Home Counties who go up there to fish and shoot, owners of airlines, princes, the head of the Liverpool Cotton Exchange who made a fortune selling khaki for use in Passchendaele and Vimy, Lords Lieutenant of various shires, 'and their friends, the loitering heirs of City directors', whom we actually saw one day, their Range Rovers parked on the roadside above the salmon river, the males in Barbour jackets and caps with nipped peaks, standing showing 'a good leg' with the foot turned out and the knee advanced, hip-flask in hand, as though a *Country Life* photographer was expected at any moment, the females with bright red lipstick and silk scarves round their hair, posing on rocks.

In hundreds of Highland journeys over 52 years I have rarely seen a landowner, and only two to speak to. On Jura in the summer of 1974 I drove as far north as wheels could go. The last four miles took an hour. As we forded a small river, a few red deer walked into a pool just upstream, put their muzzles down to drink, then stood and regarded us calmly. The island is a garden of Eden. Slow-worms and adders slide through the heather stems and twine beneath the boulders. Wild goats file past, ignoring you. Some of them, it is said, are feral descendants of herds kept by crofters evicted in the 1840s who were given no time to collect their stock. There are 5,000 deer in Jura and only 230 people. Into this paradise one morning a metal monster came snorting, a Land Rover from which an old man in a pepper-and-salt tweed jacket dismounted, clutching a rifle. He looked angrily at our tent and stalked off into the ten-foot-high bracken. A second Land Rover arrived, driven by an estate worker wearing a deerstalker. In five minutes a single shot banged out not far away. The minion walked off in that direction. Pepper-and-Salt reappeared, his rifle broken open over his forearm. He glared at us and said in a posh, congestive voice, 'Who gave you permission to be here?'

'Oh – we thought it was harmless – we're doing no damage of any kind – '

'Be sure to clean up before you go.'

He turned and snorted off. In a few minutes his man reappeared, dragging a stag by a heavy rope over his shoulder. It was already slit down the belly and gutted. Without a word he too drove off down the track to civilisation. Ever since I have thought of them as Pozzo and Lucky, but I have no idea whether this Pozzo has gone blind yet, or whether Lucky has spoken out.

My other meeting with the species was at Amhuinnsuidhe on the south-west coast of North Harris. We wanted to go up Glen Chliostair to climb on Strone Ulladale, one of Britain's greatest cliffs, and I had spent three or four days ringing the Castle, a Scottish-baronial wedding-cake put up in the 1860s to the order of Lord Dunmore, who had evicted all the crofters from the green meadows of South Harris. The story was always the same: 'I'm sorry, the master is away' or 'Try ringing tonight when the keeper might be back.' In the end we just went there. As we were lacing up our boots at the roadside, a Land Rover drew up abreast of us and we were aware of being eyed. These people too went in for the processional style – a second vehicle appeared, a large estate van driven by a heavily made-up woman with two lapdogs crouching between her thighs and the steering wheel. At this point a finger emerged from the Land Rover, extended towards us, and crooked sharply. It was like something out of a Cruickshank illustration in a Regency novel. We started to put on our anoraks. A face with slightly popping blue eyes appeared above the finger.

'Good morning. Where are you going?'

'We wanted to go up to climb on Strone Ulladale, and we could never get a clear reply, so we thought we'd just go. We'll be sticking to the path.'

'Oh. I see. Well – sorry – but not today, I'm afraid. Because my guns will be on the hill. Perhaps next month . . . '

'We'll be gone by then. And we do want to get on that crag.'

'Yes, quite. But the trouble is, it will scare off my deer.'

'I *have* been walking the Scottish hills for forty years, and I believe I know how to take care – '

'I'm sure *you* do, but most people don't – they charge about all over my hills, wearing those *things*' – his finger was doing a Cruickshank again, indicating two orange anoraks of ours. Our cause was obviously lost. The children were looking embarrassed, the pleasure of the occasion had been ruined. Stung by the phrase 'my hills', I became undiplomatic at last and said, 'It always staggers me that a mountain or a moor or a river can be *owned*.'

'Oh!' Popeye gobbled slightly. 'You're talking like a communist!' And off they processed, dudgeon whiffling from their exhausts. We had been in the presence of Sir Hereward Wake (yes!), who also owned a prime slice, if not the whole, of Rutland.

Sutherland, notoriously, has suffered since the late eighteenth century under rich people who have bought and sold sections of its vast wilderness and its fertile straths. The area is so far-flung and the people were so rigorously cleared that I might have despaired of finding any stories surviving. As it happened I was able to contact a relative of one of my oldest friends, John Manson, a crofter from Strath Fleet. I met him at university in 1951 and our discussions of literature and history have been incessant ever since. Until recently I had had no idea that he, who had been born in Caithness, was directly descended from crofters evicted from Strath Naver. In September 1988, at his suggestion, I visited his relative Daisy McEwen in Blairgowrie and she told me all she knew about her 'Hielant Granny', Minnie Campbell (in fact her first husband's great-grandmother). She had died in 1910 aged 94. Daisy was four then and had been able to hear directly about the eviction, or rather its aftermath. The factor's men had burnt their roof and cleared their township:

They went down the strath to the sea and walked all along the shore – well, near the shore. What a walk – carrying wee bairns. And they had cattle with them to start with. But when they got to Dunnet Head, the natives, the Caithnessians, pinched their cattle during the night, so they didn't even have that. And the Earl of Caithness, whatever he was – Sinclair – gave them permission to settle on a piece of bog anywhere, free of charge. It was very good of him [she laughs]. Well, they could at least sit down. And they made a divot house, in Mey, and they tried to break in a bit of the heather.

She remembered that her father started being very religious – they had meetings, religious meetings, in their house on Sunday afternoons, and one Sunday she was trying to surreptitiously sweep up some of the peat ash. Father came in, and he said, didn't she know that that piece of ash would choke her in hell yet! She was a sweet body, and I don't think she would ever be very naturally religious.

She was married very young – an older man, James Manson, quite nearby. She said that when she was newly married, on a moonlight night at harvest time she went out and danced a jig – danced a reel round the stooks of corn. Her husband was a very religious man, not daft religious but extremely strict – he wouldn't have approved of that but she did it.

She also took a goffering iron and ironed the frills of her mutch on a Thursday of the Sacrament. Two Communions a year – Thursday, Friday, Saturday and Sunday are all days when they can't work, they've got to prepare themselves. Well, on a Thursday she did the frills of her mutch, and she hung her mutch on a chair or something beside the fire, and the Lord had seen her, so a coal fell out of the fire and burned her mutch. Oh, she had to mind her step.

What further captivity was not in waiting for this girl when her family was banished from Strath Naver! In a photo taken not long before she died, she stands, still wearing her mutch but now in a widow's black dress, in front of the house at Gills, Canisbay, near Mey, where my friend John was born. A bush of honeysuckle grows up the front wall and the featureless flat lands of Caithness stretch away behind her. Her head still houses memories of the homeland in Strath Naver with its black cattle grazing round clustered houses, and her fellow-feeling with people in need moves her time after time (as I heard) to add an extra plateful of meal to the crofters' due when they bring their corn to her husband's mill.

Daisy McEwen's memories of Minnie Campbell's memories were themselves blurring a little. I talked to her in the company of her second husband, John McEwen, forester and author of the pioneering work *Who Owns Scotland?* He had designed their house himself, after a lifetime working with wood, and it was lined with holm oak brown as fallen leaves. Now his memory, which had once held all that could be discovered about Highland landownership, had gone. He sat beside us the whole evening, seeming to listen, saying nothing. Once, when his book was mentioned, he got to his feet to go and fetch copies from a hut in the garden, and as he stood uncertainly Daisy looked at him with humorous love and said, 'Don't fall, dear man.' She herself was clutching her head of short-cropped steel-grey hair as she tried to retrieve what she had been told eighty years before. In a fortnight she was dead. But, again, the story does not die because the teller was old. Daisy's daughter Margaret Hughes, who lives in London, sent me invaluable details which both corrected and filled out what her mother had told me. Daisy said that Minnie was 'not allowed' to speak Gaelic and only ever uttered one word of it – a word for 'darling'. Margaret put it like this:

My own grandmother, Williamina Innes, had been very close to her granny [i.e. Minnie Manson, née Campbell] as a child; she remembered happy times tucked up in beside Granny in a cosy bed, and that was when she asked her to teach her the Gaelic. Granny's reply was that Gaelic was the language of the past, but English was the language of the future, and she was determined that none of her offspring would learn Gaelic.

Another aspect of the captivity, natural to refugees as they try anxiously to acclimatise and be accepted. An Austrian refugee in Windermere during the War recalled recently:

Rapidly learning English, I flatly refused to speak German to anyone. If my mother pronounced so much as a sentence of German within hearing distance of another human being, I shushed her angrily. For a long time I read no German literature and only gave up my boycott when I developed a teenage crush on one of my language teachers, who convinced me that I must relearn my mother tongue.

Minnie Campbell had no such support – nothing but her own will to bend but not break under oppression. Margaret Hughes's version of her solitary defiant dancing was this:

... as soon as she turned sixteen, she was married to the son of the place [the farm where she worked]. She had her regrets about this. When you were married, you had to wear a mutch on your hair, which she found a trial, and you were not allowed to go to dances, which had been her chief pleasure. One of her tasks was fetching water from the well, with the usual two pails. The well was out of sight, down a brae, and Minnie used to set the pails a good distance apart and dance a reel of three around them.

Which is right? this highly specific memoir from a younger person? or the rather more stylised moonlit version from an older person closer to the source? Either way the story is a true legend of spirited life under bondage.

The final facet of the memoir is equally sharp and valuable:

When my grandmother's 'little brother' Alec volunteered in 1915, and was lost shortly after, their mother, who had always been a bright, active person, underwent a sad change; this was discussed among her children, who remembered their mother's mother, Minnie Campbell, telling them about how *her* mother was 'never right' after the eviction.

This, perhaps surprisingly, was not because of the physical hardships and shock involved, but because *her* two sons, Minnie's brothers, had been enlisted in the Countess of Sutherland's regiment to fight in the Peninsular War, and their mother was still waiting confidently for their return from what she took to be a long-service engagement.

Somehow she felt that the enforced move, with no means of

leaving a message for them, meant that they were indeed dead, at least in that she could never hope to see them again.

This hideous bind cropped up all over Sutherland. As a feudal superior the Countess demanded her tenants' sons for her regiment, the 93rd; the monument to its raising stands beside the village hall at Syre in Strath Naver. As a businesslike landowner she found it profitable to clear them if they refused to enlist. If they refused, she wrote, they 'need no longer be considered a credit to Sutherland, or any advantage *over sheep* or any useful animal' and she favoured 'removing altogether' any tenants in Strath Kildonan who showed a preference for regiments other than 'the two which the Marquis and Marchioness recommended'. Sometimes she tried the carrot method and offered inducements which must have been horribly attractive to the land-hungry, and to parents reluctant to make her a present of their sons. A few days into our first stay in Sutherland, Frances MacDonald of the Mill House at Gruids near Lairg (a district totally cleared in the 1820s) showed me a pathetic letter written for an illiterate crofter called John Ross of Inchvreck near Dornoch:

> ... in the year 1799 when Generall Wemess was Levying the Sutherland Regt. of Infantry your petitioner was applied to for giving his son George to be a Soldier in that Regt. and in consideration for his doing this Mr John Fraser late Factor on the Estate of Sutherland and with him Generall Wemess too, provided & engaged to put me and my said son in possession of a penny-land of Milton of Evelicks to commence at Whitsunday Last 1802 and I was to remain therein till Whits.day 1807 at the present Rent and thereafter to have a preference on equall terms ... notwithstanding whereof Mr Fraser has refused to Implement his obligation nor has the poor petitioner been put in possession of the Said Lands promised him to his very great Loss and eminent Ruin ...

Cannon-fodder being so valuable a Highland product, no wonder it was often argued as the nineteenth century wore on that if clearance left too few tenants on the rent rolls, the British Army would find itself seriously short of recruits.

Minnie Campbell's family knew the essence of her story but as they told it they made no mention of years and places. Where had she come from? and at what age? While we were staying at Helmsdale – created as a fishing village by the Sutherlands' chief manager, James Loch, to house evicted crofters – I managed to answer these questions with the help of a sardonic New Zealander called Alan Roydhouse. He was staying over here for as long as it took him to research the history of his forebears, who had been cleared from Ousdale in southern Caithness to Badbea. His living room was a rich compost of material, shelves and floor and table and chairs deep in everything from *Private Eye* to photostats of the Sutherland papers from the archive at their English base in Stafford. Sutherland was 'developed' with injections of capital from the Black Country coalmines owned by the Countess's husband. It is useful for us today that the Sutherlands' managers kept records of their shipments of people with the obsessional thoroughness of an Eichmann. Alan had photocopied lists of evictees from Strath Naver in 1819, 1,288 of them altogether. They included four Campbell families. Which was Minnie's? Two had settled in Strathy, a large dump for cleared folk on the north coast, and two had gone on to Caithness. Alan also showed me transcriptions of all the epitaphs in Canisbay churchyard (made by an Edinburgh librarian, A.S. Cowper). Williamina Campbell's gravestone gave her birth year as 1816. Her evictions must therefore have been one of those that were inflicted on the Strath in 1819, towards the dawn of her own memory. If her family lived in the township of Grummore, she could have seen a young man delirious with typhus running out of his burning house and hiding under the bushes – another setting off to carry his two little daughters twenty-five miles north to the sea at Bettyhill, 'first carrying one, and laying her down in the open air, and returning' – an old man sheltering in the mill and lying there licking oatmeal dust from the floor, defended against rats by his collie. (Presently I met a descendant of his, John Mackay of Port Gower near Helmsdale, and he was able to tell me that he had been the miller.) It happened on a Tuesday. The people were given half an hour to take out their furniture and tools. Then 'roofs and rafters were ignited into one red blaze'.

These glimpses of the chaos at Grummore were recorded by Donald MacLeod the stone-mason, whose village, Rossal, was seven miles down the strath, and by Donald Sage, minister at Achness mission, two miles nearer. One hundred and seventy years later the shells of the vandalised houses are remarkably upstanding, some of them with seven courses of stones still in place. They look like hulls of boats cast up on the broad green landing that slopes gently to Loch Naver. On its shore the stub of a massive broch signals that this has been a fit place to live in since pre-history. The sixteen families lived a life cramped and untidy by modern standards but Angus Mackay, who had been cleared at the age of 11 in the first Strath Naver burning in 1814, testified to the Napier Commissioners seventy years later at Bettyhill that they had been 'reasonably comfortable' in their old home:

> . . . you would see a mile or half a mile between every town; there were four or five families in each of these towns, and bonnie haughs between the towns, and hill pasture for miles, as far as they could wish to go. The people had plenty of flocks of goats, sheep, horses, and cattle, and they were living happy . . . with flesh and fish and butter and cheese and fowl and potatoes and kail and milk too. There was no want of anything with them; and they had the Gospel preached to them at both ends of the strath . . . and in several other towns the elders and those who were taking to themselves to be following the means of grace were keeping a meeting once a fortnight – a prayer meeting amongst themselves – and there were plenty gathering, so that the houses would be full.

If anyone is inclined to dismiss this kind of thing as rose-tinted nostalgia, consider that the Sutherland estate itself reported that the 'general level of welfare' in Strath Naver was good.

What you realise as you walk all over the cleared lands of Scotland is that they were emptied *because they were good places*: that is, fit for the new large flocks of big southern sheep to feed on even in winter. Their greenness stands out today as though lit by some unfailing sunray among the brown heather moors. They are also picked out by the pale blazes of the sheep, which still choose to browse there because ground that has once been cleared of stones, trenched for drainage, puddled by the hooves of animals, delved and fertilised over generations, maintains almost indefinitely its power to raise dense, juicy grass. If you stroke it, it feels tender. If you were blind, you would feel its resilience under your feet, as against the squelching or lumpy texture of the unimproved land round about – which also could have been improved by now, like the Yorkshire dales or the Dolomite alps, if crofting life had been allowed to go on evolving.

We worked our way north and west through Sutherland, up the narrowing coastal shelf from Dornoch to Helmsdale, through the straths that cut twenty- and thirty-mile clefts into the great central moor. There were no roads when the Countess married the Marquis of Stafford in 1785 and at first they thought they had only 3,000 tenants – actually there were 15,000. The master-plan was to rehouse them on the northern and eastern coasts or encourage them to emigrate, replacing their subsistence farming by a capital-intensive system. Leslie Bowran, the shepherd whose great-great-grandmother saw the red glow of a clachan burning, copied out for me some accounts for 1808–9 which showed that incoming shepherds – often from the north of England (Redpath, Oliver, Robinson) – were paid more than £20 a year and allowed to run 40 or 50 sheep of their own. Local men (MacDonald, Sutherland, Ross) were paid less than £10 and allowed only 10 or 15 sheep. From the estate's point of view, farming was being upgraded – and rent income raised. From the crofters' point of view, for example Donald MacLeod of Rossal in Strath Naver, the aim was to 'get rid of the natives'.

By the end of the French Wars the estate was regularly using force to expel the folk from the clachans, most notoriously under the supervision of Patrick Sellar from across the firth in Moray. He was both factor and tenant-farmer – not necessarily in that order. All over the Highlands he cleared crofters and acquired property – in Strath Naver and Strath Fleet, at Park in Lewis, in Morvern, Argyll. When the Countess grew alarmed at the ill-fame of his brutal methods and foul mouth, she replaced him by Francis Suther – whose technique was no different. As I moved about on their trail, a little rhyme grew in my head –

> I'll be judge, I'll be buyer,
> Said cunning old Sellar.
> He was followed by Suther –
> As bad as the other.

At first we stayed at Badninish north-west of Dornoch, in a cottage on the margin between cold upland fields and shaggy moor scattered with pine and birch – a place visibly dour to make a living in. Mr Goskirk, a minister at Lairg, told me that forebears of his called Leslie had had to tear out the heather with their bare hands to break in new fields here, five hundred feet above sea-level. The land-use pattern we could see on every side was becoming intelligible: broad glen-bottoms with good tilth rich in river silt, where the old townships were replaced by large spreads of sheep-farm and grandiose shooting lodges; steep, wet, rocky slopes or plateaux where nobody would ever have chosen to live, dotted with colonies of cleared people – those who would not emigrate.

At Badninish we were strategically placed near the home of Bridget MacKenzie, who had sent me the invaluable memoir of the burnings in Strath Fleet, and six or seven miles from Dunrobin Castle, headquarters of the search-and-destroy operations of 1813 and 1825. Bridget turned out to be an avid historian with a sparky militant humour. Her husband's forebears had been evicted from Dochfour on Loch Ness-side in 1870 and denied compensation for their standing crops. The new proprietor nearby was well hated, and scornfully nicknamed, for netting salmon as they swam up the River Evelix to spawn. I was reminded of Daisy McEwen in Blairgowrie reflecting, 'I suppose – a landlord – is a sort of *louse*.' Bridget's neighbour, Sandy Fraser of Fleuchary, embodied the whole history of the crofters who hung on. His great-grandfather Alexander was promised security of eviction from a croft at Clashmore, two miles south-west, which the family had 'reclaimed from brown moor'. The Sutherlands had bought the land after the estate of a humane landlord called Dempster was split up. Each year from 1819 summonses of removal were served on the Frasers but could not be carried out as there was no other croft available of similar quality. As soon as Alexander died, his widow was evicted 'without any notice at all':

The choice was four acres of unreclaimed land at Fleuchary, or emigration. A brother left for New Zealand; the family chose the four acres of bog ['Fleuchary' means 'wet shieling']. Alexander's son and his three sons had only one spade between them, but they dug the whole four acres by hand, drained and fertilised it, built a house and steading and made a fine croft of it . . . They had bitter memories of that start, and they left a small portion of the land undrained as a reminder of those days. That eviction was especially shocking to them after 32 happy years under Dempster, when they felt really secure.

Sandy has a ruddy outdoor face with bright black eyes and he is economical in speech. As expressive as his words were the little indrawn breaths of 'Aye' as he finished a point, expressing a sort of stoical 'So it goes'. He referred to the colossal statue of the Duchess's husband a few miles north on Ben Bhraggie with a sarky 'The Duke's still there – aye'. To others I presently met it was 'the murderer's monument', and one quiet, courteous crofter wondered why nobody had 'ever blown it up with – what's that the I.R.A. use? Semtex.'

The achievement of Sandy Fraser and the three generations before him was a fine example of how those who 'stayed behind' did not necessarily do worse than those who 'crossed the water'. His corn-fields stretched warmly orange below his house. Behind it were the original house, now whitened with a red corrugated roof, and the undrained portion which is still rushy. He has two other crofts nearby and works as a mason for the County Council – he was disgusted at being made to build dykes with cement instead of drystone. Sheer hard work had made up for the loss of the easy land sheltered with tall oaks and beeches and limes down on the shore of the firth. His sense of his family's stake in the land was intense and this was hereditary. He was able to show me their title-deeds back to 1809, the first few very small and tattered, the final one (drawn up in 1854) an imposing document a foot and a half long and a foot broad with ample room to specify the formidable number of things a tenant must not do and the proprietor can do if he likes. Only the laird can work mines, minerals, stone, and clay. Only he can 'cut, prune, thin, and carry away the natural and planted woods': this was crucial everywhere and led to superhuman exertions by cleared people to carry away their roof timbers. If they were made of bog fir, the ancient tanned cabers found in the peat mosses, then the estate men had no right to seize or burn them. (On Lewis and in Shetland I was told about families who carried away their timbers and floated them over the lochs to their new places.) The tenant could not 'sport, fowl, or fish' – in Raasay, South Uist, and elsewhere I constantly heard how crucial a supplement to the diet wild game was. The tenant could not 'grub up, destroy, or anywise injure' the woods, or let animals graze in them – the reports of the Land Courts set up after the Crofters' Act of 1886, which I read at Bridget's suggestion in the Public Library, refer to 'important' grazings in certain oak woods. The tenant could not 'cut Divots' – there was a real problem in many places with the flaying of good turf but crofters could not do without something to roof their houses and build up the upper halves of their walls, especially if, as happened in the islands, they were allowed to cut heather to make thatch or ropes on just one day in the year, often a day when they had to be away at the fishing. The tenant could not keep more than one dog – this must have made herding a nightmare.

Further north at Port Gower Echan Calder showed me his grandfather's title-deed to his croft at Ardens, near Bonar Bridge. It is less stringent than Sandy Fraser's – it was drawn up twenty-six years later and not by the Sutherlands' managers – but it still reserves all peat to the landlord: this was found useful on Lewis when a notorious factor called Munro MacKenzie was clearing wholesale and refused to let people who had been served eviction writs cut peats during the winter while they waited for the emigrant boats from Stornoway. It also reserves 'all sand, gravel, stone, and freestone' – a clause found useful all over Sutherland when the second Duke threw his weight against the founding of the Free Church in 1843 and refused to let churches or manses for 'recusants' be built either on his land or with his stone. Some ministers, for example at Tongue, died of the resulting hardships.

The final beauty of Sandy's title-deed was that it let me see, and touch, the signature of James Loch, the celebrated law agent to the Sutherlands, Tory Member of Parliament for Wick in Caithness from 1830 to 1852, and author of the clearance Mein Kampf – *An Account of the Improvements on the Estate of the Marquis of Stafford* (1820). Loch twice attempted, once in person in 1854, to evict Sandy's great-grandmother on the ground that tenure promised her husband did not hold good for her. The managerial system he built up was sophisticated to a degree: for example, as I found among the press cuttings in the Library, it specialised in arguing before the Land Court that the 1886 Act giving security of tenure to crofters did not apply to those who worked as tradesmen, shoemakers or wheelwrights (or masons like Sandy). This nicely flouted the profound social fact that, as peasants, the crofters were not alienated – their labour was not divided – their way of life gave scope for many skills. It is no wonder that these hearings were often crowded, with many interruptions from the 'gallery', and that the Church of Scotland sometimes refused to let its hall for such democratic goings-on. After the decades of oppression, a ground-swell of opposition was gathering, especially in the northern end of the Sutherland estate at Gartymore near Helmsdale, where they formed a Land League to resist eviction in 1882. Loch and Sellar figured as the embodiment of tyranny. When Loch fought an election at Wick in 1852, a crowd carried along the streets a model of a half-burnt croft house and bleated at him like sheep. Three years later, when a railroad surveyor called Joseph Mitchell travelled the country on his business, he was greeted everywhere with 'the quiet but exultant query "Did you hear the news? Loch is dead." '

The Duke – an Diùc Dubh, the Black Duke – had died in 1833. The Duchess seems to have been seized by a frenzy of commemoration. His monument is a 29-foot ogre on a plinth 70 feet high and it looms at you from behind impenetrable stands of fir, visible for so many miles up and down the coast that at first you think your eyes are playing tricks on you. To pay for it, the estate managers took round the hat, which is still resented: 'My great-grandfather gave the two shillings,' John Cuthbert told me at Gartymore, 'and it wasn't given willingly. It was in fear that they'd be shoved out.' I was given a hilarious insight into the whole affair by Mr Simpson, the minister of Dornoch Cathedral. Although he is Church of Scotland, he made no bones of the fact that his predecessors at the time of the Clearances had been so compromised by their alliance with the landlords that '95 per cent of the people here went over': that is, they joined the Free Church in 1843. A rare exception was a woman who had named her hens after ministers and elders. When most of these men went over, she slaughtered her whole flock except the lucky ones named after the few who stayed. One end of the Cathedral had been ruinous for many years and the Kirk Session was forever badgering the Sutherlands for money towards its restoration. Now the bereaved Duchess proposed a large statue to her husband, to be carved by Chantrey and placed in the middle of the chancel at the east end – a mausoleum to be dug out of the church floor – a stained glass window ... Here popular resentment called a halt, but a mausoleum was dug out in the graveyard and the old bones and coffins were thrown aside, which made people say, 'The Sutherlands clear you even after you're dead.' The marble statue, twenty feet high, was duly installed near the main doors. 'When I married a couple,' said Mr Simpson, 'I always had to say "Let no-one come between you" but the Duke generally had.' Luckily the church was draughty when the doors were opened and an internal porch had to be built – on the site of the statue. 'I wrote the Countess, suggesting respectfully that perhaps it was time to remove the Chantrey statue, and having no particular love for her great-great-etcetera she was perfectly agreeable. So now he's at Dunrobin.'

To Dunrobin, obviously, sooner or later, like it or not, we were bound to go. It is on the coast north of Golspie and the nearer you get the less you see it, as its Gothic pinnacles and chateau roof-lines and Scottish-Baronial pepperpot towers draw round themselves a cloak of planted conifers. Golspie is all too visibly a model village bought by a rich man out of a catalogue and the nearer you get to the Castle gates the more Christmas-cardy it becomes. Here is a Home Counties cottage, all red tiles and eaves, there is a three-storey villa with Tudoresque mullions and drip-ledges. Even the pub, inevitably named the Sutherland Arms, is under the same spell (Jacobean print drapes, fumed-oak veneer, mock cream, and chips with everything). But an amazing ikon hangs in the bar with a light directed on it from above: a landscape with a Cheviot sheep in the foreground, big nose downcurved, and leading off behind it an ochre track past a croft house with its roof-tree buckling, a dilapidated house behind it, and a slated house hull-down among hillocks beyond. The brush-work is academic, the composition is not – the sheep is impossibly big and seems to float above the ground. What could it signify other than the invasion of Sutherland by the Great Sheep? The landlady said the picture was of her husband's home at Latheron-Wheel (twenty miles north in Caithness) and 'He had the sheep put in'. Superimposed on an ordinary landscape painting? and as a celebration of the profitable animal or as an allegory of how the crofters were expropriated?

Just north of Golspie what seems to be a handsome Palladian model village stands among dense woodland – these are the estate offices, where any tenants who had not emigrated came to pay their rent. Opposite, you drive down a long, ruled avenue, park beneath bristling turrets that guard some rather bald and empty ornamental gardens on terraces above the sea, pay your money, and are admitted to a hallway three storeys high, balustraded with polished stone from Caen. In the billiard room through an archway the green baize is covered with tigers, glass eyes blazing, and the parquet floor swarms with lions and jaguars. It is not all butchery: feminine tenderness has been rendered by Landseer on a canvas eight foot high and five foot broad – Lady Evelyn Leveson-Gower and the third Duke, as children, dallying with a collared deer festooned with flowers and a spaniel begging with a rose in its mouth.

How did they pass their time in this gargantuan place? (By 1848 the additions to the original old keep had cost £41,414, as compared with £18,000 worth of Potato Famine relief – on which the estate made a profit by buying meal cheap and doling it out as payment in kind for estate works.) Well, they could have stretched out on a *chaise longue* upholstered in Gordon tartan and listened to a large pianola encased in oak. They certainly ate heavily and at length: on October 10th, 1928, the menu included *huitres*, *consommé Royale*, *filets de sole Neubourg*, haggis, *soufflés de ris*, and grouse *rôti*, rounded off by a chocolate pudding and *baguettes de Camembert*. Frequent excursions with rod and gun were made to Loch Choire lodge, where family and friends had to squeeze themselves into the usual public rooms and bedrooms plus a day nursery, a night nursery, a nursery bathroom, a butler's pantry, a wine cellar, a meat larder, a game larder, and a menservants' bathroom. All this afforded many person-hours of employment for local people – the equipment included nappy buckets with the ducal insignia on both the lid and the side and special hay-boxes to keep the soup warm for hunting parties. Honorific occasions, presentations, receptions were organised for every conceivable date: when dukes came of age, when detachments of Rifle Volunteers were raised, when illuminated addresses were tendered by crofters grateful for a 50 per cent rent reduction (1894). This 'further strengthened the cordial relations that have hitherto existed between your Grace and your Grace's tenants'. (There were regrettable exceptions from time to time, for example an old man at the Duchess's garden party who could get only a verbal assurance that he wouldn't be evicted. 'Your hand o' write ye'll no give,' he said to her face, 'and your word is no worth a damn.') In 1884 the 'affectionate respect' felt by the tenants had been embodied in a titanic chafing-dish which could almost have accommodated an undersized tenant, grilled or roasted. It was in silver-gilt and featured a brave Highlander at each end upholding a hammer, with a supporting cast of cherubs with no sexual organs, draped in laurel, surrounded by a stockade of candle-holders, antlered stags, rearing wild cats, and woolly rams. This work of art must have given employment to sculptors, silversmiths, foundry workers, and ultimately miners. Less acceptable was a table made of olive-wood looted from the Temple of Minerva in Athens.

'What's that you're doing?' An attendant gentlewoman in a tartan sash was patrolling the galleries and landings and seemed to look askance at my scribbling of notes. Maybe she took me for one of those people like Frances MacDonald of Gruids, who admits that when a guide was advising her party 'not to believe these exaggerations about the Clearances,' she whispered loudly to her friend, 'It's a shame what you have to listen to when you haven't a gun.' Dunrobin is not a place to go to for the beauty or rare quality of its furnishings, paintings, or other *objets d'art*. The first Duke, one of the richest collectors of his day and host to monarchs and their heirs at Stafford House in the Mall, must have kept his best pieces safely in England – unless they were sold during the Borgia-like family disputes of the later nineteenth century. But his holiday home in Sutherland – the name of which county he intrigued long and anxiously to have conferred on him by the Crown – does have a lot to offer as a research facility.

Our way now led north to Gartymore, Kildonan, Strath Naver, with excursions sideways up the parallel curves of Strath Fleet and Strath Brora. North of the sea-loch where the Fleet runs into the Dornoch Firth, an ample green down called Aberscross swells back into the hills. All its crofts were cleared to make yet another property for Patrick Sellar and here, I was told by the woman in charge of Dornoch Information Office, a woman was put out of her house when she was about to give birth. The minister at Lairg knew a man, a school janitor, whose Aberscross forebears were evicted with no time to remove anything but the fire-irons. This struck me particularly because in correspondence with a historian who lives in Harris I had been warned not to set too much store by 'oral tradition heavily influenced by the introduction of what I might almost term "folk tale motifs" such as the youngest child carrying the fire tongs as his share of the removal burdens'. What did the smallest people carry? Nothing? Further north in Sutherland I was told by a man of Shetland origin that when his great-grandparents' family were evicted the youngest carried a sieve across the hills. When the Strath Naver folk went back to their old place for a visit in 1884, a very old woman called Grizzell Claggan made a point of carrying a sieve with a rim made of Strath Naver oak; it must have been taken with them

65 or more years before. In Ontario I came across a mid nineteenth century memoir of a seven-year-old boy called Neil MacDougall arriving at the family's new place through heavy snow-drifts carrying the tea-kettle, the teapot, and a blanket. For that matter I have seen a 1920s photo of a Highland travelling-man carrying his fire irons on the top tube of his bike and a 1980s photo of a Beirut refugee family in which the youngest is carrying a jerry-can.

These were people who could rely on buying nothing and were used to making almost everything for themselves. When fifteen families were cleared on Coll in 1861, 'Infants carried in arms over back or in creels hung on the horses' pack saddles; the children each with his or her own load, the cattle driven in front, a shelter for the night improvised.' The tongs would almost certainly come away with such a family, because it was crucial and because it was not a thing they would expect to buy at a market or a store. I have studied as many as I can find, in the Highland Folk Museum and in the National Museum store at South Queensferry. The Highland specimens, especially those with bent and tapered ends for picking up hot peats, were nearly all blacksmith-made – two hand-forged limbs rivetted together instead of three factory-cast pieces including a special joint with a spring. The people turned out into limbo in Sutherland, poor and often with little idea of what to expect in their next place, would have carried tools made by themselves and by the local craftsmen. Among these the tongs and the sieve were prime.

The sieve for separating the coarser grains from oatmeal looks like a tambourine – calf- or seal-skin stretched on a wooden rim, with holes punched or hot-pointed in it according to a pattern. It is one of twenty indispensable tools listed by I.F. Grant in *Highland Folk Ways*, the book which has done most to show us exactly how Highland people lived. Its lightness perfectly fitted it to be carried for miles by even the smallest child. The tongs mattered even more: 'It had its ritual significance for when the bride was brought home, her husband handed her the tongs as a symbol that he made her the mistress of the house.' Here is another way in which the hearth was knit into the core of the household. This value endured through the lives of the couple: I found out recently that in inventories all over Scotland the fire-irons are listed among the wife's property. The value felt to inhere in the tongs and the sieve may have been universal. In south-east Bulgaria Patrick Leigh Fermor went to a wedding among the Sarakatsán nomadic shepherds: 'As the newly-wed couple reached the threshold, someone handed the groom a sieve, which he threw over his shoulder: a measure which is said to forfend marital discord.' The sceptical historian may be correct in holding that we can never be wholly sure whether or not the youngest carried the tongs, or the sieve. It seems to me equally true that these things would infallibly have been taken and that families would have felt bereft without them.

We were making our way up Strath Fleet towards Lettaidh. At Rogart, where I had stayed with John Manson on his croft in 1956, I got in touch with the leader of the local-history project, a vet called Angela Ross. She gave me a family tradition about her grandmother's great-aunt who was thrown outdoors when the family were being evicted 'and carried a scar on her forehead till the day she died'. Again it is unverifiable. It is not improbable. If it is a symbolic legend, it signifies how deeply the sense of being vulnerable to clearance bit into the minds of the crofters. Other forebears, she said, were evicted on a Thursday of the Sacrament when everybody was at church except an ill woman and some children. She was 'carried out of the house and left lying on a chaff mattress, beside the barn. They smashed the loom and threw everything out of the house before padlocking the door' – all this in retaliation for breaking the turf clause in their lease and cutting some divots to roof the potato pit . . . As story follows story, you gradually take the measure of how brute authority treats the powerless, picking off farms as prizes (or bribes) for its favourites, commandeering barrels of fish, making jokes about killing babies, throwing cats back into blazing houses, destroying food, wrecking machines, shooting dogs . . . Through the knot-hole of each anecdote we see into a world, like Gorky's Russia or Lu Xun's China, in which 'local bullies and bad landlords' had nothing to restrain them from gratifying their own worst selves.

Up the strath from Rogart, houses and woods become less common and you feel the bulk of the unpeopled mountains on either side exerting their silent pressure. It was not always so. Where the Tressady runs into the Fleet the great-great-grandmother of Leslie Bowran was frightened by the red stain in the sky as Lettaidh burned. Leslie spent many years shepherding at Vagastie in the midst of the mountains south of Loch Naver. The breadth of unreclaimed moorland up there is so great that as your eye follows the meander of some river, the Fiag or the Tirry, until its glistening threads disappear into the loom of the hills, you can fantasise that its source lies in Mongolia, not Scotland. Humans have made little impression here – should never have been here. Leslie's old home is shrunk to a toy by the bulk of Klibreck swathed in cloud behind it. No doubt his Inchcape forebears would have married in Lettaidh across the strath – if Lettaidh had not been razed. It is no longer on the 1-inch map. Like most of its kind it has less recognition in the official records than those stone-heaps or single liths, left by prehistoric tribes, on which the Ordnance Survey confers the dignity of Gothic script. Nevertheless a well-founded track climbs and twists beside a rock-fault filled with wild water. Hefty oaks tower over it, which Bridget MacKenzie claims to be the furthest-north oaks of full stature in Scotland. Beyond the trees, invisible from the road and railway line below, the angle eases, there is that softening underfoot, and a downland slopes and dips and pushes out green paws into the moor.

It takes many minutes to walk this ground, whether east–west or north–south. A pucker in the turf strengthened by boulders shows where the ring-dyke enclosed the homesteads and their fields. Low gable-ends of houses burnt out 180 years ago stand up amongst grasses seared by the first frosts of the year. At the upper end of the clachan there is evidence of the usual good water-supply: a deep well, fringed with fern and lined now with brick, perhaps by the sheep-farmer who took over after the clearance, perhaps by the Lettaidh Sheep Club, the crofters' co-operative which uses the grazing here in a small latter-day revival of the old community and its name.

I am now reversing the vision of Leslie Bowran's forebear – looking back across Strath Fleet to Inchcape from which she saw the firemark in the sky. There it is, ensconced on the 300-foot contour above the railway line to Lairg, its houses roofed, a well-designed row of holiday chalets at its south end, its fields neatly dyked and fenced, some blond after mowing, some fallow green. How did that community survive the clearance? According to a friend of Leslie Bowran's, a Mr Sutherland, who wrote me presently from Inverness,

It was a tradition within my family that the south side of Strath Fleet (e.g. Dalmore, Inchcape, etc) was saved from eviction by my great-grandfather James Sutherland who took it upon himself to face up to the Factor, pull him from his horse & evidently so frighten him that no notices were served & the matter was not proceeded with. A further point made was that my forebear had a substantial stone-built house on his croft (as against the old 'black' houses which were common at that time) & he evidently made out that this was a more permanent residence that could not be interfered with.

The Lettaidh men, however, were away at the war with France. And not only the Lettaidh men. As we look northward up the glen, one site after another glows faintly green, mirages that show a glimmer of settlement from just beyond the horizon of history. We follow a sheep-trod between craggy knolls and tracts of bronzed bracken and come upon a veritable clachan of sheep fanks. One is a newish concrete pen with an iron dipping trough and a ditch above it newly cut through the matted roots of wild iris. The others are monumental: four-foot walls of shapely blocks, topped with turf, insides perpendicular, outsides angled inward, corners rounded – perfect simulacra of the dwellings from whose stone they were doubtless cannibalised. Beyond, the ground is patterned with old field boundaries. Four hundred metres further on, the skyline yet again has the levelled look produced by dyking and ploughing. Beyond again, and on the far side of the river, still more of the same. It's not one forlorn outpost that they destroyed but a chain of townships – a conurbation! The spinal cord of a sub-culture was pithed out and this stony backbone remains as a telltale clue to that night, or more probably several, of torches, panicking animals, terrified children . . .

So habitation shrank downhill to the road and railway, and from there to the towns, and is now returning in the usual form as holiday or retirement homes. Near where I had parked, Fred Munro was repairing a shed for his tools and will soon be building a house on the family croft, to retire from his garage and maybe run a few animals. A transistor was singing beside him, a yellow Labrador lay patiently on the turf, resigned to the perverse inaction of his beloved human. Fred was in mellow mood as he worked steadily at the re-establishing of this foothold:

I'll do up the old house presently. It has a lot of memories for me – my uncle had it, oh, since 1890, and I was always here on holidays from Dingwall. It was like home. Yes, this *is* a good place, very well sheltered, and my croft runs right down to the meeting of the rivers. There must have been a lot of people lived up the back there – I don't know much about them – 1890, that's as far back as I can tell you about. I'm more interested in the future.

Here he looked at me, then added with the Highland courtesy, 'But I like to know about the past too. The old man at the cottage up there – he looked after this place for me – he knew all about everybody, away back he could go. But he's dead now.'

We turned back east now and made for the head of Strath Brora via Little Rogart, a hillocky upland of scattered holdings where snow lies readily and long and people would have settled only because the more sheltered and fertile lands had been taken by Sellar and his kind. To run down into the levels of Strath Brora is a relief – its grassy haughs between the links of the river cry out to be lived in – there is little but two big shooting lodges, well camouflaged in rhododendron and planted conifer. In 1825, a traveller called Sutherland passed through: 'It was from this district that many of the wanderers we saw at Cromarty had been ousted. All was silence and desolation. Blackened and roofless huts still enveloped in smoke – articles of furniture cast away, as of no value to the houseless – and a few domestic fowls, scraping for food among hills of ashes, were the only objects that told us of man.' This clearance has never been famous – perhaps because it was so thorough. An American scholar who spent some years hereabouts researching the state of Gaelic 'never encountered a single oral tradition or folk memory of the evictions experienced by ancestors of the current Gaelic speakers in Brora, Golspie, or Embo'. I felt I was overhearing the last ghost of the place as I sat in a farm kitchen in Oxford County, Ontario a year later, trying to find out from a man aged 92 called Jack Bobby Mackay what he knew about his Highland forebears. In his seventies he had been mauled by a tractor. Now he sat motionless, blue eyes washed out, skin yellowed, a cigarette barely held between his fingers. His grandfather was from Sutherland: 'I think he was pushed out. Thass what they said . . . ' A long pause, while we scratched our mosquito bites. Then, barely audible, 'Dornock . . . Brora . . . ' And sure enough, the Old Log Cemetery nearby had stones to many immigrants identified as 'Native of' Dornoch, Clyne, Creich, Rogart, and other of the good arable lands nearby which the Sutherlands' managers were avid to rent out, often to themselves.

One striking event has recently been unearthed here. In 1820 the schoolmaster at Aschoylemore, where the river bends south-east towards the loch, had warned the S.S.P.C.K. office in Edinburgh that soon there would be no more need for a school as the place was to be cleared for sheep. On May 31st, 1821, while Gordon Ross was away in Edinburgh looking for alternative work, the estate men evicted his wife and his children, who had whooping cough. The eldest was knocked down, the baby in its cradle banged against the wall, and the family sheltered at a 'dyke side where they most piteously lay for several hours trembling almost to death with cold'. One of them died three weeks later. The Marquis and Marchioness were taking their ease in Paris at the time. When they sent to James Loch for a report, he counter-accused Ross of lending the schoolhouse for anti-clearance meetings. Ross now faced destitution. He had been given no compensation for the improvements he had made to his house or the land he had broken in. He could not get another post without a character reference – from Loch. He climbed down, and retreated to Helmsdale like many of the cleared. The Helmsdale people were too poor to support a school and it was not till five years after the eviction that he was fit to work again. A Golspie minister feared he was 'insane' and 'His strong sense of sin may have arisen at this period'. For the rest of his life he believed he had to rise above 'earthly considerations' and spent most of his time counselling and praying among the fisherfolk, who were both chary and respectful of him as an uncanny seer, able to foretell whether or not a storm-bound fishing boat would get back to harbour. I dwell on the story, although I did not discover it myself, because it chimes so eerily with Minnie Campbell's father, who 'started being very religious' after the burning-out at Grummore and the forced march to Dunnet Head. People with no other refuge are driven to God, rather as the Russian countryfolk underwent waves of religious ardour during the Nazi occupation of 1942–44.

To explore Strath Kildonan we stayed for a time at its mouth in Helmsdale, in one of the parallel granite streets built to Loch's master-plan. Two thousand people had been banished from the strath by 1820, leaving Donald Sage's father Alexander without a congregation and causing Donald to leave the county for good – but not before he had noted in his diary the scenes which remain the best eye-witness account (with Donald MacLeod's) of the Strath Naver burnings. To become inward with the strath where his father is buried, to understand how its 30-mile length was once civilised at every point, you cannot do better than read the pages on 'The Topography of Kildonan' in his *Memorabilia Domestica*, which I did in the Edinburgh home of his direct descendant Camilla Bonavia. His loving knowledge is focussed in the history of each township and the features of the land whose names he translates, 'the loch of the snow-wreaths', 'the rock of light'. Many of the cleared left for the New World via Stromness and Hudson's Bay and I later went in search of their descendants in Manitoba and Ontario. Many others were dumped on the least habitable ground nearby, and especially in Gartymore, on the steeps south of the Helmsdale estuary. My guide to it was Margat MacGregor, a teacher I had heard of through her work to establish a monument to the Land League in this little place which was the heartland of the Sutherland crofters' counter-attack in the 1870s. The cairn stands at a bend in the road, on what was the croft of John Fraser, secretary of the Helmsdale branch, parent of the League in Sutherland, and the text on it says 'They laid the foundation, that we might build thereon'. During the 'Forty-five Gartymore had been so minor a place that only six men could be found in it fit to bear arms. In the 1890s a crofter called Donald Watson described his outrun as 'very dangerous and rocky and steep ... a precipice'. That was in formal evidence to the Deer Forest Commission. The same anguish lurks in the myths of the place. The Helmsdale school students have just collected local supernatural stories. Twice a small figure dressed in red was seen in Gartymore, once 'behind a dyke near a pit', the other beside a burn below a house, one by a railway surfaceman, the other by a crofter. The railwayman's aunt interpreted the omen: 'That little red person is a certain sign of death and eviction.' In both cases eviction followed.

My one eye-witness glimpse of the clearance in Kildonan came to me through Alec and Jock Cuthbert. When Margat took me up the hill to visit them, Alec was leaning against the barn, propped on alloy sticks with cups for his forearms. He was racked with pain from arthritis, through which his intelligence burns with a carbide harshness. No doubt his ill health would have been far easier to cope with if his forebears had not been forced out to a place at the maximum angle capable of being crofted at all. Alec and Jock's great-grandmother Betty Fraser was evicted with her family in 1814 and died in December 1907 aged 103. She would 'hardly talk to any-body at all about the evictions'. Certainly in her photograph, which is a speaking likeness, her gravity and contemplative downward gaze suggest a person bearing the whole weight of her people's experiences and keeping her own counsel about them. Then, on my second visit to the house, the moment of clearance surfaced unexpectedly:

> They had no shoes in those days, of course, they always just went barefoot, and when Betty was coming over the mountains there, over Eldrable [after being evicted from Kildonan], she was with her wee sister, and they each had a sheep with them – they were like a pet, I suppose. And the shepherd who kept the farm for the estate down there at Port Gower, when he saw them he set his dogs on the sheep and they worried them.

The family had been cleared from Costly, three miles below Kildonan Church. Using a sketch-map drawn by Jock, we located the township site – very much like Grummore, a wide green going deeply back into the hill, round-cornered shells of houses within comfortable reach of the burn. Stags were roaring from the slopes of Beinn Dubhain in the damson-dark October gloaming, that prolonged, demanding note like a barbarous bassoon, as I quartered the old arable land, noting the paths between houses, the striping of the old rigs. One stag had found a way inside the fencing meant to conserve the sweet townland grazing for the sheep. Now he was desperate to escape, mad that his rivals would get the pick of the hinds. He was charging up and down the fence while a golden eagle flapped slowly over and other stags bawled from Beinn Uarie and The Craggan on the far side of the river. It was the chorus of a country given over to animals, sheep and deer and grouse and salmon, and to those who pay £1,000 a week for the hunting – Barbara Cartland, for example, two of whose husbands have owned lodges there. (Two shrines honour her in Helmsdale, one in a restaurant and one in the Heritage Centre.)

The Cuthberts, still attached to Costly, wanted to know what I had made of it. Alec is precise and thoughtful about a crofter's work – he hates the exploitation it has involved. Their father had got work building 'stalls' (sheep fanks or folds) out of the vandalised houses, his granny Betty's among them. They made them circular so that in a heavy snowfall the sheep would have no angles to shelter in but would be forced to trot round and round and avoid smothering in the drifts. The stalls were only necessary because the flocks brought in by the new tenants from Northumberland would have strayed and been lost on this foreign territory. Alec's green eyes sparked bitterly and the lines in his cheeks cut still more deeply as he gave his judgement on the handing over of Kildonan to the highest bidder:

> They wanted the slave labour, that was all. They had them building all these walls, dyking and draining those farms down at the coast there, doing all the heavy work, and they were paying them one shilling a day for a ten-hour day. And they were selling them meal at £3 for a boll – that's ten stone – so that was costing them sixty days' work. Slavery, that's all it was. That's no fiction. That's the way it was.

We had been walking and driving for weeks in the autumnal lull when a blue film thickens slowly over all the vistas and the clouds heap like dunes, pale orange like snowfields at sunset, pink like eiders' wings. Between Sutherland and the low lands of Moray on the far side, the sea was a stone floor. Willy MacKintosh of Helmsdale – whose forebears had been cleared from Rossal in Strath Naver and had taken care of Donald MacLeod's wife after his eviction – told me the story of Patrick Sellar setting sail across the firth for a return visit to his native Moray. A big sea overwhelmed the boat just outside Helmsdale harbour and he barely made it through the breakers back to the beach. The story was undated, a legend of judgement on the hated factor, so there was no telling whether the storm almost forestalled the burnings – Sellar, after all, was so overweening partly because he coveted the land for himself and had outbid the crofters for it in 1814. Would a more detached factor have been less brutal? We were northbound for Strath Naver now, with a short foray past the Ord of Caithness to see Badbea. The lowlands had vanished into the dense blue water-vapour and the currents of time and change felt congealed, as though we could stare at the land or the water and see the past there in a frozen frame. Badbea means 'place of refuge' and that is where Alan Roydhouse's forebears had perched for a few gruelling years before evacuating to New Zealand. It should never have been lived in. The slope on which the crofts were made is so acute that children are supposed to have been tied to the legs of tables to stop them crawling off and rolling down into the sea. Just inland lie the fertile, almost level lands of Ousdale. The people from there and the other green lands (106 families amounting to 700 people) were cleared over two generations, as flax mills failed, proprietors' expenses mounted, and even Sir John Sinclair, *beau idéal* of the Highland grandee, went bankrupt. He evicted. His successors, a family of Edinburgh lawyers called Horne, evicted. Alan's great-great-grandfather chose to emigrate in 1839 but his father-in-law, John Badbea, was evicted. Alan had found a memoir by a man called Gunn which gave piercing details of 'the way it was':

> When he [my father] was no longer required to work at the Berriedale mill, he was afterwards evicted from Badbea. At the same time, my uncle, who was bed-ridden, received notice to quit and [was] driven from his house. He took refuge in a barn, but the laird, hearing of his still being on the estate, despatched a couple of men from Berriedale with graips and spades with orders to have the roof over the sick man's head taken off; and strange to say there were men then in Berriedale who were base enough to obey the behest of the laird, Donald Horne.

Gunn had moved south for good by the time he published his letters to the papers about the atrocities but Alan discovered that Horne hired detectives to follow him south of Edinburgh to intimidate him. Yet still Gunn testified in print: 'Their once comfortable habitations were demolished and used in building a five foot stone dyke about the place'. Six of the Badbea families, after reclaiming 'a wild piece of ground on a hillside', were 'singled out to be set adrift by next Whitsunday and to find no shelter on the paternal estate'.

The coast here is clad densely in heather, shorn close by salty updraught, like a shaggier version of the moors east of Land's End. A squat tower with a stepped top, built of stone from Alan's great-grandfather's house at his grandfather's instigation, commemorates one of Britain's harshest settlements. Below the moor a 50-metre zone of tussocky grass and the bleached skeletons of thistles and cow-parsley sloped so steeply that we had to save ourselves from plunging cliffwards by grabbing at bracken stems. It was windless yet a wind seemed to be keening – a contralto chorus sounding a melody on four or five notes, swelling, dying away until it merges with the tuning of our own blood. We wade downward through matted growth. On the skerries near the shore mottled boulders take shape as seals, a tribe of more than sixty, singing their mating arias, a liquid croon, a crescendo to an arching cadence of full-throated emotion. Now it breaks in coughs, grating as though shreds of membrane are being hawked up – choked snores – phlegmy gulpings. The distemper that has been killing thousands of seals from the Baltic to the Friesian and East Anglian coasts must have reached this far at last.

We watch and listen for an hour, taping and photographing, slithering further down through a zone of nettles to a small ledge where wind-stunted saughs hold out their hard blue-green leaves over the drop. Immediately below, at the end of a crag like a ship eaten away by salt and fulmar lime, a big dark seal with hoary shoulders lies beside a small pale mottled one. With his left hand he scratches his chest – I can see his fingernails – while she ripples over the rock and comes to rest with her nose beside his ear. A couple at their ease, seemingly healthy. From the congested skerries further out the ground-note of the croon gathers, then breaks down into tearing coughs, one of them bonily grating like the hiss a conger makes as it's hauled inboard, another transposing to a high note of agony, others ending in quacks and rattles. It's a ward of the terminally ill. The 'place of refuge', where people came in the 1770s to escape the press-gangs, is echoing to the lament of the North Sea. Forty miles north-north-east, near the nuclear power station at Dounreay, clusters of infant leukaemia have broken out. Down south the poisonous effluents from the Rhine and the Thames and the Tyne have driven away the porpoises and so reduced the seals' resistance that endemic diseases invade their undefended bloodstreams. Up here life was made impossible for the families of Kildonan and Ousdale. In this dolorous air it's suddenly startling to see a male brambling flicker among the saughs, wings dapper in orange and bright white, head glossy black. This is the only county in Britain where they have ever bred. The wee bird's fiery, unspoiled life suddenly has me envying the species whose brains are too small for them to conceive of the cruelties which first filled Badbea with people, then emptied it again.

As we drove over to Strath Naver by Kinbrace and Badenloch, mountains in the middle distance basked on the heather-ocean, sounded, surfaced again in a rhythm so gradual it seemed beyond and outside the calendar, let alone the clock. Sutherland here is the only part of Britain to stretch away with an American immensity. Donald Sage rode this way many times between his father's manse in Kildonan and his own little church at Achness. Jogging those twenty miles at walking pace must have been great for attuning him to eternity. For him Badenloch was a 'complete oasis' where the families lived among their run-rig lands 'in the midst of a desert of heath'. Nowadays the shooting lodge and the shepherd's and Forestry Commission cottages do little to relieve the wilderness and its splendid inhumanity breaks over you cleansing as the sea, pure as the air above the cloud-wrack. You come down to earth at Syre, Sellar's old headquarters. We found lodging six miles downstream at Carnachy (home to twelve families before the burning), in a caravan perched on moraine above the flood-plain. We looked out over the one place in the strath where the farming is in good heart and the barley, turnip, and hay are cropped with modern machinery. On the opposite bank a cleared township (Rhifail, five families) showed its luminous green. It was getting cold at night. One morning a dead greenfinch lay on the grass outside the window, and two nights later a thrush. Overhead the stars were so clear that the blue-black spaces between them seemed tangible. I walked to Achness (eleven families) by a road proclaimed to be 'Private', using a stalkers' bridge to cross the Naver. Its rapids were bronzed with peat and blued by skyshine in the clarified light of the north. Again the township lands stretched back deeply into the moor, even and green – after Badbea it looked luxurious.

Donald Sage rode down the strath from here to preach in the open air at Langdale on the last Sabbath before the burnings – commemorated in rhyming rhetoric by Annie Mackay, a poet from Eriboll in the north-west who died in New Zealand in 1909. A man in Stornoway had sent me a copy:

> The tune of 'Martyrdom' was sung
> By lips with anguish pale
> And as it rose upon the breeze
> It swelled into a wail
> And like a weird death coronach
> It sounded in the vale.

> Psalm 72 verse 19
> Beannaicht' gu robh gu siòrraidh buan
> Ainm glòrmhor uasal fèin;
> Lìonadh a ghlòir gach uile thìr.

Amen, agus Amen!
And echo lingering on the hills
Gave back the sad refrain.

The mission church is hard to distinguish among the many stone-heaps but the burial ground is still solidly walled. No crofters' graves – they had all been evicted long before that kind of commemoration became usual for poorer people. Gamekeepers and shepherds lie here and the most imposing stone is an employee's memorial paid for by the estate, or so I infer from the managerial phrasing: Hugh MacBeath had died in 1868 'after the respectful discharge of his several duties in the services of the Duke of Sutherland upwards of 35 years'. After all, once the 'fire brigade' had been and gone there was nobody left to work for but the Duke.

Before we left mid Strath Naver we walked through a mile of post-War forest and came out in a clearing which frames in its wide green oval the whole ambience of a township before eviction. This is Rossal, the home of Donald MacLeod. The force of the man's testimony exerted itself 140 years after his native place was destroyed: the Forestry Commission left the townland unplanted and commissioned its excavation in 1962. Now you can walk about through one of the largest townships in the strath (50 acres, thirteen families) and read labels rich in information beside the low stone outlines of long-houses, kailyards and stackyards, corn-drying kilns – all the working parts of a way of life. Looking across the shallow swell of grassland it is not hard to imagine it patched with the motley greens of oats, potatoes, and cabbages, the pale sun-glow of hayfields newly cleared, the figure of a neighbour in dark clothes standing at a house end and looking west across the river to the sculpted summit of Ben Loyal, wondering if there is rain on the way. It is excellent that the Commission have seen to it that, for once, the absolutely ordinary fabric of the past is on display in its own right, no art, no monuments, no retail outlet, no custodian – it is a thin substitute for the return of human activity to a habitable place – what would you feel if you came back as a *revenant* to your own village or suburb after a hundred and eighty years and found it turned into an empty green socket in a sombre forest as though razed by a single bomb?

These mixed feelings smouldered on as we followed the trail of the cleared people northward to Bettyhill, across the mouth of the Naver from a weird desert like a miniature Gobi, littered with prehistoric stone- and earthworks and backed by a cliff where buzzards mew and sand has been blown to a height of 300 feet. Bettyhill shows its origin as a dump for evicted families in its unGaelic name – a tribute to the Duchess – and in the strips of holdings fenced across wickedly steep ground that climbs and sinks and climbs between juts of oozing crag. At the highest house Robert Mackay remarked sardonically that a man from the estate had been round enquiring if they had a basement: 'A basement! You'd have to blast to make that.' Bettyhill faces the north with no shelter from salt sea-gust and no harbour, only beaches planed by Arctic breakers. Robert Mackay's grandfather had been cleared to here from Rossal and he himself is highly articulate but the family had kept no stories from that time: 'It was what happened.' Oppressed by shortage of material I was turning in on myself but Anne made me go and talk to a man sheltering at his house end just across the bay at Farr. He invited me in to admire his house, built by a mason for himself around 1900, with massive stone fireplaces, but he looked sourly out over his croft and said, 'You couldn't live off this – I could dig it with a bloody spade between January and May' – gesturing at the narrow strips ruled on the map by the Sutherlands' managers early in the nineteenth century. To east and west along the coast great blocky headlands stretched their limbs northward, dropped suddenly as though cleft off. It is fit terrain for sagas, not for ordinary fruit-ful living, yet here the managers had planned – it is hardly the word – they had pretended that the Strath Naver husbandmen could sud-denly become fishermen. They tried their best – in 'old crazy boats' with patched oars and no sails, fishing from the rocks, climbing for birds' eggs, carrying up sea-water to make salt. In one year, between Portskerra and Rabbit Island, more than a hundred boats were sunk or irreparably damaged, the salt-woman swept away, the egg-gatherer fallen to his death:

> Subjected to the drenchings and the beatings
> Of the furious great waves,
> Mountainous, foamy, stormy, deep-valleyed,
> Sucking, thick-lipped, blue.

So the aversion people felt for that ungovernable sea was expressed by Rob Donn, who lived twenty miles west of here and embodied Sutherland in his poetry as Burns' did the Lowlands.

Before I left Danny Thompson in Farr, he pointed across to a new house near Aird in Bettyhill where we were staying: 'Try Jim Johnston there, he's a teacher and he can tell you a lot.' And he did, not only the names of informants to the west, near Tongue, but stories about the eviction of his own great-grandparents on Shetland Mainland. This was to be invaluable later on. In the meantime our way led west by that epic coast of sheer headlands, across the Kyle of Tongue with its braided sandbars, round by Eriboll and Cape Wrath, and away south by Assynt and Wester Ross where single monstrous mountains stand up as though a great brown plain were inhabited by one mastodon, one rhinoceros, one elephant, one gorilla, one musk-ox, one dodo. It had to be like this, Britain ending in great squared precipices mined by churning waves – salt marshes and broads and gradual banks of silt belong in a gentler culture altogether. Cape Wrath, not John o' Groats, is the land's true northern end. Colossi of red rock open their gorges to a sea that moves on itself like immense crystals of cobalt grazing and fracturing against each other. You can reach it only on foot or in a mini-bus driven by a wild man who keeps the windows open so that the bow-wave flung up from the brimming potholes blows in on you in gusts of muddy water. The coastal settlements along the north – Totegan, Armadale, Kirtomy, Swordly, Farr, Skerray, Melness – would never have been chosen by settlers looking for shelter, safe harbours, or fertile bottomlands. They are spreadeagled on windblown slopes where every acre has been clawed out of black moor.

Alex George Mackay of Melness comes from four generations of ferrymen who carried people across the mouth of the kyle at Tongue where the bridge and causeway now span the tidal channel. His features are as noticeable as an actor's – jet-black bristling eyebrows, ivory-bald head, a gap in his front teeth which makes his sibilants whistle. Whatever he remembers he remembers with redolence and relish, whether it was grim or happy. The energy of his recalling is at one with the energy it has taken to live in that place. He told me about a woman, not a relative, who had died in 1948 aged 103. She had been married at 18 and her husband was drowned fishing lobsters when she was 23. Alex George remembered her living in a house 'up the back there' with a dry earthen floor spread with skins of deer and sheep:

They were walking down to Morayshire and lifting corn, making sheaves after the scythe and then after the reaper. And they worked right back up into Caithness. She was in Yarmouth [gutting herrings] and in Ireland. She made eightpence a day creeling peats off the banks – a big strong woman, and she was very happy. A bit of a midwife too, she would always be going when bairns were born. She had good courage. Och, they were just as happy then, and they had more company. And ceilidh was great [the evening meetings in each other's houses for stories and music]. They were all on a level.

This was not said nostalgically, it was steeped in a sense of hardship overcome. The narrow crofts offered to people cleared from the straths nearby had been allotted by drawing numbers out of a hat – if you drew a blank all you could do was build a little house on the edge of the moor and look round for ways of earning a minimal wage:

They weren't much, the crofts, but it was helping them to eke out a living. The fish was easy to get at that time, you'd salt them at the end of autumn. And you had carrots and cabbages. You were never looked down on for taking a stag. When the wind would blow from the north it brought the stags and hinds into the side of Ben Hope – they would always run against the wind. You'd try to avoid the keepers – you didn't abuse it, you only took when you needed it. You'd bury the intestines and you'd put the head in a bag, and that put the keeper in the clear too.

This seemed to imply a much greater degree of freedom than was enjoyed by the cleared folk of South Uist who were hounded for taking a single salmon. Perhaps it could happen more easily in the sheer expanse of Sutherland. What Alex George's people had been able to cling onto was a smattering at least of the free-ranging mountain life celebrated in the lyrics of Rob Donn from Loch Hope, a few miles away:

> . . . I used to be joyful
> Between Tongue and Cape Wrath
> At the time when I climbed the brae . . .
> And I would be well pleased

> To be in the heights of the rugged hills
> Where the tawny ones could be seen
> Running lithely through the defiles
> And the deer hounds in full chase
> Jumping playfully at their hair
> After hearing the burst of fire ...

Rob Donn had lived five miles from the head of Loch Eriboll, where Alex's Munro forebears lived till they were cleared. He emphasised that the people of Durness at the mouth of Eriboll had fought the evictions, 'especially the women'. His conversation moved in and out of poetry, which he at once translated for me, as he fired up at the thought of what his people had undergone. 'Her silk gloves will not keep the worms from her fingers,' he said quite suddenly, quoting a snatch of a diatribe against the Duchess. Then he recited in quickening rhythm a song about depopulation and translated a couplet:

> Where are the lads so dear to me?
> And the girls who were so pretty?

Now the Tongue bard was alive again and speaking through Alex – Ewen Robertson, whose monument stands at the roadside near Braetongue with this verse on it in Gaelic and English:

> 'N àit nan caorach
> bithidh tuath
> Crodh-laoigh air air'gh'n
> 'n àit damh ruadh
>
> In place of the sheep
> there will be people
> Cattle at the shielings
> in place of stags

Most of his work is lost, but Alex George was quoting his best-known lyric, which is still sung to at least two tunes of its own. It curses the *caorach mhòr*, the big sheep, in the refrain, laments the exiled folk, and bans Patrick Sellar in lines that have been rendered best by Hamish Henderson in Scots:

Justice ye've earned, and by the Book,
A warm assize ye winna jouk.
The fires ye lit tae gut Strathnaver
Ye'll feel them noo, and roast forever.

Robertson, a carpenter, testified so eloquently to the Napier Commissioners at Bettyhill, with so logical a sequence of finely-detailed grievance, that the chairman had trouble restraining him. I felt I was meeting his passion face to face as Alex George revelled in a fierce story of how he died:

He had written, 'If ever I lie down and cannot raise my elbow to lift the whisky to my lips, then put the nails into my box.' Well, he was taken ill one winter's night on the road, near where his monument is now. He lay down very ill, and it was so cold his beard was sticking to the road. And a man came by and found him and knew who he was, and when he saw a half-bottle of whisky that he had on him, he remembered the song. So he took the bottle and raised it to his own lips, but he could not get it down his throat.

Eviction, it turned out, had been the norm for Alex George's forebears. His Ross great-grandmother had been born at Toiteach, six miles up the kyle from Melness. 'There is still quite a lot of green in it. It was taken into Melness Farm and I worked as a shepherd there myself, and I always used to call it "my grandmother's" when I was speaking to the young men.' The fact was that as Alex George moved about the district, west to Durness, east to Strathy, or south along Strath Naver, at place after place forebears of his had been forced off fertile ground and sent to hack out a new life from the most severe terrain:

They were turned out of Toiteach – aye – they were ordered out, and the places were burnt. The same as Strath Naver. My family told me about it. My father's father's people came from Rossal. They were neighbours of this Donald MacLeod that wrote the *Gloomy Memories*. One time he came back and nobody was supposed to keep him a night, but they didn't want to turn him away, because he had been a neighbour. My great-grandfather was evicted twice. He went to Achnabourin [two miles up Strath Naver from Bettyhill] and they called him New William there because he had come to new territory. And then they were evicted from Achnabourin.

Ewen Robertson testified that the crofters there were forced to use pasture 'like a human being covered with smallpox – all over with rocks in every direction', that they were fined for going to cut turf on the sheep-farm because their own land was covered in sand, and that when they petitioned to rent land at a higher rate than the farmer paid, the estate refused.

. . . Flora's mother [Alex George's mother-in-law], she was living with us here, she belonged to Durness, and she'd lost her memory pretty badly latterly. She was sitting where you're sitting there, she was an old lady, she was 88. And there was a man that's dead now, he lived in the end house, Angus Mackay – oh, he was a great man for the Highland history. We were talking between ourselves and the old lady was taking no part, but we mentioned Sellar and she lifted her head and said, 'Ach, Sellar sgreataidh' – that's 'loathsome Sellar'. We thought her memory was gone but she didn't forget who loathsome Sellar was.

CHAPTER TEN

THE GRAIN AND THE BRACKEN
Tiree and Mull

Five months later the Highlands and Islands were still immersed in the cold drench of winter, with little sign of what season it was – no layering of hedges, no lambing as yet. In sodden pasture fields the brown and black beef stirks blew steam from their nostrils and chewed at what was left of the lines of baled hay scattered from the back of a trailer. The *West Highland Free Press* had been reporting on the bad winter after three wet summers, the need to buy in hay imported from Canada, the crofters' plea for a subsidy towards it. On Mull at the dock in Tobermory, waiting to drive onto the Tiree boat, I saw the big trucks and trailers stacked high with feed from the Lowlands, most of which was presently unloaded at the harbour on Coll. Bleared skies of no colour hung parallel with the sea, woods bristled dark and leafless, horizons were short – the terrain was neither fierce nor friendly, simply inhospitable.

What would I find on Tiree, if anything? This stretch of coast was unknown to me, even from childhood or adult holidays, so I had no sense of a familiar island drawing round me cosy as a quilt. It is an illusion, of course, for the outsider, this image of the island as a nest to home on year after year, an ageless veteran lends you his fishing tackle once again and reminds you of the best banks for plaice and haddock, his wife cooks you scrambled eggs at night before showing you up to the attic bedroom with its view over a west-facing bay . . . I had synthesised a few of these in my time, in Wester Ross, on North Uist, and the lack of it now in western Argyll was stealing into me like a chill of demoralisation. In the saloon I read my way slowly into *The Satanic Verses* and waited for my interest in it to kindle. Just holding it in your hands had a unique effect on other people – they came up to you and asked under their breaths, 'What's it like?' – as though the Ayatollah's secret agents might be lurking at a nearby table. Then, as mounds of clay-grey water blocked the window and were slowly, heavingly replaced by tracts of clay-grey overcast, I realised my problem. The swell left by the equinoctial gale of the past two days was bringing up the first qualms of nausea – nothing for it but to mark the place in Rushdie where Gibreel Fareeshta wakes up on the snowbound English beach and stretch out full length under my Polar jacket until we churned into the lee of Tiree and docked at Scarinish.

The day before, in much worse weather and lonelier conditions, I had felt nothing but envigorated. In rain driven horizontally by a great soughing wind from the west-south-west I had driven from Glencoe by Ballachulish and the Corran ferry to a place identifiable only by the OS grid reference 656519. I had come across it in a social history of a Highland parish, *Morvern Transformed* by Philip Gaskell. His argument that the eviction of a peasantry living in such squalid neediness was all for the best had not convinced me but I treasured his long quotation from the story of one cleared woman, 'Mary of Unnimore', who described their eviction with unique full-ness to her minister in Glasgow. It makes a complete chapter in a popular Victorian memoir, the Rev. Norman MacLeod's *Reminiscences of a Highland Parish*, which I managed to buy in Dunvegan, Ontario, a few months later. Mary's words were so perfect in their narrative phrasing that I was able to transpose them into a 44-line blank verse poem with the addition of a dozen words:

When we got the 'summons to quit', we thought it was only for getting an increase of rent, and this we willingly offered to give; but permission to stay we got not. The small cattle [sheep] were sold, and at length it became necessary to part with the one cow. When shall I forget the plaintive wailing of the children deprived of the milk which was no more for them? When shall I forget the last sight I got of my pretty cluster of goats bleating on the lip of the rock, as if inviting me to milk them? But it was not allowed me to put a cuach [pail] under them.

The day of flitting came. The officers of the law came along with it, and the shelter of a house, even for one night, was not to be got. It was necessary to depart. The hissing of the fire on the flag of the hearth as they were drowning it reached my heart. We could not get even a bothy in the country; therefore we had nothing for it but to face the 'land of strangers' [the Lowlands] . . .

On the day of our leaving Unnimore I thought my heart would rend. I would feel right if my tears would flow; but no relief thus did I find. We sat for a time on Knock nan Carn [Hill of Cairns], to take the last look at the place where we had been brought up. The houses were already being stripped. The bleat of the big sheep was on the mountain. The whistle of the Lowland shepherd and the bark of his dogs were on the brae . . .

This place had to be seen, but could I find it in the heart of south-west Morvern, amongst the birch-and-alder jungle and the recent blanket afforestation of that unfrequented peninsula? As I drove down the shore of Loch Linnhe nothing moved except the occasional big estate van. The small mansions for whose sake the Camerons had been cleared (by an Edinburgh lady who never saw the place) were blinded and shuttered – for the winter? for the century? The only other common human sign seemed to be notices on any spare roadside ground saying 'No Overnight Parking'. I had marked the grid reference in ink on the 'Oban and East Mull' OS map, in the midst of a green spread speckled with conifer symbols where Allt an Aoinidh Mhòir runs its blue thread down from the 500-metre contour to Loch Doire nam Mart. On this watershed between Loch Sunart and the Sound of Mull one wetland merged with the next. Even reaching the forest from the road was difficult, a balancing along a rotten bridge across a full black ditch, a stagger and a plouter through bog myrtle and rustling wintry grasses and scrub willow which made me think of the word 'muskeg'. Inside the stockades of Forestry Commission spruce it seemed hopeless, a permanent brown dusk devoid of birds. Was that lichenous tusk the crag from whose lip Mary's goats had bleated? Had the Camerons left no mark at all on the earth? Baffled, I turned to go back. I had had an attack of iritis and to protect my eyes, which were full of Atropine, I was wearing green clip-ons over my glasses, goggles, the hood of my anorak, a balaclava – I must have looked like a low-tech astronaut who had landed on the wrong moon. This was shameful – to be daunted where a family had managed to retreat in good order, the husband carrying his mother in a creel, the wife with a suckling baby, a toddler, and a little boy to manage. I struggled on across forestry trenches carved out by the prairie-buster plough, through entanglements of dripping saplings, and took a last look-out over the forest canopy from a rocky knoll. A slot cut through it uphill. A burn – of course – the clachan would have been *there*, next to the water-supply. I made straight for it, barging backwards where the twigs had meshed like barbed wire, and started upstream.

The banks were upholstered in sap-green moss. In each bight of the water-course the little pastures were star-scattered with primroses, as many as fifteen buds to a cluster, making the ground look spot-lit with sun even under the deep cloud. Had their forerunners decorated the Camerons' croft or had the goats eaten them all? The meanders of Allt an Aoinidh Mhòir were forcing me to cross and recross its flooding waters. Those burnside stones – surely they were too regular to be natural? They were a palisade to prevent spates from tearing away the croftland. A few yards upstream a low dyke had been built, making the straight limb of a D with the link of the burn, perhaps as a cabbage-patch – the kailyard was traditionally D-shaped. Here the tributaries had been revetted to contain their rapids. Just inside the fir-dusk a hollow oblong of stones now showed, brown and damp with that stupefied or browbeaten look of an abandoned croft-house – another a few yards away, with a small square chamber built on behind it (a barn? or a kiln for parching corn?). Here was Unnimore. I found eight houses in all, ending their time in an underworld so lightless and moist that even the whiskery grey lichens were greened by algae. Gaskell knew of 'about fifteen', home to 75 people, all cleared by stages in the 1820s.

How did the Camerons leave? Apparently by the mountainous route due south to the Sound of Mull, since they had their last look at their home from Knock nan Carn. This seems to be the crag on the 400-metre contour with a profile like a totem pole. I climbed slowly up to it, marvelling at the hardihood of James who had carried his father on his back up an angle so steep that in places I used my hands to haul up on tussocks. Below a scarp where a black cave framed a slender rowan that had shot to reach the light, I contoured along a muddied trod. Surely there were no sheep here now? As I got my breath back, sixteen deer raced off along the hill, winter-dun against cinnamon grass, melting expertly into the first fold of moor that afforded cover. At Knock nan Carn I checked that Unnimore was still visible – it was – a green cradle that would always be there by its waters among the Canadian-looking spruce. A pass or bealach split the scarp, beyond it the angle eased and I was looking out over a conifer ocean that undulated continuously for five miles down to the sea itself. To the right was Corrie Bhorradail where the Unnimore and Unnibeg crofters had taken their animals to the shielings each summer. A path snaked from it towards the Sound. Perhaps the family chose this arduous route for their exodus because it was the way the drovers had always taken their cattle to be ferried from Lochaline across the Sound of Mull to Salen, then to Kerrera, Oban, and ultimately the Tryst at Falkirk. They themselves will have been aiming for the paddle steamer from Tobermory to Glasgow, calling at Lochaline. It was called *The Highlander* (a name with a flavour of the fashion started by Scott). It had started two years before James and Mary's eviction – the coming of the Industrial Revolution to Morvern.

Near me on the ridge a TV booster pylon pointed its dishes in all directions – enabling any Camerons left around here to watch the Channel 4 series on the Highland Clearances, no doubt. Nearby, an iron fence with a moulded Victorian straining-post was in the last stages of rust, a memorial to the remarkably short span of the shepherding and deerstalking regime for which Unnimore was cleared, and I thought as I plunged off downhill, This was the victory of wire. The Saxon shepherd ran wire fences round his new big farm. The next generation made them taller to keep the red deer in their place. The wire was made in the slitting-mills which copied the systems used in the cotton mills. It was in 'a cotton work' that Mary's family found employment when they reached Glasgow. But there was a heart to their heartless situation. 'No imprecation or evil wish was heard from one of us. "The world is wide and God will sustain us," ' said her husband as they trekked down Glen Savary and along the statute road to Lochaline. ' "We are as happy, and possibly as great objects of envy, as the owner of this estate who has driven us to this wandering." ' Even eviction could be magicked into a blessing: ' "It is good for me that I have been afflicted," is his language.' In Mary's own concluding sentences the sigh of the oppressed is barely audible: 'Let neither hardships nor poverty compel them to break His law, nor to neglect His ordinances. The *higher the tempest strikes*, the closer may they flee to the shadow of the Great Rock in the weary land.'

My last night on the mainland before I took the ferry from Lochaline to Fishnish had been spent at a house in Invercoe which happened to be owned by a landlady from Tiree. Of course it wasn't chance at all, since Glencoe is on the high road to Oban from the heart of Scotland and the usual route to Tiree is via Oban, not by my old-fashioned side door through Morvern. I was following the grapevine from its origin at the house of Niall Brownlie in Larbert near Stirling. He is a bard and playwright from Tiree – a familiar name to my landlady at Invercoe – and had worked as an engineer on the Clyde. Presently I realised that the name on the gate of his bungalow, Travee, is in Gaelic Tràigh Bhì, the beach of Fee (as in MacPhee), an early coloniser from Ireland, freebooter or saint, who must have landed on the crescent of pale-gold sand which bounds the common grazing of Niall's home township, Barrapol.

Niall's stories and memoirs tapped straight into a world of fulminating grudge between the crofters and their ducal landlords, or at least their managers:

A woman went to pay her rent and the road to Island House was made up with pebbles from the beach, which are very, very sore on bare feet as you will understand. And she walked on the grass, so when she got down to the house he [the factor] turned her back and made her walk back to the gate and told her, 'Walk on the road or you don't walk at all.'

The 'he' of these stories about the factor's power and inhumanity was usually assumed to be John Campbell of Islay, installed by the Duke of Argyll to clear the island of its redundant population, to use the phrase coined by Malthus. (The population fell from 4,453 in 1831 to 3,204 in 1861 – it is now just over 1,000 – and the number of crofts was halved between 1851 and 1881.) Campbell's official title was 'the Duke's Chamberlain'. To Tiree people he is the Black Factor:

I think he must have been the most hated factor that was ever on the island of Tiree. The story goes of the blind man in the village of Kilmoluaig who he served eviction orders on. The old man barricaded himself with the help of his neighbours but the day of the eviction, which I understand was in the winter, they came along but when they couldn't get access to put him out, they took the roof off the house with the blind man inside it . . . And there was a woman in the village of Caolas whom he evicted – she gave birth to a child during the night lying outside, and they both died of course, and nobody was allowed to give them any help or succour because they would have been evicted as well.

Such stories are duplicated on page after page of the Napier evidence given on Tiree in August 1883. There Donald MacDonald, a crofter from Balemartine at the south end, puts the eviction of the blind man in the 1860s, when the Black Factor had been more than ten years gone, and records that the man's wife was crippled and two of his sons had been drowned. His neighbour, a cottar and fisherman, had seen his own parents (the mother being senile) put out onto the roadside, refused permission to build a new house, removed to Glasgow 'which city not agreeing with them' they came back to the island and were housed in a kiln. Crofters were desperate to sail to their Canaan in Nova Scotia, Ontario, or Manitoba (825 petitioned to go to Cape Breton from Tiree in 1851); the owners were desperate to slash the number of holdings and raise the rental. I was also told, again and again, stories quite different from anything that was offered in formal circumstances to visitors in tailcoats and starched collars:

When they build Island House, I think it's in 1773 or 1783, it was built by slave labour. And every crofter had to give a day's work, or two days' work, they were all commandeered to work. And a man was finishing off at night after bringing a load of building stones to Island House and he was just heading home when the factor met him. Now this would not have been Campbell by any manner of means – long before that. And he's turned him back and sent him away for another load. And the crofter says, 'Well,' he says, 'I'll do your bidding,' he says, 'but you'll never sleep a night in Island House.' So, anyway, when Island House was nearly finished, the factor took ill, and to prove the crofter a liar he asked to be carried into Island House on a blanket. And he died on the threshold – never went inside the Island House.

Again the curse figures as the fantasy-resort of the desperate. The boss is the devil and black magic is the only means of combatting his black arts.

It was also said that even in the days of the MacLeans [before Tiree was acquired by the Dukes of Argyll] the person who was last with the rent, he was hung. Now in the vicinity of Island House, not very far away, there's a place called the Hangman's Knoll and that's where they were supposed to hang them, and they said that the last man was hanged there was the son of a miller from the township of Balevulin. Now Balevulin of course is the Gaelic for 'mill town', and there's a well-known rhyme in Gaelic – it says 'The son of the miller of Balevulin, who had a mill and a quern and so on, it was to be that you were dishonoured.' That was the rhyme. His sister went to plead with MacLean, when she heard that her brother was being held and was getting hung, but MacLean says, 'Well, if you had come earlier I would have reprieved him, but he's hung now anyway.'

And Niall laughed, imitating the gloating of the tyrant.

Before I had been on the island three days I had been told this story twice more, each time with a climax in which the tyrant gets his come-uppance:

There were two people, a brother and a sister, and it was spring tide, so she went gathering whelks at low water, and her brother went to pay their rent, but he was last, so they hanged him – the gibbet was at Crossapol there, at Paterson's house. And they said they hanged him, and he was dangling there. So next time, in six months' time, there was a man stayed behind to pay his rent, after everyone else. So when he came in the factor said, 'Why have you come in last? Because you know what will be the consequence.' So the man says, 'Yes, I do, but I'll strangle you first.' And the factor jumped out of the window. And that was the end of that.

This was told me by Donald MacLean of Ardmore, near Cornaig, as I gave him a lift to the port at Scarinish where he had some business to do. And I heard the same version from Alasdair MacDonald of Kilmoluaig, who lives in a thatched house with walls seven feet thick and is reputed never to have left Tiree. 'Maybe we shouldn't be remembering such things,' he said. 'Because they're bad?' 'Because they're bad,' he agreed. But he retailed the hanging story in graphic detail: the gibbet was on a dune with a sharp edge, he said, and when he reached the climax where the 'tall man' threatens the factor, he clutched his hands round his own throat.

The striking thing is that this memoir, or legend, must relate to before 1674 when the island changed owners. It is told today as a prime chapter of the history in which clearance is only the final injustice. So Island House, headquarters for the landowner or his hated tool, has the status of Sir Isambart de Bellamy's loathed stronghold in the stories of Robin Hood's struggle against the Norman Yoke. Today it is a plain, white-walled villa or small 'big house', standing among sheep-nibbled pasture with that subdued and lonely look of a place that has lost its function. The stones of the track that hurt the woman's feet have been compacted by Land Rover wheels and there is a dip across the neck of the promontory into Loch an Eilein on which the house stands: people explain it as the remains of 'a moat where the loch used to come right round, and they had a drawbridge over it, so they were safe in there when they were doing the evicting, until things cooled down'.

By the time I was following the grapevine from one house to another, a nor'easter had blown the skies clear into a great blue hemisphere and so it maintained itself for days, a naked light cleansed of all dust and water-vapour, translucent as sapphire. The wind streamed over, rasping the forehead like dry ice, the light stung off every surface, the sea was glittering copper sulphate. Each sheep was lit white as though the sun had shorn it and at night, a few days past the equinox, the rays concentrated in the due west between cloud-shoal and sea in a corona of rubies while the last of the Hebrides, the cleared islands of Mingulay, Pabbay, and Berneray south of Barra, studded the horizon like dull-blue uncut gemstones. It was against such winds that the old houses had defended themselves by sheer thickness, a double shell of stone with sand between to receive the rainwater which ran off a roof thatched with bents, turfs, or wild iris (no heather on Tiree) and set on the inner edge of the wall so that the gusts could not get under it and rive it off.

I was living in the most westerly building on the island, 'The Glassary. Licensed Restaurant', a newish guesthouse with a cart-wheel, a plough, and an iron water-pump with a long handle set in the turf to create a rustic atmosphere. Even this building (once part of a small glass factory) had the strength of a blockhouse with its plain cement porch, little chunky 'battlements' and square concrete gateposts each with a zinc float fixed to its top. When you stepped out onto the sodden pasture channelled with old drainage lines, your anorak blew against your body like a flag on a mast and you at once fell into a crouch and began to make headway crabwise. The wind relaxed suddenly and let you stagger, then blew up again and sent you into a run. A gale blows on Tiree one day in eleven and I had always been told that it necessitated the tethering of hens, which the islanders deny. Shelter is almost nil. The highest point is only 141 metres and the midriff of the island where the airport is situated, a sunken grassland oddly called The Reef, barely reaches ten metres above sea level in its two-mile span. A nickname for the island is 'the land whose summits are below the waves'. Perching on its winter-bleached surface, surrounded by rocking blue expanses that seemed to impend above the broad, stretched fringes of the skylines, was like floating on some light home-made craft, Thor Heyerdahl's balsa-wood raft or Ally Fox's castaway home in *Mosquito Coast*, a freight of humans balancing precariously on currents both elemental and historic.

Mrs MacArthur, who ran the Glassary, was Tiree-born. Her husband Danny, born in Glasgow, knew that his mother's people had been evicted in Ardnamurchan and had had to 'build themselves a hut among the rocks and the seaweed'. He has steeped himself in the history of Tiree. He said that the Black Factor had moved the people from Sandaig, the nearest township, to the poor land near the shore when this end was enclosed for farms, so sowing seeds for the rising of 1887. The shore land drains badly; the exposure to the Atlantic winds is total. Habitation here must have been the merest perching before flight to Canada and Danny said that old people used to point out the sites of dwellings by the clumps of nettles. I crossed this ground on grass saturated by the bad winter, making for Ceann a' Bhara, Tiree's last knuckle clenched against the ocean. Perhaps there were climbing possibilities on the cliffs – I put my rock-boots in my rucksack – but no, the place looked desperate. Deep geos split it; on Land's End granite they would have made superb climbing zawns but the rock here, gneiss layered with hornblende schist and unusual limestones, presented faces slick with bird-lime whose draining smeared and blurred them, making them look like stone missiles in the act of plunging earthward. When the spring flush of flowers came to the islands in two months' time, the ledges and tops would be embroidered with thrift and wild geranium.

Just now they were dun and beaten. Directly below, as I pulled up through a band of rock, a tussocky slope had been trodden by cormorants into a mud-slide which reeked like a foul henhouse and in the deeper chasms, where direct sun never reached, layers of starling dung were mined with holes where rats had dug their burrows.

It was a relief to climb up out of a grassy cleft – strewn with Swedish timber which people were retrieving piecemeal from among the mats of seaweed debris down at the tide-mark – and stride about on the plateau, picking out the Paps of Jura fifty miles south, Heaval on Barra forty miles north-north-west, and much nearer, to the east, the weird flat crown of the Dutchman's Cap, like a Mayan temple platform floating on the sea. The real temple was the remnant of a chapel (or hermit's cell) attributed to St Patrick among the rocks nearby – sign of the beachhead Tiree had been for incomers from Ireland. The connection was still alive – Hugh MacLean of Barrapol spoke with glowing affection about ports across there which he had got to know when he was working on the coal-boats. Beyond the Treshnish Islands lay the Ross of Mull, where the Tiree people had gone to cut peats and land their cattle for droving across to the mainland of Argyll.

It was altogether a supreme vantage point, not as high as Càrnan Mòr at the far end of Tràigh Bhì, where the giant sphere of an Advance Warning Station sat like a bloodless polyp, but more atmospheric by far. For Niall Brownlie, born in nearby Barrapol, it was 'my beloved Kennavara'. Alasdair MacDonald commemorated its awesomeness in a story about the deepest of the geos, which 'runs underground the whole length of the island and comes out at Caolas. This piper went in there and commenced to walk right along the passage, and the people up above could hear him playing all the way to near the middle, and then he stopped, and he never came out. But a few days later his dog came back out, and he had no fur left on him.' This same story has found a home in various places. I felt I was hearing one more truly native when I enquired about climbing on the Ceann a' Bhara sea-cliffs and was told about 'the only person who ever went there. He was from St Kilda, and he fell in love with a missionary from Tiree who used to go over there to take a service, so he came to live here and married her, and he had brought his rope with him, that he had used to go down for birds and eggs. He climbed all over there, by himself he used to go, but when he was eighty years of age they thought he would not be safe any more, so they took away his rope.'

From this high ground Tiree looks like one of the stems oɪ the tangle, the *laminaria*, which for a time in the early nineteenth century was its most valuable crop. The rocky spurs of the cliffs are the stubs of its roots, the headland as a whole its bulbous end, anchored to the sea-bed, and the long eastward tapering of the island, smooth and dappled buff and olive, is its shank, streaming out in alignment with the North Atlantic Drift. Blown sand on the platform of gneiss has created loam all over it; 'Tiriodh' means 'land of corn'; it has been so well crofted that its herds were the first in Britain to be declared free of brucellosis. It is also painfully easy to map out the crofters' tribulations from up here. In their worst time, from 1846 till after the Great War, they were squeezed out into the rockier lands at the east and west ends, leaving the deeper, more consistent soil for the factors, ground officers, and merchants who reorganised the island's economy for their own benefit. The hardship after the Potato Famine of autumn 1846 survives in the memoirs of Hugh MacLean at Barrapol, who said that during the winter gales, when people were living on seed-corn and shellfish, 'I believe you could not get limpets, when you went fishing from the rocks.' The desperation to make a living was so acute that people would 'get up about midnight and go away down and pick up tangle out of the surf when the sea is washing over them, and take it up out of the reach of the tide on their backs over rough ground, and all they get is fourpence per cubic yard of root of tangle'. The Black Factor's solution had been draconian: raising rents (which doubled between 1851 and 1881), evicting vigorously for arrears, paying part of the passage money to Canada. More than a quarter of the island's people left in the five years after the Famine.

Hugh MacLean's whole family were among the further twenty per cent who left during the next phase. In 1874 they settled as farmers in Shoal Lake, Manitoba:

This grand-uncle of mine, he had a couple of coal smacks, and he had a bit of money – he had £1,000 in his pocket – it was a fortune in those days, and he financed the freight across, to help them. Four sons and two daughters went with their mother. I sometimes feel I'm the odd one out in this country, I should have been over there with them. Sometimes. You know – *sometimes*.

Here his speech quite changed from its usual fluency. He delights in speaking, pausing with his left hand in mid-air as he reaches a clincher, then dunting the arm of his chair as though hitting a fence-post with a 14 lb. hammer, swivelling to face you, screwing his left eye shut, tilting his head and holding the pose for several seconds as though to challenge any rejoinder. As he now thought over, for the umpteenth time no doubt, the chances of his life and the differences Canada might have made, he paused and hesitated and let his voice trail off. The insoluble mixed feelings showed in his anecdote of the grand-uncle coming back and visiting Hugh's father:

They walked the whole length of the island, there was no road, but you can walk it – I've done it myself. And they were sitting on the hill at Gott, Beinn Ghot as we call it, and it was a glorious summer's day and they could see as much as you would ever see – this whole island. And he said, 'Yes, we have done well in Manitoba, but I would prefer what that covers [pressing his boot onto the ground] to the whole of Canada!'

And Hugh went off into the passage from Scott's *Lay of the Last Minstrel*:

Breathes there the man with soul so dead
Who never to himself has said,
'This is my own, my native land' –

and I joined in:

Whose heart has ne'er within him burned
As home his footsteps he has turned
From wandering on a foreign strand.

'But,' Hugh continued, 'they *went*, and it was a good thing in the long run for their descendants that they did go. They can afford to visit us, and *we can't*!'

So emigration was the only choice, the island was impossibly congested, 'times were hard and they had to go away to find their fortune' – in such phrases the crofters I spoke to acknowledged again and again their sense that what happened was inevitable. Their quarrel was with the mean and callous style of the clearance, the humiliation and hardship it entailed. 'Clearance' was not a word they accepted, because it connoted the wholesale burning-out in Strath Naver and Kildonan, which they cited, or in North Uist and Mull, which they did not. What they bore witness to was piecemeal chivvying:

> The tenant of this croft of mine, before my great-grandfather got it, was a MacLean too, and he was flung out, and the reason was that he was riding beside the factor when both of them were coming from Scarinish, from meeting the packet there, for a letter or maybe something else they were requiring. He put his horse past the factor's — he got a month to get out — he was supposed to keep behind him!

Here he gave a characteristic quickfire cackle like the short barking laugh with which Lenin is supposed to have greeted bad news.

> There's a crofter down here by the lochside [Loch a' Phuill] was given notice to quit. 'Well,' he says, 'it's hard lines on me,' he says. 'I have a young family, and where am I going to go? I don't see how I have violated your conditions in any way.' 'Oh yes, you did.' 'And what did I do so wrong?' 'Kept a dog. And you kept a gun. And more than that — you cut turf to mend the roof of your house off the common grazing.'
>
> And there was a widow with a wee nest of children, and she had trouble paying the rent. And John Campbell wanted the place, and he and the factor were as close as two peas. So they came and took the roof off her house, and she had to go down to the shore there and build a shelter.

Such stories were legion. I was shown a copy of a notice of November 16th, 1855, signed by the agent Lachlan MacQuarie at Island House, which decreed that any tenant paying less than £30 rent — i.e. the great majority — who 'used whiskey or any other spirits at Weddings, Balls, funerals or any other gatherings' would be 'dispossessed of their lands at the next term.' The Napier evidence records eviction for keeping a pig and for sowing turnip seed one day after the date ordered by the factor. By such means were 79 per cent of smaller tenancies wiped out between the Famine and 1861.

The underdog's view of this experience was classically summed up by Sandy MacKinnon, who had built the Glassary. He had no croft, coming from a line of landless blacksmiths, and lived at Crossapol, next the airport, in a council house full of books. He was lean and aquiline with fiery, dying eyes and a mane of white hair, and he found talking painful because of a cough resulting from a recent fall onto his breastbone. Confirming that wholesale physical eviction had not taken place, he said:

> The factor would move you from Caolas to Barrapol, or from there to here. So that you could never find your feet – you could never settle. Like draughts, it was. Man's inhumanity to man. When MacDiarmid was factor, I remember him though I was only a wee boy, you had to lift the cap to him. I wanted to make the other gesture. My father had no land, but when his grand-uncle at Kilkenneth wanted more ground, the factor said [mimes a rubbing-together of hands], 'Now let me see – you have a bit at Balevullin – that's no use to you – it's inconvenient so far away. Why not give that up, and I'll give you a bit at Greenhill?' And then he divided the bit at Balevullin between the *two* on either side there. Manipulation!

In the 1890s, as land hunger reached a peak, applications for crofts flowed in on Argyll County Council. Factor MacDiarmid was also a councillor, to say nothing of owning the farm at Heylipol, and Merchant Barr was also a councillor, to say nothing of owning the farms at Crossapol, Reef, and Balephetrish. To which formidable system of control they added ingenious extras such as their practice of never competing with each other when buying cattle, so that a crofter selling a stirk had no option but to accept an agreed Barr/MacDiarmid price. I was reminded of John Manson at Rogart telling me how the auctioneer sold off the poorest crofters' lambs either early or late in the sale so that the prime time, when most buyers were present and eager, was reserved for the flocks of the bigger farmers. Man's inhumanity to man – apparently trivial, actually crucial if you live near the poverty line.

It seemed in keeping with this insidious, rather than flagrantly brutal, displacement of the crofters on Tiree that the only monument to such things was an anonymous boulder. Not an inscribed cairn of quarried stone, as at Gartymore or opposite Donald MacLeod's village of Rossal in Strath Naver, but a grey, unaltered stone three feet

1. Garthbanks, Shetland mainland, 1867.

2. Garthbanks, after the final solution, 1880.

3. Betty Fraser, Gartymore, about 1910: evicted from Costly, Kildonan, 1814.

4. Minnie Campbell, Gills, about 1910: evicted from Grummore,
Strath Naver, 1819.

5. Crofts still worked: Tarskavaig, Skye, 1931.

6. The factor at work: eviction in Lochmaddy, North Uist, 1891.

7. The moment of eviction: Lochmaddy, 1891.

8. Crofter's kitchen-room in the old style: Lochboisdale, South Uist.

9. Crofter's living-room in the new style: Callanish, Lewis.

10. Arrival in the New World: Manitoba, 1812.

11. Arrival in the New World: early 1920s.

12. William Sutherland, Beeton, Ontario: born 1816, the child of Kildonan settlers.

13. Johnny Allan MacDonald, Loch Lomond, Cape Breton Island: born 1889, the great-grandson of the Big Carpenter, one of the first North Uist settlers.

14. 'Scotland' across the water: St Bernard, Nova Scotia, 1920s.

15. Ted Gerrard, the last inhabitant of Pabbay, Harris, 1974.

high just east of the road from Heylipol to Cornaigmore, embedded in the grass, with a blind crack on one side and a central hollow on the other like the back of an elephant's skull. I wouldn't have looked at it twice but Donald MacLean made me get out of the car to study it. It had been turned right over and stood on its head by two men from Cornaig, John Lamont and John MacLean, on the eve of their emigration to Canada in 1850:

These two men, they were coming from a funeral in Sorobaigh. They were heading for their homes in Cornaig but they knew they were leaving. So they left that stone as a landmark to be written down in the history of Tiree. When the factor and the ground officer came to evict him [John Lamont], he knew. They came in a gig with a horse, so he went down to the other end of the house and he brings up a five gallon jar of whisky, that kind of a cream-and-white jar, a stone jar. And the ground officer thought, Well, that's all right, he's going to offer me a dram. And John Lamont took out the cork, that had a string on it to hold it to the handle of the jar, and he poured himself a glass. And then he drank it. And the ground officer thought, Now he'll offer me a dram, it's going to be all right. And John Lamont poured himself another dram and drank it. And he said, 'I always have that' and he put the cork in the jar with the flat of his hand. Now, do you think – you're an educated man – do you think, if he had offered the ground officer a dram, do you think they would have left him in his place?

But I did not think so and neither, I could see, did Donald.

A few hours before the boat sailed for Mull, where I was due to meet Anne off the Oban boat and begin our explorations of that island, I went for a look at one corner where I had found no oral memoirs – Balemartine and Mannal on the east shore of the southern headland. It seemed to have suffered the worst land hunger. Balemartine was the home of five of the eight found guilty of 'Mobbing, rioting, and deforcing an officer of the law in the execution of his duty' during the affray of 1887. This was a Gilbert and Sullivan scenario. A farm near the Glassary was let to a single tenant in the teeth of a demand for its land by crofters and cottars. They herded their own animals onto the ground – a police force, 37 strong, was sent from Glasgow – their gigs were turned back by a crowd and the Conservative papers, whipped on by the Duke of Argyll, turned it into an outbreak of 'savagery' in which crofters armed with spears were supposed to have lain in ambush behind hedges – there are no hedges on Tiree. The government, already paranoid about crofter militancy, sent a task force to restore order: a fleet of three led by a battleship, with 250 marines and 120 sailors. The islanders met them with cries of 'Stand at ease' as they marched past Scarinish slaughter-house and offered them milk to drink as the warm August days wore on. The *Scotsman* correspondent tried to beat the Sabbath by sending out his report by carrier pigeon – it was buzzed by seagulls and his copy scattered to the winds ... The comedy turned sour when the men were arrested and sent to prison for four months.

This was in the first year of what labour historians call the Great Unrest – modern Britain's most sustained struggle between haves and have-nots, suspended only by the Great War. In the autumn of 1892 the Balemartine and Mannal cottars petitioned for 'a small piece of ground wherein to plant a few potatoes to help us to live'. Seventy families, a few years later, were still without either land or harbour: 'The men, though willing to work, have to pass the winter in idleness.' I was shown the petition at Heylipol by Alex MacArthur. Although he was seriously worried about his sheep, which were tending to abort and needed to be medicated one by one, he took the trouble to shower me with documents and information. The landless people of Balemartine, he said, had been refugees from Balinoe and Heylipol where the clachans had been cleared to make a farm. They had made themselves homes down on the shingle just above high tide by turning boats upside down. One of them is still there, its gunwale built round with boulders, its tarry planks with their voluptuous curves soot-black under a sky of Greek brilliance. The light was blindingly reflected from the fortress walls of the proper houses a few yards away, which were freshly whitened and perfectly maintained. The sea comes to within a few feet of their back doors, a householder had had her cess-pit swept away by a storm a few winters ago, and it was plain that this settlement is on the very margin of the habitable. When I said to a man who was chopping wood at the top of the shingle, 'The village here is surely unusually huddled together,' he said at once, 'Och – they chased them down from up there – you can see the squares of the old houses between here and Ben Hynish – they had to make their living off the shore, fishing for the big cod and the ling.'

The thought of all that hardship made me grieve again that here on a seaboard of such amplitude the social arrangements should have been so merciless. Opening the eyes and mind to the fleet of islands moored in the tides and overflowed by oceanic winds brings home more fully than in any other part of Britain that you belong in the cosmos and share its physical being. This morning, in full sunlight, the island glamour opened out around me like a wide blue flower. To stand on this place, to sail away from it, was to be more aware of the planet than on any mainland stance because this little slip of land, its crest so nearly submerged, southern terminus of the gneiss that runs right down the Hebrides from Cape Wrath, brought to a focus all that we have as a species. One more surge of the tectonic impulse and there might have been a spread of land to the west instead of all that open sea, one less and Tiree might have been dragged under again or never surfaced at all. Neither quite happened, so this outpost is *here*, cattle and tractors, children, crofters, and pensioners, carved Celtic cross and Martian radar brain and Loganair wind-sock, the whole human outfit perching for a moment – but why minimise our civilisation by seeing it under the gaze of eternity? We have dug in much deeper than that, from the age of stone tools or the stone crucifixes of the seventh-century missionaries to the brand new blue metal warehouse at Scarinish harbour – as good a display of human pertinacity as you could ask for. Each island is so vulnerable. Gordon of Cluny had wanted to sell Barra as a penal colony – if that had gone through, it might be as void now as Alcatraz. In an hour the boat was tying up briefly at Coll where the 'great exodus' took place in 1861 from arable west to rock-bound east, and the guidebook writers of 1937 had heard from some of those evicted how the infants were carried on shoulders or in baskets on the horses' pack-saddles, the children had their own loads, the cattle were driven in front, and 'a shelter for the night [was] improvised till what passed for dwelling houses were later erected' – one blink of the recent past on just one site in the archipelago.

Each island blurs into a blue ideal as it recedes, refocuses as a common-or-garden fragment of our globe when you approach. Yes, that is a slab of glaciated rock patched with acid soil and edged with frets of cold salt-water. Yes, the work here is done by thick-fingered men in blue denims who pour concrete to repair shitty cement-and-alloy cattle pens. There is boredom here (no cafés or cinemas) and small enough escapes from it (coffee evenings with

Tombola or talks about birds). But the lure of the place never seems to diminish – setting off towards it is like letting a dreaming sleep close over – arriving is like waking.

The awakening at Mull set in as the boat slid towards Tobermory harbour past a black rock on which someone had painted in white block letters GOD IS LOVE. No doubt this idea was believed devoutly by great numbers of the beaten sufferers crammed into single rooms here in the late 1840s. In 1848 and 1849 alone 600 families were warned out on Mull. The nationwide campaign by Highland landlords at that time was described by the chief government relief officer, who had the incredible name of Pine Coffin, as aiming at 'the extermination of the population'. Tobermory was a main transit camp for the refugees – as were other beautiful present-day holiday places such as Plockton and Lochcarron – and its population rose by eleven per cent, while Mull's fell by more than a quarter, during the Famine and its aftermath. We're fortunate, if that is the word, that exact descriptions of the town were left by an exceptionally honest observer, Robert Somers, who travelled the Highlands for the *North British Daily Mail* in 1848.

The people he saw were in full flight from the croftlands round the western sea-lochs. An old woman in a windowless room 'so full of smoke that a candle lighted when we went in would scarcely burn' had had her 5 lbs. of meal stopped because she had an able-bodied son. He lived a long way off 'and in the present difficulties of the country may probably need relief himsel'. A bedridden blind woman had lived with her niece at Tiroran on Loch Scridain. She had been evicted in 1847 and had moved into a small tent. She and her children had measles and her granny was put into the byre end of the old house where rain poured through the roof. A family of twelve from Ardvergnish at the head of the loch were living in a room 'very bare of furniture, containing only a few things which they had carried with them over the mountain' after 'their cottages were pulled to the ground'. And still these people were forced to revisit their razed clachans, the Tiroran woman to draw relief meal, the Ardvergnish man to haul and set his herring nets. Later Somers saw the people at the end of their trek, at the Green in Glasgow, hundreds of families 'lying night after night on the cold damp grass ... or amid the still more pestilential vapours of the wynds and lanes'. It must have looked like Bombay in 1959, where I saw a woman at sunset spreading a sheet of brown paper on the pavement of a busy street as bedding for herself and two children, three among 750,000 homeless.

I had felt the merest fraction of that comfortless transience the week before as horizontal rain soaked me instantly to the skin and I went up and down Tobermory, finding all the Bed and Breakfast's still shut or reluctant to take a single person, before getting in at the last guesthouse along the front. The harbour town at the end of winter, with its crescent of tall narrow eighteenth-century houses, leafless trees on the ridge behind, and the bay empty of everything but a few prawn-fishers' boats and tarpaulined yachts, looked almost historical through half-closed eyes. The distillery has closed down, the port has lost most of its traffic to Craignure 22 miles down the coast – the smart new terminal where presently I met Anne off the Oban boat, a huge floating restaurant which disgorges the tourists for Iona through a glazed aluminium stairway that slides along the quay on rails at the bidding of a duty officer with a short-wave radio.

I was glad we were on Mull outside the holiday season, almost glad that the cloud-wrack had closed over and Atlantic showers were blinding steadily in. It made the place seem more itself. Mull is variously known as 'the Officers' Mess' and the 'g-and-t island', having long since been carved up into pads for well-to-do incomers, whom we met and mixed with (and no doubt resembled) in the tarted-up inns and the coffee shops that sold fudge and watercolours. They were like a kind of living waxworks representing a past stage of the upper-middle class, here perhaps because they fondly remembered fishin' and stalkin' parties in the castellated big houses between the Wars: women with the vowels and cadences of bygone West End actresses with names like Athene or Gwen, the men hairy in greenish deerstalkers and gingery plus-fours, smelling of pipe tobacco; the women like drawersful of scissors, the men like beached walruses wrapped in Harris tweed; all of them relentlessly letting us know what they think of the coffee, the rain, the pottery (sub Bernard Leach), their absent friends; acknowledging the rest of us with a vicar's wife's professional smile (the tweedier, more Burberried women), mincingly sweet smiles and powdered voices (the blue-rinsed), and vague glares (the men).

It would be little wonder if the Muileachs themselves had turned inwards and become rather uncommunicative, as they live on in the outskirts of exhausted villages, in the back streets of Tobermory, at the ends of unmade roads, on the fringes of enclosed estates where miles and miles of sweet, deserted grassland are banned by 'No Camping' signs. Nevertheless, with the help of a writer called Peter MacNab who had been brought up in Tobermory and now lives in north Ayrshire, we did find our way to the home of Mary Morrison whose father had been evicted from Boreraig. She lives in a small wooden house beside a stone mill near the north coast, a retired teacher of Gaelic. Although she embodies that memoir of Skye one hundred and sixty-eight years ago, she seemed, in her modern teeshirt and with her fund of radical observations, not aged at all. She had been a schoolmate of Sorley MacLean's at Portree. Her view of what the nineteenth century did to the *Gaidhealtachd* was evidently long-considered and had more of a psychological dimension than is usual:

> The sap was squeezed out of them, they were crushed, and an inhibitive feeling entered in – a *genetic* inhibition, which is what we still have. They hang back, they are depressed, as a result of the Clearances. My son is exceptional musically, though I say it myself. But he would never come forward in public. They have been discouraged in the value they set upon themselves – it was bound to be so, when your own language is not the one that has the power, that is used for the business of society.

Peter MacNab remembered the headmaster in Tobermory about 1914 saying with stinging emphasis, 'Anybody using the Gaelic within the precincts of this school will be *whipped*.' Presently Mrs Morrison's son came in for a cuppa, a sturdy, stocky man who had been ten years at sea and had come back to croft and build a salmon hatchery and take tourists over to Staffa in his boat. When he heard his mother making the usual case against the ministers for collaborating in the repression, he concurred exactly: 'They made the people think it was a penance – that they had better give in, and give up thoughts about resistance. I know this sounds like Marx and the opiate of the people, but that's what was going on.'

Mary Morrison had no specific stories of clearance on Mull. She explained this partly by her husband's grandparents' having escaped eviction because (like Norman Johnson's people in Sollas) they were weavers. They had lived near Torloisk on Loch Tuath, where there were 'quite a lot of clearances from villages down by the shore'. She also felt she had not been 'in a position to hear

many stories because I was the schoolmistress, and there was this
– barrier. It's not very great, but there is a barrier, between you
and the rest.' What she did was put me onto a man called Alan
Beaton, who lived in a council house in upper Tobermory, on a
chilly hill not far from the site of the old workhouse which figured
in a story told me by Peter MacNab. The evicting owner of Ulva
island in Loch Tuath, a lawyer from Stirling called Clark, had said
to a woman who went to him to plead against eviction, 'No no,
you must vacate your croft. But I will do my best to get you a place
in the Combination Workhouse' (an unusual thing in the Hebrides,
founded in 1862). Mr Beaton was amiable benevolence itself, with a
look of Mr Punch and a habit of chirrupping and singing to himself
as he infused the tea. He had worked as a mason in the stronghold
of the evictors, Glengorm Castle, and he had earned a Highland &
Agricultural Society of Scotland certificate for eight years' approved
services, and his conversation teemed with stories of clearances and
curses:

> 'Gorm' is the Gaelic for 'blue'. And the name of it was because
> the glen was blue with the smoke of the little thatched roofs –
> they were all cleared away, the ruins are still to be seen. One of
> these old ladies who was burnt out, or her house was burnt, she
> said that Mr Forsyth of Quinish House, who built the castle at
> Glengorm – I think he came from the Colonies – she said that
> he would see the castle finished but he would never live in it. He
> was living across the moor at Quinish, so, when it was completed,
> there was a big river [Loch Mingary] but the horse would walk
> through it but it put its foot in a rabbit burrow and he fell off
> and broke his neck.

The wicked expropriator foiled yet again. The 'castle' survived him,
a colonial businessman's dream of a seigneurial chateau, pepperpot
towers and false machicolations and crowstepped gables. As the Tiree
boat enters the narrows between Ardnamurchan and Mull, you see
the thing up there on its ledge above low cliffs and you rub your
eyes, expecting to see a film director come round the corner with
his loudhailer and order Douglas Fairbanks Snr. or Errol Flynn to
jump over the battlements before the expensive set bursts into flames.
   The striking thing about Mr Beaton's talk was the apparent
contrast between his staid image as a member of settled Highland

society and the fierce, basic struggles for the land, not far beyond living memory, which he (and Peter MacNab and Mary Morrison) knew in lurid glimpses. He had a Moderator's certificate on the wall as evidence of his forty years as a Kirk elder, beside a photo of himself in scarlet Highland regalia. He was proud that his pipe tune 'Sweet Maid of Mull' has 'gone round the world'. He also knows how viciously unsettled things were on the island as it was cleared for sporting estates, their big houses mostly mouldering now or converted into hotels and outdoor centres:

There was a Campbell, Saighdear Mòr [big soldier], who spoke up for the people against Forsyth when he was doubling and trebling the rents. He wanted them to sell their horses. Now, if there was a foal, they *needed* the two of them for ploughing. Campbell refused to sell, and some of the estate workers cut up his horses.

What sorry in-fighting – grieved over again and again by people who said to me, 'How could they get men to evict their own kind, pour out their milk, quench their fires, burn their roofs?' It was a breach in that equality which crofters feel to be at the core of their heritage (as when Alex George Mackay of Melness said, 'We were all on a level'). The same theme cropped up in another of Mr Beaton's stories of a black retribution:

There was a factor at Kilchoan in Ardnamurchan, a Mr MacColl. He ordered an awful lot of the crofters to be sent across the seas. There was one old lady, I never knew her name, she was on her deathbed, and that factor got sheriff-officers from Oban to go across to Kilchoan and order her out. Now, they carried her out and set the little thatched cottage on fire. She said, 'I don't know who brought these sheriff-officers over here but when the factor dies a blade of grass will never grow on his grave.' Now I saw that grave with my own eyes and it's as black as that fire-back – a relative of MacColl's said she'd sow grass on the grave but it's still as black as that fire. And she said, 'Those that brought the sheriff-officers over here, the sea will be their grave.' They brought them back to Tobermory here and when they were returning from Kilchoan a storm rose up and capsized the boat, and two brothers and a son were drowned.

Such black fantasies of justice done at last to the evictors and those who accepted their wages are part of the Highland pre-occupation with signs, omens, and forces not of this world. Un-fortunately the shops that sell low-priced paperbacks about second sight and fairies and whisky and Bonnie Prince Charlie rarely carry Clearance material, no doubt because it is too rankling and too recent, although I did find a well-illustrated abridgement of MacKenzie's *Highland Clearances* in the Weehavitt store at Lochmaddy. A few years ago, the Tourist Board office in Inverness was prevailed upon not to display leaflets describing a Clearance Trail round selected sites, prepared by a teacher called Rob Gibson, on the ground that it was 'political'. It is still in print, updated and selling well. To think that such matters should and can be driven outwith the pale of ordinary discourse is to make the same mistake as the apparatchiks who thought to exorcise all memoir of the labour camps from Soviet people's consciousness. When the Thaw came and Solzhenitsyn was allowed to publish *One Day in the Life of Ivan Denisovich*, the effect was therapeutic. One Soviet scholar called the novel a 'folk legend' with a rhythmic pattern: 'As if they were microwaves, these rhythms break up the stone which lies in our inner being and turn it to dust to be carried away by spiritual breezes, restoring life functions to the frozen parts of the soul – and, in particular, returning the capacity for tears and laughter.' It is the same mental freeing, and partial or ideal recompense for the old injustice, that a Muileach brings about by telling you that when the tombstone of Ulva's new proprietor, Clark, was being brought ashore, 'it could not be moved from Ulva ferry because of the weight of the evil that was in it'.

We never got to Ulva. On the day we arrived at the road end near Oskamull, the ferry, still on winter times, had finished early and we could only stare across the narrow channel at the sap-green, oddly-terraced land which had been an *exporter* of potatoes with a population of 500 until Clark reduced this by two-thirds in four years, the rest being 'herded into a corner of the island and not even allowed to plant a tree in case that indicated a desire to remain'. Peter MacNab as a boy had spoken to an old man who remembered 'being carried, as a child, on his father's back out of the family cottage' which had been 'built by the hands of his forefathers'. The factor and his men were standing outside the door with blazing torches in their hands which they thrust into the thatch as soon as the people were out.' It would have been good to see at least the evil tombstone. When we got back to Tobermory that night, there was a phone-call to say that my closest surviving relative in Aberdeen was dangerously ill. It was a Saturday. No ferries on the Sabbath. Our host told us that in emergencies a fishing-boat could be got to take you over the Sound to Morvern but this would have meant landing among those lonely forests without a car. We had to leave Argyll on the Monday, via the Lochaline and Corran ferries, with Ulva still unvisited. Luckily we had already spent some days working our way round the north-west airts of Mull, and as far south-west as Bunessan, and had been able to feel under our feet the once-tilled croftlands on the Atlantic coast.

As usual these had been effaced from the map but Peter had given me names and directions. The first was above the bay of Calgary – the very name epitomises the west of Canada, the foothills of the Rockies. Emigrant boats had indeed left from here. Now it is unpeopled, with that look that makes you stand still, listening for voices. The track to the harbour, between steep headlands, bristled with notices – NO DOGS, NO ENTRY, even DOGS WILL BE SHOT, beneath which someone had scribbled 'Balls'. The pier (notice: DO NOT ENTER: DANGER: MINISTER OF AGRICULTURE AND FISHERIES) was a bulwark of blackish local stone ending in a head of superb roseate large-crystalled blocks – granite from the peninsula nearest Iona. They were shrugging slowly downward into the sea. We climbed north-eastward up the headland to find the clachan of 'Inivea': sixteen buildings, walls still standing as high as eight feet, corners beautifully rounded, almost a street of them on an arable ledge, invisible from the sea and therefore safe from pressgangs. But not from factors. Behind the houses green ways led through the invasive bracken. As the Mull bard Angus MacMhuirich sang:

> The land of our love is under bracken and heather
> and every plain and field untilled,
> and soon there will be no-one in Mull of the trees
> but Lowlanders and white sheep.

Among shallow, rounded knolls a big 'field' was enclosed by a turf-and-boulder ring-dyke still plain to see two feet proud of the ground. The water supply was a burn now choked with weeds. As we turned back, the window-spaces in the houses framed the pier below, and away beyond it the ramparts of basalt on Treshnish Point, two miles from our next goal.

This was Crakaig, which floats on the map with no symbol to define what on earth it was, and its neighbour clachan Glacgugaraidh, 'the hollow of the dark grazings', which the map ignores. A man called Neil Paterson, who lived in a council house some distance away from the fudge-and-pottery centre of Dervaig, had told me about his father who had been born at Crakaig in 1860 and had gone to Reudle School: 'he took a peat there every day.' His mother's people had been MacDougalls and sure enough, in the ground-floor plasterwork of the ruined school – a tall, narrow black building which loomed on the hill like a Cornish wheal-tower – a graffito scratched in perfect copperplate said 'Robert MacDougall 4th May 1894', next to some expert drawings of sailboats, one with graceful timbers shown in perspective. He would have come to school by the grassy track we now followed past peat bogs and ribs of rock. Presently the bog showed straight edges of old cuttings for fuel – a threshold through a turf-and-boulder dyke – a circular lochan with some palisaded edge to it – and then the houses of Crakaig, doorways five foot six inches high, stone lintels still in place. Quarter of a mile further on, Glacgugaraidh occupied a dell just above a 200 foot bluff that fell to the coastal plain. Peter had said that there had been a blacksmith here and a communal garden. The crags to seaward of the houses were guarded by dykes built right up to their ends, the grassy gullies were similarly dyked across to keep in the herds, and in the old vegetable garden a huge moribund rowan sprawled onto its knees and elbows like a mutant octopus made of grey-green fur: the magic tree, often planted near croft houses to ward off evil.

In such places the phrase that comes to mind is 'cradle of civilisation'. This one had withered and died out, not cleared but failed – too exposed, too far from the overriding civilisation of harbour, church, shops, mainland ferries. One of its chief trades had been distilling. We scrambled down to sea level as the first sun for days glimpsed through and lit up a weave of russet bracken and olive grass as patterned as tweed. The straight lines were edges of fields where barley had been grown to make malt for the whisky. Somewhere nearby must be the cave where the vats, coil, and kegs had been hidden from the gaugers. Offshore the peculiar basalt islets of Lunga, Fladda, and the Dutchman's Cap raised their exotic profiles. The excisemen would have lurked behind them in their cutters before making a swoop or chasing a suspected vessel across to Scarinish, according to a story I had heard there in a house next the beach which was just visible from here as a pale-gold fringe on the horizon.

We worked our way along by the old barley fields, clambered in and out of a rocky geo which split the plain, and found it at last – a high-roofed cave with a glass bead-curtain of waterfall screening its mouth. The distillers would have channelled this to cool the coil or 'worm' and force it to secrete the aromatic drops. Now it watered the clumps of primrose, cliff cress, and angelica which framed the opening. A rickle of stones across the cave mouth were the remnant of the wall the men had built to hide themselves from the sea. The foundation of the still was in place, a shallow basin of big blocks, 2½ feet deep at its centre, 5 feet across, in the centre of a platform standing a yard high from the floor. At Bunessan John Campbell, a retired postman, told me how the racket had been worked at a similar site, the township of Burg on the north shore of Loch Scridain. 'People took a fiver from the distillers not to let on where they worked and another fiver from the gaugers to tip them off.' The cave at Burg had a waterfall diverted down its face to hide the smoke and the people moving about. On one occasion, as the gaugers came dangerously near, the look-out boy at the channelled burn up above quickly broke the dam as they climbed up from the shore and the torrent swept them back down into the sea.

Those were disreputable times, no doubt, and the intake of home-made whisky seems to have been formidable, often starting early in the morning as an instant source of calories. In Tiree, in Strath Kildonan, the proprietor commonly cited 'smuggling' as grounds for clearing an area – then arrogated the manufacture to themselves, as the Sutherlands did at Clyne. At least, in the time of the flourishing cottage industry, when the first efforts were made to prohibit such distilling in 1782 and Tiree exported up to 3,000 gallons a year, the income from it 'helped to maintain an over-large population when help was most needed to meet rack-renting'. When high licensing fees and heavy duty handed the industry over to men with capital, the crofters lost a crucial source of money – just when the kelp industry was being killed by the government's decision to allow the import of foreign substitutes. And now factory ships from

the Continent are wiping out the fish stocks by scooping up every-
thing, even the youngest fish, all round the Hebrides. When will the
London government learn to protect the essential resources of the
Highlands?

Burg and Bunessan were our last ports of call and they were
sources, not of clearance stories, but of remarks that reminded me
how inspiring it was to be among an eloquent people. This had first
struck me in the middle of Ireland thirty-five years before when a
countryman I had asked for directions broke off his intricate talk
of mileages and left turns to look up at the sky and exclaim, 'Now
is it rain I see hovering in that dark cloud?' It is seductively easy to
make a cult out of a few striking remarks, yet I have often found
that very old informants in remote places are able to give special
power to the most bygoing comments. It may be their age – they are
past the embarrassment of seeming 'flowery'. It may be the Gaelic
groundbass of their language, less alloyed than mainland English
by transient slang, more leavened by traditional singing, preaching,
and the Bible. The Napier evidence is full of it. We hear it from the
Great Bernera crofter who testifies, 'There is no gate there for us to
carry our dead through, and we have to carry them over the wall,
were the snow ever so deep,' and we even hear it in the piece of
Fascist wit ascribed to a factor near Ness: 'The people asked the
chamberlain at the time what he was going to do with them when
they had no homes, and he pointed to the sea, and told them their
home was there.' We heard it at Burg from Chrissie MacGillivray,
who is 94 and lives by herself at the end of five miles of unmade
road.

We walked there in continuous sifting rain, past Tiroran where
the blind woman had been put out into a leaky byre, past green
slopes where Chrissie's grandmother remembered 'seventeen smokes'
before the exodus to America. Two of Chrissie's brothers had gone to
Patagonia before the Great War and she had never heard from them
again, another had become a tugboat captain in New York. Her
great-grandmother Mary MacDonald had written the classic Gaelic
hymn '*Leanabh an Aigh*' (Child in a manger, infant of Mary) with
its sweetly tender lyric. 'Her sister', said Chrissie, 'wrote down
all fourteen verses for her as she composed it.' Chrissie's own classic
language came out as she talked about her forebears over tea in her
living-room: 'I was born at the last house, just along there, where
my grandfather's grandfather lived, and grandfathers and grand-

fathers before them. It was good water from our spring that we had here, and my father asked for a drink of it as he was dying. It was his first drink and it was going to be his last.'

I heard the same language from John Campbell, three miles across the sea-loch at Bunessan, twenty miles round by car. His house, standing by itself on the level, heathery Ross of Mull, looked deserted, its door gaping, its windows unscreened. As I walked back to the car, a voice hailed me and he welcomed me into his room, which was as cold as the air outside. He was feeding a tiny fire with pieces torn from a Nairn's oatcake box. Both doors stood open and our conversation was drowned out at times by the boney screeches of the seagulls on the roof – fighting, he said, for bits of oatcake. Through small windowpanes we looked north across blackish moors to the sea and John recalled when the peat moss there had been 'white all over with the clothes of the people who were cutting the peats', including some from Tiree. He had used to bring peats home here himself, ten loads in a day, in a box tied onto his back with a rope, and when he no longer felt up to it a young lad carted them for him with a tractor and was given some in return.

On the way round to this side we had driven under the huge, tottering cliffs of Gribun, where the western extremity of Ben More falls 350 metres to the shore in half a mile. Twisting gorges burrow up into the ragged skyline and down them chunks of the brittle lava-rocks have spewed. They litter the narrow passage of grass between cliff and shore and one of them, the largest, is called the Tragedy Stone. It fell slap onto a young couple's cottage on their wedding night and obliterated the building and everything inside it. When I mentioned this story to John, he said, 'Yes indeed, that is the stone, and my grandmother saw the timbers sticking up all round it. The minister who married them came back to conduct their funeral. "They were comely and delightful," he said, "and in death they were not separated." Dust, they will be dust. The stone will not move till the Great Day and then everything will move.' John said this with no change of tone or pace or volume from his usual conversation, which was full of dramatic escapes – the men's at the distilling cave when the gaugers came, the Jacobites' hiding from the search-and-destroy platoons after Culloden, his when he fell from an army lorry in 1942, his head split open, blood all over the road: 'After eleven days the doctor said, "There is a flicker of life" . . . ' If he had known any clearance stories he would have told them in epic style. He was able to offer just one fugitive glimpse of what the people from Unnimore must have undergone: 'The people cleared from Morvern came over by Tobermory, on their way to Glasgow, and a bard who was with them made songs to cheer them up, because they were very chary of leaving.'

An hour later we were driving east by the old droving route through Glen More in a hollow blue twilight that seemed to ooze out of the island, from the mountain whose snowcap was exactly level with the base of the cloud, from Loch Scridain which is the glen's extension seaward. On its shore at Pennycross we ate at a deserted restaurant whose only function must be to cater for summer coaches passing through on their way to Iona. Seen across the blae levels of the water, with no house lights along its edge where Chrissie's grandmother counted the smokes, Mull looked an island doomed to be evacuated, parcelled off as real-estate, handed over to officers-and-gentlemen for their seasonal pleasures. Those who had gone had left too little trace. On Tiree, in Sutherland, on Skye, at least I had been meeting people everywhere who had moved not impossibly far from their origins or were still in touch with the emigrants. The emptiness of western Mull was like a lament at a pitch one could not hear:

> Where is there an end of it, the soundless wailing . . .
> Where is there an end to the drifting wreckage . . .
> We cannot think of a time that is oceanless
> Or of an ocean not littered with wastage . . .

On the map – and I now realised that I had always seen it like this – the image of Mull is of a land blown two ways at once, simultaneously fleeing eastward to embed itself in the mainland and opening westward like a mouth gaping and shouting, like an empty trap, like handless arms held out toward America.

CHAPTER ELEVEN

'A PLACE OF YOUR OWN
AND INDEPENDANT'
South-west Ontario

Writing about Canada is as daunting as embarking on the search for descendants of cleared families from Scotland through the broad lands of Ontario and Manitoba. How to encompass the vastness? On my first evening alone in Toronto vastness was vertical, a tower twenty-eight storeys high, skyscraping the humid orange darkness. Perched on its top, at first blink seeming near as the eye of an owl, the single spark of a star or planet glowed dimly, the only one among these strips of night cut up by cliffs of building. Four hours before, the pilot's voice had told us through the P.A., 'Prince Edward Island on your left.' I hustled across to a spare porthole and there was the narrow raft of it, steady in the stream of the St Lawrence, map-flat under filtered sunlight, irregular dark-green fur of forest, gamboge of mown fields, ochre fringe of beaches, greenish-cobalt blots of lagoons. The island was a dream, I've wakened again in a hotel that was once a warren for giant oblong rabbits with square heads and electric paws, they moved out in 1934 and left their burrows smelling of bakelite and pre-War talcum powder. The recycled air, fifty-five years old, is at 28°C. I ask the receptionist, 'Can you recommend somewhere good to eat and drink?' He utters classic alienated phrases, 'We-e-ll, I dunno – I *work* here?' Then he remembers Gilson's Place on Sherbourne. It's a patio on the shore of the traffic stream, cypresses in tubs, voluble quartets of students at white plastic tables. In the window of the indoor part a manager with a French name informs us via an elegant notice on heavy buff card that the hotel has been transformed:

★ No more rock-and-roll bands
★ No more prostitutes and drug dealers
★ No more questionable characters
★ No more insanitary conditions

Pleased on the whole not to be a questionable character, I drink two shots of rye on the rocks, which helps me to drowse off again each time I wake up in the stupefied air of my burrow, hearing dance music bop and howl from an open-air party out there in the orange mist . . .

. . . Which has turned cement-pale in the morning as the Gray Goose bus to Guelph chugs in middle gear past huge words on scaffold-stilts, NISSAN, HYUNDAI – past a tall Indian and a small sallow woman bending over a hot-dog trolley at the edge of a cleared site, intently rearranging plastic sauce bottles and greaseproof paper – past a single man ghost-grey with cement dust carrying a single grey plank in his grey hands towards the stub of a bridge bristling with reinforcement rods which presently will span this freeway – past a sequence of advertisements for auto dealers, realtors, hotels picked out on the embankment in prostrate conifer on a ground of whitened stones where a lanky young man with his hair tied behind in a rubber band is squatting with a paintbrush and rewhitening a single stone . . . I'm dwelling on each little focus of necessary labour to keep at bay the inconceivable mass of the continent crushing in around me – it only half works because each focus also signals, How little each one of us alters the colossal mass . . . I'm an immigrant, flotsam on the westbound flow – well insulated against all harm by Mastercard and Visa, letters of introduction, Hertz and Rentawreck, instant International S.T.D. to Anne at home. 'Experience The Trauma Of Exile,' it invites hopefully on the brochure for a Museum of Exile planned at Greenock which a friend shows me in Guelph. The trauma of tourism is all I can experience today, as a comfortably-off white man in eastern Canada. The other acute experience is what I begin to touch, at four or five removes, as I find stories like the one about an Orkney woman in 1851 who followed her husband out from Stromness to the site of the present-day Hamilton, hitched a ride with a man hauling a steam boiler with oxen up the road to Owen Sound, asked at Fergus for William Loutitt's and was told to follow the trail till she came to a right-hand fork marked with axe-blazes on the trees, and eventually reached her husband's log house on an ox-drawn stone-boat . . .

'Pioneer' and 'settler' now begin to replace words such as 'clearance', 'eviction', 'emigrant' in the material I listened to and read. Southern Ontario, on the isthmus between Lake Ontario and Lake Huron – a chief receiving ground for Highland incomers once the American Revolutionary War had receded safely into the past – was clearly a hunting ground for me, as was Manitoba, where the Kildonan people had finally settled at the forks where the Assiniboine flows into the Red River. Still further north, 9° south of the Arctic Circle at Churchill on the shore of Hudson Bay, had been a fit place to dump refugees from Sutherland. Down here, on the latitude of Rome or Barcelona, the settlers from Scotland had retreated in comparatively good order, more or less of their own choice. These qualifications matter, since most left against the pull of custom and emotion. They felt that living in the north of Scotland had become impossible for them. A seventy-year-old crofter in Harris told Napier that he remembered a better climate when it snowed in winter and 'The frost congested the soil so that nothing of the sap was lost, but we have perpetual rains now . . . I believe that has as much to do with the deterioration of the land as overcropping.' The leading historical geographer of the Hudson Bay region told me in Winnipeg that in his view the cooling and wetting of the climate that crept over in the seventeenth century 'made the Highlands barely habitable'.

Thirty-one heads of households who chose to leave were interviewed in Lerwick in April 1772 while their ship was stormbound. They were more or less unanimous that what was driving them out was oppressive services to the landlord and raised rents. John Catanoc from Chabster in Reay was sick of 'arbitrary and oppressive Services' which 'took up thirty or forty days of his Servants and Horses each year'. William Mackay from Craigie nearby had been chafing under 'unlimited and arbitrary' services 'at the pleasure of the Factor'. John Ross from Farr – forty years before the refugees crowded in there from Strath Naver – complained that factor and tacksman (chief tenant) 'never fail to take [cattle] at their own prices', which were little more than half what he could have got in the open market. William Sutherland from Strath Halladale complained that 'the Rents were raised, as Soldiers returning upon the Peace with a little Money had offered higher Rents . . . besides the Services were oppressive in the highest Degree ... he was obliged to find two Horses and two Servants from the middle of July to the end of Harvest solely at his own Expense, besides plowing, Cutting Turf, making Middings, mixing Dung and leading it out in Seed time, & beside cuting, winning leading & stacking 10 Fathoms of Peat yearly, all done without so much as a bit of bread or a drink to his Servants.' Such men, like many on the boats to North Carolina and elsewhere during the 'emigration mania' which seized 20,000 Scotsfolk at that time, were far from destitute and some were small employers. They would 'never have thought of leaving their native Country, could they have supplied their Families in it' but now they had to 'make room for Shepherds' and the land available for cattle and grain was shrinking fast: 'The whole system seemed to be closing in, dark and portentous.' In Canada they were looking for, and they found, a way of living 'unmolested by factor or laird'. The farm people I spoke to in Puslinch, Eramosa, Wellington, and Oxford Counties, and later in Glengarry County, were quietly claiming that lineage when they said their forebears had *not* been cleared but had come out with 'a bit of money' or 'some gold'.

Guelph was founded by the Ayrshire novelist John Galt in a characteristic flight of amiable idealism which was bound to attract less capital than it needed. The region was virgin forest and some of the settlers drank heavily (25 cents for a gallon jar of whisky) to lighten the depression of living down amongst the gloom. On one occasion when Galt wanted to impress some visitors with the attractions of the area, he got his woodsmen to open up a broad ride with their axes. 'The golden sun came shining through the colossal vista of smoke and flames' and a Yankee postboy exclaimed 'What an almighty place!' A hundred and seventy years later the entire area is as open to the sun as Suffolk or Dorset, hardly an acre is unkempt, the acres of produce seem endless, the massed strawberry-blond of wheat, the trembling frosty green of oats ('Oats Equal Health', a railway hoarding claimed), the avenues of corn (maize) rustling their conical heads in the warm wind while Japanese cars hiss past at 85 kilometres an hour, never more, and leathery couples like oldies in a life insurance ad, the man in a check shirt and peaked denim cap, the woman in a flowered dress, end their days healthily on the front stoop, shaded by spreading maple trees. After the first blitzkrieg of felling and uprooting, harrowing the ground with a pine branch dragged along and sowing seed among the stumps, the later nineteenth-century generations, dismayed by the unsheltered tracts and the snow winds razoring across them, planted hedges as fast as they could to recreate the leafy enclosure of the old country.

Among the fields and shelter-belts Guelph didn't expand much, didn't fail either, and remains an ideal place to live, not to grow rich. Through it loiters the River Speed, a name which must have been one of Galt's pawky wee jokes since the water barely moves enough to urge along the pigeon's breast-feathers and lemony willow-leaves lacquered on its surface. Around it the farmland is so homogeneous that at first it was hard to orient myself. Where exactly was Toronto? (Not that I much cared.) What lands, or cities or lakes or highways, lay under that far-off rippled shoal of cloud stranded permanently up there, defining distance like the sky in some Western movie shot in Nevada? I gradually got my bearings as I moved out from Guelph in widening circles along a vine of contacts originating in Ted Cowan, a Scottish professor at the university, Hugh MacMillan, a document-collector whose exploratory instincts have all the panache and staying-power of his forebear, a MacMillan from Loch Arkaig who had worked for the Nor'Westers in the days of their fur wars with the Hudson Bay mob, and the local collection in the Public Library.

Among tall plumes of cedar and walnut trees, in the Crieff Hills south of Aberfoyle, lived people whose grandparents had come over in the 1830s and were pleased with their decision. 'We are not kept in terror by hard landlords,' wrote Daniel Stewart to his brother in Dundee, or by 'great rents, high taxes, nor by anything of the kind'. One old farmer, Donald Stewart, whose grandfather had emigrated from Kinlochrannoch in 1834, gave me a glimpse of a quite other contingent. He lives in a limestone and granite house, built for both shelter and shade, and he occupies it, aged 87 and five years a widower, like a seasoned kernel inside its ribbed, bleached, hammered casket of a shell. He called me 'Craig', looking at me with unblinking black eyes, his sparse white hair brushed hard back, his upper lip frosted with bristles. Although he had sold off his stock five years before and his hayfields were rented out to a neighbour, his hands were still kipper-brown, the bunch of fingers broader than the palm, the nails standing out from the pulps after decades of planting and harnessing and ploughing. He remembered his father carrying burdens of corn twenty miles to the mill 'with a tump band round his forehead'. The toil must have been great, for all the mellow face of the land today, and often for poor rewards when prices were low. His erstwhile neighbour, Bessie McCormack Ross from Argyll, whom I met presently at Cambridge further south, recalled that at their poorest in the Twenties they had scooped the eyes out of the potatoes for planting and eaten the rest. 'The saying around here,' said Donald Stewart, 'was "The Scotchmen made for the hills, the Englishmen got the good land, the Irishmen had to take what was left".' To my eye the Crieff Hills were shallow moraines but Donald knew they were hard to till:

> We can grow a better sample of grain than the heavy land up around Guelph but it's hard to work, it's very stony, it's chattery, and there's a lot of sidling in the hills. Down below the house there I moved stone piles and stone piles by hand. Now it's all machines – they never *touch* the hay now, not when they're mowin', nor when they're balin'.

His phrasing was continuously physical and alert – I had never heard the core meaning of 'sidling' before – and you knew he would vouch for nothing he was not perfectly sure of. He even faulted himself for not remembering the name of someone he had never even met. It did not detract from the special value of this memoir:

> Before my time people came from the island – Uist, is it? They were sent out here on the boat, I think, and they landed in Hamilton [25 miles south-east on Lake Ontario]. The landlord, or whoever, had got tired of them. They just had shacks alongside of the road – most of this side road here. Well, they had Fordyce, a weaver, and the Muileach – I dunno ... But they called them 'the shanty people'. There was Dougal MacPhee too ... They just set up a shack and the people that owned the place, they didn't seem to mind, y'know. Some of 'em worked for my grandfather. They were considered a very industrious people – they kep' a cow or sump'n'. I dunno what they done in the wintertime. There was a house in the corner of my place down here – Dougal MacPhee was there – and a log barn, I remember. Quite a number of 'em was Catholic. And there was a woman, they called her Nelly Sailor – she was from Uist ...

And Donald hammered the table as he tried and failed to remember her unmarried name.

Here was a glimpse at least – as direct as I could hope for?
– of cleared people from the driven wave of 1851. MacPhee is a
South Uist name and the people of that island are mostly Catholic;
Fordyce sounds more Aberdeenshire; and 'the Muileach' will have
been just one of many refugees from those gutted lochside lands
in Mull. Even in the country of land unlimited, they were clinging
to the fringe of the economy – existing by the grace of 'the pioneer
custom of letting cattle graze freely on the road allowance and on
any unoccupied land'. Clearly the more settled Highland incomers
had perceived them as rejects or second-class citizens while respect-
ing them for managing at all. Would I find any of their descendants,
anywhere? Would they have put down root enough, held land long
enough or been unvexed enough about their recent past, to reveal
themselves as openly as the less maltreated people who had chosen
to come here? Or would they have merged without trace into the
toiling crowds in the ports, the canals, the railroads, 'hooded hordes
swarming/ Over endless plains, stumbling in cracked earth/ Ringed
by the flat horizon only'?

For the next few weeks the Uisters, like an endangered species,
flickered elusively through such memoir as I could find. Four hundred had come out on the *Mount Stuart* in 1849, bound for Middlesex County, which is in the western end of the state, between London
and Lake Huron. Few spoke English. Many died on the voyage. A
party of the survivors became visible and audible in the words of
Nancy Jackson, who has retired to her family's elegant farmhouse
fifteen miles south-west of Guelph. She received me like a Southern
belle, in an oyster silk dress, standing beside a white birch tree. Mown
hay quilted the sunlit knolls through which the track wound its way.
It was a time-warp back to the days when the settlers were becoming
comfortable. The cuts made by their axes were still visible on the log
ends of the house built by Mrs Jackson's great-grandparents. It stood
among the hay nearby, disused, the wooden siding breached at one
corner, disclosing the massive diameters of the logs. She brimmed
with history, some of it oral, passed down from forebears who
had come here from Campbeltown, Kintyre, in the early 1830s.
She knew that immigrants in receipt of aid (most of the Uisters)
rarely got as far as Guelph, which diminished the elusive species
a little more. Of the eighty headed for the Crieff Hills area forty
died on the way: 'Cholera took its toll.' Nevertheless their piper,
Malcolm MacLennan, led them here from Hamilton and lived on

among the MacPhees, MacVicars, MacDonalds, and MacLeods like
the musical heart of his people:

> He would appear out of the woods, and from the swamps,
> he would appear at every funeral and every wedding, he would
> appear out of the blue and there would be a party right there.
> He would stand on a hill between Lots 5 and 6, at the rear of
> the Gore, and blow his pipes on a wild, stormy night.

The last of the MacLennans to live here, Sarah, a niece of the
piper's, had died in 1972 aged 103. The piper had left his pipes
to his son, who went off south to New York State.

Where did the rest of the Uisters, and other islanders, find a caravanserai? Canada had become the chief asylum, expending five times
as much on famine relief as the Americans, who would not allow
people with ship fever to disembark at all. The passage to Quebec
was the cheapest transatlantic route and the vilest: thirty per cent
of passengers died on the voyage or just after landing. Kingston, the
depot where the St Lawrence reaches Lake Ontario, was 'deserted'
for a time because people were terrified of 'emigrant disease'. This
repulsion between the two waves of incomers, both from the same
broad region of the old country, figured grievously in other memoirs I found. The Uisters went on upstate, finding work where they
could. On Highway 6, just north of Guelph, where the Fergus road
forks west to Elora, I spoke to the Blyths, whose family have farmed
here since the 1820s. Their stone house was an unbelievable treasury
of collectables – immaculate groups of flatirons, candlesticks, soda
siphons, Guelph crocks, fat stoneware jars freely decorated in blue
glaze, on which Mrs Blyth is an expert – and decoy ducks and glass
bobbles from lightning conductors, which have just recently become
sought-after, and shotguns and muskets and swords, including the
famous mercenary David Bruce's cutlass, and one that could have
been used at Culloden, and another belonging to a man who volunteered on the first day of the American Civil War . . . The Blyths
had steadily amassed, for five generations. I got a glimpse of their
position at the crown of the local tree when Mr Blyth recounted that
in the middle of last century 'two Highlanders', who had never used
an axe, were employed by his great-grandfather to clear forest and
managed to fell ten acres of maple in a day. Here was the basic labour
of the landless. I glimpsed it again in a worm-eaten cashbook I was

shown at Dunvegan, Glengarry County. Duncan MacMillan's list of his jobs expresses his weariness in little desolate touches: 'Chopping all day and so on and so forth' (November 21st, 1859). 'Putting in ashes before noon. Raining all day' (November 19th). 'Thrashing oats all day' (December 23rd). A heartfelt repetition: 'Sunday Sunday Sunday' (December 25th). And, unusually, 'Chopping fire wood *for ourselves*' (my italics: December 9th).

Ten miles north again, in Fergus, a merchant and magistrate called Fordyce, who had been a Kirk elder in Aberdeen before migrating in 1835, recorded the purgatory of the 'Uisters' in his journal year by year. In 1847 a meeting was held in the tavern to set up a relief committee to collect money for 'the destitute Highlanders'. On August 24th, 1849 'a great number of Emigrants arrive' on their way north to Owen Sound on Georgian Bay: 'All from the Duke of Argyle's property, very poor and some sick.' A year later many more came 'but whether or not to make any stay I do not know'. Next year a contingent from Stornoway 'cannot get into the Tavern for want of money'. In the next few weeks they have begun to die 'from bowel complaint'. By the autumn 'many Highlanders have the Small Pox'. By the end of the year this is 'gaining ground', in spite of generous collections among the Church of Scotland congregation. The dead were buried in unmarked graves in the Auld Kirk Yard, 27 by the end of the year, 'some without a name'. The living sheltered in sheds and stables, in the ashery, in kilns at the mill and lean-to's put up against outbuildings. Some found jobs in harness-making, smithying, weaving and dyeing. Some went on up the road to Owen Sound but 'They seemed to have nothing, and not to realise the severity of the winter they would have to go through'. They had heard of the Fergus settlement 'thro' publications in Scotland and by word of mouth'. By the end of 1851, 240 more had arrived, 'turfed out of their homes, thrown into the slums of Glasgow and Aberdeen ... They were a proud group of people who detested having to take charity, even when they were starving to death.'

Mr Fordyce and some of his fellows were good-hearted and practical. In his community opinion was as divided as ours is today when we consider whether to admit people from Uganda or Hong Kong. In the Wellington County Archive – housed in a massive fortress of a building which turned out to have been the workhouse, I looked up what the local papers had had to say. The *Elora Backwoodsman*, supposedly a Reform paper, commented with sprightly venom:

> [Owners who] have allowed the Highlanders to locate upon their
> lands ... [should do] all in their power, in future, to prevent any
> more of the same class from settling thereon ... These particular
> specimens of breechless humanity are but indifferent honest, and
> the very reverse of industrious and thrifty – they prefer beg-
> ging to working. Sturdy vagrants are they, by no means easily
> abashed, and having lived for a year or two at the expense of
> the working community are naturally unwilling to relinquish their
> Arab-like independence for a life of such toil as has enriched their
> countrymen in Aldboro, Orford and Dunwich ... Mr Galbraith
> had evidently been led away by the national clannishness, and by
> sympathy with his countrymen ... The intention of the people of
> Fergus is simply to force them to work ... Let the Highlanders
> once understand they are no longer to levy black mail upon the
> community, and they will betake themselves to axe and spade.

This was in August 1852, by which time, as we know from
Fordyce's journal, they had already taken up many trades. The
leader-writer has the view of ethnic minorities that we find in the
Sun today, though he is better educated; he comes across like a young
gentleman from Suffolk who is already tetchily tired of his job on a
paper way out in the sticks. He adroitly sounds the chauvinist note,
an attitude not confined to Englishmen. In one of a long series of
letters by Highlanders on both sides of the water which I read in a
farmhouse thirty miles west-south-west in Oxford County – well on
the Uisters' way to their destination in Middlesex – Peter MacLeod, a
settler of only ten years' standing, already wants to dissociate himself
from fellow-countrymen who are landless. He had come from Muie,
near Rogart, in 1841 – a township later famous for its Seven Men
who defied eviction in 1889. In one letter from Scotland he had given
his brother news of a neighbour's marriage to a Sutherland from
'Incheap' – presumably a relative of the Inchcape Sutherland who
defied eviction at the time of the Lettaidh burning. This origin in a
heartland of struggle against landlordism did nothing to help Peter
MacLeod sympathise with the cleared. Perhaps his own hardships
had made him anxious to separate himself from the needy.

On September 23rd, 1845 he wrote to his brother in Muie:

Our own nearest friend John MacLeod has nothing to boast of, he is sitting on a lot they call the clergy reserves, there is every fifth lot in many of the townships laid out to pay the ministers, and many of those who would write home that they had so much land and property was only sitting on these lots and still had not the least claim on them ... A man will find it very difficult for the first few years, and persons of common sense may take that to consideration, when one has to begin in wild woods to clear land, build houses, put up stock &c &c. but after a while, one will feel more comfortable and independent than being under control of Proprietors, and Factor, and troubled with shepherds ...

Six years later, proprietors and factors having done their worst to the Uisters and Muileachs, Peter MacLeod can muster no fellow-feeling for the victims:

Railway has commenced in this neighbourhood but does not get along with such speed as it did in Britain, the contractors are yankies or men from the states, the workmen are all low Irish, and western highlanders, the one is very little better than the other, there are a number of people in this neighbourhood, who emigrated the last two or three years from the western highlands, they are a disgrace to the nation, I had no idea, that civilization was so much wanting in any part of Scotland, as these wretched creatures appear to be, both in regards of cleanliness and behaviour, they are mostly papists [probably Uist and Barra], and those of them who profess Presbyterianism seem to have left their religion beyond the wide Atlantic ...

The most notable MacLeod, with quite a different viewpoint, to settle here had been Donald, the Strath Naver mason and author of *Gloomy Memories*. The Canadian edition of it was published in the nearby county town of Woodstock in winter 1857. The *Sentinel*, which helped him publish it, had been founded in 1854 and is still flourishing but nobody at its office had heard of Donald MacLeod, nor had they at the town museum. They gave me a directory and in it I found two stonemasons called Donald MacLeod listed as residents in 1852. I was now being guided by Woody Lambe, a farmer, naturalist, and champion banjo player, who traced his descent from the Lady Caroline Lamb with whom Byron had his famous affair. As I prepared to write about my time in Oxford County, a Christmas card came from him to say that they were enduring temperatures of −15°C week after week and coyotes had taken four of his sheep. While I was there, the heat built into terrific electric storms and we sat on his back porch, while he barbecued chops from one of his own animals, and the rain came surfing in across the maize-heads with a cumulative hissing roar I hadn't heard since the monsoon came at us across the tea bushes and banana palms near Kandy in 1960. Between rains he took me round the neighbourhood from one Highland family to another, driving me down the merciless straight dirt roads while bluebirds winged from power-pole to power-pole, attracted to the nesting boxes that had been put up by a farmer friend called Bernie Mackay. These roads run down the grid of that Ontario township system – with its lots, lines, and gores to fit the rectangles onto the curved shapes of the ground – which was itself a replica of the crofting pattern clamped onto north-west Scotland.

In Ontario the culture so drastically reshaped was the native-American. South of Guelph two settlements with Highland names, Moriston and Badenoch, were established at the expense of Indian villages, one becoming the site of a stone house, the other of a brickyard. So one people scorned as primitive throve at the expense of another.

> Those to whom evil is done
> Do evil in return.

The Mississauga people sold 640,000 acres to the Ontario government in 1818, including Erin, Eramosa, which meant 'dog', and 'Garafraxa', which meant 'panther country'. The early farmers used the Indian trails 'until travel began to interfere with settlers' crops. The trails were much firmer than the newly surveyed concession roads, many of which came to a dead-end in a soft swamp.' From the Winnipeg–Toronto plane some weeks later, looking down from 29,000 feet in the area south of Muskoka Lakes, I thought I saw a trace of this bald-headed disrespect for the original culture in the form of a ruled green line through the bluer forest. It made straight for a group of pools or lochans and re-emerged at the far side of them, and would be hard to explain in any other way. Up in Manitoba it was impossible to be unaware of the native-American peoples, both 'Indian' and Inuit. Down in Ontario all that was left was a handful of the beautiful four-syllable names with their light endings – Onondaga, Conestoga. It took continual effort to remain aware that the Highland folk with whom I solidarised as agonists in the Clearances had only rooted here by dint of another clearance.

In the Old Log Church Cemetery, above a marsh near Embro, Oxford County, which Woody showed me on the way to the farms of various Mackays, I could read the epitaphs of earlier Mackays, and Rosses and Sutherlands and MacKenzies and MacDonalds; one of them, Isabel, born in the year of the 'Forty-five, was the daughter of a blacksmith who had straightened scythe-blades to make swords for Culloden. For his pains his grandson Angus had had to emigrate, taking his aged mother with him. The graveyard was close-shorn but disused. Two stones were leaning together and when I pulled them apart to read some names I saw that the marble angels' wings above the epitaph for Donald and Margaret McKay had sprouted the papery flutes of a woodwasps' nest. The jet insects with their slim waists stirred uneasily. Mosquitoes came onto us from the marsh nearby, their bites raised smarting lumps and we soothed them with alcohol swabs, given us by Bernie Mackay, which were meant for cleansing cows' teats.

These early graveyards, the log houses, and even some of the stone ones were jetsam stranded to one side of Canada's newer courses and they secreted an essence of original Ontario that could almost be inhaled like perfume. At Marden, the only farm near Guelph to be occupied by one family since it was created (in 1828), Mrs MacDonald directed me to the second of the log houses occupied by her forebears. Behind a lofty wooden barn, leaning a little as though tired, was a timber building twenty feet long, ten across, and barely six feet from floor to eave. This had been home for ten people until the end of the nineteenth century. Then it became a pig house. The logs had parted along their grain and one had been fluted hollow by insects and rot. It looked doomed whereas another I was shown near Fergus had been superbly resurrected. It had been built in 1849 by Duncan Cameron and his family from Balinoe on Tiree. They were squatters and when a Toronto speculator called Black bought the land he set fire to the house to clear out the people. Before the flames got a hold they rafted it across the Grand River and put it up again on a site now under suburban gardens. A few years ago it was bought and moved again, to a leafy hill above currant fields, by a fruit farmer who is making an agricultural museum in a wooden barn as big as a cruciform priory. The Cameron house will be a studio for his wife.

So life turns into 'heritage'. It is better than obliteration. The Tiree man's great-grandson, an 82-year-old forester called Hugh Cameron, who lives three miles away, showed me over the ancestral home and congratulated its new owner on how well he had remantled it. This man was a lanky giant with the obsessional gleam of an inventor, very proud of his stainless-steel system for refining the maple syrup he tapped from towering trees along the highway. The tamarack logs of the house were wholly sound and only needed to be rechinked – the caulking between them which used to be done with clay, then whitened. With intent pride Hugh took me round the back and showed me the logs which were still fire-blackened. The char no longer came off on the fingers, of course, but it was clearly burnt. It might have been this family trauma that caused Hugh to insist that his forebears were burnt out of Tiree – the like of which I had never heard tell of on the island itself:

> At the very west end, near the ocean – in back of the Duke of Argyll's summer place – you can see the remains of houses there, like rocks in the ground. And they were burnt all right – they had black charcoal in their interstices. And in the ground – oh, I had a good look! – and there was charcoal, bits of it, in there. It doesn't rot, you know.

As squatters the Camerons must have been without resources other than their skills – Donald was a stonemason. Here at last was a place where one family from the driven wave had come to rest and rooted. With difficulty. According to Hugh:

> They hadn't got any papers. Those people couldn't speak any English. According to the Censor – I read that Census for 1851 on microfilm – they had 'Very poor English' and it was hard to tell how old they were. Well, they must have made fun of the official people because they were afraid, and they must have told them jokes instead of the real thing.

Hugh's great-uncle, also Hugh, had been born in the log house. In a photo of 1880 he is a lad of fourteen, standing amongst a great gang of men in dark clothes beside a turbid river, loggers who balanced out across a raft of trunks to chop away the key log, then race back before they were swept downstream. The house had been abandoned in 1917, then restored for living in when housing was scarce and expensive during the Slump. Now it lay gently beached above the ocean of farmlands, which were visible in dazzling layers between the logs, green-bladed close at hand, blue with the haze of their volatile oils on the horizon. Through the door-space a sign said –

U

PICK

WHITE RED BLACK

CURRANTS

FOR SALE

As Hugh recounted his forebears' travels, Tiree with its freight of families and animals and fields surfaced into sight, across there in its place on the one continuum of sunlight spanning the Atlantic. The middle-aged couple from Balinoe and Cornaigmore, having endured the six weeks' voyage, 'came up the St Lawrence with their trunks and things, and my great-grandmother, she was carrying her last baby, who was my grandfather, in her arms. But Aunty Effie was twelve years old so she could carry the baby for a piece, and Donald, who was ten, he might not carry it too far. Duncan, he was a strong man – they were all strong people, they couldn't have been anything else or they would have succumbed to the disease they were exposed to. They went right to Montreal because the cholera was very bad in Quebec. The water they were drinking was from the British Isles and it would be rotten by that time. They would have a fairly good supply of heather dew – Scottish whisky – and if they put that in the water it would kill anything.'

They landed at Whitby and walked the 45 miles north to Beaverton on Lake Simcoe, which was 'teeming with fish' and where they had cousins. The only word of their clearance from Tiree had come down from Hugh's great-aunt Mary: 'They were sent away from home, on the ship.' From Beaverton they came to Fergus 'to get a farm when this land was opened up'. They had one cow by then 'and the cow walked all the way here' (eighty miles).

They were all born with stones in their hands – able to build. And in this country you can see their work – all around Fergus. Great-grandfather was a wheelwright too [a common trade on the level land of Tiree, rare on Mull where loads had to be hauled on sledges over the rough ground]. My father had that skill too – it's amazing how the genes come down, and make a people. He built himself a sleigh, nicest looking sleigh in the township, and he had a team of horses to match. My other grandfather, he was a chopper, he would clear a hundred acres – when you look around today you cannot believe that it was all once huge, tall trees on every side.

His house was wooden too, and one night it went up in flames – whole family were all got out, and saved their things including his violin that he'd made. He went down to his sister Mary's and he said, 'Well, Mary, the bugs caught hell tonight' – the powder-post beetle would have been in the timbers, the sawdust to drop down between the logs and the siding. So he played his fiddle till morning, and they all sat around and listened to him. He got his team and he drove them all off up to Owen Sound [85 miles]. And I never heard what happened to him. You see, there was no communication – letters were very hard to get. But the graveyard up there is just full of Camerons. And on all the barns, 'Cameron Enterprise'. Those kind of people, they couldn't be beaten. Never asked anybody for anything, not the Duke of Argyll or anybody else, only to be left alone. That's the way I look at it.

Hugh's words about letters made me thankful again, as I had been on Prince Edward Island, that any correspondence had lasted at all – those single franked sheets addressed simply to 'Zora, Upper Cannada' or 'Woodstock, Oxford County, Canada West' or 'Indian Lands, Upper Canada' or 'Lot 19th, First Concesfion, near Galt, Upper Cannada, Ameraca' or (the faultiest I saw) 'Dugald Mc Maistair, Town Ship Lockale, Count of Glenary [Lochiel Township, Glengarry County], Upper Cannady'. Reading them led me in among the cross-currents of family relationship, exposed (especially if there was a whole run of letters) with the nuance and immediacy of an epistolary novel.

Some of the letter-writers are sturdy and straightforward, others shiver on the brink of migration like nervous swimmers and stay that way for years. At the sturdy end of the gamut, William Beattie from Slains in north-east Aberdeenshire writes on June 13th 1836 to his brother George, who has settled fifteen miles north of Guelph:

Der brother I writ you from the land of our birth and am hapy
to her from you that you and your Mistras are both wel and I am
hapy to her that you hav a place of your own and independant
that is what we could not any of us had her [You have] the ruts
and trubel but they must rot when the tress get cut down . . .
[Tell me] what entrist your bank gis for the hundred pound and
what depth your soil is and what avrek retorn hit will give I am
not so much afraid of the ruts of trees as you would think . . .

The man is practical, ready for anything. Had his brother stressed
the hard work of felling and stumping to get it off his chest? or to
deter his relatives from coming out and adding to the settlers' burden? Most of those who were left in Scotland sound hard-pressed,
even desperate. Neighbours are leaving ('New South Wales is more
in Vogue now than America'), food is short ('There has been a great
famine in the highlands of Scotland . . . There has been a great storm
and a great death among the sheep': June 10th 1837). Pleas for money
to help with the passage or promises to repay it as soon as possible
occur on almost every sheet: 'John McRobert is intending to cross
at Martinmas and if he do that you will get your money at that time
and if he do not cross at that time you will get it in spring when I
hope we will be the bearers of it our selves.'

It must have been acutely unsettling to live on in the homestead,
wondering whether to sell up, losing neighbour after neighbour,
hanging on each mail for positive signals from abroad, haunted
(or challenged) by visions of what was waiting for them in those
alien forests. The delay while money was scraped together gave time
for contrary emotions to ferment. A forebear of Nancy Jackson's,
Archibald MacCallum, wrote from Campbeltown to Crieff Hills on
March 3rd, 1843:

I think from the tenor of your letter as well as from others, that
there is a discontentedness among a great number that goes to that
country. The reason is not given. I think it is from the loneliness
of the place and the great distance between their neighbours, and
perhaps the want of the means of Grace [church and minister].

Without the half of the correspondence sent from Ontario to Argyll,
we can't quite interpret this. My intuition is that the discontent was
at least as much the stay-at-home's as the emigrant's. Archibald was

still tied, he felt envious, he hankered to rub the bloom off the new country for which really he was longing. There he was, stuck among old people whose time was past: grandfather 'has gathered some courage, and is much better than he was, since he began to do something for he was very dull a long time after Neil went away'. Two years later he is still stuck and palpably upset:

I made ready to go to America last year and paid £2 of the freight and the day I was going away my money was stolen and I could not get ... I would be there before a month of harvest if God spares me and as soon as this letter comes to your hand write to me without losing any time and let me know what you are going to do with me and if it be that I must lay here I must do it. I'll [hole in paper] as long as I live, my heart will be there. I hope to God this is the last letter I'll write to you from Scotland.

In letter after letter we feel this strain of distance and time-lag. The last letter received has been too long in coming and not reassuring or definite enough in its message. The families are trying hard to support each other but the occasions for bad blood are numerous. An Irish settler I heard of in Glengarry County (whose mother had carried a sock with a rock in it to protect herself en route from Quebec) played canny and wrote as little as possible: 'They didn't want good news and I wouldn't send bad news.' Most others try to carry out their ticklish obligations. The letters I read at the farm of Mrs Mackay, Woody Lambe's friend, at the end of a dirt road among copses and cornfields in Oxford County, lay bare the whole fraught experience. On April 3rd, 1839 the mother, a widow living at Muie in Strath Fleet, dictates a letter through her son Donald. She is hurt that William in Canada has written so rarely and says this candidly after her opening civilities: 'It is very surprising that you are so forgetful in writing to us, we received only one letter since you went away, you might take to consideration that nothing could give us more pleasure than to hear from you at any time, but especially in times of war' (the Rising of 1837, which must have looked much more serious from abroad than in Ontario itself). Another son, Robert, has gone away to work on the 'Rail Roads' and has caught smallpox, which has delayed a promised visit home. She craves to cross the water herself with her other (grown-up) children but first she needs William's advice, and probably his sheer welcome:

... let us know if you thought we should go there, we understand that those who are there, do not like to counsel any to go as the distance is so long, and people so liable to accidence, however, if you are well pleased there yourself, and doing well, and if you would have a thought that we would do well likewise, you may have an eye out for a good lot for us ...

Six years later, on February 15th 1845, William sounds caught as he tried to make a clear response:

I really have no advice to give any one, but people who are in a comfortable way of living there would be very foolish to put themselves to trouble to come here. Still I say, that a poor man who would be able and willing to work, would do better here, it is not easy to make money here, but a poor man will live better and more independent here than there, for my own part I have nothing to boast of as yet but I think more of this country than the mother country in many ways: though I shall never forget my native place as I love the very stones, yet I feel more liberty here, still every place has its own difficulties on this side of time.

For once the letters sent from Canada still exist, presumably carried out by the next wave. In September, Peter MacLeod – last heard of taking his mother's dictation and teaching shepherds' children in Strath Fleet – is writing back from Woodstock to Scotland, apologising to a stay-at-home brother for not saying a proper farewell:

I understand that you was a little offended at me for not informing you that I intended to emigrate to America. I own that I should not do any thing that might be offensive to you, but I was only a few days considering it myself and as soon as I made up my mind I wrote a letter to you.

Peter himself is now in the delicate position of counsellor and his exhilaration at starting afresh in Canada is alloyed by his awareness that it is no utopia:

We cut down about five acres of wood; cutting wood in winter is very pleasant work here, although the frost is very severe it is dry and there is great shelter among the trees, it was very exciting for me to go round visiting old acquaintances here for the first few days when I was considerably disappointed by the circumstances of a great many of them . . . John Murray piper is not so wealthy as we thought at home . . . I would not give my mother's house if it were rightly fitted up, for half a dozen of their houses. I do not mean to be exposing their nakedness but I use plain conversation, however there are many of them better off than ever they would be in Scotland.

His own brother Alexander, for example. On January 14th 1848 a neighbour writes to say that he is a 'dutiful and Industrious young man – no gossoping with him'. He 'has some money about him just now. But it will soon take the wing.' By April Alexander's own letter to Ontario is frankly a begging one:

> . . . this year is very slack in work here, there is very little jobs going on except a piece road between Rogart and Torroboll . . . In conclusion as my Mother is often poorly & plenty to do at home and as things is very slack, & as there is no way for me making none, I thinking to put in your mind that I am much in need of some clothes which I have know way of geting, you and Robt. will send me some assistance for what I mention. therefore when Robert will come to you I will mention my subject to him but indeed if I had any other way of getin it I would not trouble you for anything, but do not strait yourself. I only say if it was easy for you both that I am much in the need as when a person is not like his neighbours in clothes he is counted half a man.

In this case at least, the stay-at-home sounds like a born loser, dutiful, worried, tentative, unable to get out of the rut. On July 4th 1852 the ground officer takes it upon himself to write and tell the Canadian relatives that their people in Muie 'gave me no trouble but always received me with a *welcome smile*' – for a Sutherland ground officer this was no doubt a rare delight. By next spring Alexander is reporting that these nice estate people have decided 'to cut a piece of our pasture from us which will be added to his sheep farm it is a hard time for Muie tenants as they must give up there auld fashion, for our part we have know beasts on the pasture at this time'. The more his fortunes slump, the more religious he waxes. 'May the Giver of all be thanked for his Goodness to us all,' he writes, on the page which says that their stock is gone and mother is very poorly with rheumatism. As the Sixties wear away, he complains that the potatoes 'are no fit for a diet', that the Ontario folk don't write, that they never come back to see their mother . . . By the winter of 1861–2 he has missed for good his chance of escape and he almost knows it:

> I would sometimes think I might go to America and get myself some comfortable but I am fear'd there is nothing for me but wild woulds as the land is so very high. I must say, 'repent for to spend the best of my days among our stones' – I think if I had done the half in America I might have a better reward but on the other hand I do not repent for spending my time in charge of a weak and Dear Mother . . .

'Wild woulds' is an uncannily apt motto for this man who is always supposing, never quite making it. In the last of his letters (1864–5) to have survived at Mrs Mackay's he is sadly reproaching his brothers for failing to write; almost behaving as though they were still at home with him when he says that 'a good warm Winter Plaid' has been made for them; and recording illnesses and deaths: 'so many of our acquaintances is Brought to there long homes . . . May we all strive to enter in at the strait gate, and live as those that have to die.'

From the lack of any mention of it Alexander seems never to have married. He shapes himself in my mind as one of those figures from a nineteenth-century novel, more usually female, who are spectres of virtue, self-effaced to vanishing point by living for others. In an age of survival by migration he had not the hardihood to prevent the difficulties entering into him and unbending his springs of action. How different from Hugh Cameron's forebears – whose image I felt I was seeing in Hugh himself. At the age of 82 he had suddenly decided to grow a beard – the white fringe of it round a tanned face with bright brown eyes made him a Noah figure, whose ark still perched there on its hill. He had recently had his leg mauled when the motor mower ran over him but he was stumping about briskly 'to keep the wound drained'. His dog, injured in the same accident, was equally indomitable. He had been found running on the road with a bullet-mark scorched along his flank, just after a car roared off. Hugh's woodcraft, now in its fourth generation as a Cameron trade, equally represented qualities that had been vital in the creating of a new society and must have been sheer loss to the old one. The Camerons and the MacLeods had to cope with a fierce world. Pioneers in the Guelph area ate porcupine flesh raw and chased deer over the snow-crust: when they floundered they were clubbed between the antlers by the children of the family, girls as well as boys, father came to cut their throats, mother salted them down. The forests harboured wolf and lynx and the settlers shot them for bounty money. In the heavy snows a farmer would drive a team of oxen through the forest, trailing a log to clear a passage-way to school for the children – if he had oxen. Five generations later the visible remnant of that life is the well-oiled rifle on nails on the parlour wall – very likely the same wall the great-grandparents made from cedar or tamarack logs when they built their second, permanent home. Outside, the fields are immaculate quilts of produce and fleets of machinery are parked in the shade of tall harvestores. The farm people told me again and again, 'You can't make a living from a 100-acre farm anymore' and lamented some unspecified heyday. It still looks like a heyday as the horn of plenty disgorges its loaves and cereals and salads into the swelling gullet of the cities.

CHAPTER TWELVE

LEAVES ON THE VINE
Eastern Ontario

High summer was a great time to travel through Ontario, past the solid brass or bronze of wheat, the lime-and-lemon of barley ripening, the maize rustling its green plumage (but Mr Blyth on the Elora road had complained that it was 'pointing up too much' in the drought). We were driving, Hugh and Muriel MacMillan and I, from Guelph to Glengarry County in the extreme east where Ontario tapers between the Ottawa and the St Lawrence. Why go there, against the immigrant tide, when logic would be taking me north to the cleared people's first strong foothold on the Red River in Manitoba? Partly because my project was growing, inevitably, to include voluntary migrants as well as cleared people, partly because Hugh and Muriel knew the settler families in Glengarry and my policy was to follow the grapevine.

Back in Guelph there had been a bad half-hour when I had returned my hired car to the depot and was standing with my bits of luggage on the sidewalk on a scorching Sunday morning. No traffic was moving yet. Naked tarmac surfaces curved down to the bridge over the Speed. I had torn myself away from my cool basement flat at Louise Colley's in Caledonia Street. Now I felt like a grain of sand on a deserted beach. That limbo phase was setting in – I could feel it – when one phase of a journey gives way uncomfortably to another and you feel you are only as visible, as actual, as valid as your credit cards. But it was only my neurosis: here came the MacMillans at last, loaded to the gunwales with cases and boxes and books and sheaves of print-out, bound for St Pierre and Miquelon, Hugh behind the wheel like some colonial mariner in a white bush shirt and a broad-brimmed hat. There was talk of 'going to Rae's for brunch', which sounded like toast and eggs in a quiet suburb somewhere. At Argyle, east of Lake Simcoe, we pulled off the freeway at an intersection and parked behind a frame house anchored among a million hectares of serried corn. Inside, the rooms had been opened out and hung with fine original paintings – a totemistic owl figure in ink-black and ochre, portraits of people in buses and city rooms done in bleak grey-blues like Toronto in the thaw. Rae Fleming was a young connoisseur, son of the local storekeeper, professional biographer, expert cook – in a few minutes we were eating sausage he had made with meat from a pig killed locally (he pointed through the window at its old home) and the many-limbed ground-floor space was filling with characters, all bright-eyed and handsomely dressed from church. A social-history lecturer handed round stylish brochures, complete with texts of hymns, for a Presbyterian rally he had organised. The niece of a former Ontario premier, expansive in flowered silk, first-named everyone professionally and instantly began to denounce, with no apparent cue, the subsidising of students – 'Many of them should not *be there!*' An elderly minister with thin white hair and an ill, yellowish complexion was gently receiving compliments on the sermon he had just been preaching. A retired publisher's editor, English, with the cut-glass accent of a débutante, who had written the words for the Canadian edition of Monopoly in the Thirties, listened demurely as the minister began a story, 'The word "pure" reminds me of an incident in Saskatoon – ' she broke in with 'What makes you think they know anything about purity in *Saskatoon?*' and laughed like a woodpecker.

By now the traffic has hotted up and is growling through the crossroads a few yards away, making the house vibrate: great wallowing Cadillacs and Oldsmobiles, low-slung sports cars like jet-propelled arthropods, the drivers invisible behind smoked-glass windows, Titanic Mack trucks ($150,000 each, owned by their drivers) which look hammered together out of old chromium soda fountains and wind instruments by blind Cyclops and lame Vulcans with no taste, snorting their exhaust up and out from perforated pipes like pulled-out saxophones, all plying the grid of roads stamped as though with a waffle iron into the alluvial plain that attracted everybody here from congested Europe – the prehistoric lake-bed of which Woody Lambe said, 'It settled so perfectly level, if you threw a marble down here it would roll a thousand miles.' The limbo feeling is still strong in me but presently the minister, Iain Mackay, is spinning a thread of story that knits me back to Scotland. He actually has details of the emigrant voyage out:

My ancestor, John, came from Lairg – I've stood on the very ground, near Loch Shin. They moved to Bonar Bridge, and there they decided to make the journey to Canada. They talked it over with their preacher, their minister, and they sailed from Cromarty Firth in 1831. The *Cleopatra* was the ship. When they were getting ready, they prepared quite a bit of food [smoked and salted fish were standard, with 'flat bread' and grain to make flour]. And they had to carry straw as bedding for the animals. They took thirteen weeks [six was standard], and the ship ran out of food, and it became becalmed and the crew mutinied. So the settlers, who were for the most part farmers, had to bring the ship into Quebec themselves. And a lot of them did die on the way – had to be buried at sea.

They got on a smaller ship and sailed up the St Lawrence, to Toronto – they were supposed to stay on board till they got to Hamilton and then go on on foot to Zorra [where Mrs Mackay had shown me the letters]. Anyway, at Toronto they got off to stretch their legs and on the dock they heard people speaking Gaelic. So they asked them, 'Are there many Scotch people here?'

'It's all Scotch. And they speak Gaelic same as you.'

'Are there any Presbyterians?'

'It's practically all Presbyterian.'

So that's how the mistake was made – they got off the boat, the whole company of them – but they still had a hundred miles to go. My great-grandfather was pretty resourceful, he had some gold, so he bought enough wood to make a waggon, and he had enough gold left over to buy an ox. And that's why he was known for evermore – not as an insult – as John Mackay the Ox.

I had heard about him already from Mrs Mackay – he was a forebear of hers too. So the common ground unfolded, the grape-vine spread its branches. The Rev. Iain Mackay had a keen social conscience which was due partly to his solidarity with the cleared people of Sutherland. He had been 'brought up on stories of Patrick Sellar'. Some time before, his parishioners had been about to vote on whether Ontario should come in on a national pension scheme, opinion was against having to 'carry' the less affluent states, and Mr Mackay's congregation were 'conservative'. He had just been reading Prebble's *Highland Clearances* and he decided to appeal to their social responsibility by reminding them of what many of their forebears had undergone. 'I preached a strong sermon – I put my whole heart into it': on the Tuesday the district voted for the pension scheme. He also recalled his scepticism at the inscription about 'Erected by his grateful and appreciative tenantry' on the Duke of Sutherland's statue in Dornoch Cathedral – 'Whoever wrote that certainly had a sense of humour!' The real humour belonged to his own family. As a little boy he had been give his father's old chicken-house as a play-house: its family nickname was 'Dunrobin Castle' and on its whitewashed front they had painted a robin.

An hour later we were eastbound for Ottawa on the Trans-Canada. Forest took over from the fields and great breastplates of rock sloped back into the bush at shallow angles. Muriel identified them as part of the Laurentian Shield – my first veritable sight of the great North-American matrix whose name I had learned in school geography, little thinking it would so exactly answer to its name. A night in Ottawa, trying to inhale refreshment from the overheated air, and then I was checking in at the White Rock Motel in Alexandria, fifteen miles from the Quebec state border. Limbo had come again. The sign outside American hotels says not 'Vacancies' but 'Vacancy', which always suggests to me that a great deal of vacancy can be experienced in the Pine Lodge Motel, or the White Rock or the Econolodge. In the Econolodge in Raleigh, North Carolina, a few years before, we had a neighbour, a chainsmoker in a Trilby hat like something from a Forties B-movie, who had come from the Blue Ridge Mountains of Virginia – the very symbol to me of expansive America. Now he was stranded between the police station and the Holiday Inn, and did nothing all day but smoke and take his dirty washing to the launderama. The White Rock was bearable, clean towels, a tumbler in a fresh white paper bag, a TV that worked and gave out bulletins about the unprecedented forest fires that were waiting for me north of Winnipeg. It was owned by an Italian couple, middle-aged and weighty with a rich tan like varnish. They spent their days picking litter out of the roadside garden, freshly whitening the rock, and talking long-distance on the phone. Perhaps they were trying to reach out of the weird alienation of Alexandria.

On the streets I felt like a wraith. Men who looked misshapen from tractor accidents or war wounds limped slowly past in peaked caps and bleached denims, their faces ashen, or sat on chairs in the shade, leather belts curving below the sag of their guts. Out in the country little moved except for occasional sales reps in middle-sized Dodges who pulled off the road beneath shade trees at noon and dozed in their soaked shirts. 'Breakfast' was a toasted chicken sandwich and a coffee or a Labatt's Blue at 11 a.m. in the Nashville, where everyone spoke French except myself and the table mats said 'How ya doin'? Get yaself down here now!' for the live music. After sweltering days, classic plains sunsets turned the sky sheer and made the human settlement seem a still more temporary camping and scratching on the raw hide of the continent. The zenith turned dark electric blue, the layers nearer the earth glowed smoked orange and plum behind a neon sign saying ESSO DIESEL TIRE CENTRE 50.6 in burning letters a metre high, and young mechanics released from toil did handbrake turns in the dust of the goods yard behind the White Rock.

It was worth living for a while a little nearer to average America, to sample what all that journeying of people had on the whole produced. It was also a relief to sit in large shady kitchens a few miles north in places with names like Laggan and Lochiel and talk to people called MacCrimmon and MacMaster, Fraser and MacGillivray. This was a zone of deep-seated settlement, so stable over a century and a half that the original Highland groupings still lived near each other and occurred in bunches in the phone-book – MacMillans from Lochaber, MacLeods from Glenelg, Loyalists who had come north in disgust and fear after the British lost the Revolutionary War in the 1770s. A thousand Loyalists had come here in 1784 and had shortly been joined by five hundred from Knoydart led by a priest called the Reverend Alex MacDonell. Contingents of this kind were not the veritably cleared or evicted, more like what the Thatcher government calls 'economic migrants' when refusing them harbour in this country. Many more came as the French Wars ended, voyaging was safe again, and veterans on half pay led their families over the Atlantic. The great spate of the destitute ran up the St Lawrence in the Hungry Forties; 234 fetched up in the hospital at Cornwall, thirty miles from Alexandria, of whom a quarter died; the survivors found work on the canals of Dundas County. I was learning Glengarry history with the help of Marion MacMaster, farmer's wife and retired teacher. Her husband's people 'came in here across the river – we were much more water people then than we are now. And winter made the traffic easier – February was what we called the ice harvest.'

Marion herself had started to become real to me in an extraordinary way. Three hundred miles to the west, on my last afternoon in Guelph, my landlady had suggested that I went to explore Rockwood where there were 'rocks and caves'. She knew my tendencies – I had previously gone swimming in a limestone quarry upriver from Elora to get as near as possible to the nests of the cliff-swallows. Rockwood was an intricate grotto. Paths snaked between potholes filled with clouds of dark-green waterweed and bleaching fir spars. A lake narrowed under foot-bridges, spread out past cliff-sided islets tall with forest. Between treetrunks ahead of me a 90-foot limestone prow reared up. It asked to be climbed and I just made it, fingering and toeing on little polished flakes. It was sheer relief to reach up as soon as possible and grasp a dwarf-pine trunk – now I would walk off down the back. There was no way round – the prow was the tall end of a promontory surrounded by lake for 300° of the circle. I down-climbed in a sweat of fear, the salty water blinding me, buttering my fingers. As I calculated the traction on little edges and ledges, wondering with another part of my brain if I would be able to explore Glengarry and Manitoba with a broken leg, Canadian voices not far away were calling to each other about 'fixing a rappel' (a climbers' escape route down a rope). When my feet were on level ground again, calves trembling, brain humming with adrenalin, I tracked the voices to a limestone overhang where two men were climbing on a top rope. We went up and down it by all ways for three hours until exhausted contentment set in and as we sat in the dust at the water's edge and chatted, it turned out that one of them, a pilot, came from Glengarry. When I mentioned my quest there, he said, 'Then you'll meet Marion MacMaster – she was my teacher, and she sure does know a lot about the Scotch folk.' Now I sat in her parlour copying old letters, or in the kitchen while family of all ages went in and out and the rising-and-falling churr of harvest machines came through the open window.

Marion is concerned as much with the motives and feelings of migration as with the facts and she knows the difficulties of recreating a continuous memoir of migrant and settler experience. There were areas that people would have wanted to cover up. In the 1870s, she said, the family record became obscured: 'Those were hard times. They wouldn't want to talk about it.' She likened this to the local silence over troubles and feuds: 'My grandfather's brother got into a fight at a tavern down near Quigley's, four or five miles from his home. He got wounded by a man who had a hook for a hand, infection set in, and he died four days later. My mother was an old woman before she heard the facts.' This was said by way of accounting for the near silence in migrant memoir about the more desperate reasons for evacuating from Scotland (hunger, forcible eviction) and about the voyage over. Uisters or their equivalent would have come through Laggan but again it was hard to find their traces:

> There were some squatters in Glengarry – little houses here and there. The community took on responsibility for them, they were given milk and tea – some would get a cow presently . . . My husband tells of a lady they called Cailleach [old woman] Fawcett, way back in the bush, away from the society of the time. One day she was at church – the landowner burned her house. Didn't need the land – just did it out of spite or impatience . . . There was a log house on that lot and out of it there came a Presbyterian minister. His sister was a hunchback. She tethered the cow along the road, where pasture was free.

She described the site and I found it later among thickets of orange day-lilies along a creek, the ground just visibly smooth where it had been levelled to take a house. Here again were lives that we would have to represent as almost a break in the grapevine. In the *Detroit News* for July 27th, 1910 there is a mention of five Uisters (from the four hundred who came out in 1849) who were still living in Michigan. No doubt there are still MacEacherns and MacPhees in the Middle West whose forebears survived the Atlantic and the St Lawrence and whose offspring served their time in the stockyards and auto works, department stores and hotels. Their tenure of any one place would rarely have lasted long enough to make a mark. It was again a case of what Donald MacLean had said to me in Howmore on South Uist: 'These things are talked about in a community. It takes a while to build one. If you're moved – and moved – and moved, you haven't ever got a community and you haven't got a tradition.'

Here in Laggan and Lochiel the long-rooted farming families were feeling threatened and disregarded. They were complaining that the great new Museum of Civilization in Ottawa ignored the Highland contribution to Canada; there was darkling mention of 'Quebec refugees' – the influx of people from across the river to the north who were being disadvantaged by the new ascendancy of the French community. The old Glengarry sub-culture was intact, however, and in the MacMaster household it was tangible in more of those letters that had accumulated like drifts of browned leaves in the sun-dried farmhouses.

Marion showed me one letter that must have been brought back again from Perthshire by the recipient when he emigrated in his turn. It was from a weaver Hugh MacEwean to his brother in Killin, written for him by a schoolteacher in Laggan, near the MacMasters', and it was all practicality and decisiveness while being aware of how ticklish it is to advise:

> [Bring] a good quantity of oat meal for you will not loose it supose you will have some to spare lending. this will also be useful while at sea, a little old cheese, butter, tea & sugar, whiskey, potatoes and sowans and such light-meat as that ... to advise you to come forward I will not but this I tell you that I am satisfied and content in this place besides when in Scotland and much more so ... everyone has their own luck. As for to advise my aunt to come hear I do not well know *what* to say, for young people if they thrive well have pleasure hear, but as for persons of her time of life they cannot expect to see much pleasure in this place.

The nickname for the timbers of the loom was 'the four posts of poverty' and Hugh MacEwean takes care to say exactly what a weaver needed to survive:

> You will bring your reeds, from 12 porter to 45 porter, bring also your temple and shuttles all iron work is very dear here so you will better bring with you whatever your loom requires ... Endeavour to furnish yourself well with bed and body clothes.

This came back to me a little later when I was reading how the Kildonan settlers arrived at the Red River Forks, expecting to find the iron Lord Selkirk's agent had promised them so that they could make ploughs for their first crops. The only hardware they found at the Hudson Bay Company post at Fort Garry was muskets and bullets.

The Killin weavers had come to Ontario just after the French Wars were over, in 1818–20. Ten years later, Dugald MacMaster, the great-great-grandfather of Marion's husband, began to get letters from his son Duncan who had stayed behind at 'Camusein' (presumably Camasine near the head of Loch Sunart, north of Morvern). His stay-at-home blues come crying down the next 38 years. The times of course were against him:

> Dear father I will relate to you now, the State of our Country, at present our proprietors here in this kingdom in general are become a real Scurge the rents of land have got so high that it is mostly impossible for the poor Tennant and Cottar to pay, because their is no trade no Employ or demand for workmen either at home or afield; but indeed those that have hold of large Tenements Especially of sheep farms are in a better way to live because prices of sheep and wool for this year and last are pretty high.

Large tenements in lots of 50, 100, or 200 acres were available in Ontario on loans repayable after twenty-five years. But something had happened to make Duncan hang back and feel himself a scapegrace: 'providence has alotted me to be seperated as an undutyfull son from a natural father yet I still hope and expect if I am spard to become the penitent prodigal.' Duncan has lost his self-respect. He forever craves approval and as a result can never be sure of himself. In 1830: 'I would wish earnestly to hear from you before I would mary any wife'. Five years go by – he has made it through to marriage. Five more and he has 'taken a serious thought of Emigrating and especially before my family increases much heavyer I think that the sooner the better ... ' It certainly was: he now has two daughters and two sons, one of them named Dugald in what sounds like a wistful effort to atone for 'the Disobedience of my youth'. But however was he to get 'all their necessarys prepared and also the fraught paid'? There were harbingers already of the potato failure which presently became deadly: 'we have a general failure in the potato crope these few years past which we call the rot they are generraly no use after the first of June'.

In his own eyes Duncan is all ready to set off if only – if only he could afford it – if only there were not that alarming revolt in Ontario – if only his father didn't seem to think it would be better if he settled near his uncle on Prince Edward Island . . . To his nearest and dearest, Duncan did not seem ready at all. His aunt Catherine was writing letters too, from Banavie Locks on the Caledonian Canal. In 1838 'I think Duncan yr Son have give up his mind for young to se your part of the world'. In 1840 Duncan himself has 'at long last taken a serious thought of following you and leaving this place because [hole in paper] is almost gone to misery'. In 1842 his aunt writes to his father, 'I think it is as fare this year as ever from his mind'. A difference between the letters of the two is that Catherine's are wholly about others, Duncan's wholly about himself. She will have been a Gaelic-speaker but, as was usual, she could write only in English, an English in which we can hear her Highland accent: she spells 'letter' as 'lettear' and 'just' as 'chist'. It is poignant, in a letter of June 1836, to see her tender emotions stammering in the semi-alien language:

> I did never hear word about you but what Donald Kennedy told to me and I was very Sory which hapen about that the Children Died and I was very Sory about you that your Daughtair Died and your Son and I was very Sory for them . . . and I am thinking that you hard that your mother Dided about of a 6 years ago.

Meanwhile Duncan moves, and moves, and moves – never to America. In December 1866 his apologies and gratitudes and doubts and second thoughts are beamed across to his brother. Civilisation has advanced a little, blue notepaper and envelopes have been invented, replacing the old folded sheet, but so has the Gatling gun and Duncan has been put off all over again:

> In my last letter I mention that I was expecting to go to America according to the invitation I would get from you, and in reference to your letter I change my mind and Particularly as the most of the Inhabitants of America interfering into an order of Battle, that has changed my mind greatly . . . My dear Brother, I am now getting old, and very likely I must made up my mind to remain in this

country unless your Portion of the world is getting better.

'Must made up my mind' is as apt a mistake as 'the wild woulds' in Alexander MacLeod's letter from Muie to Zorra. These men's wild would's never turned into actually did's and the minds they were forever about to make up had been made up long ago.

Duncan's final letter is from Ardnastaing. All his circlings, mental and physical, have returned him to a place four miles from his old home. He has shepherded at Achanellan, which is at the remote head of Glen Loy (north-east of Loch Lochy) – then moved to Clash (the Clash near Acharacle?) but there 'I lost my situation,' although 'I was for a time allowed to occupy the house, and all this in consequence of that unfortunate heather-burning'. How big, I wonder, was the mountainside he allowed to go up in flames? And what would he have burned down if he had ever made the move to Canada – whole forests? As his voice dies away, money grievances jar the note, but 'none of you must think that I mean to reproach any of you'. Dugald has died; the two brothers in Ontario, Angus Mòr and Angus Og, have inherited the property; Angus Og has got the lion's share. All Duncan has got is a little 'assistance' from his Prince Edward Island cousin but he still pleads, swallowing his humiliation: 'none of you will turn a deaf ear to what I have said, and more especially you Angus "Og" who I understand are better situated than the rest of your brothers . . . but do not be afraid, I am not difficult to please.' It is the very voice of the 'poor relation', as Dickens might have written it. It is not the voice of someone who can pioneer his way out of the depressed society of Argyll.

While I was in Laggan, the pioneer energies come down from Dugald and the Anguses were still to be seen bubbling and fizzing in Marion's husband Keith. He must have been in his seventies, and the temperature was undoubtedly in the nineties. His own family were marvelling at the hours he spent in the full glare, tractoring home the massive cylindrical hay bales: 'Why does he still bother?' 'Because he *loves* it.' He seemed made of wrinkled brown rubber, his eyes darted and sparkled under the brim of a denim cap whose crown was printed with the complete text of Winston Churchill's famous put-down when a woman told him he was drunk: 'I'm drunk but you're ugly and tomorrow I'll be sober.' The War had been Keith's finest hour too. He had been a noted anti-tank marksman, with a big tally of German Tigers to his name, and he still loved to shoot, at groundhogs. His reason was that their burrowings disturbed the ground and snagged the teeth of the mowers but it must have been a Davy Crockett impulse that sent him stravaiging across the fields in a jeep at sunset, crazy to bag his hundredth groundhog before it became too dark to see them. Chatting to me, his talk was all physical vigour. He scorned the neighbouring farm for going to seed and almost thrilled to the possible dangers of it: 'If a fire came on, that son-of-a-bitch would all blaze to hell, wes' win' blowin' thro' that *hay*? 'Cos it's *so* high. Sure, they's a river, but a *grasshopper* c'd jump across it!'

Pioneer virtues of another kind showed in a neighbour ten miles down the line, Donald MacGillivray, whose forebears had emigrated from Strath Errick south of Loch Ness. He and his wife seemed to be quietly sitting out their days in a large dark farmhouse, which I was told to look for 'behind the north church'. Two large churches stood up half a mile apart, a result of the Disruption of 1843, which I was told angrily 'should never have happened in Canada'. The MacGillivrays were still full of vim, as they entertained me in a cavernous kitchen with a bulbous chromium stove crouching in the background, waiting for winter, and a black flue wriggling along the rafters. She was a frizzy-haired gnome in shorts who still laughed heartily at her husband's stories and defined the reason for their forebears' emigration in one word, 'Poverty'. He had a lantern-face, rasped red and gouged out by work and pain. He had lost an arm to cancer in his teens and his voice was half-destroyed through inhaling cedar sawdust, which had made cysts grow on his vocal cords. Presently he was showing me, through in the best room, some tables he had made out of black walnut. They were perfectly shaped and finished. He was so capable and self-reliant that I almost failed to realise that he had managed all this – fifty years of farming, professional carpentry in his retirement – with one arm. His had been the irrepressible life of people at home in forests, who used to climb to the tops of spruces for the pleasures of being swung about in the wind and revelled in the logging bees when neighbourhoods gathered to clear more ground: 'When a young man can pile one-fourth of an acre of an afternoon, dance twenty jigs in the evening' – to a tune they called 'Shaking off the Charcoal' – 'and wait upon his partner home, he is considered fit for a "new beginner".'

By now I had even overcome the alienation of Alexandria – in the bookshop I made friends with the owner, Harriet MacKinnon, whose forebears had come from Skye. By a lucky chance I knew the tune of a song she had always wanted to hear and I sang her Hamish Henderson's 'Fareweel to Sicily', with its plangent pipe tune, when there were no other customers about. My Glengarry days were drawing to an end among farms that struck me as half-familiar for a reason I now realised: as a boy I had often gone visiting in the heart of Aberdeenshire where untarred roads curled round and ended at comfortable houses, neither shabby nor smart. Currant bushes gave off their feline scent, hay massed behind wire fences and beech or hawthorn hedges, windfalls studded the grass, tassels of pine needles made their dark patterns on the skyline, and at the centre of this rich maze sat an 'old' person who incarnated the past, unfussed, weighty, with a language akin to mine but different. To be lapped in this kind of abundance of grain and fruit, the Lochaber and Loch Ness-side folk had had to abandon Scotland and cross the water, bringing with them everything except their houses. The MacGillivrays' neighbour Donald Fraser (also Strath Errick) showed me two things that made a quintessence of settler history. His great-grandfather had been a shepherd in Inverness-shire, with a herb garden and a knowledge of medicines. His mother's grandfather had sailed from Portree in 1840 and a brother who stayed behind gave him a snuffbox, delicately made out of two saucers of brown wood three inches across. On the lid, in black Gothic, a poem was inscribed:

> To flourish round my native bow'r
> And blossom near my cot
> I cultivate a little flower
> They call forget-me-not.
>
> Though oceans may betwixt us roar
> And distant be your lot
> Altho' we part to meet no more
> Dear youth forget me not.

This was nicely portable. The settlers also brought their heaviest things: quernstones for grinding meal, which are hard to lift unaided, and the iron gear which Donald now produced with pride from his barn. He had often wondered quite what it was – a long chain, made of figures-of-eight joined by single links, a broad flat hook at one end, a double hook at the other, one of them small and plain, the other made from a bar twisted at one end into a barley-sugar spiral with an eyelet, the other end bent to make a hook. The flat side of it had the letters 'W M T' (the smith's initials) dinted into it on one side and a zig-zag decoration on the other. It was the backbone of the Highland kitchen, a *slabhraidh* or slowrie, on which the pot hung from a roof-timber above the central fire and could be let down or hoisted up according to how much heat was needed. This one had never been used. The iron, barely rusted, was an even granular brown. 'But what did they *do* with it?' Donald kept saying, enthralled by this thing which his great-grandparents' hands had hefted, brought from the smithy, packed in Stromness or Campbeltown and unpacked in Plantagenet on the Ottawa thirty miles north. They must have half-expected conditions like those in Scotland, then found themselves cooking at a stone hearth in a log house.

The slowrie was certainly not fragile yet it could easily have slipped out of sight for ever had it not been for Donald Fraser's kind of loyalty to history. (He was going to Gaelic classes. His grandmother had read psalms in Gaelic to them every Sunday, his mother understood it but never spoke it, and Donald said, 'Gaelic words come from the back of my head, involuntary.') My other lessons in the resilience of the grapevine came from 'the MacCrimmon girls'. 'You'll have to visit the MacCrimmon girls,' said Donald. I had already been noting details from Maddy's genealogical book on the area, *From Skye to Lochinvar*. They lived, naturally, near a bend in the road called MacCrimmon's Corner, in honour of its being the only bend in the road for a good many miles and the site of a shop kept by a forebear. When I phoned them they were usually engaged. 'The MacCrimmon girls,' said Donald, 'do their talking in the afternoons.' They turned out to be two spirited sisters in their sixties who lived in a converted white schoolhouse like an ark of prettiness on the ocean of corn. I had been struck by the archetypal life lived by their forebear, Donald Og MacCrimmon from Glenelg opposite Skye. The family came from Dunvegan, then lived in Swordland, Glenmore, until Cumberland's troops burned their clachan on suspicion. Donald Og was pressganged into the Navy in 1809 while he was out fishing with his friends – served on the *Firefly* while it was guarding Napoleon on Elba – apparently let him go (and it's true that some Highland folk believed that Napoleon's rule would have been less unkind than the British Crown's) and saw him again on the *Bellerophon* as it made ready to take him into exile on St Helena. Meanwhile Donald Og's family were preparing to emigrate, via Greenock to Halifax, but their mother refused to go till her son came back from the war – a maternal gut-decision that saved her from the terrible bereftness of the mothers in the straths of Sutherland. But he had lost his discharge papers, which cost him his veteran's entitlement to 200 acres of land in Canada. Here was a life beset by history at all points. As such it had been copied down at his dictation, in the Nineties, by Donald Fraser's grandfather, then repeated in Maddy's book. Of the hundreds of lives listed there, it was the only one for which such living details were available.

It now turned out that Maddy and Kay's aunt Jane had known Donald Og, who was her granduncle, and had reminisced about him when they were girls:

> They had to clear the land, and with being pioneers they were just occupying a little knoll, not knowing if there were neighbours near them. It was all just bush and swampland. In clearing the land one day Donald Og heard wood-cutting going on some place else, so he knew there was somebody else in the area. And he listened, and he detected that it was sort of north and east of him. That morning it happened to be the sort of atmosphere when all the sounds carried clearly, so Donald Og started chopping towards the sound of that axe. And on his way he would just stop, and then he'd hit with the axe just to make a sound. And they both kept coming towards one another until they met. The other man was a Morrison – Duncan Morrison. One of his descendants is still there – you can just about see it from here. And they were just so happy to meet.

These were people from the Highlands, where low trees or no trees make every neighbour's movements visible for miles. They met each other at the exact moment of creating a settlement. And this moment in its turn nearly failed to imprint itself. Maddy and Kay's aunt Jane told them her stories fifty-five years ago. Kay said:

> Now this was the Dirty Thirties, and we would have had no chance of going on to high school in Alexandria, but Mother was anxious we should get an education, and Aunt Jane was a widow. So Dad paid her $5 a month to keep us. We brought all

our food with us every week – eggs, and butter, Mother would bake bread, and meat from the pork barrel. Aunt Jane was very retiring, and very very strict. So when she started telling her stories I wasn't listening, you know – *I* just wanted to go *out!*

And Maddy chimed in, 'Kay wasn't ready to accept that' and laughed at the memory of her sister's teenage unruliness. So Maddy stayed home nights, and so the moment of Donald Og and Duncan Morrison's carving out the new life survived as distinctly as the slowrie and the snuffbox.

CHAPTER THIRTEEN

'THE ALIEN NAMED BELOW'
Southern Manitoba

My way out to the next limbo of motel and airport and car hire office lay through Dunvegan. The air had been cleansed of haze by a blitzkrieg of electric storms and for the first time the territory across the Ottawa to the north had come into sight – sea-blue hills, the forefront of other Canadas which I now had to explore. Dunvegan held off limbo for one more day. I had been advised to seek out Thelma Franklin 'at the museum'. This suggested a stuffy brick mausoleum. It was a two-storey house made of cedar logs, the chinking whitewashed, the windows with panes of Georgian proportion intact. It stood at a crossroads among tall, bushy Manitoba maples and was the old inn, which Thelma, a farmer who lived nearby, had furnished with the cooking, weaving, and farming implements the settlers would have used. She bought nothing, it was all given and came purely from the neighbourhood. The old meeting hall had been moved onto the grass nearby and housed a good second-hand bookshop. The bodies and wheels of wooden carts stood in front of the original cedar barn. It was not quaint, it was itself, but presently a hilarious wedding party turned up in a horse-drawn carriage and Thelma allowed them to drink champagne at benches under the trees and pose for a photo with the bride's father looming over the young people from behind, holding a shotgun. Two benches away I sat in the sun and made notes from the manuscripts and books shelved in the upstairs bedroom of the inn. I was also able to handle the utensils, in particular a little horsehair sieve five inches in diameter which interested me because it could certainly have been carried by the youngest member of a cleared family.

All this was idyllic – it was the perfectly ordinary living and hard work of the past turned into an idyll – it was not the rough, motley past but a refined and privileged present. Perhaps, so long as we don't suppose we can 'experience the trauma of exile', it is reasonable to follow its spoor and inspect its vestiges. The petrol-driven, air-conditioned limbo sucked me in less than an hour's drive from Dunvegan as I tried to escape from the freeway on its concrete stilts above Ottawa. Thelma had recommended the Relax Inn as a convenient hotel in the eastern suburbs. For a moment, from the stream of cars and Mack trucks, I saw its flag on a tall staff, its elegant cypress hedges, the glass windows of Chuck and Harolds Diner (Brunch from 11 to 3) but where's the sliproad? Cut off from me by a fast log-jam of Mack trucks. I escape one intersection too far west, double back and drive for a gibbering half-hour through suburbs which *must* be near the freeway – physically near it but in another dimension, this sinuous suburb has me throttled in its grassy coils and if I escape to the freeway again the spell will still be on me and I'll turn off wrongly *again* and slither forever down the spiralling suburbs like the person who wakes up but no, he dreamed he awoke, *this* time he wakes but again it was a dream of waking . . . The freeway was standing over me. I got onto it, checked in at the Relax, swam in its pool and ate salad with blue-cheese dressing at Chuck and Harolds, and found out quite soon that the real Ottawa limbo was inside the lofty marble and light oak hallways of the National Archive, where the Public Health files for the 1840s compressed barely-imaginable miseries into their bundles of documents, box after box after box of quarto forms and little square chits, yellowish, greyish, faintly brittle but intact, blue-black ink scribed on the dotted lines.

The Emigrant Officers and their clerks had coped meticulously with the demoralised, ill, and dying people from Scotland and Ireland. The reception port of Kingston had sent on the human cargoes to wherever their paid passages ran out – Port Stanley, for example. (The map of Lake Ontario shows many ports with optimistic, or ironical, names – Port Hope, Port Credit.) The skipper of the schooner *Rose of Milton* had been paid for 'cartage of emigrants', e.g. Widow O'Brien and family (indigent) en route from Kingston to Loughborough, which is ten miles inland. The names for 1846, the year the potato rotted, were nearly all Irish. (Their monuments are the placenames: Joyceville, Lansdowne, and Fermoy are on the map nearby. So for that matter are Moscow, Sydenham, and Odessa.)

Matthew Lynch with his wife and four children was passing through to the Gut of Canso, where the bones of immigrants used to be found on islets. Widow Higgins and family were given 2/6 after being wrecked on the *James & Mary Smith*. Mary Connors's child had buckled under the strain, or perhaps had never been right: a chit recorded payment 'To the Lunatic Asylum for cash advanced to the nursing and Cloathing' of the child from June 20th, 1846 to May 1st, 1847. A teamster called Samuel Farrell had been paid for taking 'three loads of Sick Emigrants to Hospital'. How many got out again? The Quebec Marine and Emigrant Hospital had counted its patients for 1850. All the figures showed the plight of the incomers. Of the 1,223 admitted 639 were seamen and 520 were immigrants. Six hundred and twenty of the seamen had been discharged, only 461 of the immigrants. Of the 67 who died only 12 were seamen, 40 were immigrants. The seamen had spent 9,219 days in hospital, the immigrants 12,635. The deaths too had been carefully seen to and logged. Thomas Ryan had been paid for 'furnishing coffins for the following Indigent Emigrants' – 21 from June 8th to October 14th, including two for Mrs Richards's children on August 21st. A coffin cost 5/– plus 7/6 for 'digging grave and conveying the remains of the deceased son of the widow Riddle, a destitute emigrant to the place of interment'.

Hours went by. I copied assiduously. A girl went past in a flowered cream-linen dress and a straw hat trimmed with black ribbon. Her head lolled to one side, nodding on her neck like a frozen flower. She was in a powered wheelchair. It went silently on broad rubber wheels past the serried desks. People looked up, then down again as she manoeuvred awkwardly through the double doors.

Twelve immigrants had been entered as 'Deck passengers fr. St. America', which sounded gruelling. The Chief Emigrant Agent was 'confident that a great many Immigrants may be absorbed, if properly scattered over the extensive and fertile Regions, which lie in the rear of these towns', which was perfectly true. A resident was not so contented and put in for compensation because in the building of the 'emigrant sheds' the 'fencing of the field has been destroyed and I have sustained during the year the loss of profits accruing from the pasturage.' Plenty of the boat people had died, of course, which will have helped. P. Belsanger had been paid £25.0.0 for interments, which would cover at least 70 at 7/6 each. But the sheds were clearly a public nuisance: a teamster called John Kelly, who signed his receipt with a shaky cross, was paid for 'Carting Disorderly Parsons' (a pleasing misprint, possibly echoing his Irish accent) 'from the Sheds to the Public Office' at Toronto. At Hamilton the Emigrant Agent authorised the offering of a reward after the sheds had burned down, which he believed to be 'the act of an incendiary' – a maddened inmate or an aggrieved farmer, who can tell?

Time to go. No more papers could be requested after 4.15 p.m. I had a dinner date with a very old friend from Cambridge and his wife. Outside, the air was so heated it scarcely refreshed the lungs. The data of misery confounded thought. Nothing was left in my head but banalities – useless rage at what goes on (in Ireland or Scotland then, in Ethiopia today) – relief that I'm safe and free, safe from cholera, starvation, homelessness, free to eat clam chowder at Chuck and Harolds.

Winnipeg on the Red River, site of the cleared Sutherlanders' first real settlement a hundred and seventy years ago, now lay at the end of a three-hour flight west-north-west across the forests and waterlands of the barely settled Ontario that stretches from Lake Superior to Hudson Bay. In the departure lounge I passed my time with the *Toronto Globe and Mail*, whose chief local story nicely illustrated the evolution of Canada. Forty-eight hours before, in the museum meadow at Dunvegan, I had been examining the cross-section of a tree two foot across which had been hollowed out as a vat to make lye for potash. Now the Conservative government of Saskatchewan is trying to sell out of the Potash Corporation, the state's chief industry, and the New Democrats were into the fourteenth week of their filibuster: 'Armed with stacks of history books and newspaper clippings, they have dominated the legislature by talking about everything from the geological development of potash to the early use of fertilizer in pre-European times.' On the front page Grant Hodgins, Deputy House Leader (Cons.), smirks with the lop-sided smile and brazen, exposed eyes of a con-man who knows you can't prove he's lying.

Immediately outside, my plane is being fed and watered, its belly filled with luggage. A tall, rangy man is in charge of a yellow truck with tanks labelled 'Consolidated' and 'Flammable'. Festoons of concertina piping sprout from nozzles. The man connects some pipe to a manhole in the concrete at his feet and some more of it to a hatch under the wing. This isn't easy. The mouth of the pipe is hefty and complex and he has to lift it above his head. If he wasn't six foot two he couldn't do this job. He lifts the nozzle to the hole, half-turns it. No use. He waits, pipe dangling, and tries again. Still no coupling. This time he waits for a minute while the glycogen builds again in his arms, swings upward, and connects. Fuel pumps from the underground tank via the bowser into the wing.

Now a sweating man with a black moustache like a scrubbing brush and pebble lenses glides out of the plane's luggage bay. He's sitting on the conveyor belt which has carried hundreds of suitcases, golf bags, and a few guns in cases into the maw. When I look back at the fuelling, the wing-hatch has been closed and a transparent fluid is coursing down the fuselage. I almost hope it's water (but how would the plane fly on that?). The children beside me have been fascinated by the luggage: 'There's your green case, Daddy! That's our red one!' Now I'm worrying in case my luggage has stayed in Ottawa/fails to get out at Winnipeg/bursts open. It arrived from Manchester in Toronto held shut only by its strap and came last down the carrousel, which gave me three-quarters of an hour to be terrified that my card index had been sprinkled all over the forecourt.

The driver of the Marriott Chateau Air-kitchen truck has now delivered hundreds of alloy canisters of lunch and is shutting a double door on the starboard side just under the cockpit. Has he secured it properly? He seemed to turn the handle very casually ... Usually I have no paranoia at all about flying. Maybe this neurosis is an irritable reaction to several days in limbo, which aren't over yet since I am far from sure how much I'll learn from my contacts in Manitoba. This insecurity makes me latch onto the worst news in the in-flight copy of *Time*. The Pentagon want to commission 130 bat-winged Stealth jets at $530 million each. The Pakistani Army, fighting India for a few miles of high-altitude snow in the Karakoram, tied two soldiers to helicopter skids to get them onto a 7,000 metre peak before the Indians and didn't care whether the men died of exposure. A security firm specialising in protecting super-stars against crazed fans charges $225,000 a year for 'full protection' and keeps tabs on five hundred disturbed people ... In these lurid glimpses the human species down there on the ground looks insane. Are we getting worse? Comparisons could be made: did chief temple prostitutes in Babylon have expensive bodyguards? what proportion of his budget did Genghis Khan spend on weaponry? Turbulence shakes and drops us and the flight attendant's red wine only just manages to home on my upheld plastic tumbler. To the north, beyond the wingtip, thunderheads mount and bulge, Buddhatorsoes moulded in dirty snow, colossal melting pillars upholding the ceiling of stratus at 40,000 feet, buckling westward under its weight ... With a furious glimmering we re-enter the undercloud. A whine as the pilot tests the wing-flaps. Pale orange roads are ruled across dappled leaf-green ground, bluish stains like cloud-shadow sketch the virgin forest to the north.

What I have just overflown is, very roughly, the route taken by a group of Kildonan people who decided to evacuate from Red River – its shortages, its floods and frosts, its fur wars – and look for peace and easier farmlands in partially-settled Ontario. A fortnight before I had seen where they ended up and had spoken to a direct descendant, Mrs Reynolds, who lives near Beeton on the plain south of Lake Simcoe, ninety miles north-east of Guelph. I drove there with Hugh MacMillan, who thought she might have a manuscript written during the Sutherlanders' epic journey – a thousand miles of trail, canoe, and portage, guided by Indians. What she had was a photostat of the journal kept by the Hudson Bay factor, Archibald MacDonald. For me it was invaluable. The hundred and twenty people who left the Forks on June 15th, 1815 came east along what is now the Minnesota border, canoed by Lake Superior, 'St Mary's River', and Lake Huron to Georgian Bay, landed at Penetanguishene, canoed down Lake Simcoe, and came ashore for good near Hollands Landing, fifteen miles from Mrs Reynolds's home. Her farmhouse is elegant and white among shade-trees; its land has been sold off for turf farms and dust now streams in dirt-coloured clouds from the flayed fields. Mrs Reynolds's great-great-grandfather Robert Sutherland of Borobol in Strath Kildonan was married to Isabella Bannerman of Dirible by the first governor of the Red River settlement, Miles MacDonnell, at the Forks in January 1815. Her great-grandfather William was born on April 10th, 1816, which means that he was conceived on the three-month trek. In the photographs she showed me he is a white-haired patriarch in black broadcloth, sitting amidst cultured comfort, his own parents' desperate battle for life already far behind.

The Sutherlanders had withdrawn from a beleaguered settlement. A year later those who stayed fought the Battle of Seven Oaks, defending themselves against an alliance of Nor'Westers, Indians, and Métis. MacDonnell was killed, his comrades scalped and disembowelled. Twelve days after leaving, Archibald MacDonald wrote in his perfect copperplate:

> We have been driven from a country whose fertile soil, wholesome climate, natural productions and beautiful scenery, promised to us & our children *ages of happiness*, and so great was our attachment to it, that we had almost forgotten the land that gave us birth.

In Winnipeg I presently found out more about the agon they were fleeing. From MacDonald's log alone, flatly businesslike apart from that first lament, it was plain that only extremes could have forced them to so harsh a journey. In an entry for the month William was conceived it is recorded that the burdens of at least two of the party included a pair of millstones and two of the men are classed in the Occupation column as 'An ideot'. Nevertheless they completed their exodus into this Canaan, or what became one as they worked it. Mrs Reynolds, tall and straightbacked in a gown of brown and black and cream, showed us her great-grandfather's plain silver communion cup, gave me tea in her great-grandmother's cup and saucer with a handpainted flower design, and directed us to the West Gwillimbury graveyard where they were buried – my nearest point, so far, to the first victims of the Dunrobin *kampf*. We arrived at it early in the evening along a dusty yellow road. Beside a brick church with narrow shoulders, guarded against animals by a split-cedar fence, many 'Natives of Sutherlandshire' lay under marble stones the colour of old snow, some square pillars, some thin and full of text like pages from a book: William Gunn, William Sutherland, and at least one, Alexander Gunn (died March 23rd, 1839), who was explicitly identified as 'A Native of the Parish of Kildonan'.

In Winnipeg I could presumably see physical traces of the Hudson Bay outpost where the Kildonaners arrived on June 1814 – possibly hear stories from their descendants – conceivably, even, go north beyond the terminus of the road and touch their landfall at the mouth of the Churchill River on August 16th, 1813. At first sight the face of the city looked so deeply altered by many years of plastic surgery that its original features might well be invisible. At the Forks itself the Assiniboine merges uneventfully with the Red, a lesser creek of opaque brown water intersecting a greater one at right angles. From this node budded out the whole assemblage of railroad stations, department stores, Grey Goose terminals, universities, blocks of apartments, art galleries – the late twentieth century getting on with its business. The site was a wasteland till recently, as I heard from Bert Mayes, an expert on Lord Selkirk who led me from place to place along the city's fringes. Out of deference to the founding fathers and mothers, it has been landscaped. Slopes of shaven grass, tanned by the drought, seem to be waiting for some grand emblem of Manitoba's heritage to be installed. All they have so far is a blunt cairn of cement and shingle-stones with a plaque commemorating the Earl of Selkirk's proclamation in 1817, when he at last arrived to give the pioneers his blessing: 'The parish shall be Kildonan. Here you will build your church and that lot [across Parsonage Creek] is for a school.'

At a decent distance all around stood expressionless industrial blocks, rather like the Dallas book depository from which someone or other seems to have shot Kennedy. The river's edge a few yards away was still clad in the wooden wharves and cast-iron bollards from the time when this was a highway for the Hudson's Bay Company trade. The Company had controlled a territory that rivalled Catherine the Great's in Russia and its prestige is still lofty, especially in its own eyes. It publishes a stylish journal called *The Beaver*, which brims with the imagery and history of the north, and a year in its business life is still termed an 'outfit' after the idiom of the first traders. To the Company the year of my visit was not 1989 but Outfit 320. The icy northern approaches, the wilderness, the fur trade are not what they were; forest outposts at places such as Little Duck Lake have been closed down since the War and bears hibernate in their cellars. For me the Company, known locally as 'the Bay', consisted of the rather ordinary department store across the street from my hotel and the original trading post five miles downstream, which came as a savage revelation.

The post is called Fort Douglas and was defended by palisades made of great stone blocks. Inside, a sort of spreadeagled Highland township has been restored: a whitened log house surrounded by a split-cedar fence, a stone cottage with a slated roof which was pure Scotland, the Governor's splendid bungalow with its verandah and its white gateposts crowned with ornamental spikes. The grandees had foregathered here – a notorious martinet among them used to be rowed along the lakes and rivers in a big canoe, wearing a morning coat and a top hat. When he dozed off and the boatmen slackened their stroke, he jerked awake and switched them on the shoulder with a long crop. This was a company with an imperial style and what they dealt in was pelts. It sounds obvious, but my knowledge of the basic history (and reading as a boy the Canadian novels of R.M. Ballantyne, who worked for the Bay) had not prepared me for what I found in the Company store.

Outside stood one of the Red River carts, made all of wood, famous for the creak of their ungreased axles which could be heard for miles. On the river-bank was a York boat – one of the oared boats with fine sharp lifting bows which were built at York Factory six hundred miles north on Hudson Bay. Inside the long granite building the ground floor was a shop.

'Goodday, sir,' said the student in nineteenth century costume behind the counter, 'and tell me, sir, have you travelled far?'

'Many thousands of miles in truth,' I replied, 'for my home was once in Scotland, whence I came with my compatriots to settle among the savages of Rupert's Land.'

Rising above this period badinage, we reached the first floor, which was piled with stocks of tea and curing chemicals. Was there anything to see on the attic floor above? The stairwell was a rich brown shaft – it was draped with yards and yards of the supple buffalo hides magnificently called 'robes', even when they were used for bedding. The attic was the same. Room after room showed a thicket of dangling furs, the gutted and filleted cadavers of many hundreds of Canada's original inhabitants, lynx, marten, fox, bear, beaver, wolf – russet, amber, night-black, meerschaum, cream, sienna, smoky grey – pelts like flames of life upstreaming, abruptly stilled, the lustrous hair inert, legs shrivelled, ending in shiny claws – a draught of animals bunched like strings of onions or sausage in a delicatessen. On the floor stood the chunky presses for forcing the furs into bales with the least valuable on the outside.

Downstairs we had seen the grisly counterparts of the pelts – bunches of traps dangling from chains. 'Now, is that a 1 or a 1½?' a rangy 70-year-old expert was asking the 'storekeeper'. It had not sunk into me before that this is what we came here for – to decimate the animals of North America. It was still only just conceivable that so much bone-crunching and blood-licking, such lightnings, such agony of short-lived imprisonment could have been compacted into this morgue of stricken beauty.

How could I have forgotten that I was on a continent of hunters

– for adornment (since the Europeans came), not for necessity? In Ontario, Garafraxa had meant 'panther country'. Further south, in Florida, there are now thirty panthers left, as a result of 'excessive hunting'. Haunted by such evidence, I turned eagerly to the inside pages of the *Globe and Mail* for a story titled 'Buffalo Enjoying A Resurgence'. It did not mean an upwelling of new vast herds from somewhere in the prairies, however. It meant that the city of Buffalo was cleaning itself up and had 'driven its sex and drug trade to the other side of town, giving patrons of the city's new upscale hotels and offices relative safety in the Main St. shopping and theatre district'. What a monument to the animal which nineteenth-century travellers shot with repeating rifles from the train windows, leaving the dead in heaps! After all this it was unsurprising to go into 'the oldest church in Western Canada', St Andrews on the Red, built by a mason from the Hebrides, its graveyard full of stones to MacBeaths and Hendersons from Sutherland, and find that the kneeling-stools which ran the length of each pew were still covered with their original buffalo skins, now a scruffy faded brown. In 1849, when the church promised by Selkirk was finally built, the supply of animals must have seemed limitless.

'The Bay' in Winnipeg now means the big store on Portage and Colony, its windows dressed with costume jewellery and perfume endorsed by Elizabeth Taylor (and a few furs). Portage is claimed to be the longest street in the world and heads westward to a town called Portage la Prairie at the head of Lake Manitoba. On the façade of the store, day after day, serried Canadian flags with their scarlet maple leaf snapped in the overheated winds. The digital thermometer, high up on an unfinished 25-storey block with pale-turquoise reflective windows, reached 38°C. The country feared by the North Uist emigrants as 'cold Manitoba' was at its summer extreme. By the end of July 360 million trees had been burnt, 23,000 people evacuated from Indian reserves and mining communities. Each morning groups of them walked slowly along Portage or appeared at breakfast time – hotels were obliged to house a quota, at government expense. At the table next to mine a young couple had a meal with their toddler and an elder in his fifties. He sat immobile as wood, apart from a Parkinsonian tremor of his right hand. Presently he stalked slowly out, leaving his plate piled with fudge cake and ice cream. He might have been ill, but the middle-aged Indians outside seemed similarly numbed. They moved along the sidewalk with a gait that sat back on the pelvis, looking straight ahead, in an aura of silence that seemed outside place and time. I was reminded of an Ontario story about seven Indians who came silently into a log house and gazed longingly at some hams hanging from the ceiling. The woman gave them milk, they drank it and left silently, then came back later with a quarter of venison.

This silence appears to be due to estrangement or cultural distance borne with dignity. In a buffet car on the train when I was the only European among thirty native-Americans, their conversation bubbled incessantly. In Winnipeg they were as stunned as any displaced people. But then, at times, everyone out there on Portage looked displaced. Out of 80 people I saw one mealtime, 60 were native-American. Among the others were: a Thai nun; a thin woman aged about forty, her hair crew-cut, her face grey as lichen, her legs so oddly attached to her trunk that she could barely walk; a man aged about fifty with a paunch like a huge cushion under his ragged singlet, who walked along grinning broadly at nothing; a woman aged about seventy with orange lipstick and her umbrella open on a clear bright morning, the rear half of its silk collapsed and the spokes sticking into her scalp. A taxi rank stretched halfway along the restaurant frontage. The drivers were Pakistani with the exception of one who resembled a schizophrenic Scottish botanist, bald with a remnant of orange hair one foot long. He would draw up, braking violently, and sit there dragging on a mangled roll-up or taking swigs from a green plastic bottle. When the other drivers strolled along for a chat with their mates, they never once spoke to him. This was downtown Winnipeg, where people without futures slowly eddied round and round. The two nearest institutions were the long-distance bus station and the university and it wasn't hard to decide which had the stronger effect on the immediate neighbourhood.

As I let myself into this new atmosphere and waited for many phone-calls and appointments to bear fruit, I worked in my two favourite archives, the Manitoba History section in the air-conditioned Public Library and the bookshops in the Portage Mall, an enormous precinct lined with coffeeshops, jewellers, craft boutiques, and Sears stores. It had been built to revive the ailing city. Manitoba considers itself a 'Have-Not state'; the trains which used to glide into the lofty marble temple to steam-power on Main Street have been cut to the bone; farming is in trouble – the *Free Press* quoted a farmer as welcoming the compensation cheque for crops made unusable by smoke because it would 'save the expense of harvesting'. Browsing systematically through the Mall bookshops, even taking my notebook in there, pleased me because it kept to my policy of using whatever local materials came to hand. Meanness or laziness might be other words for it but I would otherwise have missed Ronald Rees's good grass-roots history *New and Naked Land*, published in Saskatoon – a photo in it featured the jingle from which my title is taken – and I also owe to McNally Robinson Books my introduction to the Manitoba novelist Margaret Laurence. *A Bird in the House* and *The Diviners* chimed so closely with my interest in immigrants from Sutherland and Morvern that my head would twang and reel at her imagery of people called Gunn and MacLeod coming over the Atlantic with their 'morsels of belongs' to live among spruce trees like dark angels.

The Gunn who became my chief guide to the ordeals of the settlers was Donald, who wrote a history of Manitoba from its 'first settlement' in 1811. As a man from Caithness who signed on with the Bay, he knew exactly how the crofters of Kildonan departed from their homeland. He sailed with some of them on the *Water-Witch* from Thurso to Stromness, its hold filled with a bin of oatmeal and a bull and a cow from Easter Ross. In Orkney the Bay employees embarked on the *Eddystone*, the cleared people (or people anticipating imminent clearance) on the *Prince of Wales*. They included a young woman whose fiancé had enlisted. Her parents decided to send her to Canada to get a home ready for them all because of 'the dread of eviction from their home, which continually haunted and distressed them'. The young man followed her to Orkney and booked a passage to Red River via Hudson Bay. A recruiting sergeant caught up with him and took him off south. By now the far north of Scotland was a chaos of uncertainty and ruptured relationships. In the two previous years, men who had signed on to go to 'the land of the cold' panicked off at the last minute and sent their chests aboard filled with stones, or jumped overboard and swam ashore. When a local man, indignant at the forced exodus, took a small boat out to the ship to persuade people not to leave, the crew dropped a 9 lb. shot through its bottomboards. The Kildonan people, desperate to realise their assets and pay to stay on by offering higher rent, had been slitting the lambs' throats so that the ewes could be driven to market more quickly. Their joint offer for the freehold in their lands, though it equalled the incoming sheepfarmers', was turned down by the landlord. On June 28th, 1813, the *Prince of Wales* set sail with Robert Gunn aboard, the Kildonan piper whom Margaret Laurence makes the spokesman for his people:

> ... my woman and I will go and rear our daughters and our sons in the far land and make it ours, and you can stay here, then, and the Bitch-Duchess can have chessmen carved from your white bones scattered here on the rocks and she shall play her games with you in your death as she has in your life.

As Donald Gunn sailed 'along the north coast of our beloved native land, one after another of its lofty mountains seemed to sink its head in the waves and disappear'. On August 17th 'we beheld the low and uninteresting shores of Hudson Bay stretched before us, presenting its narrow border of yellow sand and dark blue swamp in the front, with its dark and dismal-looking line of spruce and tamarack in the background. The scenery appeared bleak and desolate beyond the power of description.' In 1923, a woman born on the Red River in 1832 remembered hearing about a Kildonan settler 'who died from longing for her old home in the Highlands: "Oh, if only I could see a hill, I think I would live!"'

For years the settlers must have envied those who had stayed in Scotland. After a winter of near death on the shore of Hudson Bay they sledged eastward to York Factory, then on foot and by river-boat up the Nelson River and by a system of lakes and portages to Norway House and down Lake Winnipeg to the Red River forks. The Highlanders 'had to work as common labourers on the passage; to take the tow rope by turns, to tug at the oar from morning to night, and to carry the freight over the portages, and all this labour without any compensation'. An archaeologist I later met in the north repeated this trip. She told me that the haulage must have been inconceivably hard. In places the only foothold for the hauliers was a hundred feet above the river and the angle and length of the ropes must have been crippling. When they reached the Red River outpost, they found no tools or salt and had to live on pemmican and catfish, unground wheat and rancid grease. At times they ate 'nettles and other herbs'. Sturgeon would migrate upstream from Lake Winnipeg, providing a glut of food, then move off again.

Rocky Mountain locusts arrived in hordes, driving out the rabbits, the prairie chickens, even the buffalo from the nearby prairie to the south, stripping the leaves from the wheat but merely clipping off the barley heads and leaving them on the ground for the settlers to garner.

After the Pemmican War and the Seven Oaks massacre, 'the greater portion had firmly resolved on returning to their native mountains' – which would have been impossible by now since clearance was in full swing. Some of them, as I had read in MacDonald's log, moved south for good to 'Upper Canada' – Ontario – while the rest entered on several seasons of purgatory. Another Company post had been established on the Red, eighty miles south at Fort Daer near Pembina. The young and active settlers set off for it by boat with a minimum of supplies. Parents could carry nothing but their children 'which they had, Indian fashion, to bind on their backs'. The river froze and they went on over trackless snow. At the fort they found dearth; the residents could scarcely feed themselves. The Kildonaners had to trek a further hundred and fifty miles into the 'Dacotah plains' where the native-Americans were hunting buffalo. 'Freemen, half-breeds and Indians' at the hunting tents helped the Scotsfolk very kindly but they were forced to 'become hewers of wood and drawers of water' to the nomadic community. By the spring a few of them had learned to hunt and their status rose accordingly. By the time the weather had softened enough for them to return to Fort Douglas in dug-outs and coracles and sow their first year's crops they had 'suffered so much misery, that those of them, who lived after, could not relate the sufferings of that winter without a shudder'. Further desperate seasons followed, as this pastoral people learned to be self-sufficient, tilling with hoes for want of ploughs, suffering plagues of grasshoppers that ate even the bark from the willows, resorting to the buffalo-grounds again and finding that the herds had strayed far out of reach. But 'they felt that they were no longer "tenants at will", but holders of free estate, labouring on their own land, from which no tyrannical landlords could remove them'.

If only a Steinbeck had been present at that epic of endurance. At least Donald Gunn was living in the region and gathered his physically and emotionally piercing details from dozens of participants. And at least, as I waited in Winnipeg to meet descendants of early settlers, I could retrace the retreat to Pembina and see for myself the site of those purgatorial winters. The way led down Provincial Highway 75 across perfectly level plains of the rich black gumbo soil, now covered solidly with carpet-squares of maize and wheat. On the rim of the view long chains of red railroad cars stood beside grain siloes, waiting to unload. It was an absolutely normal section of prairie America. Invisible behind maples and willows to the east, the Red River unwound its earthy links. On its banks French villages as immaculate as displays in an exhibition were spellbound in the absolute silence before Mass. In the churchyard at Ste. Agathe the pioneers were commemorated in a cairn with a Red River cart finely modelled in black wire. At another point, stranded among fields, broken gravestones had been retrieved and placed round a great orange boulder 'Dedicated to the Memory of the Early Pioneers' – a monument almost as simple as the boulder stood on its head by John Lamont and John MacLean on Tiree. When I walked down to the riverside past a sun-warped wooden house, the air whirred with wings and dense airborne hordes vanished suddenly into the rushes and nettles – the grasshoppers were back in force, and were worrying the barley farmers.

The signposts began to mention Pembina and Grand Forks. Huge Cadillacs wallowed past driven by freckled septuagenarians in cream linen caps, which made me see Grand Forks as a resort where the men chugged in buggies over well-watered golf courses and women armoured to the knuckle in diamond rings played bridge. Of course – I was nearing the 49th Parallel – Pembina was just inside North Dakota. Presumably it would be all right to spend a couple of hours there gathering literary material? At the Canadian frontier post I was simply waved through. At its U.S. counterpart a uniformed man six foot three inches tall with short steel hair and a revolver on his hip leaned on my car and asked to see my passport. He pointed out the obvious – 'It's expired,' meaning the 12-month visa I had got with difficulty from Grosvenor Square in 1984. 'Where ya goin'?' he wondered, narrowing his eyes and looking off down the road.

'I'm researching the early Scottish settlers – gathering material for a book – and I wanted to see where they wintered, near Pembina.'

'Ya better come inside. Park *there*.'

He had kept my passport. Now he gave it to another armed man, seated at a desk. He actually did have small grey eyes behind steel-rimmed glasses and close-cropped blond hair. He leafed through my passport, pausing expressionlessly at visas for East Germany which had been stamped on in February.

'Purpose of your visit here?'

'I'm researching the early Scottish settlers, for a book, so I wanted to see Pembina – '

'Don' matter which town you wanna see – you got no visa.' He sat silently for a minute, staring at the empty surface of the desk. 'We-e-ll, I'll give you a paper which might help you to get back into Canada. Why don' you have a seat while I type it? You c'n certainly do *that*.' His tone was not hospitable, more a matter of setting an exact limit to the piece of U.S. territory I was allowed to occupy at this time. Ten minutes later he gave me my passport and an official blank on which he had typed 'The alien named below has been refused permission to enter the United States,' followed by my name and number.

A few hundred yards downriver, where the water suddenly turns Canadian, I went down between pine roots and tall fireweed to photograph a family angling for catfish, as the Gunns and Bannermans, MacBeaths and Sutherlands did before them, in those years of killing hardship, before the boundary was drawn, when the different peoples, Métis, Scottish, Ojibway or Dakota, could mingle and co-operate and the native-Americans visited the Kildonaners on New Year's Day in full 'war' paint, to dance and drink tea with round currant cakes.

At least there was nothing to stop my movements north, to reverse the settlers' journey of 1814 and see where they had spent the previous winter – nothing except the forest fires and the grave doubts of people I consulted in Winnipeg. Nobody I met had been to Hudson Bay and one even suggested I would 'have to take supplies'. By now I knew that York Factory, not Churchill, had been the settlers' real base. There is no road or railroad to it, only a little plane symbol on the map. This, it turned out, meant not an airline but landing for a light aircraft on Company or other business. I could fly to Churchill, or drive to some point south of it and join the train. Driving seemed a tall order. Broad spaces on the map were blank or speckled with the blue of swamp. The *Times Concise Atlas of the World* (1974) had shown no direct road north of Grand Rapids on Lake Winnipeg. An up-to-date road map corrected this but there was still the worry about fires. The railway bridge had almost burned through at Gillam on the Nelson River,

250 miles south of Churchill. I booked a sleeper to take me north from the nickel town of Thompson and briefed myself on fires.

The lightning flared daily. One evening, as I watched from my vantage-point in the restaurant, the Bay flags threatened to tear off their poles and in the strip of sick yellow-grey sky above UNITED ARMY SURPLUS SUPPLIES in incandescent letters two feet high next to the lifesize plywood Rambo figures, clouds like black smoke crawled sideways – torn sheets of charred material began to sideslip and waft downwards like great drugged bats – yellow fire-engines and Rescue Vehicles speeded down Colony, across Portage, on towards Broadway, their klaxons howling – white raindrops skited in fusillades across the tarmac – a young mother in a pink singlet cycled past, the child on the rear saddle crouching against her and covering its head. When I went up to my tenth-floor bedroom to watch the elemental show, the sky was alight. A hot pink bow would glare above the skyscrapers; my elbows as I leaned on the balcony were lifted clear off the rail by one thunderquake; and yellow light sheeted sideways behind the columnar rains advancing southward up the Red River.

Sixty-one fires were out of control and 112 were being allowed to burn because they threatened no communities. This left 50 in a menacing state. Racial ill-feeling was fanned up by the heated winds. Tom Weenusk, chief of the Oxford House band near Thompson, was complaining that the Natural Resources Department had ignored the fires in his reserve because they threatened neither property nor timber harvests. The Keewatin Tribe Council, representing 35 northern bands, demanded a change in firefighting policy and Tom Weenusk was forming his own firefighting crew. The research director for the Indian company Keewatinowin Okinakanak Inc. argued that the Cree valued trees and wildlife more than property and in any case were confined to areas where they had their trapping lines: 'Unlike their nomadic ancestors, band members cannot follow the animals fleeing the fires'. One morning the papers carried a typical story about a family near Norway House who had been burnt out. The desolate photo showed a gutted pick-up and a little boy's trike surrounded by a forest reduced to black masts.

It was difficult for an outsider to form a clear view. Some white residents of Gods Lake Narrows were bitter that the band leaders organising emergency services and the Métis organising food supplies had 'deliberately ignored' the whites and withheld information about where to go for help: ' "What it's come down to is a native versus white situation." ' Above such conflicts, one of Canada's foremost ecopyrologists argued serenely that the fires were 'only a disaster when viewed in human terms'. Happily, they destroy aged trees and harmful fungi, and burn away the duff that litters the forest floor, so that the nutrients in it are suddenly released and enrich the seedbed. There did seem to be a flaw in this argument: 65 per cent of forest fires are caused by humans and it's hard to believe that what must be a huge increase on aboriginal fires (caused by lightning) can somehow have been benignly absorbed into the cycle of destruction and renewal.

Meanwhile the politics of fire remained complex. Shortly before I left for the smoking forests, the Royal Canadian Mounted Police at Norway House charged a thirteen-year-old boy with setting a fire that cost $1m. to fight, destroyed four homes, and forced 4,000 people to evacuate. A boy of ten, too young to charge, had been referred to the Children's Aid Society. Two juvenile arsonists, like those who burn down British schools every year? Quite possibly not. A friend in Winnipeg believed that unemployed Indians set fires so that they could earn a temporary wage with the firefighting crews. When I quoted Indian spokesmen like the O'Chiese and Sunchild leaders from Alberta – 'the bands will be left with thousands of empty hectares that will take almost a century to regrow', 'You know how you feel when someone steals something from you and you feel violated?' – my friend argued that this represented only the hunting and trapping bands who take animals for meat and fur sales; the fishing bands aren't dependent on the forest and might well burn it from time to time in order to earn a few bucks. Both strategies belong to the cash economy which 'we' imported long ago.

Yet again it was hard not to be 'born back ceaselessly' to that 'transitory enchanted moment' when the 'fresh, green breast of the new world' met the sailors' eyes. In Manitoba and Dakota terms, there really was racial co-operation when Chief Péguis helped the departing Kildonaners to mount their expedition to Ontario, or when those who stayed were given shelter and employment at the wintry buffalo-grounds. But already the two business giants, the Bay and the Nor'Westers, had set whites, native-Americans, and Métis bloodily against each other at Seven Oaks, in their war for control of dead animals' skins. I got my nearest glimpse of that pioneer time one afternoon when I drove to a northern suburb of Winnipeg to have tea with Mrs Ruby Nye and the Selkirk Association archivist, Kay Gillespie. The massacre was remembered by the usual cairn, at the roadside in a copse of birch and Manitoba maple. Mrs Nye was the great-granddaughter of John Gunn from Knockfin in Kildonan and Ann Sutherland. Her father, Jeremiah MacDonald, had farmed nearby and his father had been born in a log house and worked for the Bay. Mrs Nye, born in 1896, was stylish, humorous, and a lively mimic. Her house was painted chocolate and looked out over Kildonan Park. An expert hostess, beautiful in a trouser-suit in peacock blue, cerise, turquoise and black, with burgundy beads and silver shoes, she handed sugar and milk on a silver salver, with vanilla-and-cinnamon rock-cakes she had baked herself, and apologised for being clumsy – she had broken her leg some months before and had her gall bladder removed soon after. Now she knitted her frosty black eyebrows and concentrated to retrieve each memory of the first settlers. 'My father didn't tell me much – no – he was a quiet man, and he died quite young, he would have been sixty . . .' At the far end of the vista some images of the pioneers still sparkled. Granny Gunn, who had come out in 1823 aged two, had been her '*real* grandmother'. One day, when Ruby was three, they were loading pigs. 'They were squealing and squealing – it's just in my faintest memory but I can hear the squealing – awful! And I ran the whole length of the lot, to where the old lady was sitting on a stool. And she put her arms round me.'

As Kay and Ruby warmed to their conversation, disputing the unmarried names of common acquaintances, scampering down branches of family trees, I was able to form a small mosaic of the settler community. Ruby was 'brought up on the Gunn lot, on 35, and married onto the next lot'. This was real Canadian talk, familiar from Ontario, in which the language of lots, lines, and townships is remarkably intact six generations after the properties were laid out. The lots, said Ruby, were five chains each, narrow so as to give each settler access to the Red River in the east, the Fort Douglas road in the west, fields in front and a hay-lot behind the house ('Haylot' is still a farm name in the Pennine dales). 'MacBeath the fiddler moved to 33 from his original lot so *it* could be the graveyard for the Oaks dead . . . When John Sutherland that they called "Scotchman" – he was the son of an 1813 settler, Alexander – when he left our church to go to the west coast, they were all crying, to think he would soon be gone. At least three of my uncles went out west, to Prince Albert.'

She gestured at the side window, towards Alberta, then sat up slim and erect to mimic admiringly Miss Janet Bannerman, daughter of Donald Bannerman from Helmsdale: 'She walked down the church *so* straight . . . ' She remembered the Bay's own currency, coloured to make it easy for the Indians, the crowns red and the shillings blue, and she remembered incidents that brought the wildness of the old life near. John Prebble had given me the name and address of a veteran historian of 'Kildonan on the Red', Anne Henderson, and I now learned that she had died recently. To Ruby she was Anne Matheson: 'One day Anne Matheson's grandfather went out to milk the cow – well, he never did come back, and they never found his body.' Bears were blamed, and I remembered a gravestone I had read in St Andrews churchyard: Samuel Henderson, a native of Orkney, 'left his house, sound & well July 4th 1864 and did not return nor after the most diligent search have any traces, of him been found. He was an humble minded Christian, 74 yrs.'

The two women belonged to an élite, in that they knew intimately or belonged to the first families, not in the Washington D.C. sense but quite literally and historically: their people had been here first, half a century before Winnipeg existed at all, and they had moved only a few yards from their first homesteads. Mrs Nye warned me gently against thinking too much of Donald Gunn's book, with its unsparing criticism of how the Kildonaners were treated by Selkirk's agents. 'Remember,' she said, 'to us Lord Selkirk is almost a saint.' She remembered her mother making her a cream wool dress for the founding banquet of the Selkirk Association before the Great War – 'I thought that was wonderful' – but she was amused about it all, not self-important. 'The Hendersons, Mathesons, MacBeaths – you *thought* you were all superior people.'

'Well,' said Mrs Gillespie, a little less amused, 'we *were*!'

That atmosphere was still very much with me when I went to the other end of town to visit two actual immigrants, Kate Cameron and Margaret MacLeod, 'the last two Gaelic-speakers in Winnipeg'. I had been given an address in 'a block on Kennedy off Portage'. As I walked east towards the river past bulky government buildings, I thought I was homing on a glittering new white-and-turquoise tower. In fact Mrs Cameron lived in a four-storey brick apartment block down a side street. A heavy security door had recently been installed because of 'trouble with people getting in'. As I got lost round the back in an alley lined with trash cans, a man in jeans exited briskly from a back door, started to walk off, saw me and began to hang around. It was all a far cry from the windy, open townships of Lewis, which Kate and Margaret had left for good in 1923:

> Everybody cried when we left, and every time I go home [to Barvas in Lewis] I'm always homesick leaving there. And you know – when I came to this country we thought everybody would be picking money off the streets. Well, it wasn't like that at all. But I was here, and I'm still here. And Canada has been good to us. But I usually get awful homesick watching the moon. Because I am always thinking, it is the same moon over there . . .

The two had come over in the great post-War exodus, the *Marloch* sailing from Lochboisdale, the *Metagama* from Stornoway. Margaret had married an engineer from the *Metagama*. In her phrase, 'the *Metagama* cleared the crop of the island.' Ex-servicemen and others streamed westward out of Scotland, unable to settle down again on the cramped crofts. The 1886 Act had given security of tenure but it had made no more land available to the crofters. And the whole of Lewis, of the Outer Hebrides, had felt an unrecoverable body-blow when a commandeered steamship, the magnificent *Iolaire*, bringing hundreds of men back to the islands in a storm on December 31st, 1918, foundered on the Beasts of Holm a few yards out of haven in Stornoway. Kate remembered the people of her village going down to the beach to bring up pony-loads of the dead, their clothes torn off by the sea.

The *Metagama*, the *Marloch*, and the *Canada* are still famous because they were felt to mark a turning point: the Islands had finally accepted that their population must get down to a viable level and government had accepted that emigration must be managed. Great crowds saw them off, the Territorial Pipe Band played them aboard, the Canadian Pacific Company gave a lunch for town councillors and harbour commissioners. The crofters saw them off in their own way: 'On the north shore the heather was burning and the fire smell came drifting across on a quiet wind to the *Metagama*.' Beacons were lit on the coast. Hector MacInnes of North Tolsta told his friends to set fire to his thatch as his ship sailed past the Tràigh Mhòr. Donald MacLeod of Ness saw a light flashing from the Butt which he knew to be the torch of a boyhood friend with whom he had often played at signalling. 'What ship?' the flashlight asked this time. Later his friend told him that the ship had signalled a reply: 'S.S. *Metagama* and *Goodbye*.'

Now Kate and Margaret were saturating me in the Highlands as they fed me with their own oatcakes and scones – gave me a recipe book for Anne – plied me with scalding tea and a 'refreshment' (a dram of whisky) at three o'clock on a sweltering, humid afternoon in Manitoba. They are deeply rooted here now. Margaret nursed, Kate's husband worked for the Fire Department, and it was the Scottish country dancing which had first reconciled her to the freezing winters on the edge of the prairie. At one time 'everybody' in the Winnipeg Police Force had been a Lewisman. When a police chief called Charles MacIvor had short-wave radio installed in all the patrol cars, the men 'spoke Gaelic to each other if there was some bad thing happening, so nobody else could break in'. Back home, their mothers' generation had spent half their young lives 'away at the fishing on the east coast', their brothers and cousins had emigrated one after another. Not one chance or pressure in the entire familial and social history of these two Lewis folk tended to anything but their migration westward. Now they were treating me with all the hospitable, cosy goodness of my own aunts and grand-mothers in Aberdeen. Nothing could have done more to lay bare to me the emotional root of my Clearance project: I was rebuilding, in fantasy, a homely nest in the *heimat* I had left for good myself just thirty years before.

CHAPTER FOURTEEN

ON THE TREE-LINE
Northern Manitoba

On August 6th I ate a chicken-salad sandwich for lunch in the gas-station restaurant run by native-Americans at Grand Rapids, four hours north of Winnipeg on Highway 6. For most of the morning, or at least since the forks to Steep Rock and Gypsumville, the terrain hadn't varied – not exactly monotonous, just impressively total and forever. The road ran so straight for so long that when a rare car overtook me and began to reflect the sun behind us straight back into my eyes, this dazzle didn't alter for a timed twenty minutes; like a huge yellow diamond it concentrated, apparently motionless, on the tarmac channel far ahead. During these hours I had had a one-second glimpse of still water off to the west and a second crossing of a flume between forested banks. Apart from that, nothing but the frieze of branches, needles, trunks. For the first hour and a half, I finally worked out, any curve in the road was to bypass a small settlement – Erin, Moose Horn. If the road curved back, I'd passed it. Hemmed in by dense spruce and aspen, I saw nothing else except the petrol pumps outside the Havakeen Diner, where men in peaked caps and mackinaws eyed me curiously as I drank my coffee and gave me a twinge of Peter Fonda and Dennis Hopper in *Easy Rider*. The rare side roads were ruled trenches of yellow glare. The large scale of things made clues hard to interpret. After forty blank miles a sign at the mouth of a firebreak said '53rd Parallel' and a bulldozer stood motionless on parched moss. Why?

Grand Rapids was an oasis that secreted petrol instead of water (although nearby there was a fine blue channel through from Cedar Lake to Lake Winnipeg). A sign had just warned '173

248

kms No Gas No Drinks' so I filled the tank and swallowed as much barley soup and coffee as I could (Todays Special $4.25). Behind the counter where I paid, twenty Winchesters were for sale in a locked glass-fronted cupboard and the shelves were laden with boxes marked 'Shotgun Shells'. Hunting country – the caribou and the jack-rabbits must have fled like rats in front of a reaping machine as the fires roared through. To both south and north of Grand Rapids these had jumped the road – the verges still smouldered and gave out blue wisps. The air was full of the malt-whisky smell of bonfires. Presumably because Lake Winnipeg lay so near to the east (though always invisible for hundreds of miles), the worst conflagrations seemed always to have happened to the west. The scrawny conifers lay felled in swathes like cornstalks not yet gathered by a binder. Young birches at the forest edge had kept their leaves on, sere as autumn; behind them were the charred swathes, pointing the direction of the firestorm wind, and small stands of trees so briefly scathed that they stood up with plumes of needles clinging to their tips like flight after flight of crow-black arrows shot down into the earth.

A young Anglo-French couple hitched a lift for an hour, then set off westward between (invisible) lakes, making for The Pas, where family whom the Englishman had never met were gathering for a wedding. The Pas, pronounced 'Paw', was near the mouth of the Saskatchewan and was often mentioned by Winnipeggers as a place for visits and holidays. Thompson, where I was heading, never was. The old main highway north, past settlements with French names like Dauphin and Flin Flon, had kept well west of the lakes and swamps before curving off westward again towards the impure city of Saskatoon. To the east, as the afternoon spread out its whitish haze, lay Norway House, where the political fires still crackled. The road-sign to it kept me in touch, in a notional way, with the Kildonaners, Orcadians, and others who had come south by waterways parallel with my overland route.

The infinity of trees was dulling my respect for them. Each one seemed no longer a handsome individual, rooting and branching and transpiring, holding its aureole of leafage up to the sun, but a mere hair in a pelt, a scale on a hide, an ant on a heap. And they belittled the human in me, as an ocean must nullify a lone swimmer. These were limbo feelings. To dispel the estrangement I parked on the gravel shoulder and walked for a few minutes into a wild garden where the ground was hummocky with blueberry bushes and tumps where mosses had upholstered the bases of fallen trees. Big mare's-tails and little saplings of maple, aspen, cedar, spruce made a dense tapestry stitched in all the greens, lime and sap and olive. I looked behind me, then to either side – all directions looked the same. I spied the sun, scintillating between tree-tops, and steered by it westward to the car.

In an hour and a half I was eating fettuccini in the 'hometown Pizza Hut' in Thompson, which was identical with the Pizza Huts in Preston, Sheffield, Dundee (and now they're planning one in Moscow). Unreality at last. But that's rubbish, you can't get much more real than the Pizza Hut in Thompson, 'the Hub of the North' – most of the co-ordinates of late twentieth-century life converge on the Thompson Pizza Hut and everyone should come here approximately once. It's across the road from the Royal Canadian Dismounted Police and also handy for the furthest north Y.W.C.A. in the world and the Public Library, which are both oblong. Like every other building in Thompson. The first sight of the town had been a mountain of small coal showing above the conifers. A Bureau of Tourism leaflet reminds me that 'a geologically significant vein of nickel exists' here. This must mean an economically significant vein. Nickel (and coal and money) decided that 63,000 people would live here, rather than in (say) Katowice, Motherwell, or Dusseldorf. When the company struck this nickel thirty years ago, I was told, it gave the miners at their other operation in the south a week-end to agree to come up here or be sacked. Now all these people get born or die here, injured or cured here (I've seen the hospital – it's oblong), at this random (but geologically significant) point in the great north-American forest.

The dullness of Thompson is partly a matter of historical time: there hasn't been enough of it here yet to give the place a bloom and a texture. After all, the Cree were drawn here by needs no less material than the American armament industry's demand for strategic metals. They followed the rivers, now they are following the railroad, as it carries them back to settlements like Gillam, Bird, and Sundance from which the fires had driven them. In the V.I.A. waiting room a native-American is standing – for two hours she never sits down. She has the deeply wrinkled parchment face of an octogenarian. Beside her sits her mother; her spine crooks forward through 90°. Both women are wearing vivid headscarves, blouses, and trousers, checks and Paisley patterns, scarlet and orange and blue-and-green tartan. Their cheekbones are broad, their eyes are curved slits with deep bags under them. The elder woman is silent, the younger occasionally says a phrase or two in Cree to a man of her age in jeans and unzipped yellow leather boots or to three overweight teenagers who stroll in and out. By the time the train pulls in, the native-Americans have exchanged perhaps a thousandth as many words as the white family next them, who are all fidgets and pointless questions – 'Will it be late? Will they have booked our seats? Will we get on right away?' In the sleeping-cars not a native-American is to be seen. On my way south again I found that it was their way to doze all night in the buffet.

The night was unreal, a dreamy shaking from side to side, no sense of northward progress. When I let the blind up, clear yellow light was shining from the surface of a pool. Two brown-backed Canada geese paddled across it between banks of grizzled moss. It was another wild garden but one stunted by winter's short days, long nights, and boreal winds. Small spruces stood about on wine-red heath like pennants on a battlefield. One side of each was bare of branches; from the alignment of sun and railroad I found it was the north-north-west. This was not yet the tundra, which means 'treeless', it was the taiga and it expanded in all directions as uniformly as a sea. Across its awesome purity the railroad spun its thread of culture – names, artefacts, even a joke. Every three-quarters of an hour or so a board beside the track said 'Cromarty' or 'Chesnaye' or something else often Scottish – names that seemingly applied to nothing. Once, in a peaty pool, a battered aluminium canoe lay with its bottom up. On a beach of bronze sand beside a lochan a sign daubed on scrap timber announced 'Beach Lot Property No.4'. The sky was pale and cloudless. Through it a small hawk beat southward, parallel with the running gleam of the phone-wires, which looped close to the ground on tripods of poles. These were invented to withstand winter gales and frost-heave when the track was forced through sixty years ago. Later I heard that no aggregate was needed as a found because the adamant permafrost is only eighteen inches below the surface; the ditches had to be hacked out with axes. The train rolled evenly enough at an old-fashioned trundling gait. In mid-morning, under a naked sun, it very gradually came to a halt and the few dozen of us dispersed among Churchill's clutch of dusty streets.

Here were Donald Gunn's 'low and uninteresting shores' of yellow sand — it was sifting into the angles of buildings like fine soiled snow — and 'dark blue swamp' and 'dark and dismal-looking line of spruce and tamarack in the background' — not so much of these by now after 176 more years of felling. In the sub-Arctic temperatures it takes a tree 300 years to add six inches to its girth and geographers reckon that the baldness of the terrain here is man-made. Later settlers had time to ripen a certain attachment to the place. A Caithness woman born in 1832, who married into the Bay élite, recalled in old age her sense of coming home as the ship bringing her back from Great Britain after a holiday sailed in from the north and they caught 'a faint smell of spruce from the land, though the low shore was invisible'. This sounded wishful but it turned out to be real: the world here is ceiled with a thin lens of warmer air above which it is very cold, convection is minimal, and land smells are trapped low down.

Mrs Cowan née Sinclair was living the life of a lady along at York Factory in its heyday. It was an industrial village inside a stockade, manufacturing river-boats, barrels, tinware, distilling 3,000 gallons of rum a year, and acting as the base for the Bay's 'main line' traffic in furs via the rivers and lakes to the cities in the south. Just thirty-five years ago it was closed down at last. One handsome plain white building was being conserved, and I badly wanted to see it. Churchill people I presently interviewed, who were part Highland Scottish, part Swampy Cree, described the wooden walls inside the building as being deeply carved all over with names and dates of people from the early times, some of them no doubt Kildonaners. The 1813 contingent had contracted to be landed there by the *Prince of Wales*. Foul water caused typhus to break out on board and the captain panicked. He dumped them at the mouth of the Churchill, where the company had maintained a fortified post (on and off) since 1717. They were allowed to squat outside the fort; some died; the captain ran his ship aground to make sure there was no chance of having to re-embark the immigrants before the ice closed the Bay in September. Finally the Scotsfolk were ferried up-river into safe isolation, or quarantine, and wintered in shanties — 'log tents' made of timbers fitted into an inverted V. Their graves (nine of them) were made in the same way. Just one grave could still be seen at the fort. The foundations of the shanties were buried in mud by spring floods many years ago.

These places became my goals. But could they all be reached in the time I had? Could they even be found? Fort Prince of Wales was visible across the estuary, a long stone tablet in silhouette. The Kildonaners had wintered at 'Colony Creek', somewhere upriver – fifteen miles, according to two old Churchill residents, Angus and Bernice MacIvor, twenty-nine miles according to Lily McAuley, who works for Parks Canada. But then again, Virginia Petch the archaeologist, who had spent the summer working on early Inuit settlements up the coast, believed that the Scottish camp had been at 'Haymarsh Creek, below Mosquito Point'. Days of exploration would be needed, preferably in an inflatable. As for York Factory, 150 miles to the south-south-east, a light aircraft was making a trip there soon. The Ingerbertsons, who ran the bus company – doing good business although there were only two miles of road – assured me they would do their best to get me a place on it.

In the meantime I walked through and past and along from and back into Churchill by the gritty tracks, under the amazingly pure air. It felt as though the life of plants (let alone humans) had only just begun and that whatever did manage to get a toehold on the world's surface would last for ever. The sea to the north and east, the land to the west and south were stretched into uneventful horizons. Shreds of cirrocumulus were knitted into Fair Isle patterns on the otherwise sheer blue sky. At times an easterly drew its blade gently down your skin but tranquillity reigned, calming one into a purity of simple attention to things close at hand – this carmine spire of fireweed flowers, this sledge propped up as a ladder against the end wall of a derelict shanty, that shield of greywacke (greenish-grey pre-Cambrian quartzite) scored by the ice of the last Ice Age, the grooves all pointing south-south-west between tiny blots of brilliant orange lichen. This land still rises several inches a year as it recovers from the pressure of the ice sheet – a fact that typified the terrain, benign, immense, gradual.

Churchill itself is only a few years old. Since the War it had consisted of the grain-exporting harbour and a military air base. Lily McAuley reminisced about the 4,000 personnel stationed there: 'My first three babies were all delivered by majors – after that I had to come down to a lieutenant.' When one of the babies was in its pram outside, a polar bear came down the street just fifteen yards away: 'So what did I do? I screamed and screamed for my mother, in Cree, and that was no use at all because she was hundreds of miles away at Cumberland House, in Saskatchewan' (her father is a trapper). The bear galloped off into the Legion bar and threw the tables around but hurt nobody and one hard drinker swore never to touch the stuff again. Presently I saw a bear, a white bulk sunning itself on the orange rocks at the edge of the sea a mile off, waiting in a weak and famished state for the ice to close and make seal-hunting possible again. At the bulldozed, gravelly, old-air-base end of town, the Polar Bear Jail, twenty cells in a stronghold of sheet-iron and breeze-block, housed bears that had been drugged and were waiting to be helicoptered away to a safe distance from humanity: 300 every year at $1,000 a time. Lily believed that the air base and its very big hospital had been held in reserve to keep the worst-mutilated victims of nuclear war well out of sight of the media. When it closed, the townsfolk voted heavily in favour of siting the planned new Churchill on its old place near the port, where the towering grain elevators (my first image of Churchill in a geography book at school) were now ingesting last year's crop from long trains of C.N. cars and breathing out clouds of golden dust.

The new Churchill is laid out in lines of three-storey apartment blocks with small windows deeply inset – blockhouses against the cold. The entire centre of the town – schools, public library, health centre, cafés with rows of computer games – is under one roof: an instant town, proofed against the elements. The hotels built to house railroad crews, bird-watchers, and the occasional writer look from the street like sawmills; inside they are immaculate, comfortable, no different from their southern counterparts. Under the summer gilding harshness just showed through, in remarks about winter on the dole when the jobs at the Port and Parks Canada came to an end, in worries that the big grain shippers way south in the heart of Canada would tire of sending any tonnage out through Churchill, in sights like the line of huskies who spent June to September on the bare gravel, tethered to iron stakes. We were allowed to pet them but warned to do so only at the full stretch of the tether – if there was any loose line, the dogs would tangle it round your legs, drag you down, and start eating you.

When I called in at the Ingerbertsons' office on the third morning, John had news for me – there was absolutely no room on the Cessna to York Factory.

This left a possibility or two on the far side of the river, where the Kildonaners had been dumped. It was called

'Churchill' after the Duke of Marlborough, first governor of the Hudson's Bay Company. To the Inuit it is River of Strangers. A professional wildlife photographer runs you across in his inflatable and a Parks Canada guide shows you the fort. From it the outcast Highlanders had drawn their rations – oatmeal, rice, split peas, salt pork, and molasses. The fifteen-foot palisades with their gunloops have had to be reconstructed. Being of inflexible stone, not wood, they cannot give with the frost, which levers and topples them. All the new pointing was already prised apart, the courses of stone inches out of true. They still made an archive: H. Robinson had chiselled his name onto a block with perfect craftsmanship and on a rounded foundation-boulder inside a Freemason had made his mark – the eye inside the set-square and the dividers, with sunrays spreading from it. The cleared people in 1813, however, had had to be treated as outsiders and that is where the first of their dead was buried. Lily McAuley had told her colleagues that I badly wanted to see the grave. They were reluctant to let people roam outside the fort because the exquisite fabric of dwarf fruit-bushes clothing the stony ground – bear-berry, cloudberry, dewberry, bramble, cranberry, gooseberry – is easily disturbed and takes many years to regenerate. Nevertheless Florence Beardy, a sturdy black-eyed woman of Highland-Cree descent, sat me on the rack of her three-wheeler with a Sea North lifejacket for padding, put a rifle into the holster in case of bears, and drove off across the shingle to the east side of the point.

Amongst short-stemmed willow herb, scrub willow bushes, yellow daisies, and little fiery leaves I could not identify, a yellowish-white limestone tablet 24 inches high, 15 inches across, and 5 inches thick leaned backward, almost supine, its foot among greywacke boulders that might have been used to found it until the frosts unseated them. The top portion, which I was told had borne the Christian name of John, was cracked off and nowhere to be found. The lower part bore the word 'Sutherland' and the date 1813 incised in amateurish cursive, just legible under orange speckles of lichen. To have made it and carved it at all as winter threatened was heroic. It was the most beleaguered grave I have ever seen. Presumably it is the furthest north material trace of a cleared Highlander. The splitting of the stone and its minimal quality as a marker struck me as fitting, since John Sutherland should never have been there; and it is fitting too, for the sake of his family and friends, that in losing his individual name he became his homeland, Sutherland.

On the way across the River of Strangers white gleams broke the water like floes surfacing or wave-crests curdling. Beluga were sounding and blowing all over the estuary – the 15-foot white whales which are no longer killed for their oil and are free to live here in summer, feeding, basking, having their children. Down south the papers had been running a story about some dealers who had kidnapped two beluga to sell into imprisonment. By and large they are safe and now they were swimming in from all quarters to play with us. Five males headed straight at us in arrowy formation, showing off their strength and nerve, then veered off on either side of the boat, crowing into the underwater microphone. Conversations were going on down there, a whole ceilidh of chuckles and cooings and sung notes, short chirrups which the boatman identified as being aimed straight into the mike, a sonar testing of the alien object. Beside the gunwale a double Nile-green shape shimmered two feet down, a crescent enclosing a pod – a mother with her baby less than a month old.

It was hard to tear oneself away from that concourse of genial life. At night I went back along the shore, past a line of board shacks, now foundering among drifts of fireweed, where some Inuit had lived, over the blue breastbones of the greywacke and the little troughs of willow-bog between them, and sat on a glaciated reef, just looking. Nearby, drilling had grooved the rock where stone had been quarried to make the walls and powder magazine of yet another fort, with the incongruous name of Merry. The French fighting the British, the British fighting each other, both of them ousting the Chipewya and Cree after the short honeymoon of co-operation . . . Blown breaths were sounding from the beluga out there in the water. At times the surface creamed in a hundred places, as though it was a wind ruffling it, but the calm was now perfect, the mosquitoes were whining round me. The whales were wholly at ease, in their element. Their wellbeing was as manifest as the colour of the flowers, the ripples on the water. And what was equally impossible to miss was the contrast between these mammal-people, at home in their river, and the cleared folk, warned out, sick, marooned, in isolation at Mosquito Point, where a Bay agent called Dr Auld took away the flintlocks of their muskets in case they went hunting ptarmigan for fresh food and got lost in the taiga.

I knew by now that what I could hear about in Canada was the experience of cleared folk after they landed, not before they left the old country. Except for Johnny Allan MacDonald and Dan Angus Beaton on Cape Breton, this had always been the case. It was not the time-lapse but the trauma and the sheer gulf of the ocean crossing that dropped the curtain. In any case, to retrieve authentic moments from lives lived generations ago requires nothing less than that in each generation there is at least one person with the indispensable qualities: curiosity about people, a gift for mimicry, the capacity to attend, a memory for concrete detail, a little space in which the memoir can be imparted without distractions.

In the Churchill Hotel, down the street from the Tundra where I was staying, I spoke to a maid called Barbara Gordon who was descended from Beggs, MacPhersons, Spences and Cree people. Mixed marriages had been common at York Factory. Her Begg great-grandfather had made York boats and scows, her grandfather had tried to teach her Gaelic and had pulled her out on a sleigh to fish through holes in the ice with hooks on a stick. He sang songs in the language which Barbara never learned. 'I didn't understand it,' she said, 'but I liked it' and she smiled happily and swung her head in time to the rhythm as she sang a snatch from his English repertory:

> Billy McKee Mackay
> Flapped his wings and learned to fly . . .

Grandfather had called Glasgow 'Glaschu' and smoked a curved pipe under a great white moustache. Here Barbara mimed his puffing and gesturing and I wished that old James MacPherson, with his singing and his power of captivating a child, had been able to fulfil all the conditions and carry forward memoirs from *his* elders – details of the voyage, of the family's reasons for emigrating. He had died when boiling water scalded his side, gangrene set in, 'and in those days the plane was slow to come. It got a grip on his leg and he died in the Pas.'

The York Factory people brought home to me how the harshest pioneer conditions had lasted until very recently. Barbara's family were half-breeds – the acceptable term is 'treaty people' – and as such they got no government help when they had to move out after the closing-down of York Factory in the Fifties:

Three-seventy-four, down the line – that's Weir River, that's where we came out. We lived there a while, then Mom was sick and we had to come to Churchill. On the way outta York we camped once overnight, along the trail somewhere. It was fun – for us. We were in a boat on the sled, we had ten dogs. Dad had to run beside the sled.

A cousin of Barbara's called Eleanor Sinclair, who worked in the Port office, came for a drink at the Tundra and through her words I glimpsed the same distinctive life, the mingling of immigrant and native people, the struggle for rights, the dangers of working in the wilderness. Her grandfather's mother had come 'from Scotland' and all Eleanor Sinclair knew about her personally was what her grandfather had said, that she had red hair and green eyes. Her own family live at Shamattawa, which has a land way to it only in winter, and when the smoke of the forest fires had become unbearably thick they had been evacuated to Churchill, where her mother met many people she knew at York Factory but had been cut off from for years. It had been in effect a clearance. The York band had been dispersed but they were still a band and as a member of it Eleanor now hopes to claim for her brother and herself their treaty rights – free rail travel, free health care, and hunting rights. They need these badly. In winter there is only the dole to live on unless they can hunt legally. An uncle had his arm torn off by a bear at his trapline when he inadvertently came between the female and her cub. Another time her father found a bear sleeping in the outbuilding with their dogs and walked away quietly. She herself had been to York Factory just once. She had found clay pipes and a cannon-ball near the white building, also an anchor on the verge of the river which her father remembered when it was yards away from the water . . .

With these bits and pieces I had to content myself. Flipping to York in the aircraft would have offered superb vistas over the taiga – it would have displayed to me the crushing immensity of the terrain that the Scotsfolk slowly learned to master – but what would it have been, after all (I now told myself and utterly failed to believe), but a slick substitute for the settlers' route up the Hayes River to the meeting of the Shamattawa and the Steel, up the Steel to the meeting of the Fox and the Hill, up the Hill and through Knee Lake and Oxford Lake, by Franklin and East Echimamish to the height of Painted Stone, by West Echimamish through Hairy

Lake and Blackwater Creek into the Nelson River below Sea River Falls, up the Nelson to Little Playgreen Lake and Norway House and south across Lake Winnipeg to the Red River and Fort Garry – 700 miles with 34 portages, one of them a mile long ... I duly (and approximately) reversed all this in the security of the train, which glided nervously over the charred bridge at Pikwitonei while the breakfast conductor reached into his locker and brought out a grey sweater printed with an orange flame design and the words 'I Survived Hell 1989'.

On either side of Highway 6 the ground still smoked but south of Steep Rock all that wildness faded away behind me as I turned off eastward to get as near as possible to Lake Winnipeg. Somewhere among the hazy blue levels of the woods and pastures, as dusk came down, was Shoal Lake where Hugh MacLean of Barrapol's people had settled in 1874. Too late to search them out. The journey neared its end among the wooden farmhouses and churches with onion domes built by a quite different people in the mosaic, the Ukrainians. In the gloaming it was just possible to make out the Kirillic epitaphs on their gravestones in the High Plains Cemetery and to photograph the hoary wooden crosses with no name at all. Like the barns nearby they were canting slowly sideways, left high-and-dry as the tide of prosperity ebbed from them and carried the younger generations into the cities.

CHAPTER FIFTEEN

BINDING THE RESTLESS WAVE
Barra

Going back to the Hebrides in the autumn, to visit new islands and follow up some leads on familiar ones, felt like a change of scale after Canada, a finding of history (not eternity) in grains of sand. After stravaiging over the prairies and the virgin forest, the narrow archipelago with its islets beyond islets, the intricate straits, the fretted coastlines looked like so many solution-channels grooved out by that incessant draining away of people to America (and the Antipodes). As the *Lord of the Isles* carried us north through the Sound of Mull, Morvern to the east and Mull to the west were being composed by sun and distance into imperturbable faces, their anguished lines smoothed out. Ben More was almost sleek as it rose up in its place, pap to the south, lion-haunch to the north. And as the ship reached open sea beyond the Cairns of Coll they all moved into place – Eigg's sgurr scraping the undersides of mauve clouds, Rum rearing like a single mountain, then dividing into cones, the Cuillin baring their black teeth, Canna like two tablets on the water, the thousand-metre mountains of Ratagan and Knoydart holding back the cloud massing from the east, perhaps the Torridon mountains (known to me corrie by corrie) shaping themselves in dim pyramids far into the land. The islands populating the western sea were beached animals, some dead like Mingulay and Pabbay but still lapped in the aura of their personalities. As the sun set beyond them, they turned solid, black, and cold, single vantage-points, hard places to make a living.

For many years Barra had been simply a landmark to me, the end of the Long Island, hull-down to the south. Then it became a bloodmark or a tearstain – source of those driven waves of migrants in the middle nineteenth century. Now in a very few days it became people. I had booked a room for Anne and myself by long-distance phone, simply asking the woman in the Tourist Information Office at Castlebay for Bed-and-Breakfast on a croft some miles out of the small town – following my usual escapist tendency. On our first morning at Aros Cottage, Buaile nam Bodach, Niall MacPherson sat us down in the front room to talk to us before he went out on his round as a postman and spoke for over an hour with unusual purpose. 'My father,' he said, and he gestured at a photo of an elderly man with a shrewd, noticing face and a peaked sailor's cap, 'had an unusual nickname – they called him The Coddy.' The Coddy – the celebrated story-teller of the island, whose legends, anecdotes, memoirs had been edited into an absorbing volume thirty years before by one of Scotland's finest Gaelic scholars, John Lorne Campbell of Canna. It was the wonderful luck of the grapevine once again, which is not luck at all but the genius of a people for whom story-telling and genealogy are fundamental.

The Coddy was a crofter who kept a shop and dealt in fish. Want of employment had driven Niall from the island to work on the buses in Glasgow. The croft we could see beyond the window with a few sheep grazing on it had been given by the chief MacNeill of Barra to Niall's forebear Robert MacLauchlan when he came from Aros in Mull in the middle nineteenth century to work in the walled garden of the one mansion on Barra, Eoligarry House. A sister of The Coddy occupied it after the Great War. When she emigrated with her husband to Nova Scotia, she simply gave it to a friend. In the Seventies her son, who had been in the Merchant Navy, felt no longer able to keep it up and wrote to Niall in Glasgow to offer him the holding, saying 'I have always felt you were its rightful owner'. It was a mercy, after all the displacement and flight overseas, to hear one tale of a restoration and for me it meant a providential entry into the circle of memory on the island.

Niall's talk and the talk of all the people whose houses I presently visited was of shortages and tyrannies overcome by stoicism, cunning, and sheer defiance. I had gathered already from what the crofters said 100 years ago to the Parliamentary Commissioners that on Barra, as on the islands to the north, people had been banished from the broader, greener lands and crammed into the east coast where there is little room or depth of soil between hills and rocky inlets. When I mentioned this to Niall, he said at once:

> There was great hardship. A family from here [the North Bay area] got a croft at Eoligarry [at the north end]. She was telling me a few years ago, before she died. So they had room there, but she had to get up each day and walk across to here, through all the hills there, and she filled a sack with peats, there was no coal here yet at that time – it was unheard-of – and she carried it back home all that way. And then she got the children off to school. And then she went out onto the cockle strand and gathered a sackful of cockles, to get something to eat, because that was all there was.

The logic of this – apart from the sheer image of hard living – is complex and rests on the terrain of Barra. A family cleared from good land up at Cleat, Grean, or Vaslain – all mentioned by crofter witnesses in the 1880s as the land of plenty from which they had been cast out – was likely to be settled in the narrow, poor land in the east – where we were now lodging. Farmers and factors, mostly incomers from Lowland Scotland, then farmed the north end. When their properties were redivided after the Crofters' War, the land raids, and the First World War, some families got better places once again after the long purgatory of the nineteenth century. At least there had been the peat mosses in the hilly part. Now they had to trek back from time to time to the familiar bogs to bring home their fuel.

A hard place to make a living ... Barra was bound to be struggled over, down to the last twist of bents, bush of heather, or pound of cockles from the strand. The Tràigh Mhòr, the Great Beach where the daily Glasgow plane now lands, is a mile wide at low tide and over a mile long from south to north: a plain of silver-grey as subtly tinged as birch-bark, contoured by streamers of the chalky shells that look like little moulded secretions of the curdling surf that spilled them there. As you gaze along it under single voyaging clouds as white as the shells, as blue-shadowed as Uist to the north, you feel wings opening from your shoulders, ready to spread and cruise over the breadth of the sounds, 'the mid-sea blue and shore-sea green', the Sound of Fuday, the Sound of Barra, the Sound of Eriskay. Nowadays tourists addicted to romantic poetry bring valuable income to Barra.

At the time of which Niall was speaking, the Tràigh Mhòr was being dug desperately for cockle meat and the bad blood of poverty is rife in the record.

A teacher at the school in Castlebay, a well-read researcher, told me, 'If the people took cockles, they had to do a day's work for MacGillivray' – the doctor who rented Eoligarry from the owner, Lady Gordon Cathcart. This grievance was first stated by Michael Buchanan, a fisherman from Borve, in 1883:

> ... [Dr MacGillivray's] brother-in-law, being at the time the head ground-officer on the estate – or, at least he was called so – drew up a paper with orders that it should be posted up on the chapel door, threatening the gatherers of this shell-fish with certain penalties. The officiating clergyman of that chapel did not give his assent to this proceeding, and told his congregation that he considered it an illegal act. Being thus baffled, those two gentlemen, as justices of the peace, ordered policemen to watch for fear that any of the shell-fish should be laid down above high water-mark.

A few hours later MacGillivray denied all this but allowed that perhaps his predecessor General MacNeill – the last of his name to own land on Barra – had objected to people 'digging pits in the sand'.

Who is delivering the truth (or the less biassed account of what happened)? How much does it matter? Perhaps MacGillivray's brother-in-law imposed the mean restriction without consulting his boss. Michael Buchanan was speaking for a people with so little land that their animals constantly strayed off their own exhausted grazings. If this took them onto the big farms (which still had neither fence nor dyke), the farmer put the cow or horse into his pound, 'up to the belly in mud and water', which brought on an illness they called trance: 'all the natural functions of the beast are suspended. It shakes and gets short of breath, and loses all self-command and dies in a little while.' Accustomed as we now are to walking about on the sweet, under-used turf of Barra, we might be staggered to see its former flayed and puddled state. The people needed bents to thatch their houses, and had to work for MacGillivray at twelve days' pay for 'two small cart-loads'. To MacGillivray, under his fine slate roofs at Eoligarry House, this was in any case an abuse of the bents he had had planted to stabilise the dunes, which still threaten to overwhelm the island between Tràigh Eais and Tràigh Mhòr. Besides, he alleged, they had to work only 'four short days' for a cart-load . . . Such disputes are insoluble, either at the time or as we look back. MacGillivray, I was told at Castlebay, antagonised the islanders, who are Catholic, by installing Presbyterian families from North Uist on some of the better land. When the school opened at Castlebay, the only people with enough land to vote for the School Board were the Presbyterians. So, inevitably, a Presbyterian headmaster was appointed and it was not until after the 1886 Act, which gave the crofters a vote, that a headmaster of their own faith was appointed. By an ironical turnabout, when the Eoligarry land was raided after the Great War, and enough Catholics resettled in the area to need a place of worship, they got a room in MacGillivray's old mansion, with its stone stairways and ornamental urns. When it became derelict, 'People didn't feel too badly about the house falling down. It was a symbol of greed – it was the end of an era.'

Such was the class struggle on its religious plane. Niall MacPherson was defining the thing in more basic terms when he told me about the huge black stones in the jetty at Eoligarry. They had been cut out of Ben Vaslain above what is now the main road. MacNeill of Barra commissioned the job in the 1820s to give employment and offered a stone of oatmeal for a week's work. It would seem that the job took a long time because the men had thought of a canny plan:

They walked from here at Buaile nam Bodach and everywhere from Eorsary upwards to do it, eating porridge and salt herring in the morning, and when they got home at night the same with the herring roasted over the smoke, and dry bread, with a bit of butter if there was some about. They cut those blocks to size on the hill, then they took them down and across the cockle beach on hand barrows, sometimes six men to the barrow. And to make the work last they knocked it down again a bit, so altogether it took them twenty years to finish it. The Royal Mail used to come in that way on the ferry from South Uist.

On this difficult eastern side the cleared people 'squatted in huts on the foreshore', 'living in crevices on the foreshore', 'stuck like limpets to a rock', and longed for the better places to the north and west. According to a fisherman-crofter called Michael MacNeill from Bruernish, a mile south of Niall's home, life at the north end had been satisfactory:

> All I heard about it was that they were kept well. There were no sheep in Barra at that time: the produce of the soil kept the people going, without going to Glasgow to buy a bannock; and it is very likely that the same bread should be in the land yet . . . They were shifted from it and placed on the worst places on the island. They were shifted from it at different times as they decayed out of it, and then they were shifted out of it altogether and sent to Canada . . .

Sometimes the factor would order a hut to be pulled down: Michael Buchanan testified that the evictions in places like Michael Mac-Neill's father's village of Kilbarr were 'heart-rending' – 'I have seen with my own eyes the roof of the house actually falling down upon the fire, and smoke issuing.' A generation before, Donald MacLeod from Strath Naver had published the evidence of eviction from MacGillivray's land in 1850: '[Barr MacDougall and Donald MacLean] did not remove till their houses had been partly stripped and their fires put out. Donald MacLean did not remove till his house was totally unroofed and remained for ten days within the bare walls without any covering but the sail of a boat: though he was at the time lingering under the disease of which he has since died.'

The gamut of such experiences was articulated for me by Chrissie MacDonald, a neighbour of Niall's. Her house stood facing east on a hill of awkward steepness – a site with so little easy ground to come and go in that it would manifestly never have been chosen for settlement. Seagulls went to the loch above to wash themselves after sea-fishing – if people saw them up there cleaning their beaks near a mound green with generations of their liming, they knew the herring shoals had returned and it was time to put to sea in their boats. Chrissie was slow-moving, with a heart condition, and quick-witted in every word. In her memory the old people of the township 'were heartbroken all the time' with the constant departures for abroad. In the time of her brothers – who had been in the raid on Eoligarry – there had been 39 families here; now there were five houses in full or occasional use. She had learned to weave when she was thirteen, then had to leave school because the fee of 6d. a week was too much, but she had never gone hungry because Lady Gordon Cathcart made a rule that orphans could occupy a croft rent free till the eldest was 18 and Chrissie's father had died when she was 5, her mother when she was 9. The history she knew was shot through with clearance of the chivvying kind: 'I knew a woman Mrs MacNeill whose great-grandfather was in Balnabodach. Their family was shifted to Ault, and from there to Breivig, and from there to Glen [a crowded dump for the cleared above Castlebay].' Her most vivid glimpse of clearance in action hinged on the kind of desperate effort to escape which I had read about in accounts of the man-hunts at Lochboisdale in 1850:

Some of them were being sent away from here, with the clearances. This lad, he was a MacLean, he lived down there with his grandfather. But when they came to Northbay to take some more onto the ship, to send them away, this lad took advantage of them and escaped, and came across the hill here. And they had an inlet where they built yawls, and there was a big rock there. Well, his grandfather stationed himself there and he took – he had – what do you call it? An axe with its head across – adze! – he took his adze up in his hands and when they came looking for his grandson, he said to them, 'The first one that tries to come past here, I'll have his head off.' So they went back and left him alone.

To get the measure of the contrast between the good and the poor lands of Barra we encompassed the island by car, which can be done in an hour. Eoligarry is on a rising horn which is only just attached – if global warming raises the seas, a mere twenty feet more will make it an islet. Killbarr is barely a clachan now. On the map it is Cille-bharra, the church of the island's titular saint, St Barr (Finnbar of Cork). The graveyard here is beautiful, with its well-scythed humps and hollows. The plainest headstone was Compton MacKenzie's, a granite cross with nothing but name and dates. The biggest and wordiest was a towering Celtic cross to MacGillivray's son, prudently shored up against the Day of Judgement with an iron rod at its back and inscribed with a text that seemed defiant in the circumstances: 'Blessed are the merciful, for they shall obtain mercy.' Offshore, looking like St Martins in the Scillies with its graceful heathy skyline, lay Fuday, probably the last Viking base in Scotland and one of many small isles from which people were entirely cleared to leave it as pasture for sheep. We made our way through to the west side by a pass between hills – mountains perhaps in the Irish sense – and saw the cleared lands of Cleat and Grean spread out, pure green, with a field here and there, some fencing and a tractor or two, but eery in its vacancy compared with the limpet-huddle of the settlements from North Bay down to Castlebay to which nearly everybody had gone, driven by the proprietors and pulled by the fisheries – in the boom years Castlebay was a forest of masts and sails, the biggest herring port in Britain. From the broad-shouldered headland of Aird Greian, disfigured by the concrete scabs of wartime installations, we could look right down the west coast, past beach and skerry, beach and skerry, to the thousand-foot massifs of Ben Tangaval and Heaval. Opening out towards the ocean from halfway down the west side was a pair of narrow glens, still populous, giving onto a roomy plain with the unmistakable feel of somewhere that has been well civilised for ages. Here was Borve, where Michael Buchanan, most persistent of the Barra witnesses to the Napier Commission, had lived and where fisher families still do.

We completed our round of the compass at Vatersay off the south coast, crossing to it by the Council ferry, a white-and-grey boat with a sturdy engine. A few people, a collie dog, a bag of potatoes and a bag of onions travelled with us. It was the last fine day of the year and the light stung as through a burning-glass, lighting a world of sapphire, emerald, gold. Beside the jetty a wee shop, brand-new, run by the island co-operative, Co-Chomunn Bhatarsaigh, sold teeshirts, knitwear, coffee, and from its picture-window we could see the Euclid dumpers and J.C.B.'s of R.J. MacLeod, the Skye contractor, laying down hard-core for the causeway which will link Vatersay to Barra by road. For years in the *West Highland Free Press* I had been reading statements by crofters and by Father Calum MacLellan, the priest, pressing for this link to reverse Vatersay's depopulation. A few months after our visit, at low tide on Wednesday February 28th, the first person walked across – Joseph MacDougall of Caolis, who had campaigned for the causeway for nine years. In the same village Annie MacLeod, daughter of the third of the land raiders to put up a house on Vatersay, is convinced that the link will be the saving of the place: 'It'll be easier for the crofters to get their stock across' – and building materials, and cars and petrol, and hay for the cows and feed for the sheep. On the other hand it seems a loss that the school will have to close and the pupils bus to Castlebay. As we walked past it on the two-mile road from ferry to village, the pupils, all seven of them, were in the playground and it was soon clear that the place was a focus of perky life – small was beautiful. A black-haired eight-year-old called out to us, 'Where do you come from?'

'The North of England.'

'Who's your favourite in *Neighbours*?'

Anne: 'Er – Charlene?'

Girl: 'Yes! Yes! *I* like her too.'

Dave: 'I like that older one, with glasses.'

Girl (incredulous): 'Harold? Eeuggh! He's *awful*.'

Dave: 'He's funny – I like him.'

Anne: 'The dog – he's my real favourite.'

Girl: 'He's not a person, he's a *pet*. Charlene's a p-e-et.'

Dave: 'A pest or a pet?'

Girl (exulting): 'A *pest* – Charlene's a *pest*!'

It was one of the liveliest conversations I have had, unprompted, with a child and we walked on in good spirits towards the village. It lies among perfect grasslands, sorely coveted by the crofter witnesses of the 1880s and 1890s, won by the land raiders, and now kept for 'proper' crofting, the sheep being exiled to uninhabited Sandray offshore to the south. Remoteness, however, has frayed the community to the point of dereliction. There were perhaps ten two-up two-down houses of the Twenties pattern; ten new Council bungalows with brown wooden sides, the shortest street in Scotland, with its own name, Am Meall, in accord with the dogged policy of supporting Gaelic wherever possible; and ten very poor deserted houses, a high proportion for any village. Some of them had front walls made of crinkly tin – the rusted sheets of it were shuddering in the Atlantic wind. Under the sky's brilliant lens the place had the same air of being at an utter end, physical and historical, as Churchill on Hudson Bay. The causeway has decided some crofters to stay on Vatersay but my fear is that it will maintain a half-life only, as the houses become holiday homes.

At the narrowest shank of the island on our way back, I went across the dunes to look at a slim granite obelisk above the blinding white sands of Bàgh Siar. The inscription on the plinth said –

On the 20th Sepr. 1853
the ship 'Annie Jane'
with emigrants
from Liverpool to Quebec
was totally wrecked
in this bay
and three-fourths
of the crew and passengers
numbering about 350
men women & children
were drowned
and their bodies interred here
and the sea gave up the dead
which were in it   Rev. XX 13

The emigrants were part Irish, part Highland, part carpenters from Glasgow. They pleaded with the captain to put back to Liverpool after storms carried away the topmasts. He threatened to fire on them if they got in his way, then battened them below decks to forestall a panic – or a mutiny. As the sea broke in, the few who reached the lifeboats found them secured and unable to be moved. Just one child was saved – tied to her mother's back with a tartan shawl. When the islanders (labourers for MacGillivray's brother-in-law) kindled a fire to see by as they carted the dead up into the dunes, a ship with a cargo of salt mistook it for a distress signal and sank on a rock with the loss of all hands but one as it went to the rescue of the *Annie Jane*.

The memoir I got of this episode, at Garrygall, was weirdly garbled:

There was only one man there, and he had to take his cart out over and over again to the wreck to fill it up with the bodies. There was some of the young men from Barra got into trouble down in Oban where they were saying the Vatersay people had gone out to the ship when it was sinking and they were hitting them over the head with stockings with a stone in them! There were a lot of sovereigns over there afterwards, and gold coins, and that Jew called Cohen who came through the islands, he got hold of a lot of them.

As a seaboard tale this rivalled in its savagery the stories you hear on Scilly about the islanders lighting fires which ships mistook for the old beacon lighthouses and followed onto the rocks, where they were looted. The idea that there was only one person on Vatersay was surely an unconscious cartoon of its comparative emptiness after clearance. What the wreck and its monument meant to me was the sheer omnipresence of emigration in the island culture. At times it seemed to have absorbed more life-time, more thought, more bodily energies than the economy itself.

The memoirs of clearance I heard in house after house on Barra were of a piece with Chrissie MacDonald's at Buaile nam Bodach and featured kidnapping rather than eviction as such. According to Father Calum MacLellan, a young man who was being chased, presumably by ground officers, managed to escape by jumping across the tidal inlet west of Castlebay at Nask and hid in a cave up on Ben Tangaval, where people brought him food. According to Mrs Annie MacKinnon of Eorsary, two boys from her village had 'gone to the other side of the island, after sheep. People were being put into boats off Balnabodach, and when the boys came back they heard dogs barking – there was nobody in the house – the basins of milk had been poured out onto the fire.' According to Morag MacAulay of Garrygall,

> A woman was in the field over at Tangasdale, with her two little girls with her, and she had a big skirt, it was made of the drugget – do they make it now? It was big and it stood out, so she got the wee girls under her skirt when the sheriffs came along, and they asked, 'Is there anybody else here?' And she said, 'No, there is only myself.' And a young woman was in the fields at Balnabodach, milking the cow, and they came and took her away from beside the cow, she had no coat even, she had nothing, and they sent her away on the boat.

The logic of Morag's first story presumably is that if the woman had shown herself to be a mother, the heavies would have known there was a crofter nearby who as a tenant was eligible for eviction. Yet the second woman was not saved by being single. Do we conclude that such kidnapping was fairly random? The women who spoke to me were sure of what they were saying – Annie McKinnon's eyes enlarged to their fullest as she grew appalled again at the old atrocity and Morag MacAulay was quoting her father's mother, who had seen a young man seized for expulsion at Lochboisdale in 1850: 'They put his hands up behind his neck' (she mimed the movement) 'and tied them there with two silk handkerchiefs' – the detail has a ballad force.

My sneaking incredulity was at the notion of mass person-hunts which sounded like the work of slavers in a country outside the law. By what right sustainable in court, I had been asking myself for years, could private employees (sometimes abetted by constables) seize and restrain people who were not chargeable with any crime? The explanation came at last in a memoir by Niall's father which I read in the sitting room at Aros Cottage:

[The Potato Famine] left a very bad mark on the population, and a mark of poverty, and Ground Officers came and went round the crofters and told them that they would get so much meal, oatmeal, if they gave their names to go to Canada. A great many were pressed to go – but they wanted their names before they gave them their meal, on the condition that if your name was there to go, to Canada you must go.

. . . I remember myself two old ladies, two sisters, that signed with their father to go, and they took to the hills and they were hiding up in Ben Cleat and coming down at night to Vaslan to friends' houses who used to give them something to eat. And this was carried on till the coast was clear, and their old father went. And the unfortunate part of the story, you see, he died on the way out. His name was John MacDougall, known in Barra as Iain Muillear, and he was buried at sea.

All the people from Barra were ferried over in boats from Barra to South Uist . . . I knew a man named Farquhar MacRae, who was on board the *Admiral* and witness to all that was happening . . . The captain was a burly big fellow and he gave orders to erect a sort of fence amidships, with those that were staying on this side of the fence, and those that were going out on the other side of the fence. And after he got this done he gave an order to the sailors, 'Come on, boys, now lash them out.' And the sailors got ropes and lashed the poor men and women back home, after parting with their nearest and dearest friends.

Here was the missing component. By signing to go the islanders had bound themselves over. Apologists for clearance sometimes emphasise that hundreds on Barra and South Uist 'petitioned' to leave. So why the brutal compulsions at the last minute? Because a good many of the 'petitioners' were signing on to go purely to get the meal they needed if they were not to starve to death. At the last minute, or indeed all along, they had no desire to go. Conditions as well as estate heavies (and the occasional minister) were *driving* them out.

One man named by The Coddy, Neil MacNeill, left in dismay at the rotting of the potatoes:

> The smell that was off the blight was enough to choke you, and so he decided to pack his bag and went to Castlebay to get some conveyance – a boat or ship – to take him to the mainland. And that he did. And that was his description of what happened the night of the blight. It was about the 14th of August. Well, he left, and it was fourteen years before he returned to Barra, and several who went with him never did return.

This too was puzzling. Could the sickening of the potatoes in the fields have been so sudden? Morag MacAulay's story of it – the first famine story I ever heard by word of mouth – was much the same. Her South Uist grandmother told her what she remembered:

> There was a young boy came down from the hill in the middle of the day and he said to his mother, 'There is a cockerel crowing.' And she said, 'How can the cockerel be crowing in the middle of the day?' And the next thing they knew, the potatoes had rotted in the ground, and the cows were dying. They had to bury them, but afterwards they dug them up to eat them.

This sounded ballad-like, in its telescoping of time, its resonant repetitions. Again it turns out to be veritable. In his classic history of the Great Hunger in Ireland, *Paddy's Lament*, Thomas Gallagher records that in late July 1846, near Cork, farmers with a fine green crop in their potato-gardens were awakened by a 'sulferous, sewer-like smell carried by the wind from the rotting plants in the first-struck places ... and by the dogs howling their disapproval of it. They could see nothing in the dark; they could only smell the rot.'

Morag MacAulay likened the forced exodus from Barra and South Uist to 'when they shipped off the Jews' and cited a television treatment of that, presumably the American series *Holocaust*, although paradoxically she felt that the Nazi genocide – so much worse than the Scottish – had been made too much of. She told her stories briskly, with no sentimental lingering over the martyrs or lurking sense that victimisation bore heavily on *her*. She was an elegant woman in her eighties, wearing a plum organdie dress with a high ruffled collar, a long sleeveless tunic of mallard green, and her white hair prettily curled. She made me tea with water from a battered kettle that sat on a range with a live fire in it and she rejoiced in having been the subject of 'The Fair Maid of Barra', written for her sixty years ago by a man from South Uist. She sings it herself with a skilled shaping of the phrases and the power still to hold the long poignant notes –

> Young maid of the fair hair,
> Listen to the poetry from my lips.
> Give me your promise, my love,
> And for your sake I'll return.
> Although I have been fond of many girls
> From various countries and races,
> O please consent,
> When I ask so earnestly . . .

This seems pure Hebrides in its assertion of love in spite of separation, whether due to migration or to working on the deep-sea ships. Even apart from clearance Barra is perpetually under siege by the sea. I had two people to see at Borve on the west side and to know it better I first visited the graveyard. It lies to seaward of some clustered standing-stones. Feet away, under a louring sky, breakers were blossoming like funeral flowers against slate. I never saw so much grief huddled into one place – eloquent grief, not tight-lipped and not pompous either. The three or four hundred graves were nearly all marked by crosses, crudely-moulded cement, stone Celtic, roofed with a little gable as in the Bavarian or Dolomite Alps, plain wood even (one of these was freshly whitewashed although the death had happened in 1864). A great many of the men had died in their twenties or thirties, two brothers 'Killed At Sea', a whole row of the Merchant Navy crosses with a rope loop carved in granite bas-relief, many from one ship in 1940 with an Italian '*Morto Per La Patria*' buried next them and his wife's name added thirty years later (a prisoner of war on his way to Canada, I later discovered). The language was luxuriant in the Catholic way – 'Sweet Jesus, have mercy on his soul', 'Of your charity pray for the repose of . . .', 'Mary, Star of the Sea, be with her'. A red cloth rose lay on the wet grass in front of a girl's grave, a plastic crucifix labelled 'Lourdes' with little sprays of flowers below it was fixed to a stone under a sheet of perspex. Many epitaphs were in Gaelic, mostly using the word *Tighearna*, Lord – which I had first met in a very different usage, the proverb used as the motto of the Highland Land Law Reform Association which led the crofters in their war of the 1870s and '80s: '*Is treasa Tuath na Tighearna*' – 'The People are mightier than a Lord'. One stone was inscribed wholly in Gaelic and spelt Barra 'Barraidh'. Below the outside of the wall a natural harbour was formed by two groynes of gneiss fifteen feet high – coffins could have come in that way by boat.

Next morning at breakfast Niall told us, 'There has been a terrible tragedy.' Two fishermen had drowned off Borve Point, Hughie MacInnes, whose wife was a close friend of Niall's wife Chrissie, and a lad MacFadyean from Borve itself. They had been lifting their lobster creels to bring them in for the winter and it was thought that the boat had been top-heavy with the big load and capsized in the swell. A helicopter and R.A.F. divers had been working all night and had found the boat under the water, split in two, but not the fishermen. It was clearly out of the question to go interviewing in Borve.

That afternoon, as we sat at Eoligarry eating our oatcakes and Dutch cheese and wishing that we could move up to Eriskay and South Uist by the direct ferry which still runs but carries only foot passengers, a helicopter came throbbing over and we followed it down to Borve. On the machair south of Greian Head dozens of vans, Land Rovers, pick-ups were parked. An R.N.L.I. lifeboat was disappearing into the slatey troughs and bobbing into sight again on the wind-blown crests. A few yards off the Head a low-lying white craft with lifting gear at the stern was manoeuvring to hold its position. Much closer in, just feet from the clambering and exploding white water next the cliff (where I had climbed the day before), a very small boat with a stub mast was taking the worst risks of all – manned by relatives of the dead, no doubt.

On the ribs of Sgeir Liath, the grey reef, little groups of watchers stood in orange P.V.C. trousers and dark-blue jerseys – silhouetted against the sloping grey masses of the sea with that motionless and solitary mien which seems both to stand up to the waves and to be dwarfed by them.

After an hour the lifeboat and the white craft chugged off southward and the little boat disappeared round the Head, as close as ever to the breaking waters. At the foot of the cliff more men in orange waterproofs were doing something, or nothing. Had the bodies been located? Would it be worth helping to comb the shore? Oppressed by ignorance and uselessness, I was reminded of what my last close relative in Aberdeen, my cousin Annie, had said. When there was a storm and the fishermen were out at sea – including her father and my grandfather – the headmaster at her school would choose Hymn 626 –

> Eternal Father, strong to save,
> Whose arm hath bound the restless wave,
> And bids the mighty ocean deep
> Its own appointed limits keep,
> O hear us when we cry to Thee
> For those in peril on the sea.

He meant it to be supportive but she dreaded it, it made her feel worse, not better, and I felt I knew why. The slow rise of the tune, which never quite peaks, mimics uncannily the heave of a swell and the dolour it can inflict and makes the power of the Lord seem feeble by comparison.

CHAPTER SIXTEEN

STEPPING STONES
Eriskay, Baleshare, Berneray, Harris, Lewis

The wind that had killed Hughie MacInnes and young Mac-Fadyean prevented us from reaching Eriskay two days later, which was maybe just as well. Eriskay is very small with roads like switchbacks and little room for manoeuvre. The night before, quite gently and for no particular reason, I had almost driven into the ditch. The car had come to rest at a dangerous angle just above gleaming black water and our landlady's husband had to tow us out with his tractor. Next morning at Ludag slipway the Eriskay ferryman let me drive on, then said, 'We will take you if you like, but you may not get back.' The sea was running high and throwing up bursts of spray like frenzied cockatoos. I had only one person to see (suggested by Father Calum on Barra). I gave in, reversed off, and managed to drop my offside front wheel into the turbulent water beside the ramp. '*Now* what are you going to do?' the ferryman asked with open curiosity. Perhaps he had heard about the night before. Luckily the rear wheels gripped the slipway and pulled us back and up. Next day we crossed uneventfully on the *Eilean na h-Oige*, although we had to lie low from the drenching spume in a wee saloon whose walls were decorated with computer print-out from the school on Eriskay:

Dear Domhnall Iain and Iagan,
    Thank you for taking Room 1 over to Uist and letting us see up in the wheelhouse. We were really very interested in the radar and some of us enjoyed sitting in the skipper's chair.
                                                    Yours sincerely
                                                    Primary 1–4

Jo-Jo, Martin, Duncan, and Eilidh, writing by hand, were a little more personal about it and said they had been 'very interested in the engines and also liked the smoke alarms'.

I had last landed on Eriskay in 1969 with my children, whom I had used to sing to sleep with the 'Eriskay Love Lilt'. In those days the island had no pier and slipway fit for cars. We had crossed at low tide and been landed on the beach near Ruban. On the skerry in mid-sound all the boulders turned out to be seals, who stared at us out of glossy black eyes. We jumped out of the boat onto rocks that teemed and squeaked with winkle clusters. For weeks we had been living in a fishy ambience, catching mackerel and codling by hand-line, wading in shallow channels as though strolling in a garden and gathering handfuls of buckie from under the fronds and clumps of the seaweed. Since then, tourism and HIDB grants having transformed the islands in a businesslike direction, even Eriskay has its smart pub, called *Am Politician* after the wreck made famous in *Whisky Galore* which sank with its 24,000 cases of whisky a mile east of the seal-skerry. In the bar you can look at a salvaged bottle with no label and cloudy contents and sniff from another – it smelt of riverbeds.

Donald MacInnes, now the oldest man on Eriskay, has probably changed less in these years than the island's facilities. I had been told he lived in Haun, near the new ferry pier. I went to the wrong MacInnes house at first, horizontal rain came on, and Mrs MacInnes urged me to pause for a cup of coffee. Talking about the clearance to Eriskay, she said abruptly, 'They just drove them away from Uist and dropped them on the rock here, to die.' Eriskay was the Botany Bay or Devil's Island of the clearance traffic. Only four families had been living there, for the good reason that it is steep and rocky with a minimum of arable land. Donald MacInnes, when I found him herding sheep on boggy pasture near his house, knew only that his grandparents came from 'Uist', which he defined by places 'at the back of the hill', Usinish, Lamasay, and the like. We stood at the lee end of his house to talk while the wild iris leaves writhed in the gale like snakes with their heads caught in the ground. He was not a genealogical man, more of an exact eyewitness, and what he had seen was evidence of the last stage of factor tyranny:

When they were at the kelp work, I saw it with my own eyes, the factor at Boisdale took every sack of it through his own hands, weighing it and setting a price on it. Because of course the estate considered it owned every bit of weed that came out of the sea. When they would be putting potatoes into the lazybeds, the estate officers would be coming round with their hooks – lifting up the ground (he mimed with his hazelwood crook) – looking to see what kind of weed they had put into the ground, in case it was the sort that was needed for the burning. Yes – that was hard. Och, they were just slaves.

Inevitably, as we stood near the Young Pretender's first landfall at the start of his adventure in 1745, Charles Edward Stewart came up and Mr MacInnes turned out to have a familiar difficulty – how do you name him if the winsome 'Bonnie' and the matey 'Charlie' stick in your craw? Mr MacInnes was well up in the subject. After citing details of the first abortive French expedition on the Jacobites' behalf and the French king's refusal to subsidise them after that, his judgement was:

> Charlie – I won't call him that – the Prince, whatever he was – he was what I call a young fool. He just made a fool of himself altogether. And supposing he had got all the way, he would not have lived in Edinburgh, he would have been away off to London. And wherever he had lived it would have done us no good at all.

He was turning to look me full in the eyes as he clinched each point, wiping the tear at the end of his nose, sometimes bringing his crook down for emphasis onto the cement surround of the house he had built himself (harled white walls and a red roof of crinkly tin) – a lean man with a bristle of white hair, in an old jacket and cap, focussing on one topic after another with the sceptical intelligence of Rob the miller, one of 'the last of the peasants' in Grassic Gibbon's *Sunset Song*.

The islands were stepping-stones now, leading us north. Hurricane Gabrielle from the Caribbean was reaching out her failing powers to lash the seaboard – 50 knots on Benbecula, 51 at Kirkwall, a father and son dead when their boat capsized on Loch Assynt, a Nature Conservancy researcher found dead below screes on Rum. The *Eilean na h-Oige* crabbed back across the wind to Ludag without incident but a young priest left his bags on deck beside the cars, Anne told him, and when he got over his panic at being addressed by a strange female he rushed out to retrieve them as they swilled about in six inches of salt water – turned the steel handle the wrong way and shut the door on himself instead of opening it – only just plucked his luggage out of the bilge. It is always the way – the smaller the ferry, the livelier the life on board it.

We were heading for Baleshare, a little machair island west of North Uist shaped like a bulb with a flowering top or (turned on its side) like a seal with a double tail. It was reputed to be the place where kelp-burning came into the Hebrides – for good and ill. Right up South Uist, as far as possible, we kept to the old trackway which threads the machair less than a mile from the shore, from Smerclate through the Boisdales to Kilpheder, west of Daliburgh and Askernish to Trollaskeir, by Loch Kildonan, Bornish, and Ormaclete to Stoneybridge, Peninerine, Dremisdale, and Stilligarry. This was the spinal cord of old Uist, Uist of the nucleated clachans, before the clearance to the back of the hill and the final force-pumping of people southward to 'Dalabrog', Lochboisdale, and Eriskay. The land is barely above the surf, founded on shell-sand, fertilised and nitrogenised by the close weave of the machair flowers – eyebright, speedwell, buttercup, clover, trefoil, silverweed. It is still crofted; it was like time-warping thirty years back to Skye or Wester Ross, or fifty to Aberdeenshire, to see the gilt bristle of corn-stubble woven in stripes between the greeny-yellow thickets of ripe potato shaws and, crowning the fields at intervals, the handmade stooks of sheaves, three or four feet high, each one topped with a flourish of yellow ears like a totem of harvest.

Most of these loose and fragile-seeming stooks had withstood Gabrielle, who still raved. Just yards away the combers curved up their green-glass caves, collapsed into the moil of foam in front of them with a bash like meaty wet bodies hitting a floor, while behind them at the headland of Rubha Ardvule the skerries undersea forced up the next onset and further out the water-skyline mounded out of shape like a mother's belly pushed by a foetal hand or head. Days of this had ploughed up the seabed and the tattered swathes of weed surfaced in the churning whiteness dark as seals' heads or the bodies of cormorants. As the sun spotlit them, they waved a glistening brown arm like the limb of a person going under. In the Rankins' garden at Clachan Uaine on Baleshare, the asters and snapdragons spent most of their time parallel with the ground, shuddering. According to Katey, the wind had reached 150 m.p.h.

the winter before and they almost despaired of the garden. A solid wall would only bounce the wind up and then down again onto the flowers and the leeks; they would need a hedge, and a hedge would need a plastic ribbon-fence outside it for twenty years at least to protect it from the sheep.

I had wanted to know Baleshare more deeply ever since I had walked up its western shore in 1969, looked into the thickness of the dunes, and seen the cross-section of a farmstead: chocolate layers embedded in the sand where the midden had been, veins of cockle and buckie shells, the latter up to 4 cms long, much bigger than live ones today, and a rib of large flat stones protruding, toppling onto the beach, where they contrast with the rounded shingle. The land here is sinking. Between North Uist and Heisgeir (the Monach Islands), or so it's said, you can look down into the sea on a calm, sunlit day and see the skeleton of a drowned clachan. As the sea rises and advances, it has torn off pieces of land and laid bare the old farmstead. Baleshare is a raft with its little freight of bents and pasture-fields and exposed white houses, a miniature of Tiree, tethered to Uist by a causeway now: a minimal perch for humans, you might say, if each croft were not so tenacious a centre of social life. Looking out one moonlit night from Clachan Uaine, Anne was shaken by the savagery of the terrain. The ice-sheets bull-dozed here, leaving little but boulder-clay. In the blue glare that night the low-lying moors, blanket bogs, and water-logged fretwork of the lochan system looked like a land long before civilisation, even precluding it. It has its indefatigable culture, embodied for me by John MacAulay of Illeray. He talked for three or four hours with minimal prompting, never repeating himself, telling the history of the nearby islands with a dense blend of anecdote and scrupulous documentation, balancing cigarette after cigarette in fingers almost unrecognisable with arthritis. His croft was a museum of machines, hay-rakes, binders, ploughs, all neatly arranged on the grass beside the low ruin thatched with turfs which his father had built and lived in.

John MacAulay's knowledge should be formed into a book. As it is he is an information service. People seeking their roots come to him from London, Canada, Australia. 'There was a Gordon MacDonald came here from London, and I studied for a while where the man should scatter his father's ashes. "Clachan Sands," I said to him, "because your people came from there to Claddach Baleshare, where there is a great fishing pool."' In the late afternoon of the Sunday I visited him, a young Canadian couple came to ask him about their forebears and he was able to tell the man that his great-grandfather was Tormod Ferguson of Knockintorran, near Paible on North Uist. Around 1850 he had been working one morning for MacDonald of Balranald:

> At dinnertime the carts came along and tipped salt herrings and potatoes onto the ground for the men to eat. So Tormod stormed off, he would not be taking his dinner from the ground. So next day Balranald came to their house and he said, 'Why is Tormod not at work?' Tormod's father said he would not work so long as they were fed like animals. So after that they did it right.

An alert and uncompromising feeling for the underdog was as strong in John as in anyone I met among the crofters:

> A young man called Maclean at the north end, when the Beveridge mob were coming [the rich owners of Vallay before and after the Great War], hid himself under a culvert near the mill and hammered on the underside of the arch as the horsey equipage came near. The horses checked – they wouldn't go on. Nobody knew why. They *hated* those yuppies, those sporting-fishing gentlemen.

This contrasted with Neil MacVicar, whom I had spoken to on Grimsay. He remembered that same equipage with a glow of admiration. Erskine Beveridge, a dilettante whose money came from linen mills in Fife, kept two carriages in light oak with 'yellow streaks' painted on the wheels and tan upholstery, two black horses, Baldy and Star, one with a white blaze on its forehead, and two bays, Ina and Linda. 'When they drove through the shallow water across to Claddach Vallay, it all came up in a sparkle.' Neil was grateful to a 'good landlord' and remembered thankfully Beveridge's charity at Christmas when he 'somehow found out how many there were in each house and sent round a big stocking full of stuff for everyone'. John was much more independent and the only landlord he conceded to at all was Orde, owner of the estate including Sollas many years after the battle, who was 'lenient': 'When you wanted a place there, you collected a few friends and built a house at night and put a fire in it.'

Such was the scraping life of the people who had been 'herded into Illeray' when the larger part of Baleshare was cleared to make a farm. John's forebears had been allotted this croft under the Blackadder Survey, commissioned by Lord MacDonald in 1799. People who failed to get a croft became cottars, with peat rights and a low rent:

> In ten years they wouldn't have a blade of grass on the hill [the common grazing] and they were buggering off to Canada. They would get a section, and a plough and a buggy and some seed corn, and live in an old railway carriage. They were in their glory, because they had a piece of land they could call their own, that they never had before.

John saw himself distinctly as a member of a class who were not the poorest, who did have land, but 'you never had a penny in your hand before the pension in 1912' and they were far from secure. His voice rose as he recounted an eviction in the 1840s:

> There was a man Neil MacLellan, he was married to Catherine MacAulay from Paiblesgarry. When the Church broke up in 1843, he gave his house for a preacher, a catechist as they call it. And the factor and the estate, they went to put him out of his house, and out of his croft, and they sent him away to Nova Scotia.

John sees himself as a survivor of a people who had gone west on the crofters' trail, whether by choice or because they were forced, and he was yet another who knew that only a slender chance had led to his living on this side of the water. His Campbell forebear on his mother's side had gone to Lochmaddy pier – 'to bid farewell to the rest of them – an awful lot were going – there was nothing for them here. And he was newly married, his first daughter was only a child. "If it wasn't for the girl being so young, I might go with you." And he never went. And that's why *we* are here.' John's isolation seemed to be relieved by the constant flow of people back across the Atlantic to visit – 'That's the one good thing there is just now, the communications.' It was in keeping that he should have sent to Canada for a copy of a letter from a stay-at-home forebear, Ronald MacAulay, to his brother Neil in Cape Breton Island, written on June 23rd, 1830. In it I recognised the anxieties I had seen on many sheets of letter-paper in Ontario – the pleading for relationship to be kept up, the wish to share domestic closeness as in the old days, the worries about crofting:

> This is third letter since I received your's which was only one; I am greatly surprised for not receiving more, either from you or Angus or both. I fear Angus is not alive because I never received a letter from him or rather very little account concerning him . . . I would have written before now, but being unwilling to trouble you too often in paying . . . There are sent by Lord MacDonald two gentlemen, to have all charge of kelp for new way of manufacturing it, which I think will leave the country to be worse . . . I wish to inform me of Angus, whether he is alive or not, where he is, in what place, what wages, and how the place is pleasing him. I hope whether good or bad that I will see both Angus and Donald your son, especially Angus, if good to assist and encourage us all to emigrate as soon as possible and if not let it suffice him to come unto his dear parents, who will do all what they can do with him . . . I bought Donald MacAulay's yellow horse last year for 7, but being too high for serving under creels [to carry kelp], I sold him again for 9. I hope to have a cart for the colt if she live long . . . If you have any respect for all towards your daughter I think you would provoke Donald to come for her or else you will never see her . . .

As John remarked, 'When people were cleared away, what bothered the folk who were left, when they got any word back, was would you advise us to go over there?' In the context of all this sundering, his passion for history came over like a determination to keep the threads of community woven.

Our next stepping-stone, or bone of the finger pointing north, was Berneray, half a mile off North Uist, technically part of Harris and able to be sold, bought, cleared, exploited by the same people (the Earl of Dunmore and Donald Stewart of Ensay) who were laying waste the most comfortable communities on Harris itself. These islands, Ensay, Berneray, Pabbay, Killigray, are not bleak reefs but cradles of life with a rich bedding of machair in their hollows. Pabbay had been 'the granary of Harris' and 26 families lived there well enough in the early nineteenth century. In 1834 Dunmore bought Harris for £60,000 (and sold half of it thirty-four years later at a

250 per cent profit). The people were evicted by what they called 'the Earl's *saighdearan*', i.e. his soldiers, who were a contingent of the British Army sent by one of Dunmore's friends in the Cabinet to enforce his writs.

On Pabbay a woman was about to give birth at the May term – the peak period for evictions. The ground officer took her out of the house on a blanket and nailed up the door. A late storm had left snow drifting up the dykes. The baby was born in the open and came to be called Rachel Mhòr. The family fled across the Sound of Harris, squatted in its meadows, and built a house where Rachel Mhòr spent the rest of her life. I was told this by a man from Strath Ardle near Blairgowrie, who had it from the postman's wife, who had known Rachel Mhòr in Harris. By 1858 only one shepherd and his family lived on Pabbay. There was still just the one tenant there in the 1970s. He had been 'terrible with the drink' and finally left Pabbay. Later he was found dead in a cattle-shed on Skye. Pabbay, emptied at last and owned by a Lloyd's broker 'for a help with his taxes', looked perfectly serene across the gale-torn sound, symmetrical as an Asian rice-harvester's straw hat, its hill-grazing olive, its croft-land sap-green down the sheltered southern slope. Its profile was as gradual as Taransay's off South Harris; the Rev. Mr MacKenzie of Creagorry, who was brought up on Taransay, had spoken to me lovingly about the 'peculiar aura' of that island.

Only one house on Berneray could take us. The man of it, a lobster fisherman called Angus MacLean, walked across the machair with me on a morning when a Force 10 prevented him from going out to his creels. It was ironical to think that Berneray's witness before the Napier Commissioners, Malcolm MacLeod, testified that when they began to fish lobsters after losing land to the estate, 'the factor MacDonald sent the ground officer to stop us, he being angry with us because we were not going to Australia'. The island is in halves, the hilly and rocky eastern part where the people are now and the spreading western meadowland with a burial ground at its edge. The factor MacDonald, who had cleared Pabbay, also 'cleared the half of Bernera', according to another witness, John MacLeod – himself evicted, along with two brothers and a sister, for owning the boat on which Jessie the Belle of North Uist eloped to Harris with her lover in 1851: 'A large number of the people that left these places went to Australia and died upon the voyage. Some went to America, some to Caolas-Scalpa, and to the island of

Scalpa itself, where they are now packed as thick as herrings in a barrel.'

The land they lost on Berneray, when it was taken to make the big farm of Borve, is made up of downland mellow as Dorset and fields as broad and even as Suffolk. The hard knuckles of the eastern part show striping of old lazybeds between each joint and right up to their peaks, so desperate were the crofters for potato-land. 'The women worked like horses,' said Angus, 'bringing the weed away up there on their backs.' Borve Hill and Moor Hill carry only sheep now and the good ground, regained for crofts early this century, is a blond region of extraordinary peacefulness and goodness where acres of the bristle-pointed oat shake their polished tassels and cattle graze which, like the generations before them, fetch the best prices at the Lochmaddy sales.

In Angus Maclean's lore the proprietor who most harrowed Berneray was John Stewart of Ensay, son of an arch-evictor on Harris, abetted or thwarted by his herdsman Kenny, who would have been the immediate boss of the island:

The horses the crofters kept, they had all to be tethered, of course, and they managed to stray a good deal [Angus gives his wicked grin]. And Kenny's wife would say to him, 'Kenny, get some animals into the pound – the house is without tea . . .' The farmer's sheep would be on the hill and Stewart would come over once a year to look them over. So this summer he noticed one sheep that wasn't his at all, and he said, 'Kenny, what's that animal doing there?' And Kenny said, 'Och, it's only an odd one from somewhere.' Now, it belonged to a widow, this sheep. So next year it was still there when Stewart came over, and when he saw it he said, 'Kenny – that sheep is still down there amongst my animals.' And Kenny said, 'Och, it just belongs to an old woman down there – it doesn't eat much.' And Stewart said to him, 'Would you put 365 sheep in the fold for a day, and at the end of it would you be telling me how much grass is left in it. Well, that is the quantity of grass that the widow's sheep will be eating in a year . . .'

We walked down to the burial ground near Craaknish and along past the little humpy remnants of the pre-clearance clustered villages towards the headland of Voisinish. The ground hollowed off inland in exquisitely moulded dales with their dense pelt of flowers and grasses, harebells still transparent blue, ragwort like miniature yellow trees, bladder campion withered down to papery globes. In a snap I took with my Olympus Automatic the folding and breasting of the downland, which is barely thirty feet high, seems to have the stature of the vales inland from Dorchester. On the dunes the crests of the marram whose roots hold back the sand from turning Berneray into a desert were shaking along in pulses under the equinoctial gale. We were staggering, giving up trying to walk straight, weaving about drunk on force and light and motion.

'Look at that!' Angus caught my arm. 'Do you see the movement there?' The white bursts on the dark-turquoise water made it look as though every wave had a gannet diving into it. Angus was facing into the wind and shouting above it,

> 'And a negro lass to fan him
> As he listens to the roar
> Of breakers pounding on the reef
> That never reach the shore . . .

'What's that – Alfred Lord Tennyson?'
'I doubt it. He didn't go much on negro lasses.'
'Robert Louis Stevenson?'
'Well – he wasn't as "coarse" as that – not as sexual.' At a loss for a source, I recite 'Prufrock' –

> 'I have seen them riding seaward on the waves
> Combing the white hair of the waves blown back
> When the wind blows the water white and black.
>
> We have lingered in the chambers of the sea
> By sea-girls wreathed with seaweed red and brown
> Till human voices wake us, and we drown.'

'What's that?'
'T.S. Eliot – an American – he's dead now.'
'"And a negro lass to fan him,"' repeats Angus, who is a real performer and semi-professional on the accordion. 'It was in the wee book of verse at school. I wish I'd memorised more of it.' Beside us the west wall of a ruin dropped almost straight to the

beach and I wondered if it had been too near the beach but Angus scouted this. 'No, no, the wind would have run right over it. There was nothing could bring harm to those old houses. And there's the marram that they cut for the thatch.' He was wholly at home in the wind and it was drawing out stories of how islanders braved it and whatever else was thrown at them:

A traveller was coming across and it was quite a wild day, and he said to the old man who had the boat, 'Do you know where all the rocks are?' And the old man said och yes, he knew them all. Well, they were well out into the channel and the old man wanted to steer straight for Berneray, to avoid having to tack, do you see, so when he came near a rock he just steered straight over it – bam! – and it lifted the boat right up out but of course it was all right. But the traveller said, 'I thought you said you knew all the rocks.' 'I do,' said the old man. 'And that was one of them.'

We were still in sight of Pabbay and Angus made me stop between the dunes and the cornfields to listen to the story which clearly held for him the essence of how the islands had stood up to the mainland system in the days before the Clearances:

They used to distil there, you know – great distillers. And when the Excise were coming they used to sail over there from Harris, and the man who was carrying them, he would give a wee dip of his sail when he came in sight of Pabbay, so that they knew what to do. But this one time it was a stranger was bringing the Custom men and he didn't know the bloody score, so dammit, what did he do but sail the boat straight in with never a dip of his sail, so the man comes straight up to a house where they had the still, the *poit dhubh*, you know – the black pot. Only a woman was there, and he could smell the fire on her, and he said, 'Come on, now – I know what you have there. Where is it – where is your black pot?' So she just caught her skirts right up, showing herself, and she said, '*Here* is my black pot, and if my husband was at home you would see it working.'

Harris was deeply shadowed over the water, its mountains brewing up cloud out of the Atlantic airstream. I had wanted to understand the causes of the terrible emptiness of its western meadowland ever since I had camped on the machair at Seilebost in 1975 and had been appalled by the contrast between the west of the island, unpeopled except for the manufactured villages of Northton and Leverburgh, and the east, where the soil came in flowerbed sizes yet there was a township along the side of every rockbound geo. It would have been good to take the passenger ferry straight across from Uist in the old way; the car committed us to the Calmac boat. It had been having trouble in the gale and decided to spend the night in the harbour when we reached Harris. This nearly overwhelmed the available accommodation but it was where I most wanted to stay. Somewhere or other during the previous two or three years I had heard the name of Kirstie Shaw of Tarbert as a person full of history. I found her red-roofed, white-walled house in one of the irregular streets where sheep walk about, browsing in the gardens wherever a gate has been left open. Kirstie Shaw, grey-haired in a flowered overall, was filling an old soup pan with coals from her shed.

'Who are you, now?'

'My name's Craig. I'm travelling about looking for stories about the events of last century, and you were recommended to me – '

'That is good news.'

We went inside for a cup of coffee and in a few minutes she had given me a Clearance memoir of an artistic completeness I had found nowhere before:

My father's people were from Strond – that's where Lady Dunmore saw the women dyeing the wool with crotal from the rocks – that's supposed to have started her off with the tweed. My mother – her great-grandmother was MacDonald – they were at Crago, near Seilebost, and her house was burnt to a cinder when the men came to put them out. She had to hide among the corn, in one of the furrows, with my grandmother as a baby. Early autumn it must have been, because she lay down in the furrow, beside the corn, with her daughter in her arms, and the corn was able to hide her.

Some of them went to Canada. Two old men in Cape Breton showed my brother [a minister in Ontario] the place, a lovely flat piece beside a river. They had to dig shanties out of the ground and they covered them with leaves, until they could build a house.

Some of them had died of a broken heart, they were telling my brother. They had it *here* for Stewart – my goodness – their heritage and what they loved to the last breath! Like what the Nazis did, the gas chambers – that's what it was, as bad as that.

Those were the Stewarts of Ensay. The husband wasn't so bad but the women were terrible. The husband asked the wife, 'Are you pleased now I've burnt the houses?'

'I'll never be pleased,' she said, 'while I see a wisp of smoke between here and Rodel.'

There was a bard from South Harris made a song about them . . .

Kirstie started to sing verses in a high hard clear voice, using vibrato to decorate the longer notes, looking straight ahead of her and translating from time to time:

My thousand curses on the old Stewart,
Before he comes back, that his grave will be ready for him . . .

The children were better than the parents,
I want that nothing will happen to the children,
But I hope that the one who is telling them
To be bad will not be long in the world.

Some of them went away with the boat,
Others went away overseas.
I hope *you* will never see your family
Again on the one side together . . .

There was a woman down at Geocrab, she was over a hundred years old, and she remembered how they took everything with them when they went to Canada. They took the wheels, the looms, the boiler, and the frames for the hanks of wool. And the peat irons and spades. And the big chest, the girnel. If there were couples due to be married, sometimes the parents would not like it if they left together, so the girl would hide in the boat. Annie Campbell the Scalpay tacksman's daughter wanted to marry a man called Alan – brown Alan – and he had to go. He left Stornoway by boat and he was lost on a stormy night . . .

And she sang again:

> I wish I was near where the storm left you.
> Was it the Isle of Man?
> That would not be my chosen place
> But between Uist and Harris.

Och, why did they do nothing when they were tying them for the boats in Uist? There were stalwart men there – their minds cannot have been as strong as their bodies at all.

Kirstie's speech came from her fluently and almost unprompted, as though her people's experience were using her as a mouthpiece. Not that she was some kind of eerie sybil – she was full of humour and hospitality and introduced me to a neighbour as her 'new boyfriend'. To talk and sing was second nature to her and in an Irish way the words never stopped – any pause, to go through and fill the kettle again or remember a further detail, she would fill with little verbal arabesques, 'To be sure it was' or 'Yes indeed, that was the way of it'. Her descriptions would gather momentum until they ended in a flourish of hyperbole. Describing the good fishing at Ardhasaig to which the family moved after being evicted, she said, 'Oh, I remember the croft was full of the big haddocks laid out to cure, and the ling and the cuddies. And you would not get a fish there now, no you wouldn't, not if you went upstairs to heaven itself.' She recalled that as children they had helped to bait the great-line, the mile- or two-mile line of hooks baited with mussels that the fishermen used to use. I quoted to her a rhyme from the Moray Firth –

> Faa wid be a fisherman's wife,
> Te gang wi the creel, the scrubber, an the knife,
> A fool [foul] fireside an a raivelled bed
> An awa te the mussels in the morn.

'That's it,' said Kirstie with relish, 'that's the whole thing to a T.' Her liking for lyrics was hereditary. Her great-great-grandfather had been the Chisholm standard-bearer at Culloden, married to Annie Ferguson from the Black Isle, and after the débâcle she made a song to her husband, which Kirstie sang and translated –

O Charlie, it's your cause that hurt me.
You took everything from me.
It is not cows or sheep that I lament . . .

A minister on North Uist had suggested that I went to see a man
called Norman McLeod at Leverburgh, whose father 'was a great
historian', and when I mentioned this to Kirstie she said at once,
'Oh yes, he will tell you things. His great-grandmother was cleared
from Pabbay to Scalpay and the *cailleach* [old woman] made this
song –

> My love the lovely island
> Where the corn would grow,
> If I would get my wish
> My life and death would be there.
>
> It is not the wee crooked bothy,
> The turf as the back wall,
> That I was used to when I was young
> But the beautiful beaches of sand . . . '

From those more comfortable places the people were driven east and
north. John MacLeod the Napier witness evicted after the famous
elopement had also been cleared to Ardhasaig, where I later identified the remains of the boulder walls of Kirstie's old home among
a group crammed onto the shore of Loch Bun Abhainn Eadarra
where the road starts the climb into the mountains of North
Harris.

The north, which is the high, shapely terrain beloved of Victorian
landscape painters, was the half of Harris kept by Lord Dunmore
for sporting purposes; the south-west is girt by arable and pasture
well-limed by millennia of blown shell-sand; the south-east, main
dump for cleared people, should never have been lived in. After
two hours of driving across it and all round its edges you feel your
brain has flipped inside-out, or the world has, and nothing can be
registered but the wrong side of things – Earth has the makings of
life, hasn't it, it has the vegetable and the animal possibilities, but
here there is nothing but hardened magma, its minerals locked into
an everlasting non-event. Boiler-plate slabs, giant ribs, bosses, reefs
with boulders perched on them. Hoodie crows, the scavengers of the

moor, are hardly to be seen. Are there lizards even?

At least, down there in the sea, these same rock ribs harbour the lobsters and crabs, from which a living can now be made. Five or six generations ago this wholly dour coast suddenly became the homeland of hundreds of families who had no fishing tradition, who were farming crofters faced with *creating* fields. 'Nothing can be more moving to the sensitive observer of Hebridean life,' wrote Fraser Darling, 'than these lazybeds of the Bays district of Harris. Some are no bigger than a dining table, and possibly the same height from the rock, carefully built up with turves and the seaweed carried there in creels by the women and girls. One of these lazybeds will yield a sheaf of oats or a bucket of potatoes, a harvest no man should despise.' In the Sixties he wrote that the mini-fields 'grew both potatoes and straw crops well within my own memory.' In dozens of coastal townships I saw no corn and one potato-bed, although a good many inlets of grassland between crags were pallid where a hay crop had been scythed off. From East Loch Tarbert down to Finsbay, on the crazy zigs and zags of what they call the 'Golden Road' for the employment it afforded during a Slump, the settlements looked dim, houses under-used, the whitewash grey, although one newish seafood factory was doing its best. The stickers on derelict vehicles in a roadside quarry made sad reading: 'I ♥ HARRIS, LABOUR/SCOTLAND – VOTE MCCASKILL, BLOOD DONORS LOVE LIFE' – efforts at society in a place where wilderness was bound to prevail.

The families dumped here found there was too little depth of soil in which to bury their dead. They had to trek back west with the coffins. The last resting-place was at Luskentyre, an ample green ground where the Laxdale River runs into the Sound of Taransay. Forebears of Kirsty Shaw's had been cleared from here to Canada when a big farm was made. There are two filled graveyards there and stone after stone shows that the dead had lived on the Bays side, in Cluer, Stockinish, Drinishader, Scalpay – cleared people from the west side or their descendants. The commonest text on the headstones was *Gus am bris an là agus an teich na sgàilean*, with its poignant foresight of a future without pain, 'Until the day breaks and the shadows flee away . . .'

Clearance so skewed the development of Harris that every settlement now feels wrong. Leverburgh, where Lord Leverhulme's expensive fishing station was suddenly abandoned after his death in 1925, is a maze of wharves and waggon-rails and houses dotted about on exposed rocky knolls. Northton, where the western meadows run out in the machair isthmus of Toe Head, was a Board of Agriculture effort at making an instant crofting township after the Great War – the rows of roadside cottages look alien and are unkempt. For three miles north the shore land is so vacant that passing through it you feel a sudden deafness or lack of vibration, as in a sound-proofed room. Scarastavore and Borve should be populous – they were, too much so at the end: the slopes above are striped to the skyline with lazybeds. Now the unnatural peace has made this a kind of northern *Côte d'Azur* for a very small number of tasteful incomers – the best professional cook in the Hebrides, a distinguished artist and her husband, a refined craft shop. And everyone in South Harris has to drive those wild switchbacks to the ferry port at Tarbert, which ought to have been sited down at the original haven of Rodel. There the MacLeods of MacLeod reigned until the last of them, bankrupt, sold out to his own factor, Donald Stewart.

Rodel harbour, once the base for a famous fishery – drift-netting for herring in open waters was invented here – is empty and dilapidated, presided over by the collapsing mansion where Jessie of Balranald's wicked uncle held her prisoner. In one wing a sort of bar is housed which looks like something from the more wasted parts of rural Ireland thirty years ago. The careworn man behind it said he had nothing to serve us because he had *run out of coffee bags*. We retreated to the square-towered church to read the stone archive in its graveyard. It was built in the fourteenth century and the mother-rock juts through the masonry inside. By the 1820s it was being used for corn thrashing and cart building, until Lady Dunmore had it restored. It is a museum, unused for worship, lined with superb feudal tombs, and the graveyard holds the clues to what happened. There are ordinary stones, to Neil Mackay aged eighteen, drowned on the *Iolaire*, to John Morrison, bard and blacksmith, who was able to analyse religious experience with a lyrical immediacy –

> I am drowned in the 'old' man's sea,
> in sharp dew and winter's coldness,
> the glorious 'new' man comes to his temple
> and he sets my feet a-dancing . . .

The most expensive stones (apart from the MacLeods' balustraded mausoleum) were to John MacDonald the factor, a former Army officer, died on Killigray, his personal domain, after 31 years' service, and John MacLeod, Chief Ground Officer for 35 years, served the estate faithfully etc., tomb erected by tenantry as token of esteem etc. On Baleshare John MacAulay had shown me a typed translation of a Gaelic *History of North Uist* by a minister called MacDonald. He had seen the Rodel factor once: 'His face was thin and long, his nose was prominent, knobbed, and sharp . . . he was hospitable, but in other respects like the other members of the Balranald family, worldly and utterly selfish every generation of them. Rodel [the factor] was anxious to get a lease of the farm of Sollas after the evictions in 1849, but his own brother Balranald [Jessie's father] outbid him by £5!' A local man described Rodel to me as 'an absolute tyrant – he has a bad name to this day'. His fellow instrument of clearance, MacLeod the ground officer, was the same: 'When he died, people came from miles around to urinate on his grave.' MacDonald's tomb was fortified against such treatment by a balustraded wall at the back and an iron railing round it like halberds set on end. Over the grave a rare weeping elm wreathed its branches. The gate in the railing has rusted off its hinges, animals have entered and eaten the bark off the tree all round and it looks unlikely to leaf again.

The memoir I got from Norman MacLeod of Leverburgh, a few miles north of Rodel, complemented Kirstie's. He was not lyrical but historical, a policeman who had retired early to croft and fish and so was able to play more part in the upbringing of his third child. He had spoken nothing but Gaelic to her and she is now studying at Sabhal Mòr Ostaig, the Gaelic business college in Sleat. When a white settler had stood up at a crofters' meeting and spoken in English, Norman had objected: 'You've been here fourteen years – can't you use the language of this country?' But the others had all tut-tutted and the meeting had continued in English.

Norman was a complex man, apt to disparage what he'd just said – 'But that's only bits of foolish stories' – yet trenchant with chagrin at the element of self-defeat in the Clearances. Without having heard it he suggested an answer to Kirstie's question, 'Why did they do nothing when they were tying them for the boats in Uist?' He said, 'The fascist discipline of the old chiefs' armies encouraged a deference, so that the Gaels had no guts – except when they were fighting other people's battles. That's why there was no resistance when they put them out.'

Rodel, he told me, had bid fair to be a model fishing centre, with its own tradesmen, tailor, miller, weaver (still common as a name in Leverburgh), but 'Eviction finished the whole place. When Dunmore made it his seat – before he built Amhuinnsuidhe – they didn't want anybody else there.' So the nearby crofters were cleared. The usual late retaliation – land raids after the Great War – had been attempted but 'There were people objected to raiding because it might spoil Leverhulme's scheme'. Norman's one consolation seemed to be that in the Thirties, when the last of the Stewarts were moving out, they actually met a convoy of people coming in to resume the crofts at Scarista and Luskentyre from which their forebears had been removed a century before. One of his own great-grandfathers had come from St Kilda, the others had all been cleared from Ensay and Pabbay, including the boatman who used to bring the excisemen over and warn the islanders by dipping his sail:

> When they came over they just built *bothain* [huts]. There was no point in building anything else. Pabbay had substantial thatched houses, because they were secure. The burning was meant to destroy the cabers, the rooftrees. They carried them away with them at the flitting if they could. And their querns, and the lintels. The black stones there [steps in his garden path] are all from Killigray. None of the lintel stones in Obbe [old name for Leverburgh] are local because there is no suitable rock. One *bodach* [old man] quite cheerfully said it was his ninth flitting. When they brought a teacher in, they just said, 'What croft do you want?' and kicked the people out. After the 1886 Act, when they got security, they were all building right away – the improved black houses – and this house we're sitting in is the first white house there was here: 1904, my grandmother's home, the St Kildan's daughter. The black house on this croft was a maternity hospital for decades for St Kildans escaping from the infant tetanus. She delivered them and there is one of them still alive today, a *bodach* born in 1907.

Norman's feeling for the evicted did not blind him to the elements of progress which had followed clearance. He stressed that Stewart was a good farmer, who introduced the horse-drawn precision seeder on Ensay when they were still sowing with a dibber on the mainland and won a prize with three animals from Pabbay for the heaviest Highland cattle at Smithfield. He even mooted the possibility that the cleared people presently made a better income over in the Bays than would have been possible on the west side. But 'The thing was an atrocity right enough – when they were demolishing the houses here, there were four Waterloo widows had to spend a night on the moor'.

The way to and from Norman's house led past Kirstie's Crago and I stopped to walk over the ground, a green finger curling towards the thumb of Seilebost where fifteen years before I had watched the fishing gannets fold their wings to bomb the water, covering the whole bay with white bursts like snow-devils, and the sea-swallows, the common terns, skimmed our scalps with their crimson dagger-beaks. Crago was soft underfoot, well-drained with a few faint, fair-haired stubble-lines, a combed look, clearly improved land but with hardly a ruffle in the ground to mark an old field dyke or a house. When I went in past Kirstie's again to tell her I had been there, she said, 'Oh yes – Crago – the gas chamber,' with a weird brisk nod and a mirthless glint. Then she sang me an emigrant's song from Skye:

> Although I am here in the woods
> Among the trees high and dark
> Where the cuckoo doesn't call,
> My choice would be in the glens.
>
> Give my regards over the sea,
> Over to the land of the high hills
> Where I had my early days
> At the shieling in the glen
>
> Where I can see the happy girls,
> Their singing very high
> At the pitch of their voices,
> Going out with the kegs and the tether . . .

We were now on our last stepping-stone, Harris and Lewis together, the Long Island. I could not pretend to encompass the broad black sprawl of Lewis, its tracts of strung-out croftland and peat moor and bog cotton, its stretching seventy miles north to the Butt. A very old friend, Donald MacAulay the poet and philologist, comes from Great Bernera off the west coast, and when I asked him about people who might have Clearance memoir he said with emphasis, 'There is just one man on the island who would speak to you *in English*.' When we got there he turned out to have died three weeks before. There had to be some foothold, some point of entry. Following an almost instinctive move outward to the ends of things, I chose the last possible house, on the Atlantic coast at Brenish, seventy miles from Tarbert at the dead-end of a minor road.

We spent the second half of a day working our way round the mountains, which turned to face us all the way like a suspicious herd re-grouping, until we reached a point just eight miles north along the coast from Husinish where we had been at noon. For hours it had been like swimming in a tide of light. Now St Kilda was hull-down in the west, the brown hump of it looking semi-transparent in the low beams. The leafy sycamores of Tarbert were unthinkable here – it was beyond trees, almost beyond heather at Islivig where the notorious sea-winds of this coast have pitted and channelled the moor into a barrenness like a mountain-top above 700 metres. At sea the swell left by the hurricane was conjuring a lustre of spume around the skerries as though they were metal newly tempered, steaming under the hammer. In one place which became our seamark a dark swelling would appear like a kraken emerging, white breakers rushed sideways at each other, collided and spouted – so much unbridled activity with no visible cause that the waves looked animate as polar-crested beasts, butting, goring, trampling as they contested a crucial stance.

The mountains arrayed in the east of Brenish were outlandish – Mealisval, Snodirbie, Tahaval, Cracaval, Laival a Tuath – naked as Afghanistan, inhospitable as Mercury. The house was entirely welcoming – in one window a Greenpeace decal, in another a poster with the C.N.D. logo and a joke – 'One Nuclear Bomb Can Ruin Your Whole Day'. We were in tune at once and our hosts, Kay Gillies and her husband Harley (a weaver retired early through ill health), sensed our wish to feel the place to the full and would call us out at night to see the sunset, like a furnace beyond the sea, or the Northern Lights, which Harley called the Merry Dancers – more clearly displayed than I'd ever seen, a great console of rays spread out from north-east to north-north-west. One beam, cat's-eye-green, would blur and dim, another intensify and climb higher, paling and putting out the Milky Way (*Bogha Chlann Uisne* in Gaelic), which streamed overhead like a shell-sand beach. An hour later a gibbous moon rose into sight above Mula Mac Sgiathain and its yellow blade beside the black pyramid-angle of the mountain made the scene look Saracen. Exposure to the light (and the wind) was the essence of the place – above the peat fire a large colour print showed the coast to the south, dim brown reefs, a pearly sky, an island with a pale-gold beach. It had been taken at midnight, in midsummer.

The area was dying back from its road-end. Brenish, 'the furthest away township on the west of Lewis', has no children in it now. In June 1883 Norman Morrison, a 61-year-old crofter and fisherman, told the Napier Commissioners that he remembered the people cleared from the then final village, Mealista, on the way out past his door 45 years before:

> [Our people] are crowded so much together that they have no way of living. Our places were crowded first when the neighbouring township of Miolasta was cleared. Six families of that township were thrown in amongst us; the rest were hounded away to Australia and America, and I think I hear the cry of the children till this day.

Norman Morrison is well remembered locally – Tormod Ruadh, 'red-haired like all the Morrisons'. He had been the first Brenish man to move uphill to the better croftland at the roadside from the impossibly waterlogged ground nearer the sea where the congested families at the clearance time had had to find an acre or two. His great-grandfather had had 36 black lambs, and white ones on Mealista Island, and horses, sheep, and cattle. This island, with the other grazings, had been made over to the 'big sheep and shepherds' when nine townships were cleared to make two farms, owned by incomers to Lewis.

In keeping with what I had seen everywhere, Mealista turned out to be the better ground in the area, with some machair soil and a landing-place protected by small crags. Beside the last quarter-mile of track hay had been scythed off in neat stripes and withered shaws stood ready for lifting in potato beds. Who could be crofting here? On the seaward side a weathered notice said 'Tigh nan Cailleachan Dubha', the place of the black women. Beyond it, ruins with walls still six feet high made a street paved with flat stones at the centre of a crowd of house-foundations. On the shore spectacular rock teeth, black as ravens, pointed upward beside a natural harbour – were *these* the black women, I fantasised? This made me almost as ignorant as the visitors who come back up to Kay and Harley's and say, 'There was this notice "Tie-something-or other" – does it mean "No Trespassers"?' The place had been a nunnery, with pre-Clearance families farming next to it. Stone after stone had been taken away, as at Hallaig on Raasay, to make that stigma of the post-Clearance farm, a huge rickety field wall to pen the big sheep. I made my way uphill tl rough it, starting a quartet of snipe from the rushy gutters between the old narrow fields. Another township, and maybe a third, looked down over their crofts. In the more northerly the bad wall had been built straight through the house of one evicted family. In the more southerly, Leathad an Rois, unnamed on the map, among dense, tender grass whose green glowed visibly from a distance, one homestead had a plan unique to Lewis: as the generations grew up, they built on another house behind the old one, and another – in effect a terrace running uphill with a ground-plan like a ladder.

I walked up to the 100-metre contour to see if a grass brow hid still more houses and found the tufted arc of the ring-dyke, like a necklace on the hill, curving off southward. As usual it gave good footing through rough, wet ground. It wriggled on for a full mile. Down on the sea the reefs north of Mealista Island, Greineim and Sgeir Liath, the sun-place and the grey skerry, were jet plinths and serrations on a surface smoothed out into ice-yellow and dark nacre. Presently, the dyke dipped to the Abhainn Hotarol, whose brown water ran through it by a pair of finely-masoned stone ducts with lintels. Aboriginal heather hummocked off on either side. I followed the burn down to the track by a path above a ravine thirty feet deep whose slot I could almost have jumped across and found that it flowed under the track by a little low bridge whose four arches had been built without mortar. I was reminded of places in Borrowdale, on Dartmoor, in Coldendale near Heptonstall, where the settlement in its heyday had secreted similar handsome and clever works to meet its own needs.

Nobody any longer needs to cross the Mealista bridge, except walkers from down the coast and the sporting gentry who, it appears, tend to run amok in this remote place where 'nobody' can see them. The former owner, the Rutland squire with whom I had clashed absurdly years before, used to be nicknamed 'Hereford the

Wake' and seems to have encouraged a high deathrate among small animals. Four shooters had come blazing away in line abreast across the crofts when there were cattle on them; when a neighbour of the Gillieses challenged them, they first claimed to have a right to do so, then tried to placate him with a rabbit. Four yuppies had landed from a helicopter on an island where eider breed and shot them indiscriminately. The S.S.P.C.A. man, alerted by phone, had asked a friend at Stornoway Air Control to get the chopper's number but it had got away. It was altogether little wonder that Uig, a few miles north, should have produced Iain Mac a' Ghobhainn, most trenchant of the bards, who protested a century ago at the despoiling of their country. His 'Spiorad a' Charthannais', 'The Spirit of Charity' (in the sense used by Paul to the Corinthians), makes a sustained lyric out of curses like those I had been collecting up and down the coast:

> They handed over to the snipe
> the land of happy folk,
> they dealt without humanity
> with people who were kind . . .
> Their houses, warm with kindliness,
> were in ruins round their ears;
> their sons were on the battlefield
> saving a pitiless land,
> their mothers' state was piteous,
> their houses burnt like coal . . .
>
> Though your estate is spacious
> and people bow the knee,
> Death's laws too are stringent,
> you must bow before his power.
> That landlord makes arrangements
> with equal rights for all –
> for your estate he'll give a shroud
> and six feet of green turf . . .
> In that serene inheritance
> your hauteur won't be high:
> the baillie's scolding won't be heard
> or the ground officer's anger . . .

Mac a' Ghobhainn was writing in the aftermath both of the Potato

Famine and of a change of ownership. Lewis had passed from an 'old family', the Seaforth MacKenzies, to a prime representative of 'new money', Sir James Matheson, who figures in Disraeli's *Sybil* as 'one MacDrug, fresh from Canton with a million of opium in his pocket'. His baillie, or factor, Munro MacKenzie brought efficient management to Lewis. In three years 14 per cent of the people were cleared by the carrot of paid passages on emigrant boats and the stick of eviction – 1,180 summonses of removal between 1849 and 1851. MacKenzie's diary and memoranda take us close in to the dilemmas of a poverty-stricken area and the Eichmann-like thoroughness of management's solution to them.

On April 2nd, 1851 the 'upper end of the parish of Uig' (where we were staying) is called 'the most destitute in Lews'. In his lists of townships, families, rent arrears, and stock, the entry for almost every township under 'Willingness to go' is 'Nil'. They had to go. April 5th: 'I stated that no one could compel the people to go unless they please, but that all those who were two years and upwards in arrear would be deprived of their land at Whitsunday next if not paid by then, giving them the option of emigrating'. April 13th: 'Wrote each ground officer to remove houses occupied by emigrants so soon as they leave.' May 20th: 'Had considerable difficulty getting the fishermen to get out their boats to take the emigrants out to the Steamer. But after losing much time and using entreaty and force by turns, got the emigrants out with their luggage'. May 28th: 'Had a lengthy interview with Mr Scott, Park ... He considers his farm to be a very good one if it had better boundaries, which certainly might be improved by removing a few people.' June 21st: 'Met various people from the country asking for authority to cut peats, but in most cases refused if they did not pay or find security.' July 12th: 'Took all I could get in cash and cattle. The former is very scarce at present and the people do not want to part with any cattle that have milk, as they require all they can get in the shape of food.' September 18th: 'Met the people of Breanish a few of whom pay their rents and the greater portion are in arrear, some very desperate' (the average arrears were £3.9s.5d.).

The people of Brenish are still there – just. At least they have legal security now. The contrast came home to me one night when Harley went out to help search for a neighbour's cow that had strayed. In 1883 Norman Morrison testified that when sheep strayed and a fee had to be paid to reclaim them from the pound, 'I have seen the blankets taken off the beds to pay for poinding money, and I have seen the plaids of the women taken away for the same purpose'. Crofting in such a place can never pay by itself, but that does not mean it is unfit to be lived in. A proof of this – but such a thing is incapable of proof – is a 'house warm with kindliness' such as the Gillieses'. They want to be there and their being there made it possible for us too. They defend it as best they can. Deep-sea boats are supposed not to fish inside the place where the fierce white breakers were trampling day after day – an agreement to protect inshore fishing which John Lorne Campbell and Compton MacKenzie down on Barra struggled for decades to achieve. When a boat came in and violated the limit, Kay phoned the Fisheries Protection. Nothing was done. The day we left Brenish, the year's young sheep left too, in big cattle-trucks bound for the lamb sales over in Dingwall. This is the area's chief product. Now that wool prices and the demand for tweed are both falling steeply, a crofter in the Outer Isles makes 28p an hour from his croft (against 70p on Shetland and £1.50 on Skye) and £3.50 for his work away from the croft (against £5 elsewhere). It would be pure loss if civilisation had to evacuate 'the upper end of Uig'. We heard the voice of it above the wind on a ferocious day when the trampling-place was a blizzard of white and the burn dropping over the cliff at Camas a' Mhoil never reached the sea but blew right back and over the cliffs in a horizontal rain. We all lay low and hour after hour sweet sounds unfurled through the house as Harley fingered out melodies on his Yamaha keyboard and taught Anne to play it. What a croft can be is a foothold – a bare one – for humankind of such a quality.

On our way eastward, southward, homeward I got my last glimpses of Uig's travail with the help of two more people, Anna MacKinnon of Ardroil, by Uig sands, and Kenneth John Smith of Earshader, home of Iain Mac a' Ghobhainn. Anna's great-grandfather had been evicted from Scaliscro on Little Loch Roag in what she believed to be the first Lewis clearance and she herself dwelt with a peculiar stress, dispassionate yet concerned, on the personal experience of being evicted. 'There is a legacy of non-explicit bitterness', she said, 'in the descendants of the cleared – about all things, not just the clearance.' Her phrase for what people felt about the ground officers and the incoming farmers (many from Wester Ross) was 'sheer, dreadful hatred' and she recalled that a local man (she would not name him) had sent for her on his deathbed to record a rhyme about a ground officer who rose 'from rags to riches on our grief'. I presume it was not unlike the verses about a factor recited to me by Donald MacAulay. They had been composed by a bard called Donald MacDonald who lived next door to his great-grandfather over on Great Bernera:

> I saw your mother's brother,
> Fat and with his belly protruding,
> Pouring water onto his neighbour's fire
> Until he had drowned the last ember.
>
> Look at his house now –
> Each room with the colour of night on it
> And each window-frame and pane cracked
> And the corners of it giving way.

Evictions before Munro MacKenzie's master plan of 1850 were more a matter of piecemeal chivvying and moving families from one place to another to suit the proprietor or his manager. Another great-grandfather of Donald's shot a swan; the factor came to demand the feathers to make a boa for his daughter and was refused with the nice riposte, 'Oh, but I have a daughter of my own.' The family were evicted. More widespread was the pressure to enlist in Highland battalions, on pain of eviction. Men who went were rewarded with the best crofts when they came back, if they came back, from the French and Crimean Wars. Economic pressure squeezed so hard on the townships round the Sands that there was said in Carnish to be 'only as much meal as you could blow off the top of a spoon'. The next township west, Mangersta, was earmarked for clearance even in the MacKenzies' time but it was left to the new businessman owner to do the thing in style. Carnish became 'a transit camp for the dispossessed' and was cleared in its turn – one Calum Matheson, who died in 1917 aged 97, avoided emigration only by accepting a half croft at Aird Uig in the extreme north end – a desperate move – but Malcolm MacLeod accepted eviction from Crowlista with his wife and seven children and embarked for Quebec in 1851, sailing from Loch Roag in one of the ships chartered by MacDrug. His resignation, voiced in a poem collected by Anna MacKinnon, is the same sigh of the oppressed we heard from Mary of Unnimore in Morvern:

> We have seen the day of parting
> at the church there,
> bidding farewell to the stones
> and the well-known ground.
> If we are going
> let us go
> and let God be our help.

MacKenzie chose to ship the people from Loch Roag in case they gathered support, or had second thoughts, on the thirty-mile trek eastward to the better harbour at Stornoway. The six-mile fjord of Little Loch Roag is fed by an expensive salmon river running down from the lodge built to MacDrug's orders for sporting purposes. 'There is a legend that Matheson cleared Gisla [a mile from the river-mouth] to preserve his fishing rights. Some swear it's not true because they feel it to be a stigma, but some of the more left-wing people are proud of it,' according to Anna. Such are the filters through which history reaches us. Presumably it is for similar reasons that some say the families were actually burned out from the island of Vuia (between Uig and Bernera) while others say they were not. At all events the aim of management was to empty the area of people and convert it to grazings for the new big farm of Linshader.

Kenneth John Smith at Earshader had learned through family recollection that MacIvers from Stroim, at the mouth of Little Loch Roag, had flitted carrying their roof timbers south-eastward over the moor to Loch Tangavat, made them into a raft and floated them to the south end of the loch, from there as far as possible by lochans to Loch Langavat, and so at last to the place decreed by the factor, Laxay on the east coast sea-loch of Erisort. This is a journey of something like twenty miles clear across Lewis, most of it trackless, though some of the terrain will have been known to the crofters through using it for summer shielings:

In the little houses the tenant people sifted their belongings and the belongings of their fathers and their grandfathers. The men were ruthless because the past had been spoiled, but the women knew how the past would cry to them in the coming days . . . The two men squatting in a ditch, the little fire, the side-meat stewing in a single pot, the silent, stone-eyed women; behind, the children listening with their soul to words their minds do not understand. The night draws down. The baby has a cold. Here, take this blanket. It's wool. It was my mother's blanket – take it for the baby ... And all the time the farms grew larger and the owners fewer ... And it came about that owners no longer worked on their farms. They farmed on paper; and they forgot the land, the smell, the feel of it, and remembered only that they owned it, remembered only what they gained by it ... And the owners not only did not work the farms any more, many of them had never seen the farms they owned.

Steinbeck was describing a rather different exodus, longer but less laborious; the process was the same, capital and climate converging to prise the families loose from the places where they worked together for themselves and resettle them in places where they would have to work separately for others.

Mr Smith had been speaking to me – had given me a continuous detailed forty-minute lecture on Lewis history – in the sitting-room of his house above Loch Barraglom. From a fine portrait photo above the mantelpiece a plump seaman looked out, black hair combed down over his forehead in an Edwardian dip, his moustachios spiky with wax, his hand resting on his wife's shoulder, she in her best high-collared frock and looking dutiful and apprehensive. The sailor was Mr Smith's father, of whom he had no memories: he had been drowned on the *Iolaire* when his son was six months old. That night we stayed at the Tower Guest House in Stornoway, and when we remarked on the fine glossy timbers of the front door the landlord told us they had come from the *Iolaire*, 'because it was all de luxe, you know'. It seemed to be a time of signs: on the boat across the Minch next day we met, purely by chance, Donald and Ella MacAulay on their way back from Bernera to Aberdeen – that spring I had met them for the first time in thirty years. In the morning at the An Lanntair gallery, looking through the large prints for sale, I had been stopped by an etching of the very house-shell in Boreraig on Skye where I had sheltered from the rain two autumns before. It was by Reinhold Behrens, whose three-dimensional piece 'Clearances' I had dwelt on again and again in a book called *As an Fhearann/From the Land*. At the back of this visionary work two pieces of cracked and scabby jetsam, a door and a panel, divide a broad Hebridean seascape into a triptych – a three-casement window showing us a whale-family of blue islands across the water. On the floor in front, two hundred pieces of assorted footgear fan out in lines – boots, moccasins, sandals, trainers, shoes both fancy and plain, children's amongst the adults'. Their heels are to the islands, they are coming toward us, they are the soles of the emigrants making tracks, leaving and coming and diverging.

Time and again in the previous weeks we had been seeing skeins of wild geese above the waterlands, looping sideways, almost unravelling in the savage blow from the ocean, recovering themselves, winging on south to some winter pasture, possibly on Islay. Their patterned silhouettes inscribed on the sky an ideogram that meant 'autumn – season ending'. Beside us in the ferry queue at Stornoway the big trucks, three tiers deep in sheep which doubtless included Kay and Harley's, saturated the air with a tang of wool and urine. In the hold it smelled like a farm. Horns and forelegs stuck out through the three-inch gaps; noses and black-and-yellow eyes strained to reach clear air. Near Inverness we drove between fields where still more Highland flocks were fattening for sale and slaughter. A hundred and fifty miles later, in Strathmore – at the very limit of my own original country – the biggest skeins I had ever seen, rank after rank, asymmetrical arrow-heads and long wavering trails, beat steadily towards the lowland flood-plains and water-meadows, southbound like ourselves.

CHAPTER SEVENTEEN

THE ENDS OF THINGS
Easter Ross, Sutherland

For the first twenty-five years of my life, in Aberdeen, I had been used to seeing 'the Orkney boat' beside a quay in the harbour, her funnel releasing a shred of smoke as she readied herself to sail, or watching her in the evening as she steamed bulkily past Donmouth and the dunes, dwarfing the seine-netters and even the trawlers. I never made the journey; the mountain-glamour of the west pulled us more strongly than those low-lying green islands and Shetland might as well have been in Norway. This ignorance, along with the much greater notoriety of Sutherland and North Uist as sites of clearance, even delayed my realising that Shetland was where to start out on the crofters' trail: it was cleared last of all, so memoirs should be the least blurred or overlaid. The fact is that I went on overlooking the northern islands until another curl of the grapevine made the connection. When I called on Jim Johnston in Bettyhill, expecting information about clearance in Sutherland, he gave me the gist of his great-grandmother's epic journey after being evicted from Kergord on Shetland Mainland. Printed sources show that many dozens of families were cleared. And Orkney? Edwin Muir's poem 'The Little General' reads like a fable about a hunter who came 'Across the sound, bringing the island death'. The real original, and his predecessors, had been evictors on Rousay, just across the water from Muir's home island of Wyre; one of them, I read, was still a byword for having 'blawn the reek frae forty lums'. Here were clues enough. Perhaps we should have gone to Orkney by the Aberdeen boat for this last leg of the crofters' trail but first there were still some crucial places to visit and hear about in Sutherland.

We drove up there and went to stay at the head of Strath Carron, following that impulse to get to the ends of things. Here we found ourselves in the middle of a clearance that was about to happen.

The last occupied house in the glen was also the remotest Bed and Breakfast in the area. It had the oddly unGaelic name of Forest Farm. A few yards upstream was the church of Croick, which is now almost a shrine to Clearance martyrs. Families evicted from the tributary glen of Calvie in 1845 found sanctuary in the kirkyard, under flat-topped tombs, in improvised lean-to's against the gable end, and scratched names, dates, broken phrases on the diamond window-panes: 'Glencalvie is a Wilders ... below Sheep that ... to the ... Croick ... John Rofs shepherd ... ' and most famously, 'Glencalvie people the wicked generation'. People interpret this as a morbidly religious blaming of oneself for the sins that must have brought down the punishment of eviction. Might it not be ironical – a crofter sardonically parodying what he well knew the unco guid, the righteous mob, would say about them? On either reading these traces of desperate people are uniquely poignant and the church has looked after them perfectly – framed glass round that part of the window, facsimile transcriptions inside, and an enlarged photostat of the *Times* report of the eviction dated June 2nd, 1845.

At Forest Farm Mrs Moffat showed us our bedroom and sitting-room in an ample eighteenth-century house, then said without any cue and knowing nothing about us:

Well, this is where the clearance was, a hundred and forty years ago, and we are having our own clearance here now. On September 20 the owner sold up, so now we have no idea what will happen next. This new man is talking about afforestation and that is why he bought it from Mr Wilson who had it. But there has been such a hue-and-cry in the papers, he has had to drop that – they were calling it a new clearance and he went *mad* at that. Anyway, three of the families have gone now, and it is only a small community here. Mr Wilson did not buy it very long ago and he *trebled* his money. Does money make you happy? All I know is that there has been a lot of heartbreak in the glen. If they put in broad-leaved trees, well, it would do some good in the long run. They would have to shut the gates but in twenty years they could open them again and let the animals in. But where will we be in another twenty years? We only have security until the spring. We took out a loan and bought back some of the stock. I wonder did we do right . . .

Mr Moffat, we heard, was the fourth generation of a family who had built up an outstanding stock of 7,000 ewes on Forest Farm. Moffat is a Border name – it seemed a horrible irony that Lowland farmers brought in on the heels of the original clearance should be forced out in their turn, by the latest breed of businessman (owners of newspapers, of estates in Essex and Buckinghamshire and across the mountains near Ullapool, the newly booming area in Wester Ross). Mrs Moffat herself looked Highland. Her accent was Hebridean and the particular rich black-brown of her eyes reminded me of women I had seen on Scalpay Harris in 1957, seeing off their menfolk at the ferry. I had written in a poem,

The eyes of the waiting girls are brown as peat water,
They brim with weeping. Their mothers stand in black
Facing the Minch. It looks like a funeral.
But the men are carrying strapped fibre suitcases;
Raincoats folded, faces shaved raw,
Manly and expressionless, they curve their fingers
Around their cigarettes. They file down the concrete
Like stirks to the slaughterhouse. The steel side opens,
The black boat receives them, Scalpay exports them . . .

It turned out that Mrs Moffat's mother did come from Scalpay – that island which was most cruelly congested when the people cleared from the west coast of North and South Harris were dumped into it. In the next few days, as Mrs Moffat returned again and again to her anxieties about whether they could stay and where they might have to go, she was precisely re-enacting the anguish of her great-grandparents.

I had driven up Strath Carron in a kind of dread that flowed from its history, both the expulsion from Glen Calvie and the Massacre of the Rosses, which completed the clearance of the strath eight years later. For some miles above Ardgay the river-lands are perfectly flat and fertile, well farmed for oats and turnips. Under a sky livid with rain and the dark-green gloom of blanket forest, the stubble-fields spread out a fabric of luminous gold hemmed with the green of

the alders on the river-banks. These fields had to be harrowed by
a tenant farmer during the night of March 31st, 1854 to hide the
blood of the wounded, which was being lapped by dogs. To enforce
writs of removal, a gang of drunk constables and special constables
had come up the strath to Greenyards (more properly Gruinards).
Most of the men made themselves scarce. The women defied the
thugs and were battered down with truncheons, skulls and shoulder-
blades shattered, breasts kicked, left unconscious, paralysed, out of
their minds: at least eighteen women and three men, the last and
worst injured victims of clearance in the Highlands. All this I knew
from Donald Ross's pamphlet of 1854, *The Russians of Ross-shire*.
It had so got into me that the very names of the places were fraught
– Carron smacked of carrion, Calvie of calves (to the slaughter). You
look at such a place (Craonne in Picardy, where an uncle of mine died
fighting on May 27th, 1918, or Vassieux in the Vercors where the
Wehrmacht razed a village in 1943 for harbouring the *Maquis*) and
its very peacefulness, the open sunlit face of it, turns eery, like the
countenance of a corpse in a chapel-of-rest which you could swear
is about to stir and speak to you. It seemed unlikely that there would
be any descendants left here to speak to me. Houses were few. Most
had no lights at night and by day the smartly-Snowcemmed look
of the converted holiday house – no hens, no washing on the line,
no machines in the yard. The number of expensive mini-palaces or
'lodges' was menacing – five inside the ten miles of the upper strath.
We contented ourselves at first with spying on the gentry.

For twenty years or more I had wanted to see Glen Calvie.
It turned out not to be easy. The trunk of the strath splays into
four branches at its western end. The north-western runs upstream
from Forest Farm and Croick. The western is fortified by a lodge,
Alladale, greatly enlarged by its most famous owner, the Indian
prince and cricketer Duleepsinjhi, and defended now by a deer-fence
eight feet high and a gate across the road well placarded with words
like 'Strictly', 'No', and 'Private'. This also prevents access to the
south-west branch, Gleann Mòr. In such circumstances, when I am
stopped from reaching into the wild heart of my native country, the
words that come to mind (and much more intensely, no doubt, to
the crofters themselves) are from Genesis, 3: 'cursed is the ground
for thy sake; in sorrow shalt thou eat of it all the days of thy life.
Thorns also and thistles shall it bring forth to thee; and thou shalt
eat the herb of the field. In the sweat of thy face shalt thou eat

bread, till thou return unto the ground . . . the Lord God sent him forth from the garden of Eden, to till the ground from whence he was taken. So he drove out the man; and he placed at the east of the garden of Eden Cherubims, and a flaming sword which turned every way.' The southerly branch is Glen Calvie. How to reach it? Past an ornamental pond brimming to a waterfall, a folly with designer ruins, a tarmac tennis court, a pretty black-and-white mini-mansion, all towers and points and gables, with a cavalcade drawn up beside it – new Range Rover, new pick-up, and glossy black veteran Armstrong-Siddeley. I adopt a decent-citizen approach and ring the bell, go into the hall, and have time before the servant appears to note a mahogany bear five foot high, its arms full of walking sticks, an array of gun-rests, a crash-helmet and several camouflage jackets hanging from pegs.

The servant has a green bandeau, a cook's apron over her jeans, and expertly groomed eyelashes. 'You want to see the glen – we-e-ll, it *is* private, it's not a footpath. It's *very* pretty. Afraid the boss-man' (said with a little quirk of complicity, a hint of 'We're all democrats now') 'isn't here – they're stalking. If you park – somewhere out of sight – and just . . . You *are* just walking? If you're discreet, then I shouldn't think . . . ' We circumvent the big house and take a track past an immaculate Keeper's Cottage. Nearby the Water of Calvie ripples its black muscle. Heads down against the driving rain, we rise a little, cross a bridge, and walk down into the gutted township. It is a pod of grassland quarter of a mile long, split by river and unmetalled road, whose bottoming (I learn later) was made from the crofters' houses, as was the gardener's cottage. Low humps, rather like the clan graves at Culloden, corrugate the turf in places, inscrutable stone-heaps, one of them fire-blackened. The usual wide arc of ring-dyke girdles the western slope. Here or hereabouts, according to Donald Ross, 36 families lived – cramped and poor, certainly, but not in arrears of rent.

As we neared the far end, a Land Rover snorted past towing one of those Army-looking six-wheelers which sportspersons use these days to reach their prey with a minimum of effort. A dead stag lolls in the back, pink tongue bulging out between its jaws. A square chin and a beak nose, hooded in khaki, turn towards me from the driving seat and grin slightly when I wave. Down at the house again, as we go round the back to reach the car, a teenage lad has the carcase hanging in chains just inside a game larder with louvred doors. The deer is split down the belly and he is delving in its innards, then hoisting it higher with a rattle and a clank. The antlers (and presumably the head) are still in the six-wheeler. The owner of all this, it turns out, is a newspaper magnate from London, who has 'more money than he knows what to do with'. Probably he knows very well – he charges £3,000 per head per week to stay at the lodge. This includes ammunition. He has burned down yet another lodge two miles above the clachan and replaced it with a holiday house for himself and there are not even sheep in the glen now, nothing but sport and afforestation.

The late stage of the exodus from Glen Calvie came into sight next morning as I talked to Davey Ross in Dounie, a scatter of cottages on the pasture slopes at the other end of Strath Carron. His father Robert, aged three weeks, had sheltered with his parents in Croick churchyard in 1851 among a later contingent of banished people – victims, perhaps, of the special new clause in the farmer's lease binding him 'to turn away two families every year, until the complement of cottars is extirpated'. The children, said Davey, had been put to sleep under the slab tombstones. Sure enough, when we went for another look, the ground in those places was snuff-dry, even after many drenching autumn days. The crofters in Glen Calvie had built a mill and Davey's grandfather David, a carpenter, lived there with his young family. When the eviction was imminent, the factor, James Gillanders (who next year married the daughter of the owner, a well-connected military man called Robertson of Kindeace), came to David Ross at the mill and warned him out.

'We built the mill,' said David – 'it does not belong to the estate.'

'You may own the mill,' replied Gillanders, 'but you do not own the water.' And he cut it off and forced the people out. As usual the helpless anger of the people was focussed on the factor. Years later, when Gillanders made it known that he wanted to be 'buried among my friends' in the graveyard at Croick, he was put in the ground outside the wall and rubbish from inside it was regularly thrown onto his grave until it was effaced – just as, Davey recalled with relish, when Patrick Sellar had requested to be buried 'as near Sutherland as possible, they wouldn't have him at Balnakeil, and they wouldn't have him at Ardgay, and he finished up at Elgin Cathedral'.

At Davey's suggestion I went to see Willy MacDonald at Amat a Tuath, the remnant of a clachan where the Calvie joins the

Carron. He lives on a perfectly husbanded small farm, with root crops and stubble in the fields and haystacks built in the old way round tripods of poles cut from the birch-woods and finished off with a little topknot of stalks. Beside the stackyard the gable of a house still stands with its chimney-stack intact. It had been left there deliberately, said Mr MacDonald, as a memorial to his mother's aunts, Elizabeth and Margaret Ross, who had gone to Gruinards to help prevent the serving of the summonses to quit. Margaret was felled by a truncheon, then struck again and her skull broken, compressing her brain. She was taken in handcuffs to the jail at Tain and released after 24 hours, vomiting, with severe head pains. Her sister Elizabeth was similarly clubbed down and kicked on the breast and shoulders as she lay there. Donald Ross in 1854 expected her to die but Willy MacDonald remembers her in her old age, living in the house by the stackyard and 'wearing the long clothes'. Altogether it was remarkable how many of the families had clung on in a district so maltreated. Presently I was sent news of the descendants of John Ross whose name is on the window at Croick. His son Sandy was born in the kirkyard 'in a make-do shelter built of birch branches and turfs' and lived to become the ferryman at Ardgay (his grandson Innes Fraser Ross lives near Brora); and in Ardgay I spoke to Mrs Nancy Ross whose grandfather, the same Sandy, she remembered as 'a big man, and in later life he had a white spade beard – we always knew grace was finished when we could see the end of his beard again'. She believed that the actual delivery of the baby had been 'on one of the slab stones at the north-west corner of the burial ground' – a case, no doubt, of the Lord furnishing the people a table in presence of their foes. The Rosses, then, had moved down only as far as the mouth of Strath Carron and Willy MacDonald's people were able to stay on up at Amat a Tuath because that part was owned by the Chief of Clan Ross, who did not evict. So a few crannies were left in which people could make a home and stay on, with history living in their minds. If more gates are closed and more of the land comes under the rule of the rifle and the prairie-buster plough, then still more of the Highlands will be lost to civilisation in its fuller sense.

It felt perverse to move on still further north, against the flight of the geese – and of the tourists. But Minnie Campbell and hundreds of other Strath Naver folk had left via the north and I was bent on following her trail to Gills in Caithness before going further still, to Rousay and Kergord. First there was Gruids to see, near Lairg in the south of Sutherland. Frances MacDonald at the mill house beside the Shin had brought the place further into focus by sending me transcripts of the parish records: three or four baptisms a year from 1768 to 1817 – clearance in 1821 – then one birth in 1827, one in 1833, and one in 1841: a vital community, suddenly choked.

We drove north from Bonar Bridge past the salmon leap on the Shin where the big fish, dark and arrowy against raging white water, hurl up, shudder in mid-air, writhe on the lip of the falls, never seem to make it. Moisture was gathering amongst the leaf-mould in the woods. Against their massed shadow the last of the summer's sun flared in the bunched crimson of rowan berries, the hot-metal ruddiness of cherry leaves, the luminous lemon of aspens which hovered in mid-air like apparitions of butterflies. Among the Greens of Gruids the thistle-heads were like clots of sodden rabbit-fur and spider-webs laden with dew made pockets of fog amongst the whins. Fast-growing Commission forest screens from the road a whole group of clachans, Pitfure, Plaids, and 'Kenna-kail' (the old parish minister's garbled form of Ceann na Coile, 'the head of the woods'). To older folk these lands were not 'the Greens' but 'the Touns'. Sandy MacLean, forester in charge of planting after the War, had counted 'hosts of old ruins'. Frances's neighbour had taken her for walks up the side of the fast-flowing, rocky River Grudie and she was sardonic, reliving an old impatience at being fobbed off when all Mrs Mowat's answer to questions about the Touns was, 'Oh, it was the Highland Clearances.' The forester had told her that on the patches where the clachans had been the young trees had repeatedly refused to root. A legend or a fact? Certainly there were inexplicable pockmarks of stunted growth here and there on the dark-green canopy. Between the regiments of spruce the Greens survive as grassland, a broad and gradual rise of it which we stravaiged all over, looking for traces. At the upper end a few were left, the foundation-courses of houses at least 21 paces long, as at Rossal and Achanlochy in Strath Naver. The new owner, Austrian, has put money into a sand-and-gravel road bulldozed straight up the Greens, and into the mowing of the bracken and rushes which have invaded the fields and the fertilising of them for beef-cattle pasture – use of a sort, lacking only buildings, gardens, people . . .

It had been roomy and fertile here – no wonder the women defended it as best they could. In Lairg and again at Milton of

Gruids I spoke to Renee Munro whose great-great-grandmother Isabel had taken part in the first repulsing of the sheriff's officers when they came to serve writs on behalf of the Countess of Sutherland: 'This officer – when the men saw him coming they took to the hills. But the women were ready for him, they got a hold of his papers and chased him into the inn, got him into a room, and took his trousers off, and skelped his bottom and chased him away up to Rhianbreck, and then switched him a mile on his way over to Rogart.' Delaying tactics. The Army was sent in to enforce the clearance and the entire community was banished to the east coast in accordance with the Sutherlands' master-plan. No doubt some of the women Renee remembered coming over by train from Golspie, in big white aprons and long black skirts with creels of fish for sale, were descendants of people from the Touns – which in the meantime had become yet another piece of Patrick Sellar's empire.

Had he the least conception of the culture he was uprooting? By the happiest chance Raonacloy where Renee lives was the home of Hugh Miller's aunt on the eve of the clearance and Miller, as you would expect of the most observant descriptive writer in nineteenth-century Britain, left a wonderfully complete account of the home he visited during three summers. 'It was a long, low, dingy edifice of turf, four or five rooms in length, but only one in height, that, lying along a gentle acclivity, somewhat resembled at a distance a huge black snail creeping up the hill.' The lowest room was the byre, to allow the cows' dirt to drain away from the house, and the next room was the central Ha' with 'its fire full in the middle of the floor, without back or sides ... bare black rafters ... a pale expanse of dense smoke that, filling the upper portion of the roof, overhung the floor like a ceiling'. In other words it looked like thousands of those Highland houses which encouraged sophisticated travellers (distinguished economists, journalists, Lowland clergymen) in their belief that 'the Gaels' were incurably primitive. Well – the man of the house, Hugh's uncle, had learned to lead the family in worship before the Gaelic Bible became current and he therefore translated at sight from an English Bible 'with such ready fluency, that no one could have guessed it to be other than a Gaelic work from which he was reading'. His second son, who farmed the croft, was an 'ingenious, self-taught mechanic' who could make ploughs and snuff-mulls. His youngest son, a mason and slater, wrote competent poetry and prose and was 'skilled in architectural drawing'. When the eldest son, now

a successful businessman in the south, came home on holiday, the Ha'
was filled with learned argument about the Ossian controversy – the
'elderly men of the neighbourhood' spoke up for a more authentic
Gaelic literature by reciting 'long-derived narratives of the old clan
feuds of the district, and wild Fingalian legends'. The family sounds
uncommonly gifted but it was not freakish. Its ways were of a piece
with its neighbourhood and it will have had its counterpart in hundreds of townships which the last of the chiefs and the first of the
new-rich were bent on destroying.

I should now have walked the trail from Grummore in upper
Strath Naver to Mey in Caithness, to realise in some degree just
how gruelling a trek the Campbell family and their neighbours
made after the burning in May 1819. Yet how realistic would it
have been without a burden of ploughs and tools and bog-wood
chairs, querns and slowrie-chain, sieves and fire-irons, potatoes and
meal, bedclothes, babes-in-arms? with an incapable old person in a
creel on your back, perhaps? and cows, horses, goats, and sheep to
drive ahead of you past twenty other smouldering clachans? At least
the terrain could be appreciated, if I avoided the road, so I walked
the true right bank of the Naver from Skail to Skelpick – just one
settlement in eight miles, now that the civilisation of the strath has
shrunk to a few farms and every now and then a rich man's pad,
strung out along the motor-road.

In 1883 Angus Mackay, an 80-year-old cottar and retired quarry-
man, told the Napier Commissioners how he came to live briefly at
Skail in 1814. His parents were warned to quit their home at Coille
Reidh Loisgte or Rhiloisk on the east bank (no longer on the map).
They started to move their animals down the strath. A woman came
in and told the children, 'Sellar is burning at a place called Rhistog.'
Angus started to carry his three-year-old brother across the river
to a friend's at Langdale (where Sellar was lodging). They nearly
drowned, a woman fished them out, their friends gave them refuge.
Their father came back and took them 'about a mile and a half to
the place called Wood of Skail . . . a place that never was laboured
before'. There they built a turf house and lived in it till the final
gutting of the strath in May 1819 when they trekked northward,
mingling their animals with the Campbells'. It might have seemed
easier for the Mackays to move their gear down the east bank to
Inshlampie immediately opposite Skail; perhaps the presence of
friends at Langdale was decisive. Either way the sharp elbow of the

river near Skail looked like my best place to start and the deserted east bank would time-warp me back more evocatively into the age before Land Rovers and Massey Ferguson tractors.

The latest map marks a footbridge across from Skail to Inshlampie. I made my way towards it, skirting behind a pretty white-and-blue mini-mansion called 'Hotel' on older maps, now dormant, waiting for the right millionaire to come along, and walked off into a moist world where yellowed birches wept quietly to themselves and blackbirds unused to humans dashed off low between dripping thickets. The uprights of the bridge showed between the trees, then the steel cables for its suspended footway. The planks had rotted away. The cables curved off emptily, still taut enough to ride fifteen feet above the fast black surge of the Naver. Maybe I should turn back, go upstream to Syre, and walk down to Inshlampie from Dalvina? If I added four miles to the walk I would finish after dark and see nothing. Perhaps the wire-walk would be feasible. I recalled crossing the Dee at Corrour in the heart of the Cairngorms, boots on a single slack wire, hands on another, 45 lbs. of rucksack hauling me backward until it grazed the water. This should be much easier – if the cables held. I set off astride but almost at once did the splits as my weight forced the cables apart. I would have to use one side only. I teetered off, boots splintering the rusted fibres, and it all went easily. The cables shuddered but hardly swung at all. By mid-stream both banks looked remote and each shuffle roused images of an upright collapsing river-wards, slackening the cables, dropping me in it. The structure on the east bank was creaking and shaking. It held, and in a minute I was monkeying happily down the stays on the far side.

Inshlampie was a single stone house, still with a T.V. aerial and peeling wallpaper but long since declined into a shelter for shepherds coming by to count or dose the sheep. On the top of the moraine nearby, two house-shapes with few stones just lifted the turf – counterparts of the Mackays' temporary home across the river, built perhaps by neighbours of theirs from Rhiloisk who fled straight down the east bank instead of breasting the fast current. A thread of sheep-path trailed off downstream, past the boulder-mound of a massive broch from the strath's Iron Age heyday. A mile and a half north, at Eilean Garbh, a ring-dyke on a heathery plateau above the flood-plain showed the next settlement. A mile more brought me to Rhifail: another big house with its apparatus of stables and barns, another monument to the short-lived attempt to build a farm economy on the ruin of the crofters. To employ all this plant the large walled fields would have to be in full use. Signs of husbandry were few. Behind a huge byre with rotting skylights a black garron stood among nettles, its nose two inches from an unpainted door, one fore-hoof tilted onto its front edge to avoid the liquid mud.

At this point a mile and a half of metalled track ruled due north between the neglected fields. Halfway along stood a gawky building made of crinkly tin and beaverboard on a metal frame, with a criss-crossed cement floor at one end and a cast-iron range with a stone flue at the other – a modern bothy, by the look of it, meant once to house unmarried labourers. Its lack of craftsmanship, solidity, local materials, and natural sheltered situation made me want to cry. It was a slum in the middle of a corn-factory, to use Cobbett's term. Hugh Miller's detailed argument in 'The Bothy System' also came to mind:

> It used to be a common remark of Burns's, – no inadequate judge, surely, – that the more highly cultivated he found an agricultural district, the more ignorant and degraded he almost always found the people ... [The small farmer] had to look before and after him. He had to think and act; to enact by turns the agriculturist and the corn-merchant; to manage his household, and to provide for term-day. He was alike placed beyond the temptation of apeing his landlord, or of sinking into a mere ploughing and harrowing machine. But, in many instances, into such a machine the farm-servant sunk ...

A return of the track to its old winding and a cluster of pines on the shoulder of a hill brought me to Dunviden Burn, named by Angus Mackay as the limit of Sellar's burning in 1814. The site of the clachan displayed a whole history embodied in stone: a Neolithic chambered cairn, the mass of small stones gone (for re-use nearby), five vertical chamber slabs and two partition slabs still standing up like hooded people among the heather; the massive cairn of the Iron Age broch, crowning a moraine, with a double rampart round it and the doorway still marked by the fallen slab of its lintel. The side next the clachan from which the people were evicted was almost gone – presumably the stones were rolled down the hill to build the pre-clearance village. Here there were five longhouses, one with a good fireplace and a chimney; a corn-kiln for parching oats and barley; and a well, made by lining a pool of the burn with stones. The croftland was still used; among small irregular fields big rolls of hay from a baler were lying together wrapped in black polythene. On the level ground nearby, in a link of the river, the corrugations of the old narrow fields were as plain as the bones in the back of your hand.

The next two settlements were further gone: Achanellan and Dalmor, mere humps in the heather and the low ridged arcs of the ring-dykes. The modern track has deserted them, a bulldozer has driven it through on a lower line, past the edge of Loch ma Naire where people came from all over the Highlands, until the Great War, to bathe in it and heal their ailments. The old path-line could have been one of several sheep-trods wending between the basket-of-eggs moraines. They are as distinct, these traces of the people's walking and digging and building – and also as lost and little – as the miners' footprints of ninety years ago which can still be found in the silt of the leadmines in Swaledale. The soil creeps on the pasture-slopes, puckering them back into nature; the leaf-mould layers the pounds and kailyards; moss clumps over the stones until there is no telling glacial litter from the components of a home. This strath could be as populous as Wensleydale. According to the Yorkshire historians every hill farm in the Dales has been a homestead since Norse or Danish times. In Sutherland the continuity was ruptured. The fire, the terror, the swallowed rage, the nightmare uncertainty of the trek north by Farr and east by Strathy into Caithness linger only as a darkling of the air, a fog shredded among pine-tops, a filth leaching into the ground, an uncanny half-life like radioactivity. In Bettyhill, for example, Jim Johnston happened to mention 'the gravestone that wouldn't stand up'. This is an expensive granite obelisk commemorating the Rev. David MacKenzie in the kirkyard at Farr. The stone lies full length on its back and the turf is closing over it. In the past, when it had been replaced, it was always found down on the ground again. Our landlady at Aird knew about it; Mrs Rudie, who looks after the museum, drew a plan on the shop counter where she works to show us how to find it.

The subject of this posthumous curse had been perceived as an instrument of clearance. At Golspie in 1814 he had read out and translated the first eviction notices for Strath Naver. The Countess then preferred him from the mission at Achness to the large and handsome church at Farr. A little later we find him testifying to the estate that the evicted and resettled tenants were 'well provided for, and comfortable'. In fact they were starving in temporary hovels, begging in Caithness. He repeated this in person to console the Countess when she came to Farr and was dismayed at the look of things there. He then refused Donald MacLeod a certificate of good character – virtually an insurance card or passport in those days – with a 'contemptuous and forbidding' manner, on the grounds that MacLeod's behaviour had been 'unscriptural' and he was 'at variance with the factor' – clearly the Lord in both senses must be made obeisance to or else . . . It turns out, however, that MacKenzie sent a powerful letter to the estate in March 1818 which warned against further clearance on the ground that the coastal lands were uninhabitable, cramped in extent, congested already, without limestone or seaweed for manure, without natural harbours. Clearly hating his role, he begged 'leave to be excused from giving any observations to the people of the change being so much to their advantage' as James Loch was busily making out.

MacKenzie, it seems, was doing his best in secret while appearing to the crofters like any other tool of the management. His daughter's compassion also came out many years later. The Free Church minister at Melness submitted to the Deer Forest Commission a memoir of hers which is one of the most graphic contemporary accounts of eviction. A family at Skelpick, ill with fever, were put out while the man was away: the ground officers poured pails of water down the smoke-hole in the roof: 'This created a volume of smoke, mingled with ashes, that filled the whole place, and made breathing most difficult. The neighbours learning what was going on assembled and placed the invalids each on a blanket, and four men in each case carried them down to the manse barn'. So the MacKenzies cared; it had no effect (Loch's reply was inflexible); and the crofters were denied even the knowledge that their pastor felt for them. Twenty-five years later they learned where he stood when he went over to the Free Church, vacating the charge he would have had to leave if he had openly aligned with the crofters in their crisis. Would he have effected anything if he had come out then? Pending a final judgement on the Great Day, his gravestone continues to lie under its curse.

My Strath Naver walk had ended oddly. Anne came to meet me and told me that as she sat writing in the car near Skelpick various people from the big house had driven past slowly, turned, and come back slowly, without a smile or greeting of any kind – unheard-of in the Highlands. The heir to the throne, we were told later, comes there for sporting purposes. Presumably incomers are suspected of lurking with telephoto lenses at the ready. Leaving this feudal domain at last, we now turned eastward on the fifty-mile leg to Dunnet and Mey. The road twists through the gullies and hummocks of a moor without glens, mountains, or watercourses of any stature – unrelieved Highland wilderness which to the Campbells on their trek must have seemed utterly friendless. I knew one crevice of this hinterland, Loch Meadie, where in 1948 I had seen the black-throated diver, most northerly of birds, making its long-limbed cross against a low grey sky. To the north or seaward, you would have thought, there was no room for humankind. Marginal clachans hang on there: Armadale (where Donald MacLeod perched before his second eviction), Fleuchary ('the wet shieling'), Strathy (where many evicted families looked for shelter and sheer pressure forced them northward again along a steeply angled coast to Strathy Point, which Angus Mackay from Rhiloisk called 'the worst place there is in the district').

At times the old track must have lain beneath the tarmac. At others it had avoided bogs or awkward crossings by a slightly higher line, which survives here and there as a visible groove in the moor but is being eliminated from successive editions of the O.S. map. At Melvich it must have cut straight across the Halladale River where a footbridge now crosses to the Regency chateau of Bighouse. The angle and infertility of the ground start to relent. A wood shelters Sandside House where an exceptionally humane Sutherland tenant called William Innes (who had security of tenure) gave harbour to Donald MacLeod's wife and children until, maddened by the hounding of the previous eight years, she fled back to her mother-in-law's at Bettyhill, was evicted again, and went the thirty miles east to Thurso on foot.

Over these last few miles the crofters' culture has disappeared, replaced by the mini-city round the white bulb of Dounreay's nuclear pile – council estate, white-collar suburbs, arterial roads, and all, which Lord Thurso (an Old Etonian) welcomed because 'it would mean some very nice, new, intelligent neighbours'. Presumably the poor man had been short of these before. The old borough of Thurso must have made some sort of caravanserai for Minnie Campbell's family, or were they as unwelcome as the 'destitute Highlanders' who arrived in Fergus, Ontario, thirty years later? At all events they moved on by the Links of Greenland and the Links of Dunnet, an extraordinary spread of bents two miles across and two miles long, unfarmed, dry, perfect to squat on at least for a little and let the animals browse. Here it was that 'the natives, the Caithnessians, pinched their cattle during the night'.

> The world was all before them, where to choose
> Their place of rest . . .

– a world, at that time, of broad, undrained mosses, Rattar Moss and Brabstermire, of great distances without relief in any sense of the word, expanding off towards one of the stormiest seas round Britain where nine tides clash in the firth between Stroma and South Ronaldsay.

The continuous fields of Caithness today suggest an ease of husbandry compared with all but the best bottomlands of Sutherland. The lack of landmarks and shelter must have been crushing. Minnie's great-grandson John today, though he was brought up between Dunnet and Duncansby, says that he had 'more feeling' for Sutherland, where he moved in his early twenties, and felt more solidarity, less competitive individualism, among its people. From the 1890s onwards the Strath Naver people used to make excursions back to the land from which they were expelled and some of Minnie's nine children had booked to go there by train and bus from Wick when the 1914 war broke out. As we approached the house where she ended her days, the foggy autumnal air parted for a minute and we saw an apparition in the north, a bank of gleaming golden uprights towering out of the sea.

> 'O what are yon high high hills,' she said,
> 'That the sun shines sweetly on?'
> 'Those are the hills of heaven,' he said,
> 'Where you will never win.'

They were the western cliffs of Hoy, whose maximum drop to the sea is above 350 metres. We would make the crossing from Scrabster in the evening, hopefully before the Old Man and St John's Head were immersed in darkness. In the meantime we stared at the transformation in the house since Minnie's day – the wing with picture windows, the brick garden arch, the double car-port, the hardwood 'Colonial' door, the varnished rustick labels. Just one thing was as she will have seen it: a long stone building, which was byre, stable, and shed for carts and turnips, with a roof of Caithness flags – a more solid house for animals than the family themselves had had to live in when they pitched camp, by courtesy of Lord Thurso's great-great-grandfather, on the edge of the bog at Mey.

CHAPTER EIGHTEEN

THE LONG HOMES
Orkney

A circle of connection with Canada completed itself as we walked down the harbour street in Stromness, charged with refreshment from the inlets of salt water brimming up between the yards and gardens. Near the western end we came upon a wooden frame set in a wall. Instead of a picture a surface of water glittered in the shadow inside. A chiselled stone above said 'Login's Well'. A flagstone set into the low wall beside it announced:

THERE WATERED HERE
THE HUDSON BAY COY'S SHIPS
1670 – 1891
CAPT. COOK'S VESSELS
RESOLUTION AND DISCOVERY
1780
SIR JOHN FRANKLIN'S SHIPS
EREBUS AND TERROR
IN ARCTIC EXPLORATION
1845
ALSO THE MERCHANT VESSELS
OF FORMER DAYS

WELL SEALED UP 1931

Here was the source of the water that had killed John Sutherland at Churchill in September 1813, after it had been corrupted in the foul tanks of the *Prince of Wales*.

Stromness had been the chief depot for traffic to the Red River settlement in Manitoba. Orcadians ('Arakanys' to the Manitobans in Margaret Laurence's *The Diviners*) went out there by the hundred, carrying their querns and spinning-wheels, barley seed and calves. Some, as I had learned in Winnipeg, sent back flour to needy relatives by Company ship. Cree women had married Orcadians and I had heard tell of other cultural mixing – some Inuit in the Hudson Bay area still play music which mingles their own with Orcadian fiddle styles. When the Company ships sailed into port, Stromness was *en fête*, shop windows were decorated, the house-fronts cleaned, and the 'more important young ladies of the town conducted officers and passengers to places of historic interest' on ponies, then went at night to a ball under awnings on the quarterdeck of the flagship.

That was the glamorous end of the deep-sea connection. Press-gangs ravaged the islands. Men went into hiding, one slept inside a stack of oats on Egilsay for a whole winter, some became ill from exposure or died among the rocks. One factor, on Graemsay between Stromness and Hoy, told the Navy, 'I have done everything I could except force,' then searched the houses and rough ground for three days and nights till he got a haul of four young men. From this I understood why people in the Outer Isles sometimes told me stories of escape from pressgangs as though they were stories of escape from clearance. In both cases the factor was the agent. Here was a counterpart of what had happened in my home town of Aberdeen when the baillies (magistrates) took bribes from the Navy to withdraw the constables from streets near the harbour so that the gangs could have a free hand with their kidnapping.

That was the bad old Orkney. The last serious famine was in 1782–3, when only one-sixteenth of the land was worked. The proportion now is nearly a half and it was during this improvement that clearance was bound to take place as old commons and run-rig field areas were walled and fenced to make large farms and the smaller tenants were banished to the edge of the moors to break in new ground. This might be done harshly or considerately, exacting long hours at kelping or turnip-thinning for the landlord's profit as a condition of having your rent reduced or an eviction notice withheld, or resettling people 'on, or near, the territory which their ancestors had cultivated'. A Sanday farmer, appearing before the Napier Commissioners, admitted to 'trading upon the wishes and desires of the people to remain in the place where they have been brought up'. As enclosure went on apace, grievances festered among the worst accommodated. At Evie 'two old women with no property of their own, who had always had the privilege of pasture for their geese and sheep, were so incensed by the inclusion of the waste into a neighbouring farm that they determined to set a curse upon it. Part of their ritual consisted in placing egg-shells filled with butter on various parts of the common.' By the 1880s this heritage of land-hunger drew a huge crowd to the Town House at the other end of the street from Login's Well to hear the Napier sessions. Generations of grievance spoke out at last to ears obliged to listen and the windows of the bonny crowstepped building of red sandstone had to be opened their widest so that everyone outside could hear the testimony.

On the whole the Orkney evidence pales beside Strath Naver, the Uists and Barra, Skye and Harris. The owners seem not to have been rich or distant enough to use the crueller methods. One confrontation flared up in the Town House and the rising, angry voices are almost audible as they interrupt each other. General Burroughs, owner of Rousay and Wyre, and a tenant's, son, James Leonard, mason and crofter in Digro at the east end of Rousay, could hardly be restrained by the chairman. Burroughs refused to guarantee the security of witnesses against later retaliation by the estate and voiced the classical owner's view: 'Is the property mine, or is it not mine? If it is mine, I can surely do what I consider best for it? If these people are not contented and happy they can go away.' Leonard testified that the rent of his father's croft had increased more than threefold while the hill pasture was taken from them: 'the common has been cut off at the very mark ... Although I may have to leave the land, I am prepared to speak the truth, and will not be cowed down by landlordism. I consider as Burns says – "A man's a man for a' that".' The rhetoric of a Hebridean crofter would have drawn on the Bible. To hear Burns invoked is a reminder that these are the offshore Lowlands, as we could hear in the accent: to my ear it mixes the vowels of Aberdeenshire and Geordie.

Such men would always have clashed. Burroughs was a hero of the Siege of Lucknow, able to be first through the breach in the walls because he was so small – too unpopular to get one of the Victoria Crosses allotted to his regiment when the officers were asked to vote on this by the War Office – obsessive in pursuit of this honour for the rest of his life. But 'clash of personalities' rarely explains enough. Causes speak through people. Leonard knew what was happening to his class all over, for example on Sanday ten miles to the east where another military man, Major Horwood, told his tenants: 'You will make kelp for the price named or [you] must become servants, or leave the property'. On North Ronaldsay, two miles north, the nineteenth-century owners and managers are remembered with particular bitterness, 'tough men' who were 'away in India', leaving power in the hands of factors such as the 'complete devil' still known as 'auld Scart' (Scarth). Five men capsized and drowned on their way back from Eday with a boatload of peats; their widows were warned out the next day. A crofter evicted to make room for another cleared family 'died of a broken heart'. Another had to settle on raw ground: 'they had to build the house and the first fire she lit in the house was on a "busk o segs" – the wild iris that grew in clumps, they hadn't got it cleared off the floor yet when she lit the first fire.' So she went back to her old home on a Sunday and 'prayed afore their face aun teuk aff her rivlins [rawhide shoes] aun stockings aun crept on her livs [palms] aun knees aun cursed them at their ain hearth-stane. Aun as she prayed sae gaed they oot o Howar. Auld Charlie's coffin's no paid for yet! Young Charlie was clever but weekid, aun Howar gaed tae nauthin – gaed tae nauthin!'

As on the Hebrides or the mainland, Orkney people have applied the language of curse and legend to an actual grievous history. On Rousay the struggle for land reached a peak in 1845 when the grand-uncle of the Wee General started to evict 42 families from the north-west end. George William Traill was confronted by the Free Church minister, George Ritchie, who had led the whole community out of the Established Church in 1843 – a grand demonstration of independence from the ruling gentry whose economic and political power were still absolute. Traill said he had the right to do what he pleased with the land because he owned it. Ritchie quoted at him 'The Earth is the Lord's and the fulness thereof': 'to the superstitious the text seemed like a curse for, in little over a year, he was dead, struck down by a heart attack in the lavatory of his London club.' I was amused to see that his tomb in St Magnus Cathedral in Kirkwall was made of white marble slab rather like the loos in the Athenaeum and that the epitaph praised him as 'a wise and beneficent ruler' during his years in India. In 1969 Mrs Craigie, aged 92, could still recall her grandfather's passion for the place he was banished from by Traill to make the big farm at Westside: 'that was a grievance – I don't know the outs and ins of it but that was a vexation to my grandfather because he loved it – he said, "the *bonniest* district in Rousay laid down to sheep – to *sheep*!"'

Rousay was now calling me powerfully, as we cast about and started to make sense of this strange archipelago. As we drove from Stromness to Kirkwall, or from Kirkwall to the Bronze Age township of Skara Brae one goose-grey and parchment-yellow Arctic sunset, green plains curved round shallow bays. Beyond them, past moorit headlands, further green lands just showed as though fields slid upon the sea like floes. Was that part of this island or of another? Did people still live there, or sheep alone? Only an amphibian or a helicopter – or a lifetime in small boats – could have helped us to sort out this intricate map where islands hardly a hundred feet high lie on the sea like the scattered bones of a hand. Rousay was slowly coming into focus and not before time. From years of reading Edwin Muir's poems and prose books and crossing them with a little history, I had managed to garble and fabulise its past into this myth: the lord built a wall right round the island and cast all the people to the outside of it. It was neither as simple nor as drastic as that; to simplify it so much smacks of too much zeal to seek out tragedies. But the wall does exist.

The passage to Rousay was nicely ushered in at the ferry offices in Kirkwall. The first of these, flickering greenly with V.D.Us and staffed by women in natty suits like airline staff, was the wrong one – the P. & O. The right one, a few doors along the quay, was the Kirkwall Shipping Co., which did its business behind an old-fashioned frosted glass partition. I slid back a little door in it and asked the girl about the crossing from Tingwall to Rousay. She phoned Tingwall to book us a place and said to her friend at the other end, 'Fiona? Kirsty here. Fit like the day? [How are you today?]' The smaller the boat, it seemed, the broader the language; the natty women had used not Scots but a sort of well-trained Britspeak. As we drove through the plain of Rendall, high up to our left on the flank of Milldoe were patches less rusty than moor, less verdant than the lowland – fields taken from the heather in Muir's father's lifetime which had failed back into it about the time when Muir left Orkney. His own Wyre looked all goodness (like Muir himself) with its fair-haired fields and whitened gables. Rousay over the water was dark and Highland among this family of arable islands although its high point, Blotchnie Field, is only 260 metres above sea level:

The Long Homes

Now even the hills seemed low
In the boundless sea and land,
Weakened by distance so.
How could they understand
Space empty on every hand
And the hillocks squat and low?

I had precisely failed to understand this emptiness myself, coming
nearly too late to the realisation that Orkney and Shetland had
suffered clearance like the Highlands. One thing that had lulled
me was Muir's sense of his homeland as an Eden. Island life, he
wrote in his autobiography, 'remained almost unchanged for two
hundred years'. By his birth in 1887 farms were incessantly changing
hands, rents trebling or quadrupling. Half the population left Orkney
between 1861 and 1901 and one-third from the Rousay/Wyre/Egilsay
trio in the thirty years surrounding his childhood. For the Muirs Wyre
was for a few years filled with food and peace. During Rousay's
heyday, as I had just been reading in an old notebook in Kirkwall,
'the hills [in summer] swarmed with horses, cattle, pigs, sheep and
geese. The sheep were divided into flocks or haunts as they were
called. They came to the shore in the winter season to eat seaweed
when the sea was down, and they went to the hill when it began
to flow.' At Hogmanay the young men sang from door to door,
wishing each family 'many stacks above your style,/ Some for malt
and some for meal' and 'every mare a foal at her heel' and 'every
ewe twains at her heel'. Alexander Marwick had been born there
in 1801 and remembered when the 40 or so families in west Rousay
kept 70 horses, 220 cattle, and between 600 and 700 sheep. By
Muir's boyhood nothing was left of this but the sheep, and the
Wee General was priding himself on growing turnips where none
had grown before. He gave Edwin a sixpence when he came over
to shoot 'in his neat little knickerbockers and elegant little brown
boots, a feather curled on his hat' but 'He was a bad landlord, and
in a few years drove my father out of the farm by his exactions' –
a rent of £70 which left him almost nothing to buy stock with. The
Muirs' exodus to Glasgow in 1901, where father, mother, and two
brothers were dead within four years, was only a late stage in the
process which on Rousay had herded 200 people out of the 'bonniest district' into the congested eastern slopes above Sourin and the
narrow coastal fringe where we were now to be staying.

The Taversöe Hotel at Frotoft, in keeping with the human scale of everything on Rousay, was a smallish house at the end of an untarred track and a muddy path. We drove past it twice before picking it out in the gloaming – a cottage built in 1835. Inside it was the soul of domestic comfort and it would have been easy to live there for days in a gentle trance, watching the waves pulse eastward along Eynhallow Sound past Aiker Ness, the arcs of them expanding like the ridged contours of a scallop shell, waiting for the westerlies to turn the three slim tapering sails of the giant Wellsian windmill on Burgar Hill. Rousay people nod across at it, grumble when it's still, doubt whether it really supplies one-fifth of Orkney's electricity. It is beautiful, the biggest in Europe, and extraordinary in our world because it is both very powerful and harmless.

Rousay, like a smaller Barra, was able to be encompassed; as I moved from croft to croft, people could take me to the door and point out the next likely source of memoir or a significant place – the house James Leonard built himself, still white-walled and intact, the site of Stouramira on the west side from which George Leonard, after eviction in 1846, set out with his daughter on his shoulders to walk straight over the crown of the island past the Muckle Water to his new allotment at Sourin. Our landlady, Mrs Preston, added to names I had been given at the Kirkwall Sound Archive. She suggested Mrs Marwick at Wasbister, who took me out into the stone-floored yard and suggested Dr Firth, a most venerable retired G.P. in a suit of black broadcloth who called me 'Sir' and suggested Willy Grieve of Furse 'under the Hill of Brings there, with the little cliff and the waterfall at his back'. Mr Grieve had a black gypsy beard, frosted in patches, and spoke through a choking cough. Every fact or memoir that he knew was sharpened with living detail. William Marwick who had built Furse in 1885 had been evicted twice. 'You didna get leave to pit doon a very deep root. He was a man who went high as the moon got full – he was supposed to be daft – I wish I'd people working for me were daft!' His knowledge of old toil and hardship was precise. His grandmother had lived at Flinterquoy in Quandale (pronounced to rhyme with 'Kendal') before Traill's clearance of the whole west end. Once Westness had been brought under the turnip regime, 'There was a woman walked back there to single neaps [thin turnips] for tuppence a day, in addition to which she got leave to take away a bag o nettles for the coo . . . And there were people tekken to coort for pickin up a dead braxy sheep to salvage bits of it to eat.'

Mr Grieve was able to give the Wee General's way with people a more human aspect than appears in the Napier Minutes:

My first wife's father, John Craigie, was catched poachin a grouse. So Burroughs says, 'Now promise me you won't do that again.' So John Craigie says, 'I cen't do that.' So Burroughs pats him on his shoulder and he says, 'If you *had* promised I would not have believed you.'

Och, the laird wasn't at aal bad to deal wi. But he stopped them querrying flegs – maybe it was to shaa his authority. And they made a solid roof, they didna blaa away in a gale.

In fact Willy Grieve had no illusions about how the crofters had been treated before the 1886 Act provided secure tenure. 'My father, we lived on Egilsay then, and he always called the hen harrier a Sendy Lowrence, because the factor [Alexander Lawrence] aalways demanded a fat hen if he saa it. Father never caaled it anything else, because it preyed on you.' We had seen the birds twice, for the first time in our lives, on Mainland the day before, in stubble fields near the Loch of Harray, almost brushing the ground with their lissome wings, so fiercely intent that you felt yourself rapt like their prey. 'The factor had to justify his existence – shaa he was noticin. There was a shifted crofter found he was on soil so thin he couldn't plent neaps – it was pointless – he'd have hed to heap up the drills. So he crapped it twice – he grew gress two year runnin – the factor reported him – Burroughs came and kicked him off.' So the chivvying went on. The Inkster brothers near the pier had told me how the Wee General tried to stop their father building a house at Swartafield in 1873 so he and a neighbour carted stones and built *at night*. When I told Willy Grieve that I wanted to follow to its bitter end the wall that had been built after the people left, he chuckled and said, 'You'll have a lang waak! There was a lot of work went into it. Sixpence a fethom they gave, including topping it and clearing up efter. Aald Jeckie o Mawn [John of Moan, the last croft outside the wall] had such a pride in it efter he'd made it, he used to waak aleng it in his Sunday best, putting up any stones that had faallen doon.'

Willy Grieve did not sound as though he would ever have been willing to curl up inside his fetters in that way, or internalise his oppressor's values, although his realism might have constrained him to accept the wage. What he valued was the place itself with its own life. He mimed the motion of the harrier's wings with relishing wafts of his hands, then mimed the diving of the bonxie, the great skua, which breeds only in Orkney and Shetland: 'They're veecious – they'll buzz you. It nests up there, and the great black-backed – it's veecious too. But if you go along the clifftop you'll find the *Primula Scotica* growing on the moor.'

None of this vivid life would be there today. The sky seemed to be closing down for the winter and was as darkly forbidding as a rain-wetted rockface. From Furse in the north I drove two miles south-west past Too, the last clachan before the wall, where I spoke to Mrs Clouston and her daughter-in-law, a historian who had copied the large-scale estate maps. Her husband's people had come here in 1824 and she could remember his great-aunt, who had died in 1922 at the age of 99, with 'a gey wrinkly face. When they cam in here she wasna waakin yet but they set her doon at the doorstep, because it wasna lucky if you didna waak into the new place.' Here was a rite that must have been followed by thousands of the cleared, in the Canadian Maritimes, Ontario, Manitoba, as well as in the Scottish croftlands. She remembered that houses at Frotoft had been given the names of places in Quandale such as Breek and Breck. Her own people had left of their own choice from Starling. ('Stirling' on the estate map), discouraged by the sea-gust which dropped its salt on the fields and reaches the windows in Too, a mile and a half from the cliffs. Willy Grieve had said that Quandale 'grew the best barley on the island' – in a good year, no doubt. The community had needed all the income it could get from its members overseas: 'Some of them were in the Nor'wast' – the Bay's great rival in the fur trade – 'and one of them had £300, which helped them with the move.' It was time to see this place which 215 people (equal to the island's whole population today) had been forced to leave when improvement came to Rousay.

I parked a little past the track to Moan and set out to follow the wall to its end between Bring Head and Itherie Geo. It trod straight over all the ridges and swerved just once, at the 125 metre triangulation point on Brae of Moan. After ten minutes' uphill walk it skirted a little quarry, called Hammers of Drussifer on the estate map, where aald Jeckie o Mawn must have laboured to split off pieces of the sedimentary rock with sledge and crowbar. On the wind-stunted heather sloping toward the sea, big birds with barred wings that looked like immature black-backed gulls lay dead and gutted and rabbit skulls were frequent – the bonxies had been feeding well. Ahead the sea heaved darkening blue like a night sky fallen to earth. As the wall came to its end, a great cleft opened at my feet, the rim of Rousay was splitting outwards in vertical layers and waves seethed sideways on the flag floor a hundred feet below. The wall stopped just short – a shrewd move by aald Jeckie to avoid working in a position of great danger? The end was fenced with three tottering posts and a strand or two of barbed wire. I stepped round to reach the narrow gravelly neck that still joined the outermost slice of cliff to solid ground and explored both ways along the edge. The slot was so narrow that my eyes, enthralled, almost enticed my brain to have a go – go on, jump it, you can land on that shelf of solid rock – or was it my crazy brain luring my steady eyes? Half a mile north toward Lobust a horse fell down a blow-hole into a geo like this, landed unharmed, and trotted along the shelf at low tide toward safe pasture. No, this place is fit only for rock doves and cormorants – black crucifixes fleeing along the ice-green tunnels of the breakers.

The wall itself looks daft, a mile and a quarter of stonework meeting the coast at right angles. It could not even have prevented the landlord's flocks from falling into that ferocious sea. Muir's 'The Return' remains apt –

> Their eyes knew every stone
> In the huge heartbreaking wall
> Year after year grown
> Till there was nothing at all
> But an alley steep and small,
> Tramped earth and towering stone ...

Not even a gate leads through it. It is nothing but the definitive bar between owners and crofters. I turned my back on it and walked south-west across a heath half-flayed by gales and mined by rabbits, towards Quandale itself.

On the 30-metre contour opposite Quoynalonga Ness, shallow grooves of field drainage come into focus. A few sheep are grazing – they never leave the crofts whose occupants they ousted four, five, six generations before. Ruins built of whitish stone stand up, at least 25 of them. Some lintels are still in place; roofing flags litter the hollows inside the shells. Some of the interior walls display nicely masoned niches, the sae binks or cupboards for the milking kegs. In the surrounding greens the rabbits have done good archaeological work. The little spoil-heaps at their burrow-mouths are black soil so homogeneous and rich yet free that it's a pleasure to run it through your fingers. Yet Traill purported to be moving people from poor land to better. On the slope above the houses small walled fields still keep their shape: the planticroos where the crofters sowed their cabbages, using their own seed. Down at the shore, next the reefs called Sinians of Cutclaws, neolithic burial mounds look like the features of a face dead but still recognisable.

I had seen one living face from here – George Reid, who died in 1859 aged 107. His great-great-grandson, John Mainland of Frotoft, showed me his portrait, done very plainly in oils: an old man with a bonnet set straight on top of his head, a combed white beard all round his jaw, wearing a black cutaway jacket and waistcoat made of thick home-woven tweed, black trousers and heavy shoes, looking sturdily out at you. He had been born on Westray, the next island north, and lived in Inner Quandale near Scabra Head. He died in Garson, two miles south, and his son lived in Wasdale, Sourin, so they must have been cleared. His house will have been one of a cluster at the far side of a broad green howe, 'the bonniest district in Rousay', with the artery of a burn at its centre, many veins of drainage still relieving it from waterlogging, and at its centre two sophisticated buildings: a two-storey ruin with mullioned windows, which turned out to have been a sixteenth-century principal tenant's house called Tofts, and a massive cairn which was not a burial mound but a centre for either saunas or communal cooking – firemarked stones still show at its summit. Long before the regime of the sheep and the turnip a full life had been lived here. Anne had been exploring the coast north from Westness and when we met she said there was something I must see. From the road it had looked like a disused waterworks. Inside the concrete hangar there loomed a shingle barrow so massive it looked more natural than made. It had been excavated between the wars and roofed to preserve it. We climbed steel stairs and looked down from a gangway into a passage lined with cubby-holes partitioned by tall flags set on end. Neolithic chiefs and their families had been entombed here, no doubt with a few provisions and trade-goods useful in the after-life. Perhaps they were as autocratic as George William Traill, as sure that they knew what was best for their people.

It was well into the gloaming as we left the underground darkness of Mid Howe. The light outside was making everything look ancient.

We had only just time to reach the fortified homestead of the chiefs a quarter of a mile north and walk about in their little rooms, not much bigger than their graves, their doors and partitions made out of single flags ten feet high. At the sea's edge the solid rock had been hewn to make two little docks, harbour or moat or both. Eynhallow Sound glittered darkly like oxidised silver in the last of the light and where the current of Weal Race met the wind, a *rost* six feet high peaked and seethed into overfalls. Between here and the good food and wine at Taversöe, the few orange house-lights made the frailest necklace of habitation. As you approach the ferry pier at Tingwall, the road-signs begin to say 'Rousay Monuments', as though your only reason for visiting the island would be to see the long homes of the dead, Mid Howe and Yarson Knowe and Blackhammer. If Rousay itself is a single barrow eight kilometres long and 260 metres high, then we should see it as a cairn for the 46 families of Quandale, who are not as nameless as the chiefs and whose works in earth and stone may turn out quite as durable.

CHAPTER NINETEEN

VANISHING TRICKS
Shetland

The *St Sunniva* sails west from Stromness on the emigrant trail before veering north on the long haul for Lerwick. Legs brace right away as the sea's muscle starts to heft us up and down. An hour before, in the window of a citizen concern shop in the main street, we were reading some vehement propaganda against the proposed new ferry from Caithness to South Ronaldsay – the most direct route, but an ex-R.A.F. pilot has pinned up a map and drawn bold red arrows to show that wind speeds of Force 3 to 4 in the western Pentland Firth intensify in a very few miles to 9 or 10 in the funnel between Stroma and Burwick. Sure enough, a few days before we came north the new jetty in Gills Bay was torn from its base when steel pins sheared in a gale and the ferry has still not started. In the islands, high winds, wrecks and salvages, narrow escapes are as much the staple of conversation as in Cornwall or Scilly. Mrs Clouston at Too told me about the woman who fished a hogshead of gin out of the sea at Quandale, set off through the hills with it, and was never seen again – the lochan she might have come to grief in was called after her, the Loch o Gin-jennet. Chests of tea that came ashore in the eighteenth century were a puzzle – what was the stuff for? First it was used like straw to bed the animals, then the women discovered how to infuse it and make a drink but they kept it from the men and hid the pot when it was time for them to be coming home. Today the wind is blowing enough for a steward to be reassuring people that 'it will be all right once we're out of the Firth'. And so it is, a steady churning against the sideways boost of a ponderous Atlantic swell, a resigned swallowing of shipboard fish-and-chips, a fixed stare of dazed incredulity on the face of a

336

young man who started north from Folkestone early the day before and looks ready to fall off the end of the world.

To travel north in November, at the day's end, seemed like hastening the calendar. Rousay had been wonderfully boreal – Mrs Preston had called us out one night at Taversöe to see the most wondrous aurora, not a mere arching but a canopy stretched from the zenith, warm roseate in the east and south, streaked vertically with yellow lustres as though all the constellations had loosened and were zooming down past earth. Directly overhead fine blond wisps of cirrus were lit by the polar electricity. I had never seen the height of the visible universe so defined. The world up here felt naked, an extremity laid bare to the on-ding of winter. On the *St Sunniva* a fieldfare passed us flying south in the early afternoon. They have bred on Shetland only since the early 1970s. Just before night came down another perched on the rail for a few seconds, ashen in the deck-lights, then flew off into the superstructure, letting itself be carried back north when it should have been making for the clustered haws of Cumbria, the holly berries in our own back garden. No doubt it was resting from its struggle against a headwind on this crossing that takes a powerful motor vessel seven hours.

The quays and pubs along the waterfront at Lerwick jostled with activity, the laugh and swagger of fishermen and oilmen with cash in their pockets. Down whichever alley or street you went you could still see the waves jumping up into windblown top-knots, like the painted sea on the face of a Victorian grandfather clock, and the blunt hulks of the klondykers at anchor in the Sound of Bressay, ready to go out and gulp their thousands of tons of mackerel and haul them back to Africa or Russia. The voices in the shops sounded Danish if you listened with only half an ear or caught the distinctive vocabulary – 'du' for 'you', 'peerie' for 'little'. A permanent mission for Norwegian sailors occupied a big building on the ridge above the harbour. For a day we mingled with this stir as I searched out contacts, especially the county councillor and novelist John Graham, who knew 'everybody' and spoke on the phone (though not to me) in Shetland, not in English.

At times we sheltered in the car a few yards from the water, looking at maps to get the hang of the islands with their maze of voes and headlands or simply reacclimatising to the human crowd after the quietude of Rousay. Presently a squat red

337

ship with the square stern of a seismic exploration vessel from the oilfields surged backward at an alarming speed – was this a standard manoeuvre? It hit a black-hulled inshore fishing vessel, named the *Bard* in decorative gold lettering. Timbers screeched, splinters burst from the wooden combing of the quay as the *Bard* was crushed against it, and the big red bully – which we now saw to be the *Western Viking* of Sligo – rebounded, then chugged off lopsidedly to the far side of the dock. A fisherman came from below deck on the *Bard*, looking not shattered but not pleased either. When I walked over to photograph the big white wound on the backside of the *Western Viking* a deckhand looked at me with eyes of such smouldering fury that I kept my distance. Before we moved off, a man from the Harbour Master's office arrived with a notebook to inspect the injuries to the *Bard*. Happily she still had her head above water when we came back a week later.

A mile beyond the rim of all this hubbub Shetland suddenly becomes as bare and sparsely-farmed as many a region in the Highlands. The roads that cut between the heathery brown uplands have been newly straightened and graded and equipped with steel crash barriers. Sierras and Rovers drive fast along them, carrying oil company employees to and from Sullom Voe terminal at the north end of Mainland or down to the airport at Sumburgh. Modern industry, big money, are altering the pace of life in the archipelago as they have not in Orkney. Hundreds of miles to the north and east the rigs pump out their riches. Here on this perch above the waters all that can be seen are the scattered blooms of affluence: a spruce new housing estate and supermarket at Brae near Sullom; at the terminal itself the amazingly sheer and imposing installation – a temple of power – colossal grey tanks like stumps of towers that might have reached the clouds, a slender stack blowing its tongue of orange fire into the stream of the wind and the rainsqualls that drive across in columns out of the sea. We looked at it across voes as metal-grey as itself. Under the high arc of a rainbow it seemed unpeopled, robotic, eerily releasing its energy as though it would throb on indefinitely whether or not there was a world somewhere else to receive it. This is merely fanciful: while we were there the *Shetland Times* reported that Sullom was operating at little more than half capacity, as demand for oil waned, and the docking facilities were being anxiously touted for other sorts of shipping.

Our first goal north of Lerwick was Kergord in Upper

Weisdale, where Jim Johnston's great-grandmother had been cleared in 1868. The family, following in the trail of more than thirty others, had trekked westward over the hills to a new home:

> Mother's grandmother Christina Margaret Anderson was 14 years old when she and her family were evicted from Upper Kergord. The bulk of the people had been evicted three years ago but James Anderson had a lease to his croft and could not be expelled until this expired. James and his wife Janet (she was a Laurenson), and their family of seven, had to leave the place in autumn. They carried the crops through the hills west to the Heid-of-the-Voe of Aith – they probably went by the Burn of Lunklet. And the crop and their rooftrees were flitted up the voe to the Mark, then carried down to Aithness.
>
> The timbers were too short for the new place, they had to be extended. Christina's burden was a wooden sae (tub) with the lasts for boot-making and repairing. She carried it to her Aunt Baabie at the Voe-heid of Aith. They had to shift their stock and all, including grice [pigs], and build sties for them on the outside of the yard dyke. The plough they used in Aithness was drawn by a pair of oxen with horns so long they had to turn their heads to go in the byre.

When Jim first told me this, he said that Chrissie carried a sieve. His mother (named after her grandmother) knew that it had been a sae and she confirmed this when we visited her at Upper Longaskule, four miles south of her granny's old home. As the second eldest, Chrissie would have been expected to carry a fair load. To Mrs Johnston the laden journey still seemed 'unbelievable' and she was dubious about my plan to walk the line of it on a day when hailstones were sore against the cheeks and all distances were wiped out by blinding white rains from time to time. 'It was a trokkit gait [sodden path],' she insisted, and might not be easy to find among the hills. But I would be a poor hill-walker if I could not cross over where they had gone with timbers to carry, infants in kishies (baskets) on their backs, pigs to drive – which were smaller, stronger, more colourful than they are today. Anne would drop me round in Weisdale, then drive back to meet me at Aith Voe, and we would go to Mrs Johnston's for some hot broth afterwards.

As soon as I left the car, the Valley of Kergord closed round me with the deafening silence which is the atmosphere of a habitable, emptied place – likened by Hugh MacDiarmid in 'The Glen of Silence' to what a doctor 'hears' as he auscultates a mother whose baby has died in the womb:

> Here is an identical silence, picked out
> By a bickering burn and a lone bird's wheeple
> – The foetal death in this great cleared glen
> Where the *fear-tholladh nan tighean* has done his foul work
> – The tragedy of an unevolved people.

(The Gaelic phrase means 'usurper of homes'.) Above Setter the ground was easy-angled and well grooved by old furrowings. It narrowed and climbed a little before opening out into the broad green homeland of the Andersons, flanked by low boggy hills. It had been well drained itself, with dyke foundations and the heaped stones of croft houses to be seen on every side. Jim's brother had counted 'dozens of ruins' many years before. Now there is one house with a roof, a fenced garden, flounced Austrian drapes in the windows – a shepherd's, no doubt, solitary and incongruous amid the vacant greens of the toun.

On the slope of Scalla Field to the west the ring-dyke was still plain to see. Would the families have steered round the 300-metre mountain by Scallafield Scord (pass) to the north or the steeper, slightly more direct southern route past Vats Houll and the Butter Stone? I chose the latter, then wondered for an hour if I had done right as the moor spreadeagled into desolate watersheds and the peat haggs were scored so deeply by run-off that their bottoms were worn through to quartz gravel five metres down. Memories surfaced of trekking through from Aberdeenshire to Angus via Glen Callater and Glen Doll and getting lost repeatedly as we plunged into a hagg, wearily followed its winding, and emerged no longer sure which was west and which was south. Today, as it had been then, the sun was no help, lost behind cloudwrack. At least the summit on my right was always visible and when the dark gleam of the Loch of Lunklet came into sight ahead, pathfinding lost its difficulties – the burn must feed from there and could be followed to its mouth at East Burra Firth, where the family would have floated off their timbers for the crossing to Aithness.

From time to time a hare, already white for the winter, cruised off through the tussocks, lightfooted on quaking ground where I sank to the knee and took my leg out blackened. Now a thread of path snaked roughly parallel to the burn – the families would have followed it when they came over to Burra Firth to fish. At the meeting with the Marrofield Water, on a grassy plain that in Gaelic would be called an *ùrlar*, a single ruin showed three courses of masonry and a heap of stones twenty metres long curved along a ridge nearby, gathered perhaps for further home-making by the Petersons who lived here till they were evicted. The burn was now a burly black water, like Guinness in flood, and I crossed it for the last time, leaping from one smoothed reef to another on the lip of the high white waterfall called Ramnaholl which is a landmark for the cleared folk in John Graham's novel *Shadowed Valley*.

It had been a rough, wet three miles. According to Mrs Sandison at Whirligert in Aith, whose great-aunt was also an Anderson evicted from Kergord, the families had to make the journey repeatedly to bring away all their gear and the baby would be carried uphill by the eldest brother or sister, then downhill by a younger one. Her husband's mother's people had been evicted too, from Voe on Olna Firth a few miles north of Kergord to Sullom; as he said, more sadly than angrily, 'It always seems as though the better the soil, the more were sent away from it.' Jim and Mrs Johnston's people had been 'lucky' in that their lease gave them grace in which to find a new place. Most Shetland evictions were on forty days' notice because the annual lease had been verbal and unrecorded. The Andersons' well-being was of course at the expense of the sitting tenants of their new place at Aithness, including a woman called Margaret Dalziel and her baby who had been living in the barn. At the time when the landlord (a Lowland lawyer called Black) was putting his tenants through this unfestive game of musical chairs, it was said, according to Jim, 'that the third generation would never enjoy the possession of the new place that had been given them, and so it happened in Aithness'. In his mother's time the family left it in their turn as though the curse was working itself out. One son died of yellow fever in Australia, another (along with his brother-in-law) was drowned when they 'went off in a sailing boat to move a few sheep to a different part of the farm, it was a windy day and they had been wondering whether to go or not. However when on the homeward journey the boat capsized with all hands.' Cursing is only to be expected between tenant and landlord. Over in Weisdale, according to Mrs Sandison, two old women called Huxter had refused to leave their home and the estate men walled them in to starve them out, 'so they laid a curse on it, and it stands there empty today'. In *Shadowed Valley* an evicted woman curses the factor in words like those the Sutherland folk used against the Countess: '"Deil sneck dy finger-points an may he swee dy evil krang" ["May the devil chop your fingers off and sting your evil carcase"].' The factor was fair game but it is grievous to think of one crofter family laying a ban on another one.

Our way north to the last of the islands followed a mazy line enforced by the terrain – balancing across isthmuses not a mile wide, sidestepping voes that draw the tides miles inland from the open sea. From Kergord I had been able to spy along the north-south grain of the land almost into Olnafirth. 'By Shetland standards it is an inland place, whose main stay of life in days gone by was the land.' These days went by rather rapidly in the middle nineteenth century when crofters' rents were no longer 'sufficient to keep the landowner in the grander style to which he had grown accustomed since he had embarked upon a life in commerce'. Only rents from sheep farmers 'could offer the profits which the lairds considered worthwhile'. A fifth of the parish was cleared. The people's spokesman, a crofter called Thomas Henderson, told Napier that some families 'settled down on the hills, and others along the shores. Some fell into pauperism.' The younger people emigrated:

> You are aware that in this country we consume peats, and not coals, and if an eviction takes place we don't know that it is to be until November. Now our peats must be cut and cured in summer, and not winter, and if we get notice to leave there is no resource but to stand and face it – we have no alternative but to face it, or go to the fields. Shelter we might get, but not fire.

Today this history exists as short, piercing stories. David Sandison crippled himself hauling his crop away from his croft, then built himself and his family a shelter in a gravel pit, where his youngest child died of pneumonia. (When the Commissioners asked him whether he had been compensated, he held up his crutch and said, 'This is the compensation I got!') Jane Anderson was lured out by the ground officers with a story about her cow having strayed into the corn – she left her child and went after the animal – when she came back the child was outside on the ground and the thatch was burning. That is what happened.

Again and again for years this question had been forced up into sight – not 'How could they do it?', since it is late in the day to be marvelling at our inhumanity toward each other, but 'Why did *they* do it?' and 'Who, in a community, was willing to?' Evidence about this and every other strand in the experience came pouring in abundance from Robert Johnson of Yell, a crofter who writes history. When I phoned him to ask for a meeting, he suggested we stay at his house, Snuastadr, at Setter, where the island is almost severed by Whale Firth in the west and Mid Yell Voe in the east. By now the drenching autumn was so far on that water seemed omnipotent, the islands like so much flotsam amongst tides and rains and winds. Yell was a mere chance surfacing of moors and little fringes and veins of arable above the swell of the ocean. Clouds like squat grey ogres were slouching off beyond the horizon, having spewed their last full gobs of water onto the saturated peat. The branch track to Setter was six inches deep in silt where Robert had been ditching and a mud-boltered tractor with double tyres leaned like an exhausted beast in front of the house. We would be snug for the night but the dusk-light, reflecting coldly from caked earth and boggy pools and dripping cuts in the peat, at least took one a mite nearer to the dread of nightfall that must have faced Robert Peterson with his wife and aged parents, twice evicted from North Olnafirth, forced to live in a turf hut on the moor.

Robert Johnson was brusque and eloquent, strong and paunchy, scholarly and still speaking broad Shetland little moulded by printed English. His articles are sheer fact, fed from below by the first-hand experience which pulses in his talk:

Grandfather came from Camb to Hevdagarth on the voe there in 1868 – he was warned oot sae aaften it broke his hert. He had dug most of that park [at Camb] by moonlight. The hoose he cam into, it was supposed to be disinfected but it can't have worked and the boy died – his oldest son, Charles. Grandfather was buildin corn in the yard when they got the forty days' waarnin. The peats was brought hame o coorse. The taaties wasna up but they were allooed to tak up the taaties. They had the boat, they could drag it down to the voe. When they were pit oot o the hoose, the dinner was boilin. The roof was torn aff – they could get no men in the island to act as sheriff officers, they brought men from Larwick. Was it like that in the Highlands?

John Smith fae Kirkabister [on Basta Voe], he had three rafters pit in so he took them wi him. The sun shined in on the next man. He could tak the corn because he had cultivated it. But no fixtures. On Fetlar a man caalled Gairdner was takin wood oot o the laft and the Nicholsons took him to coort. Once it was dug into the waa it had to stay. The box beds they could tak because they were loose – nae nails were used. My grandfather was carryin for weeks. The grand-uncles had to be led, John and David, because they were blind – every ither sight was intensified, they could set the nets.

Robert was equally interested in the neighbour islands a mile or less across the water, Fetlar to the east, Unst to the north. What seemed common to them all was a severity in the evictions, a rage in the (short-lived) retaliations, which still comes off the facts in a rank odour. The factor who was instrumental in clearing Unst and Yell, as well as Olnafirth, was John Walker. 'Walker wronged every person,' Andrew Spence, a crofter, told Napier. He was burnt in effigy in the 1860s, when sabotage was rife. The father of our landlady at Gerratoun on Unst had told her that Walker went round at night digging up sheeps' heads from middens to check whether the earmarks belonged to the croft he found them on or had been filched from one of the new farms. It happened so much that only the minister's flock was allotted the *full stou* – the whole ear removed; if anyone else had been entitled to this, according to the factor, he would only have abused it by stealing other people's sheep and cutting off whole ears to efface the distinctive marks. To enforce eviction, doors were taken off their hinges, water thrown onto the fires. The dovetailing between Church of Scotland minister and laird was exposed more plainly than I had seen anywhere. Simply, they belonged to the same class and it is this, rather than any archaic nonsense about driving moneylenders out of temples, that typifies these Christian proprietors. According to letters Robert showed me, the Rev. William Watson owned Bouster, west of the voe-head of Whale Firth. In the summer of 1852 he wrote to a farmer who factored for him, 'I hope the woman Smollet has taken her departure from my house at Bouster. If she has not you will

344

oblige me by causing the house to be unroofed, or by adopting such means as may be effective to move her out.' Eleven years later there had been a change of owner, the Rev. David Webster had taken over but the policy was unchanged. On October 12th, 1863 he wrote regarding a recalcitrant tenant, John Omand: 'If John Omand has taken the loft and wood fixtures he will just have to bring them back and fit them up again as they were before. I understand that William Anderson cut his peats as well as Charles. If he has cut them that fixes him with the rent and I do not doubt he could also be made to fire the house.' That is, the Andersons had taken fuel from the minister's moss and were therefore beholden to him. Even this whiphand couldn't automatically force a crofter to do the owner's dirty work. On November 16th Mr Webster is still being thwarted: 'As to the thatch of the houses in Bouster, I have already sent them word to do it but it seems that they have not done it. I am not sure whether they can be made to do it or not . . . '

I came a little nearer to those primitive fights over an acre, a timber, the carcase of a sheep through the words of a very old woman in a council house at Mid Yell. Grace Mann was immobile in her chair beside the cooker and the words came from her like a lesson learned by heart in early childhood, in this case from her mother, who was evicted from Bixsetter above Basta Voe, and her father, who was evicted from Vollister near the mouth of Whale Firth. 'What they had they took with them. I think it was the month of October. It was a good place. They had plenty of sheep and grew good crops. I saw the ruins once – just stones. It was poor days.' That was all – phrases like an inscription on a weathered stone. And then, talking to a Mr Williamson in Lerwick Museum shortly before the boat sailed for Aberdeen, I was hearing details which brought to pinpoint brilliance all that experience of clearance from the lands east of Whale Firth. His grandmother had been born at Dalsetter during the Potato Famine and she had told him how the men from Lumbister, next to Vollister, used to come to the mill for oat and bere seed because 'the Lumbister seed was getting lang and green and nae seed-feardie [fertile]'. Lumbister was cleared and fenced off to preserve it as pasture for a large farm: 'Sheep are very territorial, especially Shetland sheep. And the evicted sheep trod a mirey track along the Dalsetter side of the new fence, and they lay down alongside it and died with their faces towards Lumbister.'

Yell had been so stark and dour that it took close thinking to realise why people were attached enough to it to resist uprooting. As we reached the far end of Unst, where we were to stay in the furthest north Bed-and-Breakfast in the British Isles, Mrs Ritch's at Gerratoun, the sun streamed through at last between cloudwrack and sea and laid long swathes of light as golden as barley across the planes and folds of the land. As we explored, Burra Firth received us, a fjord reaching two miles into the land from the very north end at Herma Ness. It was one of those places that look shaped with loving expertise for habitation. The parallel sides facing each other across the tidal reach should be mirror images. The east-side croft at Budabreck was perfectly farmed, wire fences strained taut round fields that striped the land immediately above the clifftop with yellow tweeds of oat stubble and hay aftermath, luminous with fertility under the fading wine of the moor. Opposite, the croftland called locally West-the-Burn was deserted – a blank sward, a green shroud. Parallel ridges of fail-dyke divided it into fields unused for a century. When I walked up it, the toun (like Achness or Grummore in Strath Naver, Lettaidh in Strath Fleet) stretched back and back, a roomy place, all cleared by a laird called Edmonston whose descendants still own North Yell. Alan Fraser at Crosbister, a few miles south, had heard how Edmonston behaved. He went in person to get 're-compense' (arrears of rent) from a woman in Colvadale and found her milking. 'She raise up. He kicked the milk over: "That doesna beleng to thee." Then he took the cow: "An that doesna beleng to thee either."' Mrs Sutherland, who lives on the hill above Burra Firth-head, knew many more details of how the thing was done. A family called Johnson at Cliff, the next township south – who had previously had to move from Yell – came home and found their roof gone and the old folk sitting on the ground amongst their gear. An old woman living on her own, who had refused to give up her place, was sent on a message to Uyeasound at the south end and when she got back her house had been pulled down, its stones built up into a dyke. 'When West-the-Burn was cleared, the people came to this side and room was made by taking in from the hill. They mostly moved in with relations. But there was a big wave of emigration when they came to see there wasna room. They went to New Zealand and Australia – there was an agent in Lerwick.' In the ten years to 1881 the Unst crofters lost to the big estates 111 homes that housed 540 people and one-third of the island.

I had seen a likeness of West-the-Burn in its heyday on the

wall of Alan Fraser's house: a painting made on the eve of the clearance, looking north along the firth, in a light yellow as buttered eggs which gave a look of permanent goodness to the two sidelands each with its crofts full of corn. Mr Fraser, an expert breeder of Shetland ponies, had bought it at a sale down at Belmont where a family called Sandison had lived – rich owners of fishing boats and kippering kilns, fond of driving round London and Bournemouth with a pair of Shelties in the shafts of their trap. The picture, perhaps a century and a half old, radiated a late-summer harvest light. Now it had thinned to a clear amber, in which Unst lay fixed. As I looked across the floor of the firth, yellowed blue where the sand-coloured cliffs and stubble fields tinged the water, a gull turned above the shell of a ruin: in the photo I took it is a white body with blurred wings, the migrant spirit of the place. The sea was so calm it barely managed to toss up a white crest on the reef at the head of the voe. Above this, on a perfect pasture, a football pitch was marked out, two goals with orange nylon nets. Four Shelties were grazing in the penalty box at the home team's end, one white, two Irish-setter bronze, one clouded grey. At that moment the Third World War started, ululating from the three-bulbed installation over on the hill called Sothers Fields, making my back shiver with memories of wartime sirens in Aberdeen when bombs smashed half a church in the next street and gravestones near the university were sent flying through the air. Only practising – the Shelties browsed on and in a minute the All Clear sounded its level note.

The R.A.F. were an important presence at this end of Unst – a sort of replacement for the herring fishing based at Balta Sound which had once been the core of the island's cash economy. The Sound and Harold's Wick had teemed with boats. Now Norwick village is 'the camp'. It reminded me of Churchill with its look of an outpost: brand-new oblong buildings in matt brown and Prussian blue, a leisure centre with cinema, squash courts and bar, named with Brit humour 'The Ice Cap'. At a gateway into the military quarters a sentry sat with his bum on a pile of sandbags – in case the I.R.A. hit Unst? 'If it wasn't for the R.A.F. I would not be on Unst,' said Mr Ritch, our landlady's husband, who worked for the NAAFI at 'the camp'. This far end of Britain has been a fortified bulwark for many years. We went to see 'the last house in Britain', the Haa of Skaw, one roofed house among small ruins on a green just above a tidal rampart of sand, and on the way back we walked out along

347

Lamba Ness where the laird had 'encouraged' the survivors of the North Unst fishing disaster of 1832 to leave, then walled off the headland for a pasture. Such blows were crucial; in North Yell we had visited Gloup, where 58 men from all these northerly fishing villages had been drowned in a gale in 1881 and their monument, a broad-hipped woman holding a child and looking out to sea, towers above three bronze plaques with their names. The elements and the laird having destroyed the community of Outer Skaw on Lamba Ness, the military took over and equipped it with blockhouses, air-raid shelters, radio masts. An unheard-of number of ravens, thirty or more, were hobbling about on the sheep-shorn grass among blast-walls and bunkers, as though auditioning for a remake of *The Birds*. One rusting sheet-metal door was padlocked and the lock was *freshly greased*, which gave me the eery feeling that there might still be a group of Second World War squaddies sitting in there playing cards, with Woodbines in their mouths, their eyes sagging wide open and glassified by cold like Franklin's men who have recently been found in the ice on Greenland.

Amongst all this the good crofts at Burrafirth seemed perfectly wholesome, the best possible monument to all those aborted homesteads up and down the west and north of Scotland. Should I have left it at that? On our last day we visited Garth Banks at the other extremity of Shetland, near Fitful Head. I knew it because of the photographs. George Washington Wilson, best photographer of the Highlands soon after the Clearances, had taken its picture in 1867: the close-built clachan with smoke blowing from chimneys in the thatched roofs, the sheltering dykes and beehive kilns for parching grain before grinding, the strips of ploughland, the huddled stooks, the planticroo full of greens. In 1880 a local man, James Profitt Isbister of Dunrossness, had the wit to repeat Wilson's photo. The vanishing trick has happened, as completely as the disappearance of Trotsky from the famous photo with Lenin on the podium. No houses, no crops, no walls. A wire fence replacing the ring-dyke on the hill behind. The physical fabric of a community abolished as utterly as Lidice. In 1871 Arthur Irvine of Garth Banks and 28 fellow-crofters testified *in favour* of their landlord Andrew Grierson at an enquiry into landholding. Two years later he evicted them all.

In a gale of rain I walked over the greens of Garth (pronounced 'Gerth'). Looming ahead was the dark profile of land-mass familiar from the photos. It turned out that the clachan in Wilson's picture was only the core of the township. Its stones had been cannibalised to make the usual large square field for the sheep-farm. There were a good many other houses, some still showing their gables, here and there on the broad and gently-angled saddle of grass between Garth Ness and The Cleap. A good burn watered it and fell 50 metres into the sea at the lower end. The kailyard of the 1867 photo was still clear, an oblong of stones bedded in the turf. For all the fearsome crags immediately to seaward, it was a comely site, above the reach of the worst salt-gust and sheltered by 150 metres of hill to the west. It is nameless now, a non-place, but the oddest monument was standing up in a patch of segs: a very old timber, with a shaped curve in it and a row of square-headed blacksmith's nails down one side. It had clearly been planted there and it had no function as a fence- or gate-post. Conceivably some Gerth descendant had come back from New Zealand and raised it as though to say, Human beings once made a life here.

As I let the gale hurry me back to the car, I was composing an epitaph:

> Clubs were not used on Gerth
> Or guns or fire.
> This was the victory
> Of capital and wire.

Sitting in the steamy car at the ferry dock I wrote this on a postcard and sent it to John Graham. Later I heard that in 1890 the crofters ten miles north of Gerth, at South Cunningsburgh, defeated the encroaching wire at least for a time. They won legal actions against the landlord and prevented him from fencing in hill grazings to make them his own. To celebrate, they sounded the looder horns that they used to signal to each other on fishing trips and whale drives and kindled a big bonfire on the hill-top:

> Loud and prolonged cheering rent the air, and some of the men recited a primitive war-song . . . While we write Mr Bruce's servants are still proceeding with the removal [of fences] . . . and the lasses are proposing to put on another bonfire to crown the victory when the job is completed.

Now there was nothing for it but to settle into the 14-hour trudge southward to Aberdeen – the voyage it had taken me fifty years to make. Presumably we would be safe. The Shetland paper had been filled with the case of an oil-field supply-boat skipper who, being understandably tired, had gone to sleep, wakened up in a fog, and only realised where he was when his ship hit Score Head. His ingenious defence was that he could not have been really drunk because on his way north to join his ship at Lerwick he had been drinking with some highly responsible people – the captain and engineer of the boat on which we now found ourselves ... Not a thing my grandfather would ever have done as he sailed his trawler, the *Strathairlie*, time after time on this same run.

We slept peacefully as the gale blew itself out. In the oyster grey of morning familiar landmarks on the Aberdeenshire coast solidified slowly – the Bullers of Buchan, Ythan mouth with its throngs of eider, the long range of dunes at Balmedie where I had gathered Neolithic flints as a little boy before the War. The chalk-white pillar of the lighthouse at Girdle Ness was the sign of Aberdeen and set me looking for the four-lugged tower of Nigg Kirk where the remains of my parents and grandparents lie buried. Now we were abreast of things I had never seen from the sea: the South Breakwater at the harbour mouth where waves were flowering suddenly; the stubby pier called the Skate's Nose; the white fingers of the leading lights next to the fisher-toun of Old Torry, granite cottages which became a slum, as fishermen prospered and preferred the new respectability up the hill, and were demolished recently to make room for petroleum tanks. There would be few trawlers in the harbour, now that the place is given over to the floating machinery of the oil work. As crewmen in oilskins and yellow hard-hats laid out lengths of hawser on the wet metal of the after-deck, my Aberdeen, already bygone, seemed to leave me as finally, in a long backward zoom, as all the other lives I had been tracing.

NOTES

EPIGRAPH

Ronald Rees, *New and Naked Land* (Saskatoon, Saskatchewan, 1988), CPR Corporate Archives 8454.

CHAPTER 1: Watching the People's Mouth

P.3: 'Watching the people's mouth': Brecht's phrase for Martin Luther's style. Bertolt Brecht, 'On Rhymeless Verse with Irregular Rhythms' in *Brecht on Theatre*, ed. John Willett (1964), p. 117.

P.3: James Hunter, *The Making of the Crofting Community* (Edinburgh, 1976), pp. 4, 282.

P.3: George Ewart Evans, *Where Beards Wag All* (1970), p. 92.

P.4: John Prebble, *Mutiny*, 1975 (1977 ed.), pp. 403–31; Kenneth J. Logue, *Popular Disturbances in Scotland, 1780–1815* (Edinburgh, 1979), p. 101.

P.4: Alexander MacKenzie, *The History of the Highland Clearances*, 1883 (Glasgow, 1946 ed.), pp. 198–200; John Prebble, *The Highland Clearances*, 1963 (1969 ed.), pp. 257–60.

CHAPTER 2: 'The Thing That Would Make Dross of Meadows'

P.15: Eric Richards, *A History of the Highland Clearances* (1982), p. 376.

P.16: Sorley MacLean, 'Screapadal': *Cencrastus No. 7* (Edinburgh, Winter 1981–2), p. 19.

CHAPTER 3: Pouring Away the Milk

P.18: Hunter, *Making of the Crofting Community*, p. 116.

P.19: F. Fraser Darling, 'Ecology of Land Use in the Highlands and Islands' in *The Future of Scotland*, ed. Derick S. Thomson and Ian Grimble (1968), pp. 51–2.

P.19: *West Highland Free Press*, May 13th, 1988; A.T.A. Learmonth, 'The Population of Skye' in *The Scottish Geographical Magazine*, Vol. 66, No. 2 (Edinburgh, September 1950), p. 93.

P.19: The five tenants from Dalavil were evicted in the early 1830s. Eight crofters were evicted from Caradal in 1879. *Minutes of Evidence Taken Before The Royal Commission (Highlands and Islands, 1892)*, 1895: hereafter cited as 'D.F.C.': Question 8024.

P.23: Iain Fraser Grigor, *Mightier Than a Lord* (Stornoway, 1979), p. 70.

P.23: *Evidence Taken by Her Majesty's Commissioners of Inquiry into the Condition of the Crofters and Cottars in the Highlands and Islands of Scotland* [hereafter cited as 'Napier'] (1884), Question 5179.

P.23: Napier Q. 5546.

P.23: Napier Q. 5535.

P.27: Archibald Geikie, *Scottish Reminiscences* (Glasgow, 1904), pp. 226–7.

P.28: MacKenzie, *Highland Clearances*, pp. 204–7.

P.28: Prebble, *Highland Clearances*, p. 272.

P.29: Collected in South Uist by Alexander Carmichael: Napier Commission Report, Appendix A, p. 474. A Barra version is printed in Helen MacGregor and John Cooper, *Barra* (Edinburgh, 1984), unpaged.

P.29: Prebble, *Highland Clearances*, pp. 277, 280; Napier QQ. 10322 ff., 14465, 14744, 14874, 15017, 15070, 16153, 17840; QQ. 24603, 28229.

P.29: John MacKenzie, *Pigeon Holes of Memory*, ed. Christina Byam Shaw (1988), p. 36.

P.30: Richards, *Highland Clearances*, p. 430. Suishnish was taken over by the Department of Agriculture after the 'Crofters' War', reapportioned to crofters after the Great War, and worked until the 1960s: interview with Neil MacKinnon, Elgol, in John Muir Trust *Journal* (July 1997), p. 22.

P.33: A Gaelic version is published by Michael Newton, 'The Sense of Place in the Gaelic Tradition': John Muir Trust *Journal* (Summer 1998), p. 24.

P.34: Donald MacLeod, *Gloomy Memories in the Highlands of Scotland: versus Mrs. Harriet Beecher Stowe's Sunny Memories . . .*, 1841/1856/1857 (Glasgow, 1892 ed.), p. 167; Prebble, *Highland Clearances*, p. 80.

P.34: *The Christian Watt Papers*, ed. David Fraser (Collieston, Aberdeenshire, 2nd ed., 1988), p. 27.

P.35: *West Highland Free Press*, February 17th, 1989.

CHAPTER 4: Handfuls of Earth

P.36: D.F.C. QQ. 198–206; Richards, *Highland Clearances*, vol. 2 (1982), p. 464.

P.37: Sorley MacLean, *Spring Tide and Neap Tide* (Edinburgh, 1977), p. 94.

P.39: *MacLean, Spring Tide and Neap Tide*, pp. 142–4.

P.41: See above, p. 8; see below, p. 56; Prebble, *Highland Clearances*, pp. 85, 89.

P.41: D.F.C. QQ. 499, 503, 510.

P.42: *West Highland Free Press*, May 5th, 1989.

P.44: D.F.C. Q. 530.

P.44: D.F.C. Q. 482.

P.45: *Boswell's Journal of a Tour to the Hebrides*, ed. F.A. Pottle and Charles H. Bennett (1936), pp. 242–243.

P.46: MacKenzie, *Pigeon Holes of Memory*, pp. 33–4.

P.47: D.F.C. Q. 361.

P.48: *From the Farthest Hebrides*, ed. Donald A. Fergusson (Toronto, 1978), pp. 46–8.

Notes

Chapter 5: The Loom and the Tweed

P.56: Richards, *Highland Clearances*, vol. 2, p. 264.

P.57: Sorley MacLean, *The Cuillin*, Part 1, in *Chapman* No. 50 (Edinburgh, Summer 1987), p. 162.

P.58: Prebble, *Highland Clearances*, p. 260.

P.64: Horace Fairhurst, 'The Surveys for the Sutherland Clearances' in *Scottish Studies* vol. 16 (Edinburgh, 1968), p. 16; Fairhurst, 'Scottish Clachans' in *The Scottish Geographical Magazine*, vol. 76, no. 2 (Edinburgh, September 1960), p. 73.

P.64: H.A. Moisley, 'North Uist in 1799' in *The Scottish Geographical Magazine*, vol. 77, no. 2 (Edinburgh, September 1961), p. 92.

P.64: J.B. Caird, 'The Reshaped Agricultural Landscape' in *The Making of the Scottish Countryside*, ed. M.L. Parry and T.R. Slater (1980), pp. 204, 212.

P.64: Alan D. MacMillan, *Native Peoples and Cultures of Canada* (Vancouver/Toronto, 1988), p. 280; *Manitoba Pageant* (Winnipeg, September 1963), p. 11.

P.64: Napier QQ 3045–6, 13221.

Chapter 6: 'Banished from Everywhere'

P.69: J.B. Caird, 'The Making of the Scottish Rural Landscape' in *The Scottish Geographical Magazine* vol. 80, no. 2 (Edinburgh, September 1964), p. 75.

P.72: MacLeod, *Gloomy Memories*, pp. 137–9; MacKenzie, *Highland Clearances*, pp. 213–222.

P.76: John Prebble, *Culloden* (1961), pp. 173–6, 190–200, 214–24, 233–5.

Chapter 7: 'The Isle of Contentment'

P.79: Daniel Gillis, *Measure of a Man* (Philadelphia, 1982), p. 3.

P.80: Adapted from Margaret MacDonell, *The Emigrant Experience: Songs of Highland Emigrants in North America* (Toronto, 1982), pp. 107, 109.

P.81: *From the Farthest Hebrides*, ed. Fergusson, p. 300.

P.85: All quotations from Selkirk's diary are based on a typed transcript given me by the Belfast Historical Society, P.E.I.

P.93: Hunter, *Making of the Crofting Community*, p. 159.

Chapter 8: 'Boats Against the Current'

P.100: 'Johnny Allan MacDonald of Enon' in *Cape Breton's Magazine*, No. 48 (Wreck Cove, Cape Breton Island, n.d.), pp. 10–11.

P.101: Richards, *Highland Clearances*, pp. 405–8.

P.101: D.C. Harvey, 'Scottish Immigration to Cape Breton' in *The Dalhousie Review*, pp. 319–20.

P.101: James Cameron, *The Old and the New Highlands* (Kirkcaldy, 1912), p. 25.

P.102: Napier Commission Report, p. 127.

P.106: Prebble, *Highland Clearances*, p. 197; *Guelph and Galt Advertiser*, January 27th, 1847; *As an Fhearann/To the Land*, (ed. Glasgow, 1986), p. 13.

P.106: Cameron, *Old and New Highlands*, p. 22.

P.106: Harvey, 'Scottish Immigration to Cape Breton', pp. 313–4; D. Campbell and R.A. MacLean, *Beyond the Atlantic Roar* (Toronto, 1974), pp. 66, 93.

P.107: Abraham Gerner, *The Industrial Resources of Nova Scotia* (Halifax, 1849), pp. 310, 333–4.

P.109: Campbell and MacLean, *Beyond the Atlantic Roar*, pp. 66–8.

P.109: John Prebble, *Glencoe (1966)*, p. 236.

CHAPTER 9: 'Local Bullies and Bad Landlords'

P.122: Daniel Defoe, *A Tour Through the Whole Island of* Great *Britain (1962* ed.), 11, p. 416.

P.123: John Mercer, *Hebridean Islands* (1972), p. 37.

P.127: Hella Pick, 'Passing time and emotion' in *The Guardian*, October 22nd, 1988.

P.128: *Papers on the Sutherland Estate Management 1802–1816*, ed. R.J. Adams (Edinburgh, 1972), vol. 1, p. 65.

P.129: MacLeod, *Gloomy Memories*, p. 17; Donald Sage, *Memorabilia Domestica* (1889), p. 292.

P.130: Napier QQ. 25589–90; *Sutherland Estate Management*, vol. 1, pp. 16–17.

P.131: MacLeod, *Gloomy Memories*, p. 5.

P.134: Napier Q. 13684.

P.134: Extracts from Munro MacKenzie's diary ed. Joni Buchanan: *West Highland Free Press*, June 10th and July 8th, 1988.

P.135: I.M.M. MacPhail, *The Crofters' War* (Stornoway, 1989), p. 92; Joseph Mitchell, *Reminiscences of My Life in the Highlands*, 1884 (Newton Abbot, 1971 ed.), p. 6.

P.137: Eric Richards, *The Leviathan of Wealth* (1973), pp. 268–9; *Sutherland Estate Management*, vol. 1, p. 73.

P.137: Mitchell, *Reminiscences*, p. 6.

P.138: Richards, *Highland Clearances*, p. 359.

P.139: Coll guidebook, 1937: quoted by Noel Banks, *Six Inner Hebrides* (1977), p. 110.

P.139: I.F. Grant, *Highland Folk Ways* (1961), pp. 99–100, 189.

P.140: Patrick Leigh Fermor, *Roumeli*, 1966 (1983 ed.), p. 11.

P.143: A. Sutherland, A *Summer Ramble in the Northern Highlands* (Edinburgh, 1825).

P.143: Nancy C. Dorian, *Language Death (Philadelphia*, 1981), p. 46.

P.144: A.S. Cowper, *Gordon Ross 1791–1868* (Edinburgh, 1981), pp. 1–4.

P.145: Donald Sage, *Memorabilia Domestica*, pp. 79, 99.

P.145: D.F.C. Q. 24969.

P.145: *Stories of the Supernatural from Helmsdale and District* (*c.* 1985), Nos. 48–50.

P.150: Sage, *Memorabilia Domestica*, p. 79.

P.150: Sage, *Memorabilia Domestica*, pp. 290–1.

Notes

P.152: MacLeod, *Gloomy Memories*, pp. 26–7; Ian Grimble, *The World of Rob Donn* (Edinburgh, 1979), p. 50.

P.152: Grimble, *World of Rob Donn*, pp. 53–4.

P.154: Ian Grimble, *The Trial of Patrick Sellar* (1962), pp. 158–60; John MacInnes, 'A Gaelic Song of the Sutherland Clearances' in *Scottish Studies*, Vol.8, (Edinburgh, 1964), pp. 104–6.

P.156: Napier QQ. 26157–26161.

Chapter 10: The Grain and the Bracken

P.159: Philip Gaskell, *Morvern Transformed* (Cambridge, 1968), p. 155.

P.159: David Craig and David Paterson, *The Glens of Silence*, (Edinburgh, 2004), p. 89.

P.160: Norman MacLeod, *Reminiscences of a Highland Parish*, 1863 (S.W. Partridge ed., London, n.d.), pp. 294–5.

P.162: A.R.B. Haldane, *The Drove Roads of Scotland* (1952), pp. 86–7; Gaskell, *Morvern Transformed*, pp. 20–21, 24, 169.

P.162: MacLeod, *Reminiscences of a Highland Parish*, pp. 295, 303.

P.164: Napier Q. 33607.

P.164: Napier Q. 34184; T.M. Devine, *The Great Highland Famine* (Edinburgh, 1988), pp. 235–6.

P.169: Devine, *Great Highland Famine*, p. 240.

P.173: This also happened at the first clearance of Rum, in 1826. A man 'rolled an enormous boulder – probably the Clach Cuid Fir, the manhood stone – to a prominent place not far from Kilmory where it still stands near the road': Camille Dressler, *Eigg: The Story of an Island* (Edinburgh, 1998), p. 68.

P.174: Local informants; Cameron, *Old and New Highlands*, pp. 96–9; MacPhail, *Crofter's War*, pp. 188–91.

P.174: Cameron, *Old and New Highlands*, p. 94–99.

P.175: Hector MacDougall and the Rev. Hector Cameron, *Handbook to the Islands of Coll and Tiree* (1937), pp. 23–4.

P.176: Devine, *Great Highland Famine*, p. 181.

P.176: Devine, *Great Highland Famine*, p. 193.

P.176: Robert Somers, *Letters from the Highlands*, 1848 (Inverness, 1985 ed.), pp. 157–9.

P.181: David Burg and George Feifer, *Solzhenitsyn* (1973 ed.), p. 212.

P.181: Devine, *Great Highland Famine*, p. 183; P.A. Macnab, *Mull and Iona*, 1970 (1983 ed.), p. 75.

P. 182: Sorley MacLean, 'The Poetry of the Clearances' in *Ris a' Bhrutaich*, ed. William Gillies (Stornoway, 1985), p. 64.

P.184: W.H. Murray, *The Islands of Western Scotland* (1973), pp. 218–20.

P.185: Napier QQ. 14741, 15459.

Chapter 11: 'A Place of Your Own and Independant'

P.190: *Older Voices Among Us*, ed. Alvin Koop and Sheila McMurrich Koop (Erin, Ontario 1981), p. 16.

P.190: Napier Q. 13327.

P.191: *Emigrants from Scotland to America 1774–1775*, ed. Viola Root Cameron, 1930 (Baltimore ed., 1980), pp. 6–22, 91.

P.191: T.C. Smout, 'Problems of Nationalism, Identity and Improvement in Later Eighteenth-century Scotland' in *Improvement and Enlightenment* ed. T.M. Devine (Edinburgh, 1989), p. 16.

P.191: Bernard Bailyn, *Voyagers to the West* (1986), p. 516; Campbell and MacLean, *Beyond the Atlantic Roar*, p. 91.

P.192: W.H. Graham, *Greenbank* (Peterborough, Ontario, 1988), p. 215.

P.192: Letter of October 10th, 1836: reproduced in *Erin Advocate*, March 23rd, 1839.

P.194: Graham, *Greenbank*, p. 111.

P.194: MacDonell, *Emigrant Experience*, p. 199.

P.195: D.H. Akenson, *The Irish in America* (Kingston and Montreal, 1984), pp. 241–2.

P.195: Kerby A. Miller, *Emigrants and Exiles* (New York, 1985).

P.199: *Morriston County History* and *History of West Garafraxa Township* (in Guelph Public Library).

P.199: *Older Voices Among Us*, ed. Koop and Koop, p. 25.

CHAPTER 12: Leaves on the Vine

P.216: MacDonell, *Emigrant Experience*, pp. 198–9.

P.221: Gerner, *Industrial Resources of Nova Scotia*, pp. 94, 191.

P.224: Madeleine McCrimmon and Donaldson R. MacLeod, *Lochinvar to Skye 1794–1987* (Alexandria, Ontario, 1988), p. 148.

CHAPTER 13: 'The Alien Named Below'

P.233: *Sunday Times*, January 28th, 1990.

P.235: For a single 'winter's take' of pelts, brought in to a Pacific depot of the Hudson's Bay Company by a Gaelic-speaking trapper in 1855, see James Hunter, *Glencoe and the Indians* (Edinburgh, 1996), p. 137. The animals slaughtered numbered 15,815.

P.236: *Older Voices Among Us*, ed. Koop, and Koop, pp. 24–5.

P.238: Margaret Laurence, *The Diviners*, 1974 (Toronto, 1988 ed.), p. 60.

P.238: W.J. Healy, *Women of Red River* (Winnipeg, 1923).

P.239: Donald Gunn, *History of Manitoba from the Earliest Settlement to 1835* (Ottawa, 1880), pp. 89–96.

P.239: Gunn, *History of Manitoba*, p. 105.

P.239: Gunn, *History of Manitoba*, pp. 135–5, 144.

P.241: Gunn, *History of Manitoba*, pp. 193, 197, 201–7.

P.247: Jim Wilkie, *Metagama: A Journey from Lewis to the New World* (Edinburgh, 1987), pp. 70–74, 78.

CHAPTER 14: On the Tree-Line

P.252: Michael Payne, *The Most Respectable Place in the Territory* (Ottawa, 1989).

Notes

P.253: Angus and Bernice MacIver, *Churchill on Hudson Bay* (Churchill, 1982), p. 149.

P.255: Gunn, *History of Manitoba*, p. 100.

CHAPTER 15: Binding the Restless Wave

P.263: Napier QQ. 10193, 10761.

P.265: Napier Q. 10324; D.F.C. QQ. 38332–6; MacLeod, *Gloomy Memories*, p. 136.

P.267: *West Highland Free Press*, February 23rd 1990.

P.269: Cameron, *Old and New Highlands*, pp. 14–17.

P.271: *Tales of Barra Told by the Coddy*, ed. J.L. Campbell (Edinburgh, 1961), pp. 92, 94.

P.272: Thomas Gallagher, *Paddy's Lament: Ireland 1846–1847, Prelude to Hatred*, 1982 (Swords, Republic of Ireland, 1988 ed.), p. 4.

CHAPTER 16: Stepping Stones

P.285: Napier QQ. 13116, 17783, 17816, 17819.

P.292: F. Fraser Darling, *West Highland Survey* (1955), p. 44; Darling, 'Ecology of Land Use' in *Future of Scotland*, ed. Thomson and Grimble, p. 36.

P.293: Iain Gobha na Hearadh, 'The New Birth, or the Struggle of the "Old" and the "New" Man' in Derick Thomson, *An Introduction to Gaelic Poetry* (1974), p. 222.

P.298: Napier QQ. 13850,13911.

P.300: Thomson, *Introduction to Gaelic Poetry*, pp. 237–45.

P.301: Extracts from MacKenzie's diary ed. Joni Buchanan, in *West Highland Free Press*, April 22nd, 1988 – January 27th, 1989.

P.301: Napier Q. 13860.

P.305: John Steinbeck, *The Grapes of Wrath*, 1939 (1951 ed.), pp. 79–80, 139, 213.

CHAPTER 17: The Ends of Things

P.307: George Marshall, *In a Distant Isle* (Edinburgh, 1987), p. 143.

P.310: Donald Ross, *The Russians of Ross-shire*, 1854 (London, 1977 ed.), pp. 9–21.

P.311: Richards, *Highland Clearances*, p. 377.

P.315: Such learning is dealt with in rich detail by Ian Grimble, *The Trial of Patrick Sellar* (1962), pp. 134–40.

P.316: Hugh Miller, *My Schools and Schoolmasters* (1854), ch. 5.

P.316: Napier Q. 25592.

P.318: William Cobbett, 'Tours in Scotland' in *Rural Rides*, ed. G.D.H. and M. Cole (1930), vol. III, pp. 762–3; Hugh Miller, 'The Bothy System' in *Essays* (Edinburgh, 1869), pp. 201–2.

P.318: Kevin J. O'Reilly, *What to See Around Bettyhill* (no date or place), p. 21.

P.320: MacLeod, *Gloomy Memories*, pp. 18, 29, 52–4; Richards *Highland*

Clearances, pp. 320–1; D.F.C. Q. 28229. Sellar was furious with MacKenzie for supporting the crofters. The minister's 'position was complicated by the fact that his stipend (which had fallen behind) was paid by the Sutherland estate through Sellar himself': Eric Richards, *Patrick Sellar and the Highland Clearances* (Edinburgh, 1999), p. 175.

P.321: Napier Q. 25618.

P.321: *Glasgow Herald*, September 19th, 1988.

CHAPTER 18: The Long Homes

P.325: Ernest Marwick, *Journey from Serfdom* (typescript in Orkney Library, Kirkwall), pp. 92–7.

P.325: Marwick, *Journey from Serfdom*, pp. 105–7; Alexander Marwick, MS Reminiscences (in Orkney Library, Kirkwall, D8/1/22).

P.326: Marwick, *Journey from Serfdom*, p. 142: Napier Q. 23457.

P.326: W.P.L. Thomson, *The Little General and the Rousay Crofters* (Edinburgh, 1981), pp. 74–8.

P.326: Napier QQ. 24823–8, 24797, 24803: Thomson, *The Little General*, pp. 45–52.

P.327: W.R. Mackintosh, *The Orkney Crofters* (Kirkwall, 1889); Sidney Scott in Orkney Library Sound Archive 125/3; Mary A. Scott, *Island Saga* (Aberdeen, 1967), pp. 83–5.

P.327: Thomson, *Little General*, p. 52.

P.328: Mrs Craigie in Orkney Library Sound Archive.

P.329: Edwin Muir, 'The Return' in *Collected Poems* 1921–1951 (1951), p. 97.

P.329: Muir, *The Estate of Poetry*, quoted by Marshall, *In a Distant Isle*, p. 57.

P.329: Marwick, *Journey from Serfdom*, p. 184.

P.329: Edwin Muir, *An Autobiography* (1954), pp. 15, 63, ch. 3.

CHAPTER 19: Vanishing Tricks

P.340: Hugh MacDiarmid, 'The Glen of Silence' in *Lucky Poet* (1943), p. 296.

P.341: Susan A. Knox, *The Making of the Shetland Landscape* (Glasgow, 1985), p. 167.

P.342: John J. Graham, *Shadowed Valley* (Lerwick, 1987), p. 185.

P.342: A.J.R. Tait, 'Olnafirth Till the Clearances' in *Shetland Folk Book*, ed. John J. Graham and Jim Tait, vol. VIII (Lerwick, 1988), pp. 20, 28–32; Napier QQ. 22402, 22413.

P.342: Napier Q. 19721.

P.345: Robert Johnson, *A Shetland Country Merchant* (Lerwick, 1979), pp. 4–45. The homing instinct of sheep is also recorded in Cumbria, among the Herdwick breed: Andrew Humphries, 'Folds in the Landscape', in *Andy Goldsworthy Sheepfolds* (n.d.), p. 64.

P.346: Robert Johnson, 'Clearances in Unst' in *The New Shetlander*, no. 157 (Lerwick, Hairst 1986), pp. 10–11.

Notes

P.348: James W. Irvine, *The Dunrossness Story* (Lerwick, 1987), p. 113.

P.349: *The Shetland News*, December 1890, quoted by Brian Smith, 'Shetland and the Crofters' Act' in L. Graham (ed.), *Shetland Crofters* (Lerwick, 1987), p. 7.